Legal Decisions That
Shaped Modern Baseball

Legal Decisions That Shaped Modern Baseball

Patrick K. Thornton

McFarland & Company, Inc., Publishers
Jefferson, North Carolina, and London

Publisher's note: Patrick K. Thornton died on January 15, 2012, after completing the writing of the manuscript for this book. Special thanks are given to Jackie Faccini and Michael Flint, who subsequently proofread and indexed the book for him.

LIBRARY OF CONGRESS CATALOGUING-IN-PUBLICATION DATA

Thornton, Patrick K.
    Legal decisions that shaped modern baseball / Patrick K. Thornton.
        p.   cm.
    Includes bibliographical references and index.

    ISBN 978-0-7864-3780-1
    softcover : acid free paper ∞

    1. Baseball — Law and legislation — United States — Cases.
I. Title.
KF3989.A52T46   2012
343.73'07879347 — dc23   2012001991

BRITISH LIBRARY CATALOGUING DATA ARE AVAILABLE

© 2012 Alison K. Thornton. All rights reserved

No part of this book may be reproduced or transmitted in any form or by any means, electronic or mechanical, including photocopying or recording, or by any information storage and retrieval system, without permission in writing from the publisher.

Cover images © 2012 iStockphoto

Manufactured in the United States of America

McFarland & Company, Inc., Publishers
   Box 611, Jefferson, North Carolina 28640
      www.mcfarlandpub.com

To my wife, Alison, and sons, George and Samuel

Acknowledgments

A good book needs good input from a variety of people and this book was no exception. There are many people to thank for this project. My wife, Alison, has had to listen to me talk about baseball for twenty years, even though it is not her favorite subject. I probably have had more conversations about baseball with my father, Jack, than anyone. Also, I owe a large debt of gratitude to my mother, Jennie for all her support throughout the years. As well as to my sister, Candy.

Jackie Faccini, Emma Tsai, and Michael Flint deserve special acknowledgment as they assisted in the research, preparation, and reviewing of the manuscript and have given great input and advice throughout this project. Thanks to my father-in-law, Gene Hewett, for his keen insight and use of the English language.

A special acknowledgment goes to my long-time friend, attorney and former center fielder Mark Schwartz for the many discussions we've had about baseball. Dr. Larry Ruddell, too, provided many valuable insights. I was also fortunate to receive contributions and advice from several outstanding legal scholars along the way.

I also had outstanding contributions from Dr. James (Jimmy) Disch, Mark Willis, Dr. Mike Bourke, E. Brian McGeever, Joe Branch, Kevin Erwin, Steve Elkington, Seth Daniel, Nick Nichols, Ronnie Ren, G. Ray Thornton, Tim Purpura, Mike Janecek, Massimo Coccia, John Thorn, Dr. Richard " Hutch" Divorak, Doug Gerhman, Mike Laramie, Kenny Waldt, Joseph Promo, Waco Thornton, David Brickey, Cheryl Thornton, Sam Webb, Oliver Luck, Maury Brown, James Taylor, Jessie Marcos, Jack Dolphin, Dr. Doni Wilson, Kathleen Stischer-Burnette, Jon Maire, William Little, Kurt Kilman, and Bryan Teel.

Thanks to all the deans who let me teach "Baseball and the Law": Richard Alderman at the University of Houston Law School; Lylene Pilkenton at South Texas College of Law; Mandi Gibson at South Texas College of Law; Dr. Clark Haptonstall at Rice University; Marian Dent at Pericles in Moscow, Russia; and my good mate Gordon Walker at Latrobe Law School in Melbourne, Australia.

Table of Contents

Acknowledgments vi

Preface 1

1. *Popov v. Hayashi*
   The Legal Battle Over the Barry Bonds 73rd Home Run Ball — 5

2. *Metropolitan Exhibition Company v. Ward*
   Baseball's First Significant Legal Case — 21

3. *Philadelphia Ball Club v. Lajoie*
   Napoleon Lajoie Bolts to the American League — 41

4. *O'Connor v. St. Louis American League Baseball Co.*
   The Legendary Dispute Over the 1910 American League Batting Title — 59

5. *People v. Cicotte*
   The Black Sox and Baseball's Most Famous Trial — 77

6. *Rose v. Giamatti*
   The All-Time Hit Leader Is Banned from the Game — 109

7. The Arbitration Case of John Rocker
   John Rocker Speaks His Mind About Race Relations — 126

8. *New York State Division of Human Rights v. New York–Pennsylvania Professional Baseball League*
   Postema v. National League of Professional Baseball Clubs
   Bernice Gera and Pam Postema Try to Break Baseball's Glass Ceiling — 140

9. *Flood v. Kuhn*
   Curt Flood Takes His Challenge Over Baseball's Reserve Clause to the U.S. Supreme Court — 158

10. Andy Messersmith/Dave McNally Arbitration Case
    Players Win Their Freedom in Arbitration ... 178

11. Baseball's Collusion Cases
    Free Agents Take On the Owners ... 194

12. *Schentzel v. Philadelphia Baseball Club*
    Benejam v. Detroit Tigers, Inc.
    A Day at the Ballpark Isn't Always a Can of Corn ... 217

13. *C.B.C. Distribution and Marketing v. Major League Baseball Advanced Media*
    Baseball's Battle for the Box Score: A Constitutional Question ... 233

14. The Arbitration Case of Steve Howe
    Testing Baseball's Patience ... 251

Chapter Notes ... 269
Bibliography ... 319
Index ... 331

Preface

Baseball and the law are natural relatives. They belong together. John Roberts drew an analogy between an umpire and a judge in his senate confirmation hearings on his way to becoming the Chief Justice of the United States:

> While many advocates on the left and right would like a Court that promotes their agenda, what we must have, what our legal system demands, is a fair and unbiased umpire, one who calls the game according to the existing rules and does so competently and honestly every day. This is the American ideal of law. Ideals are important because they form the goals to which we all strive. We must never abandon our ideals of unbiased judges, judges who rule fairly without regard to politics.
>
> The role of an umpire and a judge is critical. They make sure everybody plays by the rules. But it is a limited role. Nobody ever went to a ball game to see the umpire. Judges have to have the humility to recognize that they operate within a system of precedent, shaped by other judges equally striving to live up to the judicial oath.[1]

Former commissioner of baseball and Yale president A. Bartlett Giamatti clearly understood the perfect balance of baseball and the law: "With all these elaborate rules and regulations and customs and wrongs and rights and fair and foul, it's the most highly moralized game in the world, at least to Americans. That's why Americans love it so much. It's a kind of people's legal system."[2]

Maybe it is the rules of the game or the umpire acting as a judge on the field of play, or the manager who, like a trial lawyer, tries to stay a step ahead of the other side, anticipating moves and countering them with his own strategy. Whatever it is, for over a century U.S. courts have discussed, analyzed, and ruled upon legal issues facing the national pastime.

The sport has had its share of lawyers who have impacted the game, among them Branch Rickey (University of Michigan Law School), Moe Berg (Columbia), Hugh Jennings (Union Law School-Chicago), James O'Rourke (Yale), John Ward (Columbia), Miller Huggins (Cincinnati), Happy Chandler (Kentucky), Bowie Kuhn (Virginia), and recently Tony La Russa (Florida State).

With so many interesting and influential cases to choose from, it was difficult to select only a handful for discussion in this book. I eventually selected cases that best represented a variety of areas of law and that also would be interesting for the baseball fan. The cases deal with umpires, players, spectators, fans, owners, and managers. They address issues that have been hotly debated, some of them for more than a century, such as gambling, the reserve clause, player salaries, and drug testing. The cases represent some of the greats of the game, including Lajoie, Ward, and Rose, as well as some good players like Messersmith, Howe, and Flood.

The dates of the cases range from 1890 to 2007, 117 years of baseball law. The first case is a lawsuit dealing with a baseball struck by the all-time home run leader, Barry Bonds. The Bonds home run began a legal dispute between two fans who both claimed ownership to the ball. The case has now become a staple for law school professors teaching the law of personal property.

The next three cases in the book deal with contract law. John Ward's 1890 lawsuit is baseball's first significant legal dispute. Ward, the Hall of Fame pitcher-shortstop and leader of the Brotherhood of Professional Base Ball Players, was also a lawyer, and in 1890, he put his legal training to use by suing the owners over the reserve clause, which bound players to their teams in perpetuity (or so the owners argued). Ward's lawsuit dealt with the reserve clause, but he won his case based on contract law. After Ward prevailed against his club, he started the Players League. *Philadelphia Base-Ball Club, Limited, v. Lajoie* has become one of the most famous cases not only in sports law but contract law, and is studied by a large number of law students every year. When Lajoie attempted to "jump" to the American league his club sought an injunction against him. Lajoie's legal woes spread over three years and two states. The battle between Lajoie and Phillies owner John Rogers is one for the books. The third case in the contract section deals with Jack O'Connor, who brought a lawsuit against his former club, the Browns, because they fired him as manager. O'Connor's actions in a double-header on the season's final day would produce controversy and lead to an investigation by the league. The facts surrounding the O'Connor lawsuit have to do with the notable Cobb-Lajoie race for the 1910 American League batting title, and specifically with O'Connor, Lajoie, and Cobb all playing dynamic parts in this episodic story.

The next set of cases involve overlapping legal issues, but they all deal to a large extent with the rights of the commissioner to protect the best interests of baseball. Since the inception of the Office of the Commissioner of Baseball in 1920 there have been legal disputes concerning decisions made by commissioners.[3] Three of those decisions stand out and deserve special attention. Each explores significant legal issues. Even casual baseball fans have heard of the Black Sox Scandal which surrounded the 1919 World Series. The case that rose out of it has no legal opinion to review and analyze, but it is nevertheless the case that has been the most written about. There have been numerous books, articles, and movies depicting the events surrounding the 1919 World Series. Players on the Chicago White Sox allegedly gambled away the series even though they were favored to beat the Cincinnati Reds. "Shoeless Joe" Jackson was the most famous White Sox player, but many others that allegedly participated in the scandal have gained fame over the years. Jackson, along with some of his teammates, was banned from baseball for life by Baseball Commissioner Kenesaw Mountain Landis even though the players were found not guilty by a jury.

The Pete Rose case explores the limits of the authority of the baseball commissioner. There is no dispute that Pete Rose was a baseball icon. Nicknamed "Charlie Hustle," Rose defined for many fans and players alike the way the game of baseball should be played. He is baseball's all-time hit leader with 4,256 base hits. He was the idol of many young baseball fans that grew up in the 1960s, 70s, and 80s. However, he has become well known in baseball circles now for his gambling activities and his head to head match-up with Commissioner A. Bartlett Giamatti. Rose still remains an outsider to Baseball's Hall of Fame. This chapter discusses Rose's legal troubles with the commissioner, the multiple court decisions involving the parties, and Rose's eventual suspension from baseball for gambling by Giamatti.

John Rocker, the Braves reliever as famous for his objectionable comments as for his fastball, is at the center of an arbitration case that deals with the best interests clause, and the extent to which the commissioner can discipline a player for off-the-field conduct.

The next two cases deal with issues of discrimination and gender equity in baseball. Most baseball fans know Pam Postema and her quest to become a major league umpire. However, fewer know Bernice Gera. Both filed discrimination lawsuits against baseball because they were prevented from following their dream. Gera's fight against baseball would go through multiple courts. Postema's fight against baseball would result in a confidential financial settlement in her favor but she would never umpire a game at the major league level.

Curt Flood's antitrust lawsuit against baseball over the reserve clause is regarded by many scholars as the seminal case in sports law. Flood's case would force him out of the game that he loved and even thought he lost, he paved the way for free agency in baseball.

The Messersmith/McNally arbitration decision followed Flood's lawsuit and gave the players free agency status. With Flood's help, Messersmith and McNally were able to achieve at the arbitration table what Flood and his lawyers could not achieve through the courts. The role of Marvin Miller in baseball labor relations is also explored in this chapter.

Collusion by the owners came on the heels of the Messersmith/McNally arbitration and led to an award of damages to the players for the clubs' illegal attempts to hold down player salaries. The collusion cases took over five years to settle with the players receiving a large financial settlement.

There is nothing like a leisurely day at the ballpark. That is unless you are hit by a bat or ball! Both *Benejam* and *Schentzel* explore the duty of the stadium owner to provide a safe place for the spectator to watch a game. These two cases were selected among the many baseball tort cases because of the legal issues they pose and also because of their precedential value.

Statistics have played a large part in the history of baseball. So why not a federal lawsuit over the ownership of statistics? The CBC lawsuit against major league baseball is a hybrid lawsuit dealing with issues of copyright law, right of publicity and an alleged breach of a licensing agreement. CBC prevailed against major league baseball, allowing fantasy league owners the freedom to use players' statistics.

The last case, but certainly not the least significant, involves Steve Howe's long-running dispute with baseball over his drug use. Howe's arbitration case explores the extent of the commissioner's powers to deal with drug use in baseball and also tells the sad tale of major leaguer Steve Howe.

There are sixteen cases in all, some better known than others — but all influential and fascinating. It is clear baseball touches a wide variety of areas under the law.

I was fortunate to write this book about two subjects I enjoy the most, the law and baseball. I hope you enjoy it.

1

Popov v. Hayashi[1]
The Legal Battle Over the Barry Bonds 73rd Home Run Ball

> Giving it to a lawyer, I think that is ridiculous.—Barry Bonds, outfielder

It is the middle of September in a leisurely ballgame between the Royals and Twins with both teams mathematically eliminated from the pennant race. In the seventh inning a Royals batter fouls off a pitch that soars and hangs over the crowd. A few souvenir seekers position themselves for a catch but are unable to complete it. The ball skids off the end of a middle-aged man's mitt and goes scurrying down the aisle. Several fans make an effort for the ball but it eludes them. A teenager eventually secures it with her bare hand as it slowly rolls right to her. The other fans, realizing she now has captured the ball, give up their futile chase for the souvenir and recognize she is now the owner of the ball. Another fan congratulates her as she enthusiastically shows the ball to another teenager sitting beside her. Just another foul ball at the national pastime. That is the common law of baseball.

The Game

When Barry Bonds hit a 3–2 knuckleball served up by Dodger pitcher Dennis Springer[2] on October 7, 2001, over the right-field fence into the arcade at Pac Bell Park in San Francisco, no one could have anticipated the legal ramifications resulting from the historical home run. Patrick Hayashi and Alex Popov were among the ball seekers on the day Bonds established baseball's all-time single season home run mark at 73. Just a few years earlier, Mark McGwire had broken Roger Maris's long-standing mark of 61 home runs when he blasted 70 long balls in 1998.

The record home run ball would create a legal dispute that would result in a three-week trial with numerous witnesses and noted property law experts debating the legal definition of possession.[3] The dispute over the ball would become a nationwide debate with the litigants appearing on national television. The events surrounding the ball and the court's ruling would soon become a subject of discussion among first-year property law students and law professors alike.[4]

The case has all the components of a great story. Two men struggling over a historical baseball hit by baseball's all time home run leader. Both seeking a lottery-style recovery for the ball. After all, the ball hit by Mark McGwire breaking Roger Maris's single season home run record of 61 was purchased by Todd McFarlane, creator of the "Spawn" series, for $3 million.[5] McFarlane also purchased Sammy Sosa's 66th home run ball and would eventually become the highest bidder for the Bonds 73rd home run ball.[6] Sports memorabilia experts estimated the value of the Bonds 73rd home run ball value at more than a million dollars. It was the ultimate American lottery and the odds had been narrowed to those fortunate few who were standing in the arcade at Pac Bell Park on the day Bonds hit the home run.

Fans arriving at Pac Bell Park on October 7, 2001, came prepared to catch a Bonds home run.[7] Expectations were running high. Fans in the outfield seats donned baseball gloves in anticipation that Bonds would hit the record setting home run in their vicinity. Both Popov and Hayashi came prepared to cash in, bringing their gloves to the game, hoping to get an opportunity to catch the valuable baseball. Bonds hit most of his home runs in 2001 into the arcade area,[8] and a standing room only section located in the right-field stands, on the day of the game the Giants had limited access to the area to only those who held tickets for that section. Outside Pac Bell Park is an area called "McCovey Cove," named after Giants Hall of Fame slugger, Willie McCovey, who belted 521 lifetime home runs. McCovey Cove is located beyond the right-field stands and is a section of San Francisco Bay.[9] On October 7, Giants fans arrived in McCovey Cove in boats, kayaks, and other seagoing vessels, hoping to catch a Bonds home run.[10]

Popov actually brought his girlfriend's softball glove to the game, which by all standards was an extremely large glove. Both Popov and Hayashi were standing in the arcade section of right field at Pac Bell Park before the game began. Popov had a reserve ticket but chose instead to stand in the arcade area. At some point prior to the home run ball entering the arcade area, Popov and Hayashi were actually standing right next to each other talking. That is something they would not be able to do once ownership of the ball became the subject of a lawsuit.

In the first inning Bonds drove his 73rd home run into the arcade section. A massive pile-up of bodies ensued, all clamoring for the valuable ball, each hoping for their personal lottery.[11] Giants security personnel began to remove individuals from the large pile of people that were still struggling for the ball.[12] Eventually Patrick Hayashi emerged, holding the ball proudly in the air to signify he was the ball's rightful owner—or was he? Hayashi had kept the ball hidden until Josh Keppel, a cameraman who was also in the arcade filming the event, pointed the camera at Hayashi.[13] Once the camera focused on Hayashi he revealed he was holding the record-setting ball.[14] He was immediately escorted by ball park security to a nearby room in the park where the ball was verified to be the actual ball hit by Bonds for the 73rd home run.[15] Kathy Sorensen was a fan in the arcade section on that day and stated that she heard the crowd chanting, "do the right thing," to the police and the Giants security personnel, indicating they should give the ball to Popov.[16] Witness Kevin Griffin stated in his sworn statement that he told a television crew member, "That's not the guy."[17] He believed they were taking the wrong person to security with the ball.[18]

The ball was placed in a transparent plastic case and Hayashi was told the ball was his to keep. Major League Baseball had marked each ball prior to the game, using a unique pen with an invisible and water-resistant ink that could only be seen with an ultraviolet light. MLB wanted to ensure they could verify the genuine home run ball.

Although Hayashi emerged from the scrum as the possessor of the ball, did that make him the legal owner of the ball? Not according to Alex Popov. The ball had initially landed in the upper portion of Popov's glove when he extended it above those around him. The Keppel tape shows Popov extending his glove above the crowd and the ball going into his glove. The ball landed in the webbing of the glove and, by most accounts, stayed there for a very short period of time. Could that constitute ownership of personal property under the law? As Popov began to close his glove around the ball, he was pushed to the ground and a mad rush ensued for the ball.[19] Popov ended up face down on the cement in the arcade.[20] He was kicked, punched, and hit as a struggle for the ball continued.[21] The Keppel videotape shows an out of control mob scrambling for the ball.[22] Hayashi was standing near Popov and was also forced to the ground. According to Hayashi, while he was on the ground he saw a loose ball and grabbed it, placing it in his pocket.[23] While on the bottom of the pile Popov can be heard on the Keppel tape yelling, "Get off me" and "Help!"[24] When Popov was eventually able to get back to his feet he immediately began to demand that he was entitled to the ball.[25] When Hayashi displayed the ball to the camera, Popov actually attempted to grab it from him but was stopped.[26] Popov went to the security office where Hayashi was taken and allowed in the same room as Hayashi. Paul Padilla, Major League Baseball's manager of security operations, telephoned the director of security operations for Major League Baseball concerning Popov's claim to the ball. After the conversation Padilla told Popov he could not help him. When Popov emerged from the room he was swarmed by the media. When he was asked what happened, he told reporters that he was told he could pursue the matter "outside of baseball and the Giants." He was also asked if he would file a lawsuit. He responded, "I don't know what I am going to do.... We'll see."

Popov actually did end up with a baseball in his glove while he was on the bottom of the pile but unfortunately it was not the Bonds 73rd home run ball. The ball in his glove had the word "sucker" written on the ball in large black ink. It is uncertain how it ended up in his glove. Jeff Hacker was one of the people on top of Popov also going for the ball. As he got off of Popov he saw Popov open his glove and he could see the letters "suc" written on the ball and Hacker yelled "that's not the ball."[27] It was later discovered that many fans had actually brought fake balls to the game that day. The "sucker-ball" was never found.[28] Popov was determined that he was entitled to the Bonds ball. He believed he had no other option other than to file a lawsuit to prevent Hayashi from disposing of it.

The Lawsuit

Not many people know what they are getting into when they file a lawsuit. It can be a long tedious process with no clear winner in the end. That did not discourage Popov as he forged ahead with his claim to possession of the ball. He asserted that his original contact with the ball gave him possessory rights to the baseball and challenged Hayashi's claim that he was the true owner. Popov claimed that multiple eyewitnesses and the Keppel videotape confirmed that he had caught the ball and that it belonged to him.[29] On October 24, 2001, a mere 17 days after the game, Popov was in court seeking an injunction to prevent Hayashi from selling or disposing of the ball. Popov needed the court to grant the injunction so he could ensure the ball would not be sold. After all arguments were heard the court agreed with Popov and issued its ruling:

IT IS HEREBY ORDERED that:

a. PATRICK HAYASHI, together with his agents or any persons acting in concert with PATRICK HAYASHI, is forbidden from transferring, encumbering, hypothecating or concealing Barry Bond's 73rd home run baseball (hereinafter THE BASEBALL), pending, the completion of trial in this matter or further order of this court;

b. PATRICK HAYASHI, together with his agents or any persons acting in concert with PATRICK HAYASHI, shall place the BASEBALL into a safe deposit box requiring a minimum of two keys with the keys held by the Court (Department 301), pending the completion of trial in this matter or further order of the Court determining title to THE BASEBALL....

JUDGE OF THE SUPERIOR COURT[30]

Popov had won the first battle, keeping Hayashi from getting rid of the ball. Now he was ready to pursue his legal claim of ownership to the ball.

Lawsuits are expensive and typically take several years to resolve. Popov actually borrowed in excess of $100,000 from his parents to fund his lawsuit. Popov asserted legal claims for conversion, trespass to chattel, injunctive relief, assault, battery, and constructive trust. The California Superior Court would eventually dismiss Popov's causes of actions for assault and battery against Hayashi, finding that he was a "victim" just like Popov.[31] The court succinctly framed the legal issue it had been called upon to decide: "The deciding question in this case then, is whether Mr. Popov achieved possession or the right to possession as he attempted to catch the ball."[32]

Popov claimed in his lawsuit that he "successfully caught the baseball in his baseball mitt and brought the mitt containing the baseball to his torso."[33] He further alleged that once he was thrown to the ground he felt the baseball in his mitt and also felt the ball pressing against his rib case.[34] Popov claimed that Hayashi and others fans assaulted him and committed a battery upon him while he was in possession of the ball.[35] He stated he had "successfully obtained possession of the baseball."[36]

Several witnesses, including Evan Knight, Maurie Bennet, and Kevin Griffin, submitted sworn statements that Popov caught the ball. Even cameraman Josh Keppel submitted a sworn statement that Popov caught the ball.[37] John Creech was a big fan of the San Francisco Giants. He had season tickets to 17 Giants games. On October 7, 2001, he was sitting about six to seven feet from Popov. He described the incident in his sworn statement of November 19, 2001:

> I saw the baseball descending at a very sharp angle as it flew over my head and directly into Popov's glove. Popov's glove was the only glove that went up for the ball. I heard the sound of the ball hit the leather of the mitt. Popov caught the ball firmly in his glove before being knocked to the ground by the crowd. There was no loose ball.[38]

Popov believed he had a solid case for conversion based on the number of witnesses who saw him "catch" the ball, as well as the videotape showing that he had caught the ball. Hayashi responded to Popov's lawsuit by denying he had assaulted or battered Popov or that Popov was in any manner the owner of the baseball.[39] His position was that he emerged from the scrum with the ball and that he in fact was the sole owner of the ball.[40]

The Alleged Bite

Every lawsuit has some interesting facts and this piece of litigation was no exception. Taking a page from the theater of the absurd, Popov alleged in his complaint that "the video film shows DEFENDANT HAYASHI biting the leg of another individual and that individual reacting with sudden movement consistent with pain from a bite."[41] Hayashi vehemently denied he ever engaged in any illegal behavior in his attempt to get the ball and that included biting anyone. Kathy Sorensen was on the arcade that day and she testified that she saw Hayashi bite a kid.

> While POPOV was beneath this pile, I saw three people, next to the pile, ripping, scratching and tearing at POPOV. Two of the people were near my feet. HAYASHI was behind and to the left of POPOV. HAYASHI came up between POPOV's legs and under him in the pile. While HAYASHI was trying to reach the BASEBALL, a twelve to fifteen year old child came up behind POPOV. This child's leg was interfering with HAYASHI'S ability to reach the ball. I saw HAYASHI bite the child's leg. I heard the child say, "OUCH!" and saw the child back out of HAYASHI's way. HAYASHI continued digging and then stopped. HAYASHI now had the ball and placed the ball unto his mitt.[42]

Dr. Doug Yarris was also on the arcade that day but instead of coming home with a souvenir he became a witness to the event. In a sworn statement he gave to the court he stated:

> I saw DEFENDANT PATRICK HAYASHI on his hands and knees very near POPOV. I lost sight of HAYASHI and heard a child yell out in pain. I then saw HAYASHI reaching underneath POPOV's body in the direction of POPOV's glove with the Baseball. I lost sight for a moment of HAYASHI'S hand, because of the ongoing assault and battery of POPOV. Within seconds, I saw HAYASHI'S hand again. HAYASHI had something in his hand as he was pulling away from the direction of POPOV's glove. The ball was no longer in POPOV's glove.[43]

Oddly enough, Yarris was a dentist in the bay area.

The kid that was allegedly bitten was 15-year-old Brian Shepard. No one could find Shepard until days before the trial. Prior to the trial, both lawyers talked to Shepard, who could not remember if he had been bitten. But at trial he testified he was bitten during the melee. If Hayashi did bite another fan in his rabid pursuit of the ball that would certainly affect any claims Hayashi might have. He would no longer be a victim but a "bandit." Did Hayashi bite a child to gain possession of the baseball? After Shepard testified, Judge McCarthy struck his testimony from the court record, finding it unreliable.[44] The court found the evidence of the bite unconvincing and declared Mr. Hayashi a victim of bandits just like Popov.

Settlement Discussions

Lawyers understand that a trial is expensive and can be a gamble. However, sometimes clients can be stubborn. Could the parties arrive at a reasonable solution to the division of the baseball before the trial? After all, wouldn't that be best for all parties? In a settlement both parties are virtually assured they will walk away with something. A trial is a "roll of the dice" for both parties and one party might walk away empty handed.

Hayashi demanded an apology from Popov for several things Popov said about him. Hayashi said once he received the apology he would then discuss how to divide the proceeds from any possible sale of the ball. Popov offered Hayashi $5,000 if he would give up all rights to possession of the ball. Popov submitted a sworn statement to the court, stating that if he was awarded the ball he would not sell it.[45] The parties did have some discussions prior to the trial but a settlement never materialized. The parties even hired a retired judge who charged the parties $9,000 a day to attempt to strike a settlement between the parties but they just could not arrive at a solution.[46] Popov's lawyer said the parties were "not in the same ballpark" when it came to settlement negotiations. Barry Bonds even injected his opinion into the fray, offering the following Solomon-like solution:

> My thing is, if there is a dispute you guys got a better chance at splitting the money than going to court. Giving it to a lawyer, I think that is ridiculous. Those two guys could have just said here, take it to an auction and what we get, just split it.[47]

Both parties continued to assert they were the rightful owner of the ball but neither was prepared to resolve the case and give in to the other's demands. Popov continued to assert he was the original owner of the baseball because he came into contact with it first and Hayashi claimed ownership because he currently had the ball in his possession. With the parties entrenched, the matter would proceed to a trial.

The Trial

The trial lasted approximately three weeks with more than a dozen witnesses testifying. Former Major League Umpire Ricky Garcia would testify, along with Popov and Hayashi, as well as noted property law experts, numerous eyewitnesses and the teenage boy who was allegedly bitten. In almost a surreal fashion the World Series featuring the Giants and Anaheim Angels was taking place just down the street from the courthouse.[48]

Judge J. McCarthy of the Superior Court, San Francisco, County of the State of California, would be forced to grapple with case law from the 1800s dealing with the possession of wild animals and sunken treasure and also sit through a trial, listening to eyewitnesses as well as expert witnesses, and arrive at an equitable result for all parties. He would be called upon to make a decision consistent with the law of personal property. Whatever his eventual ruling, it most likely would not make all parties happy.

When Is a Catch Really "a Catch"?

How was the judge to rule on possession? How is it determined when a fan has made a catch? Is a catch by a fan to be judged differently than a catch by a Major League player? Rich Garcia was a major league umpire for 25 years and umpired five World Series. In a sworn statement he provided to the court he referred to Major League Baseball's rule 2.00, definition of a catch:

> A catch is the act of a fielder in getting secure possession in his hand or glove of a ball in flight and firmly holding it.... It is not a catch however, if simultaneously or immediately following his contact with the ball he collides with a player, or with a wall, or if he falls down, and a result of such collision or falling, drops the ball.... In establishing the validity of the catch, the fielder shall hold the ball long enough to prove that he has complete control of the ball and that his release of the ball is voluntary and intentional.[49]

After reviewing the videotape it was his professional opinion that Popov did not catch the baseball "Based upon my review of the videotape and my experience as an umpire, it is my opinion that the videotape does not show that Mr. Popov caught the baseball."[50] Garcia said the ball was not completely in Popov's glove and that the last frame of the videotape actually showed the ball moving "upward and out of his glove."[51] He further stated that when a home run is hit into the stands it was his experience that "until someone establishes possession and control of the baseball" it is "fair game" and "up for grabs" to the fan who can establish complete control of the ball.[52]

At the preliminary injunction hearing Popov took the position that MLB does not set the standard by which to judge whether a fan obtains possession of a ball hit into the stadium stands. He argued that "[t]he analysis of ownership and possession of a baseball caught in the stands is governed by legal principles of possession rather than rules of professional baseball."[53] Judge McCarthy never mentioned MLB rule 2.00 in his final ruling, choosing to rely instead upon the common law of possession.

The Common Law of Baseball

What are the rules of the ballpark? Is there a common practice or tradition established by fans with regard to balls hit into the stands? What is the law concerning a baseball hit into the stands at a major league game? Professor Paul Finkelman, a noted expert on baseball and the law, has argued there is a common law of baseball.[54] At most ballparks, teams allow fans to keep baseballs hit into the stands.[55] Furthermore, teams urge fans to bring their gloves to games. One of the reasons fans can keep a baseball is once they go into the stands, they are scuffed and damaged. A scuffed baseball is illegal and the umpire will toss any scuffed ball out of the game. Football, on the other hand, typically prevents footballs from going into the stands by the use of nets. In basketball, if a ball goes into the stands, fans will merely toss the ball back to the referee. The National Hockey League allows fans to keep pucks that go into the stands. Interestingly, baseball is the only sport where a team can score by hitting a ball into the stands. What effect would that tradition of the ballpark play in the court's ruling?

Defining Possession

The law of personal property has a long history in the law. It might seem that the question of who actually owns personal property would be a relatively straightforward and easy question to answer. That would not be the case for the ball struck by Bonds. Just like settlement, Popov and Hayashi could not arrive at an agreement about the definition of possession under the law either. Both agreed that before the ball was hit it was owned by Major League Baseball. However, a common definition of possession remained elusive. It is usually the home team that supplies the baseballs for the game, therefore it would actually be the owner of the ball. However, MLB had provided the baseballs for this game. After it was hit, the ball became intentionally abandoned property under the law.[56]

Judge McCartney was clearly a hardworking judge who wanted to make sure his decision was consistent with the law. He called a conference of noted law professors who were experts in the area of property law to assist him in defining possession under the law. An official session of the court was held at the University of California Hastings College of Law.[57] Experts in property law attended along with first-year law students who were following the case to further their understanding of property law.[58] After much debate among legal experts, the professors could not agree on one definition either.[59]

The court opinion quoted the following definition of possession offered by Prof. Roger Bernhardt in one of his books:

> Possession requires both physical control over the item and an intent to control it or exclude others from it. But these generalizations function more as guidelines than as direct determinants of possession issues. Possession is a blurred question of law and fact.[60]

The court also quoted the definition of possession proffered by Ray Andrews Brown in his book, *The Law of Personal Property*:

> The orthodox view of possession regards it as a union of the two elements of the physical relation of the possessor to the thing, and of intent. This physical relation is the actual power over the thing in question, the ability to hold and make use of

it. But a mere physical relation of the possessor to the thing in question is not enough. There must also be manifested an intent to control it.[61]

The court eventually adopted the rule urged by the defendants as the rule defining possession in the case. The court referred to it as Gray's rule, since it was proposed by professor and legal scholar Brian Gray:

> A person who catches a baseball that enters the stands is its owner. A ball is caught if the person has achieved complete control of the ball at the point in time that the momentum of the ball and the momentum of the fan while attempting to catch the ball ceases. A baseball, which is dislodged by incidental contact with an inanimate object or another person, before momentum has ceased, is not possessed. Incidental contact with another person is contact that is not intended by the other person. The first person to pick up a loose ball and secure it becomes its possessor.[62]

The newly proclaimed Gray's rule would certainly seem to support Hayashi's claim, or would it?

Judge McCarthy's Decision

After hearing all the evidence and all the witnesses' testimony, and taking into consideration the oral arguments of both parties, Judge McCarthy emerged from his chamber and read his decision. He also produced a lengthy written opinion outlining the basis of his decision. The judge noted that Popov sued Hayashi for wrongfully converting the ball. The court defined conversion as "the wrongful exercise of dominion over the personal property of another."[63] Conversion operates as the civil aspect of theft. Individuals can be liable for conversion even if they lawfully come into possession of property if that possession interferes with plaintiff's ownership of the property. When a person who is entitled to possession of the property demands its return, the unjustified refusal to return the property to its rightful owner can constitute the tort of conversion. Conversion is classified as an intentional tort under the law. The remedy available to the wronged party is either to sue for damages or seek specific performance, that is, the return of the property.

Judge McCarthy noted Popov also sued Hayashi for trespass to chattel. The difference between conversion and trespass to chattel is one of intent. Trespass to chattel occurs when an individual takes another's property but does not have the requisite intent to convert the property to his or her own use on a permanent basis. Judge McCarthy said Popov's claim was only for conversion, stating "There is no trespass to chattel. If there was a wrong at all, it is conversion."[64]

The judge then noted an action for conversion does not exist unless a party has title or right to possession. The judge noted that different industries have different standards for possession but that there were some fundamental concepts that could be stated regarding possession.

The judge described possession as more of a journey down a path. He posed the question with reference to Popov, "Were his acts sufficient to create a legally cognizable interest in the ball?"[65] Judge McCarthy noted that Professors Finkelman and Bernhardt were correct when they stated that certain cases do recognize that possession under the law can take place even though the potential possessor has not gained actual control and dominion over the item. If individuals show they were actively involved in establishing complete control over the property, they may have a claim to possession if they can show their efforts were significant and would have led to dominion and control in the near future. Judge McCarthy also cited several cases in his written opinion dealing with the hunting of wild animals in his struggle to arrive at a just decision for both parties.[66] He noted that in these cases a hunter who wounds an animal but then fails to capture the animal might still have some possession rights under certain circumstances. He noted that "[i]t is impossible to wrap ones arms around a whale, a fleeing fox or a sunken ship,"[67] but

> [t]he opposite is true of a baseball hit into the stands of a stadium. Not only is it physically possible for a person to acquire unequivocal dominion and control of an abandoned baseball, but fans generally expect a claimant to have accomplished as much. The custom and practice of the stands creates a reasonable expectation that a person will achieve full control of a ball before claiming possession. There is no reason for the legal rule to be inconsistent with that expectation. Therefore Gray's Rule is adopted as the definition of possession in this case.[68]

In applying Gray's rule, Judge McCarthy noted that Mr. Popov did not show that he achieved full possession of the ball in his attempt to catch the ball:

> We will never know if Mr. Popov would have been able to retain control of the ball had the crowd not interfered with his efforts to do so. Resolution of that question is the work of a psychic, not a judge.[69]

But finding that Mr. Popov did not retain control of the ball did not resolve the dispute between the parties and did not mean that Hayashi could retain possession of the ball. The reason why Mr. Popov could not show full possession was because he was attacked. "His efforts to establish possession were interrupted by a collective assault of a band of wrongdoers."

Professor Gray had indicated to Judge McCarthy that Popov still had the right to sue those individuals who assaulted him. The judge found this possible solution "unworkable," stating it was impossible to separate those engaging in lawful acts from those engaging in unlawful ones. Notwithstanding, Mr. Popov did name as defendants in the lawsuit "Defendants, John Does 1–25."[70] This is a particular way of pleading that is allowed by law if a plaintiff has suffered a wrong but is uncertain about who actually committed the wrong. A court would then allow a plaintiff a reasonable amount of time to locate the wrongdoers and name them in the lawsuit. Mr. Popov chose not to pursue other potential defendants in his lawsuit.

The judge continued: "We are a nation governed by law, not by brute force."[71] He found it was only fair to give Popov an unimpeded chance at catching the ball. "To hold otherwise would be to allow the result in this case to be dictated by violence. That will not happen."[72]

After finding Mr. Popov had never been given this opportunity, he stated:

> The legal question presented at this point is whether an action for conversion can proceed where the plaintiff has failed to establish possession or title. It can. An action for conversion may be brought where the plaintiff has title, possession or the right to possession.[73]

The court fashioned a unique rule of law for the case by finding a "pre-possessory interest" on behalf of Popov:

> Where an actor undertakes significant but incomplete steps to achieve possession of a piece of abandoned personal property and the effort is interrupted by the unlawful acts of others, the actor has a legally cognizable pre-possessory interest in the property. That pre-possessory interest constitutes a qualified right to possession which can support a cause of action for conversion.[74]

In applying this rule to the facts in the case, Judge McCarthy noted that, as Popov began his journey to possession, "he was set upon by a gang of bandits, who dislodged the ball from his grasp."[75] He found that Popov did in fact have a legally protected "pre-possessory interest" in the ball. But what about Mr. Hayashi? If Popov had a pre-possessory interest in the ball, what did Hayashi have? Judge McCarthy found Hayashi was not a wrongdoer but a victim preyed upon by the same "bandits" that assaulted Popov. When Hayashi emerged from the pile with the ball he found he had "unequivocal dominion and control" of the baseball.

Judge McCarthy wrote that "[a]n award of the ball to Mr. Popov would be unfair to Mr. Hayashi…. An award to the ball to Mr. Hayashi would unfairly penalize Mr. Popov."[76] He continued:

> Both men have a superior claim to the ball as against all the world. Each man has a claim of equal dignity as to the other. We are, therefore, left with something of a dilemma.
> Thankfully, there is a middle ground.[77]

Citing the concept of "equitable division in the law," Judge McCarthy found "both plaintiff and defendant have an equal and undivided interest in the ball." To support his decision to divide the ball equally, he relied upon a 1896 New

Jersey decision, *Keron v. Cashman*.[78] In that case, five boys were walking home along a railroad track in Elizabeth, New Jersey. The youngest boy in the group, a nine-year-old, was walking ahead of the group and found an old stocking tied at both ends. He began to swing it around when the oldest boy in the group took it from him. The boys began to pass the stocking between one another. The oldest boy was beating another boy with the stocking when the boys began to suspect the stocking contained some money. They all looked inside the stocking and found some rags and clothes and $775 in bills. The boys decided how to divide the money and began to distribute it when they were interrupted. The boys then went home and one of the fathers of the boys found the money and turned it over the police to discover its true owner. The true owner was never located. The oldest boy's family sued, stating he was entitled to the entire amount while all other boys claimed an interest in the money. The New Jersey Court was in a quandary. How should the money be divided? Who had actually taken possession and control of the stocking? Who actually exercised dominion and control over the stocking and its contents? Who owned the money? The presiding judge did what any fair minded person would do under the circumstances — he divided the money equally between all the boys. He stated in his ruling:

> I am of the opinion that the money within the stocking must be treated as lost property, which was not "found," in a legal sense, until the stocking was broken open during the play. At that time, and when so found, it was in the possession of all, and all the boys are therefore equally finders of the money, and it must be equally divided between them.[79]

In the same manner as the New Jersey boys who found the money in the stocking, Judge McCarthy noted that Popov had the intent to possess the ball when he made physical contact with it. In finding the parties equal owners, Judge McCarthy stated:

> *The court therefore declares that both plaintiff and defendant have an equal and undivided interest in the ball.* Plaintiff's cause of action for conversion is sustained only as to his equal and undivided interest. In order to effectuate this ruling, the ball must be sold and the proceeds divided equally between the parties. (emphasis added)[80]

Aftermath

On December 18, 2002, the court ordered the parties to agree on a method to sell the ball and divide the proceeds. With a new baseball season approaching, Hayashi and Popov met alone without lawyers or public relations representatives and actually began to talk to one another. They discovered they both graduated from the same college. On March 12, 2003, Popov announced to the press that he and Mr. Hayashi had come to a resolution. "We have come to an agreement that the best thing to do is get back to what this is all about, which is that this is a historical moment in baseball history that we are both part of it."

Hayashi actually noted that Barry Bonds' original idea of selling the ball, splitting the proceeds, and not giving the money to lawyers was part of the impetus for the settlement between the parties. The two agreed to retain Barnes Sports Group to sell the ball on their behalf. The Barnes Group had been the agent that sold the Mark McGwire 70th home run ball for $3.2 million. The ball had been insured for two million dollars. The auction was broadcast live on ESPN on June 25, 2003. All parties anxiously waited as the bidding started, hoping that they were sitting on a winning lottery ticket. Sports fans nationwide tuned in to see how much the ball would bring and who would be the highest bidder. The auction went quickly and in the end the ball sold for a mere $450,000.[81] Disappointment was clear on the faces of both Popov and Hayashi, not to mention the lawyers. Todd McFarlane was once again the high bidder. McFarlane commented after the sale:

> The funny thing [is] [t]hese two guys have two sets of lawyers that they've got to pay court costs. These two guys could actually be in debt when it's all said and done. They could actually be worse off for having that ball. Add up two sets of lawyers. I'm being generous if those lawyers fought in court for a combined total of less than $500,000.

Why did the ball not sell as high as once thought? Was it that Popov and Hayashi looked too greedy? Was it because Barry Bonds hit it? Was it because the market value of the ball was actually $450,000?

After more than a year of fighting over the baseball, the parties, lawyers, experts, and witnesses could now move on with their lives. If that had been the end of the tale of the 73rd home run ball, that itself would have been an interesting story involving the national pastime. However, once the ball was sold and the proceeds divided, the topic of attorney fees became an issue for both parties. Both parties were sure the ball would sell for in excess of one million dollars and were willing to pay lawyers to argue they were entitled to rightful possession of the ball based on that premise. Lawyers do not guarantee results and can be entitled to a fee regardless of the outcome of the case. Popov's lawyer was working on an hourly basis while Hayashi's lawyer took the case on a contingency fee basis, only getting paid if Hayashi received any money.

Don Tamaki, Hayashi's lawyer, was a civil rights attorney. He stated that he would be reducing his fee because of the low dollar figure the ball retrieved at the auction. He said this would leave Hayashi with a "significant amount" of money after attorney fees were deducted. Popov's lawyers were not so generous. When Popov refused to pay his attorneys, they sued him for $473,530.22.[82] Martin Triano, Popov's lawyer, said, "I think that Alex is speaking up now basically because he is disappointed with the proceeds of the auctions."[83]

Noted property law expert Professor Roger Bernhardt testified as an expert witness on Popov's behalf. He never received the $19,000 he was entitled to and sued Popov for his fees as well.[84] Popov has never paid either party.

Popov eventually filed for bankruptcy.[85] Triano obtained a preliminary injunction prohibiting Popov from disposing of any of the money he received from the sale of the ball.[86] Triano filed a claim in the bankruptcy court for $777,356.89. The bankruptcy trustee objected to Triano's claim, saying his fee agreement was unclear about the fee structure. Triano appealed the decision to the United States District Court for the Northern District of California. That court overturned the decision of the bankruptcy trustee that Triano's fee contract was deemed legal because Popov "had actual notice of the lien provision before he agreed to enter into the fee contract...."[87] A unique ending to a very unique lawsuit.

This case made new inroads into U.S. property law. Law students and professors will now debate the legal ramifications of the ownership and possession of personal property in the context of the 73rd home run struck by Barry Bonds. Hours will be spent by those preparing to become lawyers debating what possession actually means and wondering if Mr. Popov could have actually retained control of the ball if he had not been mobbed by "bandits." In the end, who prevailed? Popov? Hayashi? The lawyers? Maybe the parties should have taken the advice of Mr. Bonds from the beginning and divided the proceeds equally immediately after the ball was struck and all would most likely have been better off. The anticipated lottery never came to fruition for either Popov or Hayashi.

Epilogue

Since the Popov litigation, the ownership of other balls has come into dispute. The odd case of *Boston Red Sox Baseball Club v. Mientkiewicz* presented new issues in the ownership of balls.[88] Doug Mientkiewicz fielded the final out for the 2004 Boston Red Sox World Championship team. He jokingly referred to the ball as his "retirement." The Red Sox argued that they were entitled to the ball and sued their first baseman for the right to the ball. The Red Sox argued that Mientkiewicz, as their former employee, came into possession of the ball through his course of employment with the Sox organization, and therefore the Red Sox were the rightful owners of the ball.[89] Mientkiewicz was traded to the New York Mets three months after the Red Sox won the World Series. Mientkiewicz had agreed to loan the ball to the Red Sox for display along with the World Series trophy. The Commissioner's office filed a grievance against Mientkiewicz claiming he had no ownership rights to the ball.[90] The Red Sox and Mientkiewicz eventually agreed to settle the matter. According to Red Sox president Larry Lucchino, "An amicable agreement was reached several weeks ago when it was suggested that the Baseball Hall of Fame and Museum become the custodian of the ball."[91] Of course, that ball never left the playing field.

2

Metropolitan Exhibition Company v. Ward[1]
Baseball's First Significant Legal Case

He is by long odds the most popular player in the profession. In this city he is looked upon as the Napoleon of the diamond field sport. He is a dyed-in-the-wool enthusiast, and would rather play baseball than eat. He is a strict disciplinarian, but works harder than any man on his team.—*New York Times,* February 11, 1893, on John Montgomery Ward

There was a time when the National League stood for integrity and fair dealing; today it stands for dollars and cents.—John Montgomery Ward, Giants Shortstop

The National Brotherhood of Base Ball Players had been originally organized by John M. Ward in 1885. Its declared purpose, at the beginning of its career, was simply fraternal, and had to do rather with the relations between players, as such, than with those between players and the clubs to which they belonged. The effect of this organization, however, was to breed dissatisfaction—Albert Goodwill Spalding, *America's National Game: Baseball's First Official Bible: America's National Game 1839–1915* (Cleveland, OH: Halo Books, 1991).

Let the wine flow. We are the people.—John Montgomery Ward, January 29, 1890

Much has been written about John Montgomery Ward and his contribution to the game of baseball. He was well known in baseball circles as a great player, manager, writer, and baseball executive. Ward had three great loves: baseball, the law, and the stage actress Helen Dauvray, whom he married and then unfortunately later divorced. Ward was the most important man in his profession in the 1890s. He would battle baseball's behemoths in court over his contract and baseball's onerous reserve clause. His chief rival would be Albert Goodwill Spalding. Spalding was a giant of early baseball and would use his knowledge of the game and his business acumen to eventually dispose of Ward's Brotherhood union and prevail against the newly established Players League.

The 1890 lawsuit between the Metropolitan Exhibition Company (New York Club) and Ward was a dispute over the reserve clause in Ward's contract, as well as legal issues relating to the fairness of a player's contract.[2] Ward would fend off the legal challenge of the National League and lead in the formation of the new Players League. The league would last only one year but the events leading to the establishment of the league and the Ward case laid the foundation for legal precedent. Ward's case presents an interesting examination of a player's contract in 1890, as well as issues about the enforceability of the contract.

Baseball's Renaissance Man

John Montgomery Ward was sued by the Giants after he walked away from his contract to start the Players League, which would operate without a reserve clause (National Baseball Hall of Fame Library Cooperstown, New York).

John Montgomery Ward was baseball's Renaissance man.[3] A graduate of Columbia Law School, Ward would challenge baseball's owners by organizing the game's first labor union and lead the charge to establish the Players League in 1890. The Players League would fold after only one season of play, but it still remains a great episode in baseball history and was significant in the evolution of labor relations between owners and players. Ward was early baseball's superstar. If he would have played a hundred years later, Ward would have been a media darling. He would have been sought after by the press to give his opinion on the state of game because of his extensive knowledge of baseball, his stature in the game, and his great ability on the field. He wrote extensively about the game for top flight newspapers, including the

New York Times, and was interviewed many times about how to play the game and on the business aspects of baseball.[4] He wrote one of the earliest books on baseball, *Ward's Baseball Book, How to Become a Player*.[5] In it, he showed his in-depth knowledge of the legal and business aspects of the game, as well as how to play the game. He dealt with subjects such as the history of the game, baseball for ladies, and training for ballplayers, and he analyzed each player position on the field. His book was considered an excellent source for those who wanted to fully comprehend the intricacies of the game. Ward clearly understood that baseball was not merely a game but a business:

> [Baseball] is not a Summer snap, but a business in which capital is invested. A player is not a sporting man. He is hired to do certain work, and do it as well as he possibly can.[6]

Showing his wide knowledge of subjects outside of baseball, Ward cited *Homer* in the first page of his book on baseball as describing one of the first episodes of individuals playing with a ball.[7]

Ward entered Columbia Law School in 1883 at the age of 23 and graduated *cum laude* with a degree in law in 1885.[8] His legal training and education would assist him throughout his career as a player, manager, and, later, as a baseball executive.[9] Ward was clearly a man ahead of his time. He attempted to sign a black player, George Stovey, to a contract for the New York club in 1887, but A.C. Anson was opposed and Stovey was never signed.[10] Ward also spoke five to six languages.[11] He played two positions on the diamond extremely well, organized a players' union and a new league to compete against the National League, and after his playing days were over stayed close to the game in an executive capacity. Ward was the first to use the intentional walk and was known to be one of the first pitchers to signal for a pitchout on an attempted steal.[12]

Ward's grandparents enrolled him at Pennsylvania State College in 1873 when he was only 13. He would not complete his first year at Penn State but returned in 1874, a more mature student. While at Penn State he organized the university's first baseball team and became well known as a great ball player on campus.[13] He was suspended from school in 1876 because he missed class to play in a semi-pro game[14] and was permanently suspended from Penn State in 1877 at the age of 16 when he and a friend were accused of stealing chickens from a nearby farm. He denied the charges but Penn State suspended him notwithstanding his denial.[15] He left Penn State without graduating.[16] Ward continued to play semi-pro ball and developed a very good curveball.[17] He is credited with being the first college curveball pitcher.[18] He traveled and played for several teams and, at the age of 18, signed a professional contract with the Providence Grays of the National League.

In 1878, at the age of 18, Ward dominated the National League. In his rookie year, Ward posted a 22–13 record as a pitcher and led the league in ERA at 1.51.[19] In 1879, he would pitch 587 innings (3rd in the league) and complete 58 games (5th in the league).[20] In his second year he led his team to the National League pennant, leading the league in wins, winning percentage, and strikeouts (46, .712, 239).[21] In 1880, he posted a 39–24 record, leading the league with eight shutouts, finishing second with 595 innings pitched, and third in complete games at 59. Although Ward knew a lot about baseball, he most likely would be befuddled by today's baseball parlance of a "quality start," "hold," or why a "fireman" was getting an award.[22] He still holds the record for the longest pitched shutout, an 18-inning, 1–0, blanking of Detroit on August 17, 1882. Ward would pitch 25 shutouts, win 164 games, and complete 245 of the 262 games he started in his career. He pitched a perfect game against the Buffalo Club on June 17, 1880, winning 5–0. He possessed a minuscule lifetime ERA of 2.10. In 1882, Ward went 19–12 with a 2.59 ERA for Providence, but was sold to the New York Club after the season. Ward began his career as a pitcher but played outfield when he did not pitch. He developed arm problems so he switched to shortstop in 1884, and he mastered that position as well. He has been referred to as the classic shortstop.[23] He finished his career with a .275 lifetime batting average, with 1,408 runs scored, 231 doubles, 867 RBI's, and 540 stolen bases.[24] He twice led the league in steals, once with 111 swipes.[25] It is known that he had at least 45 steals in four other seasons, but records of stolen bases were not kept prior to 1887.[26] As a manager for four different teams over a 13-year span, Ward's win-loss record was 412–320.[27]

In his playing days Ward lived the life of luxury residing in a downtown New York apartment. He married Helen Dauvray who was a well-known New York stage actress. The wedding was a well-publicized event in New York, but unfortunately the couple would divorce in 1893.[28]

Ward was an extraordinary player on and off the field. Who would not have wanted to be John Ward? He was an Ivy League lawyer, married to a beautiful stage actress, wealthy, and a great pitcher and shortstop for a New York baseball club.[29] He was living the American dream in the late 1800s. Many early ball players came from the working class and some worked in saloons in the off-season. Ward was an intellectual and also a pretty good ballplayer. He was the perfect candidate to lead a player's revolt.

The Brotherhood of Professional Baseball Players

John Ward was an idealist and a natural leader. He believed ballplayers should have rights just like any other American and often referred to them as "working men." The period of 1885 to 1889 has been referred to as the "golden age" of baseball[30] because of the growth in popularity of the sport. Ward sought to capitalize on that increased popularity. In October 1885, John Ward and some of his teammates formed the National Brotherhood of Professional Baseball Players, the first union of baseball players. Chapters of the Brotherhood were quickly formed in every city in the National League. By 1887, the Brotherhood had over 125 members with each member paying five dollars in monthly dues. Over time the players would slowly become more aggressive in presenting their demands to management, especially the need for a new standard player contract. The Brotherhood plodded along and, in September 1887, Ward wrote the president of the National League, outlining the concerns of the Brotherhood and requesting recognition of the players' union.

After some discussion, Albert G. Spalding and other National League owners would finally formally recognize the Brotherhood in November 1887.[31] During a meeting of the owners on November 17, 1878, Ward was sent for by the National League president.

> Dear Sir: I am instructed by the league in annual meeting convened, to state that they will be most happy to meet you and your associate of league players this evening at 8:30 o'clock, for the purpose of ascertaining the objects of the association for which you claim recognition. Respectfully,
> N.K. Young, President[32]

When Ward arrived at the meeting he quickly got to the point:

> Gentlemen, Mesars. Brouthers, Hanlon, and myself are a committee of the Brotherhood of Ball-Players, although we are not unconscious of the fact that in your invitation you have failed to address us as such. You have taken advantage of the technical points, but we do not desire to follow in your footsteps. We come as players to show our perfect good faith. You do not recognize our Brotherhood, but if you ask us what we want you must recognize our organization. As players we represent Hanlon, Brouthers and Ward. Both sides have been misrepresented in this matter. For your opinion, formed by hearsay, we are not responsible. We represent a reputable organization.[33]

After a discussion of a revised contract and the reserve clause, Spalding said the following:

> I am favorably disposed to Mr. Ward. He said the Brotherhood is beneficial and protective. I see no reason why we should not recognize them. I move that a committee of three be appointed to meet them.[34]

In November 1887, Ward wrote a letter to the members of the Brotherhood giving them the good news that they had been recognized as a viable labor union by management.[35] He informed the members that a new standard player contract had been agreed to by the parties. He detailed the specific paragraphs that had either been revised or added as provisions in the standard player contract. Ward noted section 6 of the contract was "an effort to stamp out dissipation, a thing to be wished for by every self-respecting player."[36] He wrote that section 7 of the contract was new, and provided a defense for a player "in case he considers himself unfairly treated."[37] He noted that section 8 guaranteed a player's pay if he was "injured in the service of his club or while performing any duty for it."[38] Ward conceded that the union was not able to obtain all the items the players desired but bragged that the contract was the first time a player had "the reciprocal right of annulling the contract for any material violation of its terms by the club."[39] Section 16 was revised to state a player no longer had to pay $.50 a day while traveling. Ward noted section 18 of the new contract "takes from the right of reservation much of its scorning injustice to the player...."[40] The player could only be reserved at a salary equal to or greater than his previous season.

Ward ended his letter by stating that the committee had secured for the Brotherhood a "recognition and a standing" and that it had negotiated "a contract whose terms it believes to be equitable to both parties and more than all, it has dispelled the illusion that the organization of ball players was a dangerous thing." He ended by saying, "If you find there are some things still to be desired remember the world was not made in a day. In practical life, ideal reform must compromise with expediency. If you are satisfied with our work, the committee will feel itself, fully rewarded. Yours fraternally, John M. Ward, Edward Hanlon, Committee, D. Brouthers."[41]

The Players Revolt

The Brotherhood was now recognized. But the question still remained to what extent the owners would negotiate with the Brotherhood and what concessions, if any, they would make to them. The Brotherhood would get a quick response and learn a hard lesson about the business of baseball from the owners.

The world tour of baseball was organized by Albert G. Spalding in the fall of 1888 and its purpose was to showcase major league players to the world and create an international demand for baseball. All-star players traveled overseas to promote baseball.[42] Ward was the captain of one squad and his rival Cap Anson captained the second squad. They would play games in Australia, Egypt, Italy, and England,[43] but the tour would lose money and baseball did not catch on in any of the places the players visited.[44]

While the players were on tour, the owners of the National League were busy attempting to get an edge on the players. In the players' absence, they implemented a new salary structure, which in today's terms would be deemed a form of a salary cap. The Brush classification plan, named after the president of the Indianapolis Club, John T. Brush, set salaries for players based on their baseball skills. The players would be paid according to a formula and would be categorized. The classification plan stated:

The compensation for all League players for services as players shall be limited, regulated, and determined by the classification or grade to which such players may be assigned by the secretary of the League, after the termination of the championship season, as follows: Class A, compensation $2,500; class B, compensation $2,250; class C, compensation $2,000; class D, compensation $1,750; Class E, maximum compensation $1,500. But this section shall not prohibit the payment of extra compensation for the services of one person to each club, as field captain or team manager. In determining such assignment batting, fielding, base running, battery work, earnest team work, and exemplary conduct, both on and off the field, at all times shall be considered as a basis for classification.[45]

Clubs would be allowed to lower a player's classification if his personal conduct was unacceptable to management. A player's classification could also be lowered if he committed errors or went into a slump. Players in the C, D, and E categories could also be given the additional tasks of sweeping bleachers or collecting tickets. The plan was adopted by National League owners by a six to two vote.

Ward learned about the plan while in Cairo, on Spalding's world tour, and felt betrayed and outraged by the owners' actions. It was reported that he confronted Spalding about the plan but Spalding claimed he had nothing to do with it. Many players were opposed to the system and considered it degrading. Under the plan, most players would receive a reduction in salary for the 1889 season. Ward and the Brotherhood attempted to negotiate with the owners regarding the Brush classification plan but had little success. Early in the 1889 season, Ward attempted to meet with management but they denied his offer, saying they would not meet with him until after the season. Ward began to see the handwriting on the wall and declared the Brush plan as the "last straw."[46] Although the players considered striking, they voted against it on July 2, 1889. Finally, in November 1889, the Brotherhood issued a public manifesto which stated in part:

> At last the Brotherhood of Ball Players feel at liberty to make known its intentions and to defend itself against the aspersions and misrepresentations which for weeks it has been forced to suffer in silence. It is no longer a secret that the players of the League have determined to play next season under different management, but for reasons which will, we think, be understood, it was deemed advisable to make no announcement of this intention until the close of the present season; but now that the struggles for the different pennants are over, and the terms of our contracts expired, there is no longer reason for withholding it....
>
> The reserve rule and the provisions of the national agreement gave the managers unlimited power, and they have not hesitated to use this in the most arbitrary and mercenary way.
>
> Players have been brought, sold, and exchanged as though they were sheep instead of American citizens. Reservation became with them another name for proprietary right in the player.... Even the disbandment and retirement of a club did not free the players from the octopus clutch, for they were then peddled around to the highest bidder.

That the players sometimes profited by the sale has nothing to do with the case, but only proves the injustice of his previous restraint....

Then, upon their final refusal to meet us, we began organizing for ourselves and are in shape to go ahead next year under new management and new auspices. We believe it is possible to conduct our national game upon lines which will not infringe upon individual or natural rights. We ask to be judged solely upon our work, and believing that the game can be played more fairly and its business conducted more intelligently under a plan which excludes everything arbitrary and un–American, we look forward with confidence to the support of the public and the future of the national game.

NAT. BROTHERHOOD OF BALL PLAYERS[47]

The National League responded to the players' manifesto:

TO THE PUBLIC

The National League of Base Ball Clubs has no apology to make for its existence, or for its untarnished record of fourteen years.

It stands to-day, as it has stood during that period, sponsor for the honesty and integrity of Base Ball.

It is to this organization that the player of to-day owes the dignity of his profession and the munificent salary he is guaranteed while playing its ranks.

The good name of this League has been assailed, its motives impugned and its integrity questioned by some of the men whom it has most benefited....[48]

Ward had attempted to meet with the owners but to no avail. He was now backed into a corner. The battle lines had been drawn and the parties began to prepare for baseball's first labor war.

The Players League

Ward and others decided they would form their own league.[49] They had anticipated the owners would not budge, so they met during the 1889 season to begin to develop a plan for a new league.[50] They were able to obtain substantial financial support and, on November 5, 1889, Ward and team owners announced the formation of a new league, the Players' National League of Base Ball Clubs.[51] The league was to be a "democratic alliance of workers and capitalist."[52] The league would not have a reserve rule but each player would receive the same salary they received in the 1889 season. The league had 127 players, 72 from the National League, 22 from the American Association, and the remainder from the semi-professional and amateur levels. They included stars such as Ward, Dan Brouthers, "Pud" Galvin, and Hugh Duffy. Spalding essentially offered baseball great Mike "King" Kelly a blank check but Kelly turned him down, issuing his own famous statement, "I need the money, [but] I can't go back on the boys."[53] Teams were formed and the Players League was on its way to begin its inaugural season. Ward said the following about the league:

> The men figure that it will be to their interest to manage themselves, and a general surveillance will be kept up by the members of each team on their fellows. A man's interest in the association will be continued as long as he is a member of it. For bad work he will be released and his share turned over to his successor. A structure to last forever is to be reared by the brotherhood. The profits and losses being pooled, a general pooling of interests and players must follow. All extra men unemployed except at intervals under the present state of affairs, will be utilized under the new plan and extra talent put where it would do the most good.... So the great baseball deal stands to-day. The players are united and present a strong case. They number about one hundred and thirty. The league club owners, practically eight men, say: "Let me go at fighting at once. We can beat you. If you put in a team here we will fill your places with new men, cut down the prices, and see how smoothly your craft will sail in rough water." The League men do not know, however, how broad the movement among the players is. They expect that only part of each team will go out. In this they are mistaken. The brotherhood has some hundred and thirty members. All are "in this play." And in all the eight League clubs not ten men will be left.[54]

When the National League owners realized that the Players League was moving forward and was actually viable, they organized a "war committee" to battle the newly formed league. Spalding led the committee, saying, "I am for war without quarter. I was opposed to it at first but now I want to fight until one of us drops dead."[55]

In a gesture of good will, the Players League sent a copy of its schedule to the National League in early 1890 to attempt to avoid conflicts with National League games. In response, the National League attempted to duplicate the Players League schedule to try to drive the league out of business. It was clear that the Players League had superior players, was well capitalized, had better stadiums than the National League, and had the possibility of becoming the predominant baseball league. The league sold 75,000 copies of the *Players' National League Base Ball Guide* for its inaugural season.[56] On opening day in 1890, the New York franchise of the Players League drew 20,000 fans against Ward's Brooklyn's club, while only 860 were present for the National League's Brooklyn team.[57] Ward was presented with two "floral horseshoes" when he came up to bat in the first game.[58]

The Ward Lawsuit

The Giants needed to stop Ward and the Brotherhood from establishing a competitive league. After considering all its options, the National League would turn to the courts to try to stop them.

Ward was served papers at his residence on West Seventy-Sixth Street in New York on December 23, 1889. Even though he was represented by counsel, Ward picked up the legal briefs for the temporary injunction himself at the law offices of Duysters on January 21, 1890. It was reported that Ward was "recognized by hundreds as he walked down Broadway...."[59] Ward was confident he would win his case.[60] He said even if he lost and an injunction was in place, the "Brotherhood clubs will go along and make preparations to play ball during the coming season."[61]

Under the law, a party can seek the equitable remedy of an injunction to enjoin a party from engaging in conduct which could be harmful to another party.[62] A trial will still be held between the litigants, but if a court grants a party's request for an injunction, the opposing party is prevented from continuing the conduct until a trial is held. In Ward's case, if the court granted the club's motion for a preliminary injunction, then Ward could not play for another team, but a trial on the merits of the parties' positions would still be held. A preliminary injunction could turn into a permanent injunction. A preliminary injunction is an extraordinary remedy and a court must believe the party who is requesting the injunction will most likely win the case at trial before it will grant the injunction.

History of the Reserve Clause

The reserve clause was first introduced at a meeting of the owners in September 1879.[63] The owners secretly agreed that they would each keep five players off the market. The owners would agree to not attempt to sign or employ the five reserved players of other clubs. It was baseball's first collusion between owners but would not be the last. With the rise of the American Association in 1883, which established itself as a rival to the National League, owners were even more concerned about reserving players because of the potential of players signing contracts with the new league.

In 1883, the first year of the American Association, each team could reserve eleven players, and the National League followed suit by allowing the reservation of eleven players as well. The number was eventually increased to fourteen in 1887. In practical terms, this meant the entire team in the 1880s.

Metropolitan's Arguments for a Preliminary Injunction

The first, and essentially the only, court hearing to take place in the case occurred on January 16, 1890, in front of Judge O'Brien. The primary focus of the argument by the Giants for an injunction was the enforcement of the contract against Ward. The Giants argued several points in support of the motion for preliminary injunction.

1. They argued paragraph 18 of the contract was "clear and unambiguous upon the face of it," and was not ambiguous in any way that required "explanation or elucidation."
2. The word "reserve" simply means to "hold, to keep for future use."[64] The contract was clear, Ward had to play for the Giants.
3. Since the form of the contract was drafted by Ward "it should be construed most strongly against him and in favor of the Giants."[65] Using his legal training, Ward most likely had a large part in drafting the contract.
4. Paragraph five of the contract gave them the right to enjoin Ward from performing services for other clubs. They said Ward should be not able to benefit by "objecting to the enforcement of a right which he has expressly granted."[66]
5. "There [was] no want of mutuality in the contract" and in its simplest terms the contract was "An agreement on the part of the defendant to render services as a ball player during seven months of the year 1890, in consideration of a salary of $5,250."[67] They further argued "that amount of money for a ball player cannot be considered unfair."[68]
6. Ward had argued that there was an established practice of players leaving the National League going to other associations notwithstanding the reserve clause. However, the club pointed out to the court that Ward could not cite to one case to support this proposition.
7. The applicable laws of both England and America clearly showed an injunction should have been issued. "Where a person has entered into a contract to render services to another of such a nature as not to be easily replaced, and the loss to the employer would be a loss not to be compensated for in damages, a breach or a threatened breach of such contract may be restrained by injunction."[69]

The Giants submitted affidavits that Ward's position could not be easily filled.[70] It certainly would be interesting to read those affidavits and see who signed them. Ward was in the awkward position of arguing he was easily replaceable.

The Giants wanted to hold Ward to the contract. If they were unable to prevent him from breaking his contract and going to the Players League, other players might take the same path as Ward.

Ward's Arguments Against a Preliminary Injunction

In response, Ward argued the injunction should not be issued because of the following reasons:

1. Ward's attorneys argued that the word "reserve" in the contract should not be defined by examining the contract and that the word was used in the contract in a "technical sense."[71] They argued that when a meaning of a word is not clear in a contract the parties must look to other sources to define the word found in the contract. Ward argued that a past history of the use of the word was necessary to gain an understanding of what the parties intended when they entered into the contract.
2. Ward's attorneys said that "no club has ever relied upon reservation alone as a good contract for the next year."[72] The word "reserve" did not prohibit a player from playing for another club but merely was referring to the practice of reservation exercised under the National Agreement. They argued the "sole objective" of the reserve rule was to ensure that a club who had a well-known player and who won the championship would not have to suffer the loss of the player to a rival club for the next season. If a club wanted to keep a player, it signed a contract with him, and if the club wanted to keep him from a rival who was competing for the championship, then it reserved him.

Three years before the lawsuit, in 1887, Ward provided interesting insight into the reserve rule in his book on baseball:

> The most important feature of the National Agreement unquestionably is the provision according to the club members the privilege of reserving a stated number of players. No other club of any Association under the Agreement dares engage any player so reserved. To this rule, more than any other thing, does base-ball as a business owe its present substantial standing. By preserving intact the strength of a team from year to year, it places the business of baseball on a permanent basis and thus offers security to the investment of capital.... The reserve rule itself is a usurpation of the players' rights, but it is, perhaps, made necessary by the peculiar nature of the base-ball business, and the player is indirectly compensated by the improved standing of the game.[73]

3. Ward then turned to the issue of the fairness of the contract. He argued that the contract was "grossly inequitable in its terms" and could not be enforced in a court of equity.[74] He pointed out to the court that the club could, by plaintiff's interpretation, bind the player for life while the club was only bound for ten days. Ward, through his attorneys, stated:

> If the plaintiff's construction is correct, every player who signs a League contract is bound for the current playing season, and also for the ensuing season, and at the close of the latter season, to sign another contract for the then approaching season, and so on, to the end of his life.[75]

4. Ward argued that an injunction should not issue unless there was "irreparable injury" to the plaintiff and that did not exist in this case. He pointed out to the court that "the general rule is that an injunction will not be granted in aid of a contract for personal services." The sole

exception is where a profession requires "extraordinary personal ability."[76]
5. Ward also argued he should prevail based on legal precedent. A case very similar to Ward's had been decided nine years earlier in favor of a player. In *Allegheny Baseball Club v. Bennett*,[77] Bennett signed a contract with the Allegheny Club of the American Association prior to the 1882 season stating he would play for Allegheny. He instead signed with Detroit. Allegheny filed a lawsuit seeking a preliminary injunction against Bennett. In baseball's first real case of contract litigation, the court held in favor of the player.

The parties had made their arguments and all that was left was for the court to rule.

The Court's Opinion

Although the judge disagreed with some of Ward's arguments, the court ruled in his favor, dismissing the plaintiff's request for a preliminary injunction against Ward. After the ruling, representatives from the National League and American Association met to discuss its ramifications. They viewed the decision as a setback, not a defeat, and agreed to continue to fight in court to keep their players.[78] Judge O'Brien noted the standard of review for the granting of an injunction: "A preliminary injunction will not be granted except in cases where there is the strongest probability that the court will ultimately decide that plaintiff is entitled to the relief which it demands in its complaint."[79]

The court must believe that the plaintiff has a good chance of prevailing at trial to issue a preliminary injunction. The issuance of a preliminary injunction is considered a remedy of "extraordinary relief." The court discussed the difference between a permanent and preliminary injunction, noting "that while final injunctions are matters of right, preliminary injunctions are matters of discretion."[80] The judge said he would issue the injunction upon a "showing that a contract exists which is reasonably definite and certain, and that for a breach thereof no adequate remedy exists at law, and the probability of plaintiff's finally succeeding in the action is free from all reasonable doubt."[81]

The decision of the court was issued on January 28, 1890. Judge O'Brien was faced with the decision of whether Ward would be bound to his contract with the New York Club or would be free to move to another team or another league. More lawsuits dealing with the same legal issues would likely follow this one. Judge O'Brien knew his decision would set the legal precedent for other cases filed by the clubs or league against players. In fact, several cases were later filed and the Ward case did indeed become legal precedent, with several courts citing the Ward case as binding legal authority in support of their decisions. After reciting and discussing the provisions in Ward's contract, Judge O'Brien quickly indicated that the meaning of the word "reserve" was one of the principal issues presented before the court.[82] Although finding in Ward's favor, Judge O'Brien adopted the argument of the club with regard to the definition of the word "reserve" as used in the contract.

He relied upon *Daly v. Smith*[83] in support of his decision. That case involved an actress who agreed to act during the seasons of 1874–1876. She breached the contract and the court granted a preliminary injunction in favor of the plaintiff. The court found that an actor and baseball player were similar in nature but Ward's lawyers disagreed. Judge O'Brien stated:

> Each is sought for his particular and peculiar fitness; each performs in public for compensation, and each possesses for the manager a means of attracting an audience. The refusal of either to perform according to contract must result in loss to the manager, which is increased in cases where such services are rendered to a rival.[84]

The court noted the question that must be asked: "Is there such a definite contract existing between the parties that can be enforced?"[85] Judge O'Brien said a court will not enforce a contract that is not definite.

The court then turned its analysis to paragraph eighteen of the contract, the reserve clause. In examining that paragraph and the supplemental contract dated April 23, 1889, the court concluded:

> It must be noticed that these provisions standing alone fail to disclose what are to be the terms and conditions of the agreement between the parties in the event that plaintiff shall exercise its option, which is accorded, to reserve defendant for the ball season of 1890.[86]

It then posed three questions:

> What are the terms and conditions of the alleged agreement for the season of 1890 now sought to be enforced?
> What does the defendant Ward agree to do?
> What salary is to be paid him?[87]

In answering these questions the court noted there were no fixed terms or conditions in place for Ward's 1890 contract. Judge O'Brien said that all Ward had actually contracted to do was to give the club the right to reserve him, with the terms to be agreed upon as a later date. He did not agree to enter into a contract for 1890 on the same terms and conditions he did for the 1889 season. The reserve clause gave the club the right to reserve him "at a salary of not less than $3,000," but it did not state what his salary would actually be.

The court then turned to the legal question of how a salary is to be determined in case of a dispute between the parties. Should the court assume the parties meant the terms and conditions to carry forward to the next contract year? The court answered no to that question, saying:

> The failure in the existing contract to expressly provide the terms and conditions of the contract to be made for 1890, either renders the latter indefinite and uncertain, or we must infer that the same terms and conditions are to be incorporated in the one to be now enforced, which necessarily includes the reserve clause, for no good reason can be suggested, if all the others are to be included, why this should be omitted.[88]

The court then turned to the second legal issue, whether mutuality of contract existed. The court found it unfair that the club could terminate the contract upon ten days notice while the player was bound to the contract for years.

In summary, the court sided with Ward on the grounds that the contract lacked mutuality and definiteness. The court had serious doubts about whether the plaintiff would be successful at a trial, principally because the contract was indefinite and uncertain. It was too vague and uncertain because it provided for no set salary or definitive conditions for the reserved year. The court noted with regard to mutuality that the club could terminate the contract with a mere ten-day notice while the player was bound to the contract indefinitely.

Ward's Contract

The court's opinion provided a detailed outline of the complete contract between the parties, not merely the provisions in dispute. A summary of the contract is insightful with regard to the court's decision.

On April 23, 1889, the Giants and Ward entered into a contract whereby Ward would play baseball for the Giants for $2,000. The term of the agreement was from April 1, 1889, through October 31, 1889. The court detailed each paragraph of the contract.

Paragraph 1: Stated the names of the parties.

Paragraph 2: This section contained the term of the contract as well as stating that Ward "agrees to perform such duties pertaining to the exhibition of the game of base ball as may be required of him...."[89]

Paragraph 3: Ward agreed to comply with requests of any officer, manager, or field captain for the Giants. The contract stated the player would "yield a cheerful obedience to all directions that may be given to him...."[90]

Paragraph 4: This paragraph allowed for the imposition of team rules for discipline and further allowed the team to suspend the player if necessary. The contract allowed for discipline for "dishonest play or open subordination" and also allowed the team to discipline or suspend a player for conduct deemed careless or indifferent. This provision of the contract concluded by saying the player was "...to cheerfully obey all rules and regulations ... and to absolutely refrain from any excess or dissipation whatever."[91]

Paragraph 5: The parties agreed that a player could not leave the team, agree to play, or actually play for another team unless he had the written consent of his current club. The paragraph also gave the club the right to terminate the contract if the player was "guilty of offering, agreeing, conspiring or attempting to lose any game of ball, or if he shall be interested in any pool or wager thereon...." Another provision of paragraph 5 enunciated the right of the club for a player who breached the contract. The Giants would rely upon this paragraph in their attempts to obtain an injunction against Ward. It gave the Giants the right to seek damages for breach of contract, as well as the right to seek specific performance of the contract.

Paragraph 6: This section dealt with "excessive indulgence in malt or spirituous liquors." The fines for violations were $25 for the first offense, $50 for the second, and $100 for the third. A further violation would result in a season-long suspension. There were also provisions which allowed the team to suspend a player for such a definite period of time as may be just and reasonable for "gambling in any form, insubordination, or any dishonorable or disreputable conduct...."[92]

Paragraph 7: This paragraph states that if a player is disciplined he must receive in writing "the character of the offence charged, the time and place of its alleged commission, or omission, and the character of the penalty."[93]

Paragraph 8: If the player becomes ill the team can deduct from his pay whatever amounts were to be paid to him during the time he was ill. However if the player "meet[s] with any accident or injury while in the service of, or performing any duty for the club, and be incapacitated," then no deduction from pay would be made. However, the club still retained the right to discharge the player if they were in an accident or injured.

Paragraph 9: If the player does become ill from "natural causes" he must submit to a medical examination by a physician to be selected by the team but the player must pay for the medical exam.

Paragraph 10: This section gave the team the right to fine the player "for any disobedience[,] ... violation of rules ... or for any insubordination or neglect of duty...." The fine was capped at $50 per offense.

Paragraph 11: By this paragraph, the club had the right to deduct from the player's contract the amount of any fine that may have been imposed by an umpire or league official.

Paragraph 12: This paragraph obligated the player to keep "informed fully" of all playing rules and regulations of the league.

Paragraph 13: This paragraph obligated the player to be under the "control and direction of the captain of the 'nine' ... and ... cheerfully and promptly obey his directions." The player was also contractually obligated to respect the authority of the captain "in the management and control of the 'nine.'" Furthermore, unless the player was excused by the captain or became incapacitated because of illness or "lack of any sound physical condition," then they must be ready to play.

Paragraph 14: This section allowed the team to terminate the contract upon "reasonable notice" for a material breach by a player. The team would no longer have to pay the player if the player breached the contract.

Paragraph 15: This was the reciprocal paragraph to paragraph 14, allowing the player to terminate the contract if the team breached a material condition of the contract.

Paragraph 16: The team would provide uniforms and the "necessary outfit" to the player. The club could deduct $30 from the player's pay for uniforms. The club would pay for the player's lodging, meals, and other traveling expenses while the team was on the road.

Paragraph 17: This was one of the most hotly disputed of the contract's clauses in the lawsuit. This paragraph allowed the club to terminate the contract with ten days notice to the player and both parties were free from further obligations under the contract. If the team terminated the contract "without any fault or neglect of duty on the part of [the player]," then the player would receive an additional ten days of pay in addition to what the team already owed him.

Paragraph 18: This paragraph became the most disputed contractual provision in the lawsuit. The team reserved the right to the player for the next year if certain conditional precedents were met. First, the Giants had to offer Ward at least $2,000, which was what he was making for the 1889 contract year. Second, the number of reserved players was to be limited to only fourteen players.

Paragraph 19: This paragraph stated that the contract contained the entire agreement between the parties and no other documents would govern their agreement except the contract.

Paragraph 20: Ward's salary would be payable on a semi-monthly basis.

A supplemental contract was executed by the parties on April 23, 1889, revising the original agreement. The supplemental contract stated that the Giants must offer Ward at least $3,000 to be able to reserve him for the 1890 season. It was agreed by the parties that the supplemental contract was to be made a part of the original contract.

Ward played for the Giants in the 1889 season and the Giants won the championship, beating Boston by one game. Ward batted .299, striking out only seven times in 479 at bats. He also stole 62 bases and drove in 67 runs. At the end of the 1889 season, Ward make it clear to the Giants he would not play for them in 1890. The Giants said they had the right to Ward's services for the 1890 season by virtue of the reserve clause in his contract.

Ward had fended off the first wave of the legal onslaught from his club. The court had denied the club's request for a preliminary injunction. Ward had gained his freedom temporarily. However, a trial of the matter would still be scheduled for the parties. Judge O'Brien stated:

> While, therefore, I think that this is not a case in which a preliminary injunction should be granted, it is proper that the rights of the parties should be determined by a trial before the ball season begins, and to that end, on application made, I shall assist in securing a speedy trial, upon which a final and deliberate judgment upon the rights of the parties can be pronounced.[94]

The court said that the playing season did not start until the middle of April and that the case could be tried before that time. "A final judgment before the playing season opens will secure every possible right of plaintiff."[95]

The Judge then scheduled the matter for a trial. Because the matter was considered equitable in nature (the plaintiff was not suing for money damages but rather an equitable remedy), the matter would be decided by a judge and not a jury. A footnote to Judge O'Brien's opinion provides some insight to the final disposition of the case. The club's lawsuit was dismissed on March 31, 1890, and Judge Lawrence issued a very short memorandum regarding the decision:

> As I am informed by counsel for the plaintiff that they do not intend to submit a brief in this case, and as I am of the opinion that the contract referred to in the complaint is one which a court of equity will not enforce, judgment will be granted dismissing the complaint with costs.[96]

The lawsuit was over and Ward had won. Even though he had not filed a lawsuit challenging the reserve clause, Ward had prevailed against his club on the enforceability of the reserve clause found in his contract. The Ward case involved only a denial of a preliminary injunction motion brought by the club, no trial was ever held.

The players won almost every lawsuit that was brought by the National League in its war with the Players League. Notwithstanding the loss to Ward, the Giants continued to be aggressive in their attempts to hold players to their contracts. They also sued catcher Buck Ewing and were unsuccessful in securing an injunction against him as well. Ewing's case was decided on March 25, 1890, almost two months after the Giants sought a preliminary injunction against Ward, but a week before the final decision on Ward. The court in *Ewing* cited to the Ward case in support of its decision. In *Philadelphia Ball Club v. Hallman*,[97] the court again examined the reserve clause and found that plaintiffs were not entitled to an injunction. Despite being the victor in court, however, the Players League would only last one season. Both the National League and the Players League suffered as a result of the 1890 season.

A poem of the day provided some perspective on the status of the game:

> Who Killed Baseball?
>
> Who killed baseball? "I," said John Ward: "of my own accord, I killed baseball."
> Who saw it die? "We," said the slaves; "from our own made graves, we saw it die."
> Who'll make its shroud? "I," said Buck Ewing, "I'll do it well, I'll do the sewing, I'll make its shroud."
> Who'll dig its grave? "I," said Brunell, "I'll do it well, I'll dig its grave."
> Who'll be the parson? "I," said Cub Stricker, "I'll let her flicker, I'll be the parson."
> Who'll carry the link? "I," said Jay Faatz;* "I watched the gates, I'll carry the link."
> Who'll be chief mourner? "I," said Tim Keefe; "I'm filled with grief, I'll be chief mourner."
> Who'll sing a psalm? "I," said Comiskey; "though it's rather risky, I'll sing a psalm.

Who'll toll the bell? "I," said "King Kell"; "I'll toll it
like _____, I'll toll the bell."
And now all the cranks have forgotten the game
And the ex-slaves perceives that D. Mud is his name.
   *Non-playing manager of the Cleveland Players League team.[98]

Ward Aftermath

Ward would return to the Brooklyn Club of the National League as its player/manager for the 1891 season. Upon his return he would play four more years in the National League under the same reserve clause which he had previously disposed of in a New York courtroom.[99] After leaving baseball Ward would become a top-flight Manhattan lawyer[100] and one of the best amateur golfers in the United States.[101] He would also represent players in lawsuits against their clubs. One might argue that Ward was the first player agent. After leaving the game, Ward was still thought of as a stalwart of the game. In 1912, he commented on the state of game, saying, "Baseball is much the same as it was 20 years ago. There are good and bad players, always will be. Clubs get men who work hard and enjoy team success and then again you find the indifferent to club-triumph crowd just the same as in days gone by."[102]

In July 1909, the National League President Harry Pulliam shot himself in his room at the New York Athletics Club.[103] The coroner arrived at the scene and asked Mr. Pulliam how it happened and all Pulliam could say was, "Am I shot? I didn't know it."[104] Pulliam had been in a sanitarium the previous spring but all thought he had recovered. He had been recently restored to the position of National League president in June 1909. John Ward was essentially nominated as a "protest" candidate to replace Pulliam.[105] After all, Ward had battled the establishment in court and started the first players union. There was much opposition to Ward's nomination by Ban Johnson, president of the American League. He vehemently objected to the appointment of Ward and threatened to resign from the National Commission if Ward was elected. Johnson was still angry about Ward's representation of a player, who White Sox owner Charles Comiskey had signed to a contract, in a 1902 lawsuit. The case was litigated and although the club prevailed, Johnson was still angry because he was forced to spend money on legal fees. Johnson thought Ward's conduct in the 1902 lawsuit was unethical. Johnson issued a statement indicating that Ward's appointment might cause some problems between the leagues.

Ward was not selected and he later became angry about statements that Johnson made that Ward thought impugned his integrity. Johnson called Ward a "trickster" in a newspaper article. Ward was always up for a good fight against the owners and fought for the things he thought were right. Ward sued Johnson for libel and won a $1,000 jury verdict even though he had asked for $50,000.[106] Ward always said he was not interested in the money but just wanted a retraction to clear his name. After the trial Ward said:

> A vindication was all I was after. If Johnson had retracted what he had said I wouldn't have sued him. I have already said I don't want Johnson's money. What I wanted was to clear my name as a man and a lawyer, and I think the verdict has done that. I had more evidence that Johnson had made those statements and that he had traduced me, the case, as I already had more than sufficient evidence against Johnson and was sure of the verdict. I'm not disappointed about the throwing out of the other charges, as this last clause is what we built on chiefly, it containing all the libel and the principal facts of the case. The proof of that was vindication, and vindication has come.[107]

Ward had once again taken on a baseball owner in court and was the victor. Even though he would not become National League president, he would become the part-owner and president of the Boston Club in 1912.

Ward died at the age of sixty-five in 1925 after he contracted pneumonia on a hunting trip. He was enshrined in the Baseball Hall of Fame in 1964. Ward could have been inducted as a pitcher, shortstop, baseball executive, or as the Brotherhood president. However, Ward's Cooperstown plaque tells what a great ballplayer he was but, interestingly, fails to mention his involvement with the Brotherhood of Professional Base Ball Players or the Players League.[108]

Flood v. Kuhn case may be the most famous case dealing with the reserve clause, but Flood initiated a lawsuit while Ward was actually sued by his team to prevent him from going to another team. However, unlike Curt Flood, Ward actually won his case. Ward made great contributions to baseball both on and off the field. He was by any standard a great ballplayer, a scholar and a student of the game. He wrote extensively about the game both from a legal standpoint and how to play the game. John Ward will long be remembered as baseball's first renaissance man and a pioneer of the game. After all, who wouldn't have wanted to be John Montgomery Ward?

3

Philadelphia Ball Club v. Lajoie[1]
Napoleon Lajoie Bolts to the American League

> When it comes to great hitters, what was the matter with Napoleon Lajoie? If the big Frenchman hit the ball that they're using today, he'd have been the greatest hitter baseball ever knew. He always hit line drives. The greatest ever. That's what I think; that's what I said and that's what I believe. He ripped that ball something terrible. But he never did get a shot at the lively ball.—Ty Cobb,[2] 1954

> What a ball player that man was! Every play he made was executed so gracefully that it looked like it was the easiest thing in the world. He was a pleasure to play against, too, always laughing and joking. Even when the son of a gun was blocking you off the base, he was smiling and kidding with you. You just had to like the guy.—Tommy Leach, on Napoleon Lajoie

The Unique One

Napoleon Lajoie may be the greatest second baseman to ever play the game.[3] He was called the "most graceful"[4] ballplayer to ever don a uniform and he dazzled fans and players alike with his extraordinary and unique baseball playing skills. Unbeknownst to Lajoie when he began his baseball career, he would become the most significant player in a legal war between the National League and the newly established American League and become involved in a legal battle that would eventually become binding legal precedent in American contract law for the next one hundred years.

In 1896 Lajoie was working part time as a hack driver and playing baseball for the Woonsocket Baseball Club.[5] Fred Woodcock was pitching against Lajoie and gave up two long home runs to him. Woodcock was a former pitcher for the St. Louis Browns and recognized a ballplayer when he saw one. Woodcock traveled back to Boston and talked about the great hitter he had faced on the

Woonsocket Club. The owner of the Fall River Club, Charley Marston, heard about Lajoie, hunted him down, and signed him for $100 a month. When he signed Lajoie, Marston failed to bring a contract with him so the two consummated the deal on an envelope.[6] Lajoie would keep the envelope his entire life as a keepsake. He would play in 80 games for the Fall River Club, batting .429, with 185 hits, 34 doubles, 16 triples, and 16 home runs.[7] After three months in the minors, 20-year-old Lajoie was on his way to the major leagues. He appeared in 39 games for the Philadelphia Phillies in 1896, batting .326. For the next four seasons Lajoie would be one of the game's best players. In his first full season in the major leagues he would lead the league in slugging percentage. The following year he would lead the National League in doubles and RBIs. His batting averages from 1897 to 1900 were .361, .324, .378, and .337, respectively.

Lajoie was clearly the best player in the American League after its creation in 1901. When Ty Cobb arrived in the league in 1905, the two would engage in a fierce rivalry on the field as well as vie for multiple batting titles. Lajoie would win four batting titles (including 1910) and Cobb eleven. The 1910 American League batting race between Lajoie and Cobb was one of the most

Napoleon Lajoie, who was wanted by two Philadelphia clubs and, as a consequence, ended up in Cleveland. His 1901 season was considered one of baseball's best (**National Baseball Hall of Fame Library Cooperstown, New York**).

hotly contested in baseball history. Both men wanted the title because the winner would receive a new Chalmers automobile.

Lajoie finished his career with 3,242 hits, 1,599 RBIs, 380 stolen bases, and 1,504 runs scored. He led the league in hits four times, slugging percentage four times, total bases four times, extra base hits four times, and RBIs twice. His lifetime batting average was .338. At the time he retired, he was the all-time leader in doubles with 657. The *Sporting News* ranked him as the twenty-ninth greatest player of all time[8] and he was the sixth player elected to the Hall of Fame in 1937. Lajoie was such a great player that they changed the name of the Cleveland franchise to the Cleveland Naps in his honor.[9] He was the player/manager of Cleveland Club from 1905 to 1909, compiling a managerial record of 377–309.[10] He resigned as the team's manager in 1909 but continued as a player for Cleveland until 1911. He rejoined the Athletics of the American League in 1915, still being managed by Connie Mack, and retired in 1916.

There was no question Lajoie was a great player. The question of how great was a question that several courts would have to decide.

Summary of Lajoie Litigation

The litigation involving Lajoie began rather simply when the Philadelphia Phillies of the National League filed a bill for injunction against its second baseman, Napoleon Lajoie, and several other players to prevent them from playing for the new American League club, the Philadelphia Athletics.[11] The court of common pleas of Pennsylvania refused to grant the injunction requested so the club appealed to the Pennsylvania Supreme Court. The supreme court found in favor of the club, enjoining Lajoie and other players to prevent them from playing for clubs other than the Philadelphia Phillies of the National League. The question then became what force the legal decision of the Pennsylvania Supreme Court had in other states. Could Lajoie and his teammates still play baseball outside the state of Pennsylvania and stay out of the grasp of the Pennsylvania injunction? Lajoie eventually signed with Cleveland of the American League so Philadelphia Phillies owner Col. John Rogers sought a ruling from a trial court in Ohio in an attempt to enforce the Pennsylvania injunction in Ohio but the court dismissed the case. Lajoie would continue to play baseball for many more years, but he never played for the Phillies again.

The Story of the Lajoie Case

Where the lawsuit against Lajoie was litigated and how it progressed through the court system is just as insightful and entertaining as the multiple court decisions the litigation produced. Law can be categorized as either substantive or procedural. Law students study substantive legal subjects such as torts, contracts, and criminal law while in law school, but they also are required to take both criminal and civil procedure courses to gain insight into how a case progresses through the legal system. The Lajoie case could be a case study on civil procedure, as it meandered through several courts and across state lines while lawyers, judges, and players battled for the legal high ground. Lawyers and non-lawyers alike have had difficulty following the legal journey of the Lajoie case. With legal issues such as injunctions, equitable remedies, full faith and credit, and multiple appeals, the case can be difficult to digest.[12] The procedural aspects of the Lajoie case actually show the true nature of the parties as each party struggled to gain the legal advantage.

Ban Johnson was the driving force behind the establishment of the American League in 1901. Johnson had been the president of the Western League, a minor league outfit, and saw an opportunity when the National League reduced the number of its teams from twelve to eight after the 1899 season. He changed the name of the Western League to the American League and set out to attract star players for the league's inaugural season of 1901. Johnson refused to sign the National Agreement with the National League before the start of the 1901 season and a free-for-all began. When the smoke cleared, the American League had fared well in raiding the rosters of National League clubs. In fact, 111 of the 182 players who appeared in American League games in 1902 were from the National League. Some of the star players included John McGraw, Clark Griffith, Cy Young, and John Collins. However, it was the signing of Lajoie that gave the American League instant credibility, popularity, and guaranteed success. Lajoie would dominate the American League, winning the Triple Crown in its inaugural season. He led the leagues in hits (229), doubles (48), home runs (14), runs scored (145), RBIs (125), on-base percentage (.463), slugging percentage (.643), total bases (360), and batting average (.422). Lajoie also had the highest fielding average for second basemen (.963). His .422 average still remains an American League record.[13] Lajoie's 1901 season is still considered one of the all-time best single seasons by a ballplayer.

After the 1900 season was over, Lajoie considered "jumping" to the Philadelphia Club of the American League. After much negotiation, Lajoie signed a contract for the 1901 with the American League's Philadelphia Athletics who were being managed by Connie Mack.[14] At the end of the 1900 season Lajoie was earning the National League maximum of $2,400, plus an additional $200 that was being secretly paid to him by Col. John Rogers, the owner of the Phillies. After he signed the contract with the Athletics for $3,000, it was reported that the National League offered him $3,500.[15]

Rogers, along with Al Reach, was the original owner of the National League Philadelphia Phillies in 1883. Rogers gained sole ownership of the team in 1899. He took much pride in his ownership of the team. Battling players through the courts was not new to the Colonel. He was a lawyer and understood the legal issues involved in holding players to their contracts. He had fought players during the Brotherhood wars in 1890,[16] and was involved in discussions to stop John Ward from going to the Players League.[17] After Ward's lawsuit was over, Ward and Rogers exchanged pleasantries in New York:

> John Ward and John J. Rogers of the Philadelphia Club met in New York just after Judge O'Brien had rendered his decision.
> "I heard you said you would like to have me on the stand under cross-examination," said Ward.
> "Yes" replied Col. Rogers, "and I hope to have you there. I will ask you a hundred questions which I think will mix you up."
> "I can ask you ten questions which would knock your side of the case out," said Ward, "if I only had you on the stand under oath."
> "Well, I am no hypocrite," replied the league lawyer, "I will answer the questions now if you ask them."
> But Ward declined the challenge.[18]

Two baseball lawyers, Rogers and Ward, going head to head; what a legal battle that must have been. Col. Rogers was admitted to the bar in 1865, the last year of the Civil War, and at one time served as the Judge Advocate General of the National Guard for the State of Pennsylvania.[19] He also served as a poet in the military. As unique as Lajoie was on the field, Rogers was unique off the field. Rogers had taken on John Montgomery Ward, the Brotherhood Union, and most likely numerous military tribunals in his day.[20] So he must have been confident that a ballplayer he already had signed to a contract would pose no legal problem to him. Rogers wasted no time in showing Lajoie he meant business and that he would never play for anyone but the Philadelphia Phillies. Before the beginning of the season, on March 26, 1901, Rogers appeared in the prothonotary's office of the Court of Common Pleas in Philadelphia to file the necessary legal papers to enjoin Lajoie from playing for Connie Mack's American League team.[21] It was the opening salvo of the legal war that would go all the way to the Pennsylvania Supreme Court, venture across state lines into Ohio, and take almost two years to resolve. To Rogers, the Lajoie situation was very personal. Rogers would represent his own club in legal matters against Lajoie as he attempted to hold the player to the Phillies contract.

The lawsuit filed in March 1901 was against Lajoie and two other players who also intended to break their contract with the Phillies. Lajoie wasted no time in filing an answer to the plaintiff's lawsuit, responding that his contract only bound him for the 1900 season and, furthermore, that no "mutuality of obligation" existed between the parties.[22] Those were the same arguments made by John Montgomery Ward in the 1890 case with the New York Club in which Ward prevailed. Lajoie also claimed that "the contract is upon its face contrary to public policy, and in violation of the constitutional rights of American freemen, and is an attempt to subject the defendants to continuous servitude for an indeterminate period."[23]

The matter was originally set for a hearing on April 20; however, after some testimony was taken that day, the case was continued to April 27, 1901.[24] Lajoie wanted the case to be heard right away so he could play for the Athletics. At the hearing on April 20, Lajoie testified that he decided to sign a contract with the Philadelphia American League Ball Club because the salary he was earning was "insufficient."[25] He further testified that he contacted the Athletics on his own and had never been approached by anyone from the American League. It was reported that John Rogers "gave some unimportant testimony."[26] At the close of the hearing, Rogers asked the court to restrain Lajoie from playing for another club.

Three weeks later, on May 17, 1901, the Court of Common Pleas of Philadelphia County rendered its decision dismissing the case, refusing to grant the club's request for an injunction.[27] Lajoie was now free to begin his great season and he became an immediate drawing card for the American League. The "Frenchman" was the face of the new league. In May 1901, the *Chicago Daily Tribune* noted that "the star second baseman of the country will make his first appearance in an American League uniform at South Side Park today at the head of the Philadelphia team...."[28] Lajoie completed his fantastic 1901 season but the Athletics finished in fourth place in the American League.[29]

Col. Rogers refused to give in to the American League or Lajoie and filed an appeal with the Supreme Court of Pennsylvania on November 14, 1901.[30] An interesting event occurred in the off-season. It had been reported that Lajoie died on an operating table after a railroad accident in California. The report proved to be a hoax: Lajoie was alive and well and ready to duplicate his 1901 season.[31]

After his superb 1901 campaign, Lajoie was once again enticed to return by the National League, with the New York Club reportedly offering Lajoie $10,000 a year for three years.[32] Lajoie turned the offer down, saying he would remain loyal to his American League club.[33] As the 1902 season approached, the parties waited anxiously for a decision from the Pennsylvania Supreme Court on the status of Lajoie. The Phillies' appeal had been argued by the lawyers in February 1901, but months had now passed and there was still no decision from the court.[34] Finally, on April 21, 1901, two days before opening day, the court rendered its decision. A reversal of the lower court's decision in favor of the Philadelphia Club of the National League![35] An injunction would be issued against Lajoie as well as two other players, Bernhard and Fraser, prohibiting them from playing for another team.[36] Col. Rogers was elated. He took winning and losing personally and gloated in his victory over Lajoie and

3. Napoleon Lajoie Bolts to the American League 47

all the players who had broken their contract with the Phillies. It would later turn out to be only a Pyrrhic victory. Colonel Rogers commented:

> I am vindicated at last. Perhaps the ball players will now admit that I knew what I was talking about when I warned them against jumping their contracts. We have enjoined all twelve of the players who turned at once. Lajoie, Bernhard, and Fraser cannot play with any club in any part of the State of Pennsylvania except the Philadelphia National League club. Should they play in any other State with any other club they would be in contempt of court and would be punished upon their return into Pennsylvania. Unless the other players report at once we will immediately take action against them.[37]

Rogers sent a message to other National League owners gloating over his victory:

> Here was Lajoie case, which covers all others. Our higher court upholds league contract in every particular; injunction ordered; opinion wide and sweeping. Congratulate National League on our great victory.[38]

Rogers was very serious about enforcing the Supreme Court's ruling and made it clear that not only were the defendants not able to play elsewhere but the ruling applied to other contract "jumpers" not named in the lawsuit."[39] Rogers said players who failed to obey the injunction would be prosecuted for contempt of court if they came into the jurisdiction. He would consider anyone who failed to follow the court's order "an outlaw and a fugitive from justice."[40] President Hart of the Chicago National League Club went even further and said "'Larry' [Lajoie] will not play with the Athletics unless he wants to go to jail."[41]

Lajoie sat quietly by as lawyers and baseball executives battled in the press over the enforceability of the Pennsylvania Supreme Court decision. Once the court's decision was made public, other American League clubs began to show immediate interest in Lajoie. The management of the Boston club of the American League said they would be more than happy to have Lajoie play for them because they did not believe the Pennsylvania Supreme Court decision could be enforced anywhere but in Pennsylvania.[42] Boston would just not use Lajoie in games played in the state of Pennsylvania.

The Supreme Court ordered the record of the case be remitted back to the trial court "for further proceedings in accordance with this opinion." Therefore, on April 23, 1902, Col. Rogers was back in Common Pleas Court No. 5, the very court which had given Lajoie the victory in the first legal battle between the two.[43] Rogers' appearance in court that day was merely procedural. He was securing a permanent injunction against Lajoie pursuant to the Pennsylvania Supreme Court ruling. The Court of Common Pleas would merely enter the order as instructed by the Supreme Court, thereby prohibiting Lajoie from playing anywhere but for the Philadelphia Phillies of the National League.[44]

On the same day the Court of Common Pleas Court entered the order, the Athletics were playing the Baltimore Club in Baltimore. In the eighth inning of the game, Athletics manager Connie Mack received a telegraph from his attorney, William Jay Turner, stating the court of Common Pleas in Philadelphia had issued a five-day temporary injunction against Lajoie.[45] Mack did not really know what to do, but erring on the safe side, he immediately took Lajoie out of the game pending "a conference with counsel." It would be the only game Lajoie would appear in for the Athletics in 1902.[46] The box score for the April 23 game shows Seybold batting for Lajoie in the ninth inning and Connie Mack replacing Lajoie at second base with Lupe Castro.[47] Lajoie would not play another game for the Athletics for 13 years, finally returning for the 1915 season.

American League president Ban Johnson immediately issued a statement regarding the Lajoie matter. "I am advised that whatever the judgment may be in the Pennsylvania courts, it cannot have any effect outside the State. In every other State where these questions may arise it has been determined that an injunction of the character would not lie." The American League fought back claiming they would take the matter to the United States Supreme Court.[48]

The five-day preliminary injunction had expired and the parties were back in court. When the court reconvened on April 28 some baseball greats stood before Judge Ralston: Colonel Rogers, Ben Shibe, Ban Johnson, Connie Mack, and Napoleon Lajoie. Any lawyer or judge certainly had to be impressed with the lineup of baseball men appearing in the Philadelphia courtroom that day.[49] The *Chicago Daily Tribune* headline for the day said it all: "Lajoie is out of the Game."[50] The Common Pleas Court No. 5 had issued a permanent injunction in compliance with the Pennsylvania Supreme Court's ruling. The injunction was now final against Lajoie, Frazer, and Bernhard and kept them from playing.[51]

Lajoie and other players had become baseball's wandering souls. They had lost their court battle. Not really knowing what else to do, Lajoie, Frazer, and Bernhard rejoined their teammates in Washington, D.C., for a game on April 28, 1902. Lajoie said, "We're here ... but we don't know what for."[52] The three players were told by Connie Mack not to put on their uniforms. As the Athletics prepared to return to Philadelphia, it was not known if all thirteen members of the squad would go back to Philadelphia because of the injunction. Four players, including Lajoie, were not going to go to Pennsylvania because of the possibility of deputy sheriffs serving them with writs of execution for the injunction.[53] They were intending to go directly to New York and wait for their teammates for the next series of games.[54] One writer of the day summarized the feeling of many at the time: "With baseball being played in the courts and on the field at the same time the average fan is much like the fellow who undertakes to watch a three-ring circus and eat peanuts and drink red-headed lemonade all at once."[55] In the midst of all the legal wranglings, rumors continued to circulate about where Lajoie might play during the 1902 season.

Chick Fraser finally gave up his legal fight and signed a contract with the Philadelphia Club of the National League for $2,400.[56] Lajoie left the Athletics unexpectingly, which fueled rumors he too would re-sign with the Phillies.[57] Ban Johnson even announced that the American League would no longer fight to keep Lajoie, Bernhard, or Fraser: "We are willing to fight their battles for them, but they were afraid to take any chances with the courts. All we can do is to let them go."[58] It looked as though Lajoie had nowhere to go except back to the Phillies of the National League. Lajoie even practiced with the team and it looked to all the world that Lajoie would once again become a Philadelphia Phillie.[59] Col. Rogers certainly knew he was in a good legal position "and hoped to reel in the star on the cheap."[60] Rogers and Lajoie began negotiations to return to the Phillies. Rogers offered Lajoie $3,000 plus a year end bonus of $500, but Lajoie was bitter and still wanted the $400 Rogers owed him from the 1900 season.[61] Just when it looked as though the two competitors would strike a deal, Rogers got greedy.[62] He told Lajoie if he signed with the Phillies he would have to pay a fine for the time he missed. Lajoie was reported to have said, "[Rogers] had the chance to do what was right ... and failed to take advantage of the opportunity."[63]

In the meantime American League teams were still vying for the services of both Lajoie and Bernhard. It was reported that Detroit would sign Lajoie to a contract[64] but Lajoie and Bernhard would both eventually sign with Cleveland.[65] In response to rumors that they were signing with Cleveland, Rogers said:

> I can hardly bring myself to believe that Lajoie and Bernhard would do such a foolhardy trick, but from what I read in all the papers I must confess that it looks pretty much as if the men had put their heads in the lion's mouth. I shall go into Court and ask for an attachment of contempt against the players at once, and shall also consult attorneys to see what action can be taken against those who are the instigators of this crime against the law.[66]

On June 4, 1902, Lajoie made his debut in Cleveland before an enthusiastic crowd of 9,827.[67] He had a double and scored a run in his first game with Cleveland. At the time he joined the club their record was 12–24, good enough for last place in the American League. Cleveland would finish the season at 69–67, in fifth place, 14 games behind Lajoie's former team, the Philadelphia Athletics. The National League's Philadelphia Phillies would turn in a record of 56–81, 46 games behind league-leading Pittsburgh.

The 1902 season was in the books but Col. Rogers was still after Lajoie and Bernhard. On June 11, 1902, Rogers was back in the Court of Common

Pleas asking it to hold Lajoie and Bernhard in contempt of court.[68] He had promised that if they signed with Cleveland he would seek to have the injunction enforced against both of them in Ohio and he was making every effort to keep his promise.[69] "Colonel Rogers promises to go into every court in the country to land Lajoie or keep him from playing with any other club than his own. This being the situation, lawyers are looking forward to full pocketbooks."[70]

Rogers had to be angry. Lajoie had signed with Cleveland and he could not stop it. Rogers' philosophy was simple and his actions showed he was true to his beliefs: "We lawyers have to stand together.... I would rather spend a couple of thousand with lawyers in getting back Lajoie and Bernhard than pay over $500 to the player to secure him at his own figure."[71]

Rogers continued his legal onslaught and being true to his lawyer nature filed another legal action, this time in federal court in Cleveland.[72] He filed an application for a preliminary injunction to keep Lajoie, Bernhard, and Flick from playing for the Athletics. The court denied his request in a hearing on July 9. Notwithstanding their legal setbacks, the Phillies continued to attempt to negotiate a new contract with Lajoie behind the scenes. On July 24, Rogers offered Lajoie $10,000 to play for the Phillies.[73] The offer was made by the manager of the club in a face to face meeting with Lajoie while the two were in Atlantic City. Not able to persuade Lajoie to sign, Rogers continued his legal endeavors, this time in the Common Court of Pleas for the State of Ohio, again seeking to restrain Lajoie and others from playing outside the state of Pennsylvania.[74] Arguments were made to Judge Strimple of the Common Pleas Court in Cleveland on August 7. Ironically, Rogers did not attend the hearing for fear he would be arrested. Evidently, Rogers had made some inappropriate remarks while in front of Federal Judge Wing the month before, when his case against Lajoie and others had been dismissed by the Federal Court.[75] Rogers was held in contempt of court and a warrant was issued for his arrest. If he had gone to Cleveland he would have been arrested. In a rather ironic twist, Rogers was seeking an order from a court preventing Lajoie from playing in Ohio when Rogers himself could not venture into Cleveland to argue the case for fear of going to jail. On August 10, 1902, the court denied the injunction requested by the Phillies, stating that it would not "interfere with the internal policy of a sister state."[76] The Phillies never appealed the ruling from the Ohio trial court, most likely thinking it would lose again.

The 1902 season ended with Lajoie as the only unanimous choice by the baseball writers for the "all American League Nine."[77] He would complete the 1902 season second in the league in batting and first in fielding for second basemen. The American League actually outdrew the National League in the 1902 season: 2,206,456 to 1,683,012, even without a team in New York.[78] The National League knew it had few options but to make an agreement with the

American League. A settlement was finally reached on January 9, 1903.[79] It was a major victory for the American League. Rogers was still reluctant to lift the injunction but finally agreed to do so in June 1903 at the urging of another owner. Lajoie was actually free to play anywhere he wanted once the National Agreement was signed by the leagues. Lajoie finally played a game in Philadelphia on June 12, 1903. "Lajoie's re-appearance here helped to swell the crowd to-day for 7,342 persons were present."[80]

With the procedural matters in mind the actual legal decision can be examined. There were three different court opinions concerning Lajoie and the Phillies and each one is instructive in its legal analysis and final decision.

Court of Common Pleas of Pennsylvania, Philadelphia Court

If there was a baseball litigation Hall of Fame the Lajoie case against Rogers and the Phillies would be a first ballot entry. The Lajoie and the Ward cases deal with the critical issue of ballplayers being able to move from one club to another. They were the precursors to the modern free agent market. From the 1880s through the early 1970s, clubs attempted to restrict player movement using the reserve clause contained in the player's contract and elsewhere. The Lajoie decision cemented the league's power over its players. It assured clubs that they could require a player to comply with his contractual obligations notwithstanding the enforceability problems of the Supreme Court's decision. It firmly established that a ballplayer was presumed to be unique and provided clubs equitable relief through a negative injunction.

Contract law states that individuals cannot be required to perform a personal services contract against their will.[81] However, a grieved party may request an injunction to prevent a party to play for another club.[82] To prevail in the Lajoie case, the Phillies had to prove that Lajoie's skills were "unique and extraordinary" and that the calculation of money damages would be difficult or inadequate to compensate the club for its loss.

The Phillies began the litigation, suing the star second baseman in a Pennsylvania state court called the Court of Common Pleas. Lajoie had already begun his great 1901 season when he heard the good news that the trial court had ruled in his favor. He continued to play for the Athletics. The opinion was issued by Judge Ralston who had been present for the testimony given by Lajoie, Shettsline, and others. The court based a large portion of its decision on a very famous English case dealing with a well-known opera singer, Johanna Wagner.[83] Wagner had entered into a contract with Her Majesty's Theatre to sing with the Royal Italian Opera. She then breached the contract by agreeing to sing at the Covent Garden Theater. The plaintiff sought the equitable remedy of specific performance against the singer. The court ruled in favor of the plaintiff, saying that while it could not force Ms. Wagner to sing for the plaintiff, it could prevent her from singing at Covent Garden. This would, in essence, force her to keep her contractual obligations. This is commonly referred as a "negative covenant." The Court of Common Pleas said: "Courts of equity have been frequently asked to enjoin breaches of negative covenants in contracts for personal service where, from the nature of the case, specific performance of the contract could not be enforced."[84] In order to issue an injunction, the court would have to conclude that money damages would be inadequate to compensate the plaintiff for its losses and furthermore that the player's skills were "unique" or that the player could not be replaced. Thus, in relying on *Lumley v. Wagner*, the court stated: "The defendant's services must be unique, extraordinary and of such a character as to render it impossible to replace him; so that his breach of contract would result in irreparable loss to the plaintiff."[85]

The court found that based on the testimony of the parties it was clear Lajoie was an "expert base-ball player." It further found he had a "great reputation as a second baseman" and "that his place would be hard to fill."[86] If he was not on the team, the team would be "weaker" but that would be true for any "good" player. It also found that Lajoie's absence "would probably make a difference in the size of the audiences attending the game."[87] Notwithstanding, the trial court said that this was not enough to issue an injunction under the standard set forth in *Lumley v. Wagner*. The trial court determined that Lajoie was not "unique" enough or impossible to replace so it denied the club's request for injunction.[88] If Lajoie was playing for a team outside the city of Philadelphia maybe the court would have been under some pressure to keep Lajoie playing ball in the city of Philadelphia but that was not the case. Lajoie was just playing across town for an American League Club, so whatever decision the court rendered, the "Frenchman" would still be playing for a Philly club, and most likely keep most of the fans happy.

The court then turned its attention to the second legal issue involved in the case, the legal concept of mutuality of obligation in a contract. The court stated:

> There is another principle which is controlling in this case. A court of equity will not decree specific performance of a contract which is lacking in mutuality. Thus, where one party only is bound, as in cases under the statute of frauds, specific performance will not be decreed.[89]

It further noted that a court will not issue a decree for specific performance if the contract lacks "mutuality of remedy." The court would examine the fairness of the contractual provision which allowed the club to terminate the contract on only ten days notice while the ballplayer was perpetually bound to the contract.[90] Lajoie argued that the contract with the Phillies was "one-sided" and therefore lacking in mutuality because the club could terminate the player's contract with ten days notice while the player was obligated to an indefinite duration. This was the same argument made by John Ward in his famous case in 1890. In essence, Lajoie did not have the same right to terminate the contract as the club. Does that make the contract enforceable and illegal?

In arriving at its opinion the court cited to the *Ward* decision, saying that almost the exact contractual language was in dispute in that case and the court denied the club's request for an injunction and found in favor of Ward. After examining Lajoie's contract and existing legal precedent, the court denied the Philadelphia Club's request for an injunction on the ground that the contract lacked mutuality. "[F]or a court of equity will not enforce specific performance of a contract, or enjoin the breach of it, where one party is bound for a series of years, while the other may annul it at any time upon giving ten days' notice."[91]

What was said in the courtroom on the morning of April 20, 1901, to persuade the court to rule against the Phillies?[92] It was reported that Col. Rogers offered a ninety-minute opening statement, giving the history of the option clause, a clause he had a part in drafting. What a great sight that must have been for the baseball fans who crowded into the courtroom to grab a glance at the great Lajoie and listen to Col. Rogers' opening statement. Rogers argued to presiding Judge Martin and his associates, Judges Stevenson and Ralston, that the clubs had purchased the option rights of players because of the "fabulous salaries" received by the players.[93] He concluded his arguments about the reserve clause by stating, "Every dollar of capital now invested in professional baseball will be withdrawn."[94] He argued that the purpose of the ten-day notice provision was so the player would do his best and not become "listless,"[95] and further argued that it provided incentive to the player. One wonders what Rogers might think of today's guaranteed contracts in sports.

The defendants countered by saying the contract was illegal because it was a violation of their constitutional rights not to receive the most money they could for their services as ballplayers.[96] After a short recess the parties began to call witnesses. Lajoie was called to the stand. Phillies lawyer John Johnson attempted to get Lajoie to admit he was a "rare and exceptional talent" and that the Phillies could not replace him. Lajoie was not college-educated man but evidently he had been well "coached" by his lawyers. He responded to Johnson's question, "Shucks, who, me? Why, I'm just a hack driver from Woonsocket."[97] His response may have been a bit understated considering his ballplaying ability. Charles Dryden,[98] a well-known sportswriter for the *Chicago Tribune*, wrote, "Larry Lajoie, in low tones and with a modest mien that paralyzed the fanatics, said that he had never heard of himself."[99] Shown his contract while on the stand, Lajoie said he had never received a copy. Phillies manager William Shettsline testified players were not usually given a copy of their contract. He also said that Lajoie signed the 1900 contract "at the grounds while in uniform and wrote his name with a lead pencil."[100] On direct examination, Johnson asked if Shettsline thought Lajoie was a star. Shettsline answered, "Yes, we've played him at second base, but you can't hook him up wrong anywhere."[101] Under cross examination by Richard Dale, the attorney for the players, Shettsline testified:

> DALE: "How much have you invested on the grounds?"
> SHETTSLINE: "Two hundred thousand dollars."
> DALE: "You have spoken about the expert playing of the different men. Can you mention any player on last year's team who was more expert than another?"
> SHETTSLINE: "They were all experts. No, I mean, not so expert as Lajoie. I might say that Petey Childs [a reserve infielder who never played in a game with the Phillies] was not an expert."[102]
> DALE: "Isn't Joseph Dolan, who is now playing second base for you an expert?"
> SHETTSLINE: "He's a good ballplayer, but not as good as five or six other second baseman in the league."
> DALE: "Do you think Lajoie is?"
> SHETTSLINE: "Yes, sir, I do. I think he's the best thing that ever happened."[103]

Lajoie had been injured during a fight with a teammate on May 31, 1900. He had been out of the lineup for five weeks. At the time of the injury the Phillies were in first place at 27–10, but while he was out of the lineup, the Phillies went 12–19. This information would provide fodder for questioning by the lawyers at the trial. Shettsline testified on direct examination: "Before Larry's injury the team was in first place and after that dropped off and never recovered its lost position."[104] The player's lawyer drew laughter from the crowd when he posed: "Isn't it a usual thing for the Philadelphia Club to do, to lead for a while, then drop behind whether Lajoie plays or not?"[105]

After his court victory Lajoie played the 1901 season for the Athletics. After the season was over the Phillies appealed the trial court's decision. The parties were headed for a showdown in the Pennsylvania Supreme Court.

Philadelphia Ball Club, Limited v. Lajoie, Supreme Court of Pennsylvania, April 21, 1902, 51 A. 973 (1902)

The majority of prior cases, including John Montgomery Ward's case, denied clubs seeking an injunction against players. However, in the Lajoie case the Pennsylvania Supreme Court allowed the club's request for an injunction against Lajoie. The Court of Common Pleas had found Lajoie was replaceable and that his skills were not "unique." Lajoie did not help himself in establishing his mediocrity with his brilliant 1901 season. The six justices of the Pennsylvania

Supreme Court would be called upon to determine whether the lower court had made the right decision by refusing to grant an injunction. With Lajoie's 1901 season fresh in their minds, the Pennsylvania Supreme Court justices ruled that the Phillies should have been granted the injunction and overturned the lower court's decision. The Supreme Court found that the lower court had taken the "extreme ground" when it said that it would only grant the injunction if Lajoie was irreplaceable. The Supreme Court held that it still must be proven that Lajoie was "unique," but concluded the Phillies could meet this standard if it could show he was not "easily replaceable." The Supreme Court thought the lower court underestimated Lajoie's ability. "We think that, in thus stating it, he puts it very mildly, and that the evidence would warrant a stronger finding as to the ability of the defendant as an expert ball player."[106] The court noted that Lajoie was "well known" and was an "attractive drawing card."[107] It then issued those now famous lines with reference to Lajoie's ball playing ability: "He may not be the sun in the baseball firmament, but he is certainly a bright particular star."[108]

Lajoie did not have to be the greatest player in the game (even though he probably was at the time), rather the inquiry was whether he was "easily replaceable." In all fairness, Lajoie has just won the Triple Crown in the American League's inaugural season.[109] Who knows if the lower court's decision would have been different if he had just done the same before it rendered its opinion? The Supreme Court found that

> the evidence in this case justifies the conclusion that the services of the defendant are of such a unique character, and display such a special knowledge, skill, and ability, as renders them of peculiar value to the plaintiff, and so difficult of substitution that their loss will produce "irreparable injury," in the legal significance of that term, to the plaintiff.[110]

The court next turned to the question of mutuality of obligation under contract law and reversed the lower court's decision on that issue as well. The Supreme Court said the concept of mutuality did not mean that both parties had to have the same rights or available remedies under the contract. The court ruled:

> We are not persuaded that the terms of this contract manifest any lack of mutuality in remedy. Each party has the possibility of enforcing all the rights stipulated for in the agreement ... but mere difference in the rights stimulated for does not destroy mutuality of remedy.[111]

The court found the parties were free to negotiate what duties and obligations they had under the contract and as long as the contract was fair it would be enforceable.[112] The court found Lajoie was paid for his services as a ballplayer and that operated as consideration under the contract.

The Phillies had hit the ball out of the park, a victory in the Supreme

Court of Pennsylvania. However, uncertainty and confusion would soon set in about the enforcement and applicability of the Supreme Court's decision in other jurisdictions.

Philadelphia Baseball Club Co., Limited, v. Lajoie, Court of Common Pleas of Ohio, Cuyahoga County, August 16, 1902

Col. Rogers was fresh off a victory in the Pennsylvania Supreme Court and felt invincible. He was adamant that Lajoie would not play for anyone except the Phillies. After Lajoie and Bernhard signed with Cleveland, Rogers filed a petition for preliminary injunction against Lajoie in the trial court for Cuyahoga County in Ohio. The Colonel presented the Ohio court with a certified copy of the record from the Court of Common Pleas No. 5 from the County of Philadelphia, the court had that entered the permanent injunction against Lajoie. The court order presented to Judge Strimple stated:

> It is hereby ordered that the special injunction granted against defendant, Lajoie, on April 23, be made perpetual, restraining him from giving his services as a baseball player, for the season of 1902, now current, and continuing until October 15, 1902, to any other club or organization, person or persons whatever, other than the plaintiff, the said Philadelphia Ball Club, Limited.[113]

After being presented with the order of the Pennsylvania court, the judge faced a dilemma. Could he enforce a court order from the state of Pennsylvania in Ohio? After all, it was just a supreme court that had made the decision to enforce the injunction and Judge Strimple was a local trial judge. Would Judge Strimple disappoint the Cleveland fans and send Lajoie to Philadelphia? In a rather meandering and somewhat complicated opinion, Judge Strimple said no to the Phillies. Lajoie was in the clear once again. The U.S. Constitution does require a state to give "full faith and credit" to another state's decision.[114] Faced with this constitutional challenge, Judge Strimple said the full faith and credit clause was confined solely to "judicial determinations as possess the quality of *judgment*, and does not extend to orders or proceedings in the nature of execution, or to orders merely ancillary to some special form of relief."[115]

Did Judge Strimple render a "crack" or creative legal decision?[116] Whatever it was, it sure had to make the fans of Cleveland happy. Did Col. Rogers really believe when he walked into Judge Strimple's courtroom that day that the judge would give him what he wanted and send the 1901 American League Triple Crown winner from Cleveland back to Philadelphia? If Judge Strimple was running for re-election, he probably won.

Col. Rogers knew he would never win on appeal. Still, it had to be extremely frustrating to a topnotch Philadelphia lawyer like Rogers. A "Philadelphia lawyer" has always had the reputation of being one of the finest in the legal profession.[117] He had won a decision at the Supreme Court of Pennsylvania but Lajoie and his teammates were still playing baseball and it was not for the Phillies. He must have wondered what else he had to do to "win" his case. He would finally throw in the "legal towel" and accept defeat.[118]

The Legal Significance of the Lajoie Decision

What significance does the Lajoie Supreme Court decision have? After all, was it just a case about a ballplayer who wanted to go to another league to play baseball? One of the reasons the case was significant is because it would be the first time a court would issue a negative injunction to enforce a professional sports contract. Lajoie's case was significant in the continued evolution of baseball's cartel. In the litigation involving John Ward, the court agreed with Ward that mutuality of obligation did not exist in the contract. However, the court in Lajoie found for the club, saying there was consideration for the 10-day notice provision in the contract. Although the Lajoie case was against the great weight of legal authority at the time, its legal principles have stood the test of time and been adopted by numerous courts in multiple jurisdictions over many years as binding legal precedent. One of the case's most lasting contributions to the law deals with the concept of mutuality of obligation or remedy. Generally, mutuality of remedy between the parties does not have to exist to enforce a player's contract.[119] The concept of mutuality is essentially a non-issue in professional sports contracts in the modern era. The Lajoie case also set the standard when granting injunctions against athletes who want to play elsewhere.[120]

The court's ruling and analysis with regard to mutuality of obligation and uniqueness have been adopted by courts throughout the United States and continues to be applicable today. Even as recently as 2003 a court relied upon the *Lajoie* decision in deciding a case. In *Marchio v. Letterlough*, a promoter sued a boxer claiming the boxer breached a contract by agreeing to box in matches being arranged by other promoters.[121] The promoter sought a preliminary injunction against the boxer. The court in *Marchio* spent a substantial amount of time discussing the applicability of the *Lajoie* decision, noting that it had been followed by at least eight other Pennsylvania court decisions.[122]

The *Lajoie* case is one of the most significant legal decisions in baseball history and sports law for several reasons. First, it involved one of the greatest players in baseball history, Napoleon Lajoie. Much attention was paid to the case because of the stature and popularity of the "Frenchman." It was also significant because the case and Lajoie himself became the focus of the war that was occurring between the National League and its new rival, the American League. Lajoie's entry into the American League would give the new league its best drawing card.[123] The case also provides precedential value in contract law and for the legal concepts it established dealing with mutuality and uniqueness.[124]

Aftermath

During his major league career, Lajoie never played on a pennant-winning team. However, in 1917, he managed the Toronto Club in the International League to a pennant. He also played for the club, batting .380 at the age of 42. Did Lajoie possess "unique" baseball skills? Was he irreplaceable? Maybe Baseball Commissioner Ford C. Frick answered those questions best. Upon hearing of Lajoie's death, he called him "one of the greatest hitters in baseball history" and "a great athlete and a great man."[125]

4

O'Connor v. St. Louis American League Baseball Co.[1]
The Legendary Dispute Over the 1910 American League Batting Title

The Setup

The 1910 American League batting race proved to be the most controversial, exciting, and disputed batting title in the history of baseball.[2] Who won the 1910 title for best batsman? Was it Cobb or Lajoie? The mystery still prevails today.[3] According to Major League Baseball records, Ty Cobb was the official winner; however, doubt still lingers today about who actually holds the title. Baseball icons Cobb and Napoleon Lajoie went head to head throughout the 1910 season vying for the batting title. Not only was the title at stake but so was a new 1910 Chalmers "80" automobile which had been promised to the leading batsman in baseball by the president of the Chalmers car company, Hugh Chalmers.[4] Cobb and Lajoie both desperately wanted to win the car as well as the title of best batsman. Ty Cobb won batting titles from 1907 to 1915 and three more from 1917 to 1919.[5] The 1910 title was number four in a series of nine consecutive titles for the "Georgia Peach."[6] He would win a total of twelve titles.[7] Napoleon Lajoie won four batting titles during his career.[8]

The historical race would produce nothing less than an investigation by the president of the American League, the institution of the Most Valuable Player award beginning in the 1911 season, and a lawsuit by a St. Louis Browns manager against the Browns for breach of contract which would almost take six years to reach a conclusion.[9] Events surrounding the 1910 title would lie dormant for more than 70 years, but would once again create a ripple in baseball circles in 1981.[10]

The Characters

The batsmen involved in the 1910 batting race were two of baseball's all-time greats, Ty Cobb and Napoleon Lajoie. The race would also involve a crusty veteran catcher who would manage only one year in the Major Leagues and would later seek vindication through the courts against his former team, a rookie shortstop who was playing out of position at third base, a St. Louis Browns scout, an official scorer, and the president of the American League. Altogether, quite a line-up.

Ty Cobb has always been considered one of baseball's greats.[11] He was not always the most well-liked person on the diamond but he certainly was respected for his baseball skill.[12] Branch Rickey once noted, "Cobb lived off the field as though he wished to live forever. He lived on the field as though it was his last day."[13] Cobb desperately wanted to win the 1910 title and the car.

Napoleon "Nap" Lajoie was one of baseball's first superstars.[14] Lajoie was loved by all fans. He started his career in Philadelphia, playing for the Phillies of the National League, but after playing one game for the Philadelphia Athletics of the American League in 1902, he moved to the Cleveland Broncos.[15] In 1903, the team was renamed the Naps in honor of Lajoie.[16] Lajoie seemed to have a pretty good deposition. Early in his career, while playing first base in a game in Boston, a fan ran onto the field and asked him, "Nap old boy, I've got to get that 5 o'clock train back to little old Woonsocket. Stake me to $2, will you?"[17] He obliged the fan with $2 without any real interruption of the game.[18] Lajoie also wanted to win the title and the car for the 1910 season.

St. Louis Browns Manager Jack O'Connor was a veteran of the Major Leagues.[19] He was born on June 2, 1869, and played his first Major League game at the age of seventeen.[20] He appeared in 1451 games with a lifetime batting average of .263 and 19 home runs.[21] He was known as either "Peach Pie" or

Ty Cobb, whose much-disputed 1910 batting crown also earned him a new automobile (National Baseball Hall of Fame Library Cooperstown, New York).

4. The Dispute Over the 1910 AL Batting Title

"Rowdy" Jack O'Connor depending on who you asked.[22] Before arriving as the Browns manager in 1910, O'Connor had already established a sordid reputation in baseball. The *Spalding's Official Baseball Guide* of 1892 discussed O'Connor's conduct:

> On July 3, President Kramer of the American Association expelled John O'Connor of the Columbus club from the Association, for habitual drunkenness, disorderly conduct and insubordination. He was suspended by the club the day before without pay, for disgraceful conduct.[23]

O'Connor was thought of as the consummate baseball man. In his classic work, *The National Game,* Alfred H. Spink wrote the following about O'Connor just before he began the 1910 season as the manager of the St. Louis Browns:

> Jack O'Connor is one of the best baseball men in the country, and there is every reason to expect that he will prove the success with the St. Louis Americans that President Hedges anticipates. No one knows the game any better and he has had the experience to build up a first-class team.[24]

He further stated:

> As far as baseball knowledge goes, O'Connor bears the highest reputation among the best judges of play in the world. Baseball men say that he is without doubt one of the cleverest judges of play that has ever graced the game.[25]

O'Connor's first and only managerial job in Major League Baseball was with the Browns in 1910. The team finished last in the American League with a record of 47–107 and a .305 winning percentage, 57 games behind the front runner.[26] O'Connor's actions on the day of the doubleheader, October 9, 2010, the last day of the 1910 season, were viewed as suspicious by several parties, including the president of the American League, Ban Johnson.[27] O'Connor was eventually terminated as

"Rowdy" Jack O'Connor never backed down from a fight, even against his own team (National Baseball Hall of Fame Library Cooperstown, New York).

Browns manager on October 15, 1910, for these actions.[28] He later sued the Browns for breach of contract.[29]

Ban Johnson was livid over the events which happened in the doubleheader and would start an investigation into events surrounding the batting race. The player in the spotlight and on the hot seat was Browns rookie John Corriden. He would be questioned by Johnson about his play in the doubleheader.[30] Corriden would play four more seasons in the major leagues and finish with a lifetime batting average of .205.[31] He actually became a teammate of Ty Cobb's on the 1912 Tigers club. Browns owner Robert Hedges was also at the doubleheader on October 9, 1910, and would give a statement to Ban Johnson for the investigation. The official scorer for the doubleheader was E. V. Parrish. He claimed a Browns scout attempted to bribe him to give Lajoie an advantage over Cobb.[32]

The Race

Throughout the 1910 season Cobb and Lajoie battled for the title and the car, each man fighting to keep the lead. At mid-season, it looked as though Lajoie had the title virtually locked up.[33] He was batting .399 while Cobb was at a mere .372.[34] However, Cobb made a mad rush at the title and the car. For all games played through August 4, Cobb had a 13-point lead over Lajoie, with Cobb at .381 and Lajoie at .368.[35]

American League
BATTING AVERAGE

Player and Club	G.	A.B.	R.	H.	S.B.	S.H.	Av.
Strunk, Athletics	11	32	7	14	2	1	.438
Cobb, Detroit	95	357	71	136	49	10	.381
Lajoie, Cleveland	96	356	51	131	18	15	.368
Speaker, Boston	84	316	60	108	19	9	.342
Laporte, New York	80	281	33	89	10	14	.317

(Averages as of August 4, 1910.)

Two weeks later Cobb's lead had increased to 19 points, with Cobb at .377 and Lajoie at .358.[36]

American League
BATTING AVERAGE

	G.	A.B.	R.	H.	S.B.	S.H.	Av.
Strunk, Athletics	11	32	7	14	2	1	.438
Cobb, Detroit	108	395	82	149	55	11	.377
Mcloan, Chicago	16	55	4	20	1	1	.364

4. The Dispute Over the 1910 AL Batting Title

	G.	A.B.	R.	H.	S.B.	S.H.	Av.
Lajoie, Cleveland	115	427	59	153	20	16	.358
Speaker, Boston	99	379	66	129	21	9	.340

(Averages as of August 18, 1910.)

A calculation of their averages through September 1 showed Lajoie narrowing Cobb's lead to just three points.[37]

American League
Batting Average

Players and Clubs	G.	A.B.	R.	H.	S.B.	S.H.	Av.
Strunk, Athletics	11	32	7	14	2	1	.438
Cobb, Detroit	119	442	92	160	60	11	.362
Lajoie, Cleveland	126	473	64	170	23	16	.359
Speaker, Boston	110	418	73	145	23	9	.347
E. Collins, Athletics	123	470	72	155	63	22	.330

(Averages as of September 1, 1910.)

Cobb would miss ten days in September due to an eye ailment requiring him to wear "smoked" glasses to filter the sunlight.[38] On September 6, in Detroit, Lajoie and Cobb went head to head. The Tigers prevailed 6–2, but both Cobb and Lajoie went 2 for 4, with Lajoie getting a double and Cobb a triple.[39] The next day in Cleveland the Naps prevailed 4–3.[40] Lajoie had a perfect day at the plate with a single, two walks and a sacrifice, and he also stole two bases.[41] Cobb did not play.[42] On September 9, in Cleveland, the Tigers turned the tables on the Naps and won 5–2.[43] Once again Cobb did not play but Lajoie went 1 for 4 with a double.[44] On September 13, the Tigers grabbed a 6–0 lead, but the Naps scored 7 runs in the sixth inning and won 8–7.[45] Both stars went hitless — Lajoie 0 for 5 and Cobb struck out in a pinch-hitting role in the eighth inning.[46] The next day in Detroit the Tigers won 9–8.[47] Once again Cobb did not play, but Lajoie was 2 for 3 with a double and was hit by a pitch.[48] As of September 15, Cobb was still leading Lajoie by three points.[49]

American League
Batting Average

Player and Club	G.	A.B.	R.	H.	S.B.	S.H.	Av.
Cobb, Detroit	125	459	95	167	60	13	.364
Lajoie, Cleveland	141	526	79	190	28	18	.361
Speaker, Boston	122	468	81	160	26	10	.346
E. Collins, Athletics	136	518	75	164	66	24	.317
Oldring, Athletics	126	515	73	161	16	19	.313

(Averages as of September 15, 1910.)

Lajoie picked up the pace on September 19 with a 3 for 3 day, including a double and a stolen base, in a 5–4 win over the Athletics.[50] The batting records through September 22 showed Lajoie finally overtaking Cobb and leading the race by seven points.[51]

American League
Batting Average

Player and Club	G.	A.B.	R.	H.	S.B.	S.H.	Av.
Lajoie, Cleveland	147	548	83	202	29	18	.368
Cobb, Detroit	128	468	97	169	60	13	.361
Speaker, Boston	127	485	85	167	27	10	.344
E. Collins, Athletics	142	544	78	177	73	24	.325
Knight, N.Y.	107	376	52	116	22	17	.309

(Averages as of September 22, 1910.)

Lajoie continued his torrid pace on September 26 with a 3 for 4 day in a 5–5 tie with Boston.[52] The next day in a doubleheader against the Red Sox Lajoie was 3 for 4 in the first game and 1 for 4 in the nightcap.[53] In the first game Lajoie doubled, hit a home run, and stole a base.[54] On September 28, Lajoie did not play against the Red Sox due to an injury.[55] Cobb kept pace on September 29, with a 3 for 3 day and a stolen base in a 6–5 loss to the Yankees.[56] With the end of the season less than two weeks away, Lajoie went 3 for 4 with a triple in an 8–5 win over the White Sox on October 1.[57] The two stars faced each other again in a doubleheader in Detroit on October 5. Cobb and Lajoie each gathered three hits in the doubleheader as the Tigers and Naps split the games.[58]

First Game

CLEVELAND	AB	R	H	PO	A	DETROIT	AB	R	H	PO	A
Turner, 3b.	5	1	1	0	4	D. Jones, lf	4	0	0	1	0
Graney, lf.	5	1	1	2	0	O'Leary, 2b.	5	1	1	2	3
Jackson, rf.	4	2	2	0	0	Cobb, cf.	3	2	2	2	0
Lajoie, 2b.	4	0	3	3	6	Crawford, rf.	5	0	3	1	0
Hornhorst, 1b.	5	1	1	14	0	Mor'ty, 3b.	3	0	0	0	2
Birmingham, cf.	5	1	1	1	0	Bush, ss.	3	0	0	2	5
Smith, c.	5	1	1	4	2	T. Jones, 1b.	3	0	1	13	1
Sall, ss.	5	1	3	6	5	Casey, c.	3	0	1	9	1
Mitchell, p.	5	0	2	0	2	Mullin, p.	4	0	0	0	4
Total	43	8	15	30	19	Total	33	3	8	30	16

Second Game

DETROIT	AB	R	H	PO	A	CLEVELAND	AB	R	H	PO	A
D. Jones, lf.	3	1	1	1	0	Turner 3b.	3	0	1	1	2
Kirke, 2b.	2	0	1	1	2	Graney, lf.	3	0	1	2	0

4. The Dispute Over the 1910 AL Batting Title

DETROIT	AB	R	H	PO	A	CLEVELAND	AB	R	H	PO	A
Cobb, cf.	3	1	1	1	0	J'kson, rf.	3	0	1	1	0
Crawford, rf.	2	1	1	0	1	Lajoie, 2b.	2	0	0	2	1
Mor'ty, 3b.	1	1	0	2	2	Hohnhorst, 1b.		0	0	7	0
Bush, ss.	1	0	0	1	4	Birmingham	2	0	0	0	0
T. Jones, 1b.	2	0	1	7	1	Land, c.	2	1	0	2	0
Stanage, c.	2	0	0	2	2	Ball, ss.	2	0	1	0	1
Summers, p.	2	0	0	0	1	Blanding, p.	2	1	1	0	3
Total	18	4	5	15	13	Total	21	2	5	15	7

The Chalmers automobile became a major focus in the batting race between the two players. They even posed in the car on the day before the doubleheader between the two clubs.

Continuing his torrid pace, Lajoie gathered three more hits in a 6–5 loss on October 6.[59] League records for the games played through Thursday, October 6, showed Lajoie with a slim two-point lead over Cobb.[60]

American League
BATTING AVERAGE

Player and Club	G.	A.B.	R.	H.	S.B.	S.H.	Av.
Jackson, Cleveland	17	66	14	25	4	2	.379
Lajoie, Cleveland	156	580	93	219	29	20	.378
Cobb, Detroit	139	503	106	190	65	15	.376
Madden, Boston	13	31	4	11	0	1	.355
Speaker, Boston	141	539	93	182	33	11	.338

(Averages as of October 6, 1910.)

On October 8, Lajoie went 1 for 4 and his averaged dipped.[61] On the same day, in Chicago, the Tigers were shutout 4–0 and Cobb did not play.[62] On October 9, 1910, the *Washington Post* displayed a picture of Cobb with the caption, "Ty Cobb, has quit to join McAleer's picked team at Philadelphia. He leaves the Tigers with an unofficial batting mark of .378 a fraction of a point in advance of Lajoie, who has a chance to go by at St. Louis today."[63] With Cobb now gone, Lajoie had two games to win the batting title and the car.

On October 9, the St. Louis Browns were scheduled to play a doubleheader against the Naps and Lajoie. The stage was now set. Cobb did not play the last two games of the season, hoping his lead would still be intact when the season came to a close. On the last day of the season Lajoie started the doubleheader at .376, seven points behind Cobb.[64]

Lajoie responded with four hits in the first game of the doubleheader and four hits in the second game as well.[65] Eight hits would seem to be more than enough to pass Cobb but Lajoie would still come up short of the title. Eight hits in a doubleheader is a great day for any player, but the manner in which Lajoie got the hits would come under suspicion. As of October 10, the batting race was still to be decided.[66] The Chairman of the National Baseball Commission, August Herrmann, was still waiting on the official averages from both leagues.[67] Herrmann stated that because of the Lajoie-Cobb dispute no more prizes or bonuses would be permitted under the rule for the National Commission.[68] The box score for the doubleheader of October 9, 1910, showed the following[69]:

First Game

ST. LOUIS	AB	R	H	PO	A	CLEVELAND	AB	R	H	PO	A
Truesdale, 2b.	5	0	0	1	3	Bronkie, 3b.	3	1	1	1	1
Corriden, 3b.	5	2	3	1	1	Graney, lf.	4	1	1	4	0
Stone, lf.	5	0	2	1	0	Jackson, cf.	4	1	2	1	0
Griggs, 1b.	5	1	0	13	1	Lajoie, 2b.	4	1	4	4	1
Wallace, ss.	3	0	1	3	6	Easterly	4	0	0	1	0
Northen, cf.	4	0	0	2	0	Stovall, 1b.	4	0	2	7	0
Hartzell, rf.	3	2	1	1	0	Smith, c.	4	0	0	4	1
Stephens, o.	3	0	2	4	4	Peckinpaugh, ss.	4	0	0	2	6
Nelson, p.	3	0	1	1	6	Blanding	4	0	0	0	1
Total	36	5	10	27	21	Total	35	4	10	24	10

*None out when winning run was scored.

Errors — Truesdale, Wallace, Bronkie

```
St. Louis    1 1 1 0 0 1 0 0 1 — 5
Cleveland    3 1 0 0 0 0 0 0 0 — 4
```

Two-base hits — Jackson, Corriden, Griggs, Graney, Stephens. Three-base hits — Lajoie, Griggs. Sacrifice hit — Stephens. Stolen bases — Bronkie, Stovall, Griggs. Wild pitch — Blanding. Bases on balls — Off Nelson, 1; off Blanding, 4. Struck out — By Nelson, 4; by Blanding, 4. Left on bases — St. Louis, 12; Cleveland, 5. Time of game — One hour and forty-two minutes. Umpire — Mr. Evans.

Second Game

CLEVELAND	AB	R	H	PO	A	ST. LOUIS	AB	R	H	PO	A
Birmingham, 8b.	4	1	2	1	5	Truesdale, 2b.	4	0	0	2	0
Graney, lf.	5	2	0	1	0	Corriden, 3b.	4	0	2	3	1
Jackson, cf.	4	0	2	1	0	Stone, lf.	4	0	1	0	0
Lajoie, 2b.	4	0	4	0	4	Griggs, 1b.	4	0	0	10	0
Easterly, rf.	4	0	0	2	0	Wallace, ss.	3	0	1	1	4
Hohnhorst, 1b.	3	0	1	18	0	Northen, cf.	3	0	0	2	0
McGuire, c.	3	0	0	2	1	Hartzell, rf.	3	0	1	2	0
Peckinpaugh, ss.	4	0	1	2	4	O'Conner, c.	0	0	0	1	0

4. The Dispute Over the 1910 AL Batting Title

	CLEVELAND						ST. LOUIS				
	AB	R	H	PO	A		AB	R	H	PO	A
Falkenberg, p.	3	0	0	0	5	Malloy, p.	3	0	0	0	5
Killifer, c.	3	0	0	6	2						
Total	34	3	10	27	19	Total	31	0	5	27	12

Errors — Truesdale, Corriden, Malloy, Graney, (2.)

| Cleveland | 1 | 0 | 2 | 0 | 0 | 0 | 0 | 0—3 |
| St. Louis | 0 | 0 | 0 | 0 | 0 | 0 | 0 | 0—0 |

Two-base hits — Birmingham; Corriden. Sacrifice hit — Lajoie. Double plays — Malloy, Truesdale, and Griggs; Lajoie, Peckinpaugh, and Hohnhorst. Passed balls — McGuire, Killifer. Stolen base — Stone. Hit by pitched ball — By on balls — By Malloy. (McGuire.) Wild pitch — Malloy. Bases on balls — Off Malloy, 4. Struck out — By Malloy, 6; by Falkenberg, 1. Left on bases — St. Louis, 4; Cleveland, 10. Time of game — One hour and sixteen minutes. Umpire — Mr. Evans.

On October 9, the *New York Times* noted, "Lajoie Leads Cobb In Batting." The paper referred to Lajoie's eight for eight day and the unofficial averages showed Lajoie at 386.8 and Cobb at 383.4.[70] On October 10, 1910, the *Chicago Daily Tribune* headline read, "Lajoie's Bat Wins Prize Automobile."[71] It showed the "unofficial figures" as[72]:

	G.	A.B.	H.	Pct.
Lajoie	159	592	228	.385
Cobb	140	508	194	.382

The headline in the *Washington Post* on October 9 read, "Corriden Helps Lajoie to Seven Out of Eight Hits."[73] The article read in part:

Cobb Is Not Popular

At this stage of the game Lajoie had piled up only five hits. In the fifth Larry beat out a bunt to Corriden. In the seventh Malloy, after passing two batters, struck out Graney and Jackson. Lajoie then laid down his seventh bunt, a little roller to Corriden. Easterly fanned.

In the eighth inning Hornhorst walked, McGuire was hit by a pitched ball. Peckinpaugh fanned, Falkenberg forced Hornhorst, Birmingham was out. This left just three men to come up in the ninth, and Lajoie was the third man to step up to the plate. Graney fanned, Jackson was out on a tap. Lajoie bunted to Corriden and was safe getting his eighth hit.

For some reason Cobb is not popular in St. Louis; while Lajoie is held in high esteem and has been able to fatten his batting average beyond the pale of discretion. It is figured by local experts that he has won the coveted prize.[74]

Lajoie's day consisted of seven bunt singles and a triple.[75] It was noted Lajoie that was not "considered highly fast."[76] Lajoie was also credited with a sacrifice on the day which was later questioned as to whether that may have been scored as a hit as well.[77]

In the first inning of the first game Lajoie struck a line drive to center field which soared over the centerfielder's head, giving Lajoie a triple.[78] Some spectators in the stands thought a more experienced outfielder might have caught the ball.[79] In the third inning of the second game of the doubleheader, a batboy was sent to the official scorer to determine if the scorer had given Lajoie a hit on a ball that Corriden had fumbled.[80] The box score shows Corriden with one error. At this point, Lajoie only had five hits and needed more to catch and overtake Cobb.[81] He proceeded to get hits in the fifth, seventh, and ninth with two outs by bunting down the third base line and beating the throw to first.[82]

St. Louis Browns manager Jack O'Connor appeared in 1,453 games from 1887 to 1907.[83] However, he evidently still had one game left in him behind the plate. Oddly enough he waited three seasons to make his last appearance on October 9, 1910, in the second game of the doubleheader. He registered one putout but did not bat. Not to be outdone, Naps manager Deacon McGuire also caught the second game, going 0 for 3. It was the only game McGuire appeared in all year as a player.

On October 9, the *Chicago Daily Tribune* reported Lajoie had unofficially won both the batting title and the car.[84] It noted that the Browns third baseman Corriden played a short left field every time Lajoie stepped to the plate.[85] Five local sportswriters charged that the Browns allowed Lajoie to get the hits he recorded.[86] The next day Lajoie stated all his hits were legitimate:

> Every hit I made in the double-header played in St. Louis Sunday was made on the square.
> I did not speak to a St. Louis player about my batting average. I asked no favors from any one, and worked my head off to make the safe drive I collected.
> After my first hit, a clean drive to center for three bases, the St. Louis players played deep, expecting me to pound the ball out every time. I fooled them the next time up by beating out a bunt, and, knowing that a bunt would be the unexpected every time up, continued to lay the ball down and beat it out.
> I am sorry that some persons are inclined to think that the batting championship has been decided in a questionable manner. I worked hard to achieve the honor.[87]

Umpire Billy Evans weighed in with his version of what occurred, stating on October 10:

> Not until yesterday have I seen anything to make me believe that Lajoie was being helped to win the batting prize. I have heard that the pitchers of various clubs were out to get the auto for Larry, that they would put the ball in the groove for him with nothing on it, whereas Cobb would be asked to swing against the best stuff they had in stock. It sounded plausible but I can truthfully say that not until yesterday have I seen Lajoie helped out.[88]

Lajoie wanted the car as much as Cobb.[89] In fact, he even admitted to calling the official scorer at his home to determine if he had nine hits instead

4. The Dispute Over the 1910 AL Batting Title

of eight.[90] E. V. Parrish was the official scorer on October 9 for the doubleheader. He said Harry Howell, a Browns scout, approached him during the doubleheader and asked him how one of Lajoie's at-bats was scored.[91] Parrish said Howell wanted him to change Lajoie's sacrifice to a base hit but Parrish would not change it. Parrish reported later in the day a batboy brought him an unsigned note promising a new suit of clothes if he would change his scoring.[92]

As with many other moments in baseball history, the Cobb-Lajoie episode produced a poem. Maybe not as famous as "Casey at the Bat" or "Tinker to Evers to Chance" but, nevertheless, still entertaining and insightful.

Cautious Corriden's Funny Fests Now Embalmed in Immortal Verse[93]
Edgar A. Guest, in *Detroit Free Press.*

I'd like to be as popular as Larry Lajoie.
I'd like to have a lot of friends to ease my weary ways;
I'd like to have them do for me what they have done for him;
'Twould make this life of mine, I'm sure, less burdensome and grim.
How Nice 'twould be for me if I were entered in a race,
To have them trip the other man and kick him in the face;
My cheeks would flush with manly pride as in I walked to get
The prize I had so bravely won, and yet, and yet — and yet —

I'd like to be as popular as Larry Lajoie,
I wouldn't have to sit up late or rise at break of day;
I wouldn't have to struggle hard or sacrifice my joys,
But while my rivals worked I could be mingling with the boys.
Serene and happy, feeling sure that when the race began
My friends would do their very best to beat the other man;
In spite of all his skill and strength I'd win the race you bet,
And have the glory and the prize, and yet, and yet — and yet —

I'd like to be as popular as Larry Lajoie,
At present no one likes me enough to smooth the way.
Nobody gives me hits that I am not entitled to,
They play my bunts for all they're worth, the way they ought to do.
The curves come whizzing o'er the plate, the fielders are keen,
And all the hits I ever get are sizzling ones and clean.
And if I ever win a prize I earn it, you can bet!
Nobody hands a gift to me, and yet, and yet — and yet —

The more I think about it now the better satisfied
I am that things are as they are. I'd rather keep my pride,
I'd rather strive to win and fall, I'd rather Ty Cobb be
Than Larry Lajoie today with such a victory.
I'd rather lose a motor car than lose my self-respect,
I'd rather lose a fight then fail to keep my head erect.
I don't want my friends to hand me hits or win fights for me,
If I can't win it on the square I don't want victory.

The Investigation

Although all those involved in the doubleheader asserted their innocence, the president of the American League began an investigation into the matter. The day after Lajoie's extraordinary batting exhibition, Ban Johnson stated that no more prizes would be permitted and that he was undertaking an investigation into the events surrounding Lajoie's success in the doubleheader on October 9, 1910.[94] Johnson stated, "Even if the assertions proved unfounded the merest suspicion of crookedness works irreparable injury to the game, and from now on no more individual contests for prizes will be allowed."[95] On October 12, Umpire Billy Evans filed a report with Ban Johnson regarding the "Lajoie Incident."[96] Notwithstanding his previous statement reported in the *Washington Post*, Johnson stated that Evans gave Lajoie a "clean bill" with regard to his hitting performance in the doubleheader.[97]

In the midst of the uncertainty President Johnson was already mulling over a possible solution to the batting dispute. He was contemplating returning the prize automobile to Chalmers, having the league declare a tie between Lajoie and Cobb for the batting race, and awarding a league prize to both players.[98] He would meet with St. Louis Browns owner Robert Hedges,[99] Browns rookie John Corriden, Browns manager Jack O'Connor, and official scorer E. V. Parrish in an effort to get the "real story."[100] At the request of Johnson, Corriden appeared at President Johnson's office on October 14. Corriden stated to Johnson that he was respectful of Lajoie's hitting and that was the reason he was playing so far back.[101] Ban Johnson found Corriden's statement "satisfactory"[102] and issued a statement:

> I found that Corriden had a perfectly logical and, as I believe, an absolutely truthful explanation of the reason why Lajoie made so many hits.
> There have been some misrepresentation over the character of the hits. One that was represented as a bunt was a low rifle drive, which it would have been dangerous to field. Others were cleverly placed bunts that a veteran fielder would have difficulty in getting, and a player new in major league company might be excused for missing them.
> Any one familiar with Lajoie's skill as a batter can understand how it would be quite possible for him to make hits against a recruit when he can turn the trick against the most experienced veterans of the game time and again. I give Corriden a clean bill, and do not think that any suspicion of blame should attach to him. I am very glad to find the facts as they are.[103]

Jack O'Connor received a telegram from President Johnson telling him that he was to report to Chicago within 24 hours to explain what happened in the doubleheader.[104] After meeting with O'Connor, President Johnson stated, "As far as I know there are absolutely no charges of unfairness to be made against Mr. O'Connor, and no official action on my part will be taken."[105]

4. The Dispute Over the 1910 AL Batting Title

Notwithstanding Johnson's investigation, O'Connor and Howell, the Browns scout, were both fired on October 15, 1910.[106] Browns President Hedges stated, "The investigation has proven beyond doubt that there is none guilty of misconduct or dishonesty."[107] Regardless, Hedges gave O'Connor his unconditional release, saying he would not allow any conduct that even seemed "suspicious" to be connected with the St. Louis Browns.[108] Hedges also said with regard to Howell, "no man ever worked harder for success of the St. Louis Browns...."[109] President Johnson stated he received a letter from Hedges discussing the "Lajoie affair" and that O'Connor would be replaced.[110] In the letter Hedges indicated O'Connor was not involved "in any irregular scoring deal."[111]

On October 15, President Ban Johnson declared Ty Cobb the batting champion of the American League for 1910.[112] Cobb also laid claim to the Chalmers automobile.[113] Cobb stated, "That's bully news. I am glad that I won, because I worked hard to be the champion batsman of the two leagues, but it is equally pleasing to know that Larry will get a machine, too. The rivalry between us was very keen, but it was of a most friendly character so far as I am concerned. I am certainly glad Lajoie will be rewarded for the battle he gave me."[114] The Chalmers Car Company had decided to award cars to both men, which President Ban Johnson permitted.[115] Lajoie later noted "that the automobile I got ran a lot better than the one they gave to Ty."[116] Of course, human nature being what it is, Sherwood Magee of the Phillies, who won the National League batting championship, complained he should have received a car as well.[117] He said, "There was no reason why a beaten contender in the American League should be treated better than a champion in the National League."[118]

The final official batting averages were fairly calculated and posted[119]:

Official Figures Given.

The batting record of Lajoie and Cobb, as turned in by the official scorers and approved and promulgated by Mr. Johnson, is as follows:

	At bat.	B.H.	Pct.
Cobb	509	196	.33506
Lajoie	591	227	.33409

With Cobb the declared winner and both players in receipt of new cars, it would seem that the whole matter had been put to rest.[120] That might have been true if not for Browns manager Jack O'Connor. O'Connor was out to clear his name and get the remaining money he believed the Browns owed him on his two-year contract. He declared his innocence in the Cobb-Lajoie episode. After all, he had received a clean bill from umpire Billy Evans, the American League president, and the team owner. No one involved had pointed the finger at him as a guilty party.

O'Connor Litigation

O'Connor always asserted his innocence in the "Lajoie incident," although several writers of the day hinted that O'Connor was aware of a "frame up" and "winked at it."[121] O'Connor was ready with an answer. "Lajoie outguessed us ... we figured he didn't have the nerve to bunt every time. He beat us at our own game. I will not send any of my players to play up close to Lajoie when he tries to bunt."[122] After the season was over, O'Connor indicated he would ask baseball's national commission to award him a year's salary based on his contract with the Browns.[123] He believed he was still entitled to one year's salary on a two-year contract.[124] O'Connor clearly stated his intentions:

> [Ben Adkins] has scheduled the annual meeting of the St. Louis American League Club next Tuesday, when I think he will appoint Bob Wallace as my successor. Until he names the 1911 manager of the Browns I can't bring suit, as I will have to offer him my services for next year. But when he names the next manager I will enter suit for every cent of my 1911 salary.
>
> I have never lost a fight in baseball or in any other line, and if I didn't feel as though I would be successful in going after Hedges this time I wouldn't try to collect the money from him. I haven't a chance in the world to lose this suit.[125]

O'Connor continued by saying if Hedges did not like the way he ran the ball club he should have said something and stated a reason for his firing.[126] He also noted:

> I said a few days after the season closed that I had a two-year contract to manage the Browns. I served one year and will be on hand next year if wanted unless I break a leg or am killed. I will be ready to fulfill my end of the transaction and Hedges must let me or come up with the dough. That's in black in white.
>
> But I intend to call on him personally or write him and offer my services for next year. Of course, I know they will be refused. If they are, I will file suit.[127]

O'Connor had made it known to Hedges he would sue and was confident he would win.[128]

O'Connor received a salary until January 1, 1911.[129] The Browns had an annual meeting on December 6, 1910, and the directors of the ball club discussed O'Connor's situation at that time.[130] To complicate matters further, a corporate transaction occurred on December 20, 1910, when President Ban Johnson approved the transfer of the club's majority stock.[131] Robert Hedges transferred stock to several individuals but he was still to serve as the president of the club until January 1911.[132] The new owners considered O'Connor's claim and showed some interest in staving off a potential lawsuit. They also said O'Connor would be retained in some capacity with the club, most likely as a scout.[133]

However, it was clear O'Connor was not in the long-term plans for the Browns.[134] The syndicate which now owned the Browns indicated in late

4. The Dispute Over the 1910 AL Batting Title

December 1910 that the new manager of the Browns must have social standing and be a man of integrity.[135] If the Browns were looking for sophistication, then O'Connor was probably not their man. "O'Connor, of course, is impossible. He is an uncouth person, of no social aplomb, and qualifies for a job, according to the interview, 'because he has too large a following in North St. Louis not to have him on our side.'"[136]

Notwithstanding promises of employment in the Browns organization, O'Connor never again worked for the Browns. O'Connor said no one in baseball would hire him. It should be noted that there may have been some personal animosity between O'Connor and the Browns. O'Connor married a 17-year-old Kentucky beauty, Isabella Cora, in the late 1890s.[137] After a tumultuous relationship, the marriage ended in divorce.[138] A few years later the former Mrs. Jack O'Connor married St. Louis Browns club president Ralph Orthwein.[139]

O'Connor eventually did file a lawsuit as promised.[140] Approximately two and a half years after the doubleheader, on May 12, 1913, a jury returned a verdict in O'Connor's favor for $5,000, the amount the Browns owed him for his second year under the contract.[141] The jury deliberated a mere thirty minutes in arriving at their verdict in favor of O'Connor.[142] O'Connor was the last witness to testify at the trial.[143] Two fans, Sidney Cook and Julius Cronheim, had testified they overheard O'Connor giving orders that would assist Lajoie over Cobb.[144] Cook testified he heard O'Connor "instruct his players to favor their opponents."[145] Cook further testified he heard O'Connor tell his pitcher, Malloy, to give base on balls to Cleveland batters so Lajoie could be brought to the plate more often.[146] Cook also said he heard O'Connor tell Malloy to hit the Cleveland manager with the ball.[147] Malloy's pitching line included four walks, a wild pitch, and a hit batsman. Cook also testified he heard O'Connor swear at Corriden for touching a ball hit by Lajoie which resulted in a sacrifice and not a hit.[148]

President Ban Johnson testified at the trial by way of deposition that was filed with the court before the trial.[149] Johnson stated he ordered that O'Connor be dismissed because he had instructed third-baseman Corriden to play back while Lajoie was batting.[150] This seemed to be inconsistent with his finding after his investigation that O'Connor did nothing wrong. President Hedges testified at the trial as well. He mentioned he was at the doubleheader and made no protest about how the Browns players were playing.[151] At trial, O'Connor adamantly denied that he favored Lajoie in any manner.[152]

The Browns appealed the St. Louis circuit court's ruling.[153] On appeal, the Browns argued that O'Connor's contract had expired "on or about October 15th, 1910."[154] They also argued that O'Connor was in breach of his contract by "instruct[ing] one Corriden, who played the position of third baseman of the defendant club, to play so far back of his regular and ordinary position as third baseman as to allow Lajoie to make what are known as 'basehits,' which

Lajoie could not and would not have made had it not been for the instructions by plaintiff to Corriden."[155]

At trial, O'Connor testified that he gave instructions to all players to play back for Lajoie, not just Corriden.[156] He further testified he "played that game of ball the same as any other game of baseball he had played in his life; that it was as square as he had ever played and he had not given any player any instructions that he ought not to have given to have them play an honest game of baseball...."[157] The court of appeals said that "[t]o have sustained these charges, the jury would have had to act on the vaguest suspicion."[158] Many publications asserted that O'Connor had some influence over the events which occurred in the doubleheader on October 9, 1910, but a jury, as well as a state court of appeals, found he was not in breach of contract and had done nothing improper during those games.

A jury only needed thirty minutes to find O'Connor was not in breach of his contract by favoring Lajoie and that O'Connor had a two-year contract with the Browns.[159] O'Connor may not have been the most sophisticated guy in the world but evidently he was persuasive. He won his case at the trial court level and that verdict was upheld in his favor over three years later. O'Connor had called his shot. He said he had no chance of losing and that he had never backed down from a fight before and would not back down from a fight with the Browns.[160] The court of appeals found "no substantial evidence that plaintiff [O'Connor] was desirous of favoring Lajoie in his contest for batting honors over Cobb, or that he, in disregard and in violation of his duties, and to favor Lajoie, instructed Corriden to play so far back of his regular position as to allow Lajoie to make successful hits, and which he could not otherwise have made."[161] The jury's verdict was upheld by the Missouri appeals court on January 4, 1916, over five years after the doubleheader.

All issues arising from the October 9, 1910, doubleheader and the 1910 American League batting race were now resolved, or were they? Baseball is a numbers game and people have debated baseball statistics for over a century.[162]

1981

Seventy-one years later the 1910 batting race would once against be subject to debate.[163] In 1981, the *Sporting News* historian Paul McFarlane discovered that Cobb had actually been given two extra hits during the season.[164] Under those circumstances Lajoie would have taken the crown. Major League Baseball, however, refused to take the crown away from Cobb.[165]

On April 18, 1981, the *Sporting News* published a story once again examining the 1910 race. The article said that Lajoie was the actual winner of the 1910 batting race based on research performed by McFarlane.[166] Commissioner

Bowie Kuhn and American League President Lee MacPhail opposed any move that would take the title away from Cobb.[167] The writer stood behind his story: "Readers of the *Sporting News* have known for decades that this paper provides the most accurate, most informative news possible.... The revisions in the Cobb and Lajoie records are in keeping with TSN's philosophy."[168] After reviewing the situation, the Official Baseball Records Committee did not change the records and affirmed Cobb's 1910 title.[169] On December 16, 1981, the Official Baseball Records Committee rejected the appeal by the *Sporting News* over the Cobb-Lajoie matter.[170] As a result, the 1982 edition of the *Sporting News* lists Cobb as the 1910 batting title winner. But the *Sporting News* was not satisfied with the decision and noted, "The score isn't final yet."[171]

Prior to 1981, publications consistently showed Cobb as the leading batsman for the 1910 season. For instance, the 4th edition of Joseph L. Reichler's *The Baseball Encyclopedia*, published in 1979, showed Cobb winning the title at .385 and Lajoie at .384. However, John Thorn and Pete Palmer's *Total Baseball*, published in 1989, shows Lajoie at .384 and Cobb second at .383. In yet another twist, the 4th edition of Gary Gillette and Pete Palmer's *The ESPN Baseball Encyclopedia*, published in 2007, put Cobb first with .383 and Lajoie second at .384. It addresses the discrepancy in Cobb's batting record:

> Nevertheless, there is a paradox inherent in the historical accuracy of baseball statistics. Too many people mistakenly believe that baseball stats are engraved in stone, like birth and death dates on a granite tombstone. If the Macmillan Baseball Encyclopedia showed that Babe Ruth hit 714 home runs, or that Ty Cobb finished with 4,191 hits and a career batting average of .367, most people believe that these are immutable facts.
>
> Not so. At least four mistakes have been found in the past twenty-five years in the official batting records for Cobb. The net result in correcting these errors in pre-computer record keeping is that "The Georgia Peach" has 4,189 hits and a career .366 average *to the best of our knowledge*. So, when the nation watched as Pete Rose broke the all-time hits record on September 11, 1985 with his 4,192nd base hit, few knew that Rose already had broken Cobb's record three days earlier. By the way, the first edition of the Macmillan encyclopedia showed Ty Cobb with 4,192 official career hits, though that was changed without explanation to 4,191 in subsequent editions.[172]

The 1910 American League batting race has been put to rest but, for many, it still remains unresolved.[173] The 1910 batting race was historical and provided the catalyst for baseball to institute the Most Valuable Player Award.

Conclusion

Who should hold the title for 1910 American League best batsman? Did Lajoie receive some assistance along the way from Jack O'Connor because of the hatred for Cobb? It is pretty well documented now that Cobb's average was only .383. Did O'Connor give Lajoie a helping hand in the doubleheader? Two courts said O'Connor did nothing wrong and that is the way Jack O'Connor would have wanted it. Why did O'Connor insert himself into the second game of a doubleheader between the Browns and the Naps? The real answer may never be discovered. It will remain one of baseball's mysteries.

5

People v. Cicotte[1]
The Black Sox and Baseball's Most Famous Trial

Introduction

The criminal trial arising out of the events of the 1919 World Series may be the most famous event in sports history and certainly in baseball.[2] Even the most casual baseball fan is familiar with the notorious events surrounding the 1919 World Series. The Black Sox scandal has been investigated, discussed, and written about extensively, and has even become the subject of several Hollywood films.[3] Lawyers and baseball fans have been fascinated with the Black Sox trial and its connection to baseball for over 90 years.

1919 World Series

The 1919 World Series was not anticipated to be a very competitive series. After all, the 1919 Chicago White Sox were thought to be one of the greatest teams in baseball history with Eddie Cicotte on the mound, future Hall-of-Famer Ray Schalk as backstop, and Shoeless Joe Jackson roaming the outfield and terrorizing pitchers.[4] The 1919 White Sox went 88–52 (.629) finishing 3½ games ahead of second-place Cleveland and 7½ ahead of the third-place Yankees. They had won the World Series in 1917. The White Sox led the league in batting average (.287), runs (668), RBI's (571), stolen bases (150), and hits (1,343). Their opponent in the World Series, the Cincinnati Reds, were a very good team as well, winning 96, losing only 44 (.686), and finishing 9 games ahead of the second-place Giants. The Reds were a good ball club but it was the lineup of the White Sox that made them famous.[5] The Reds would, however, not be intimidated and they beat the White Sox in a nine-game series that would become the talk of baseball and the subject of baseball lore. There had been some rumors that the series might not have been on the "up and up" and rumors of gamblers fixing the series were rampant. Many kept a keen eye on the players to see how they would perform. The vast majority of those covering the series thought it was being played on the "square."[6] The publisher of the *Sporting News*, J.G. Taylor Spink, was an official scorer at the 1919 World Series and thought it was played "square" but noted a few suspicious plays that occurred during the series.[7] Tris Speaker, manager of the Cleveland Indians, wrote a series of articles for the *Washington Post* about the 1919 World Series. After game one, Speaker wrote:

> The Chicago team that led us to the wire had Eddie Cicotte working like one of the greatest pitchers I had ever seen in action. The Sox, who showed us the way, played smart ball. If the Cicotte who pitched against Cincinnati today looked like the Cicotte who beat us so often during the American League campaign, then I better quit center-fielding and go to pitching myself.
>
> If the White Sox played smart ball today I am going to recruit the Indians for next season from some place over in Europe, where they never saw our national game played.... There are a lot of things that are generally taught in the minors. For instance, we learn to protect base runners when they make attempts to steal and we so arrange our infield on base hits to the outfield as to cut off the return throw and nip the batsman in case he makes an effort to go down to second.[8]

The 1920 season was coming to a close when the Black Sox Scandal broke. On September 19, 1920, a well-known Chicagoan, Fred Loomis, penned a letter to the editor of the *Chicago Tribune*:

> **What's Going to Be Done?**
>
> I am intensely a lover of the game. I am constrained to write to inquire just what is going to be done to clarify this situation, which at the present time seems so badly confused.
>
> There is a perfectly good grand jury located in the county. The citizens and taxpayers of Illinois are maintaining such an institution for the purposes of investigating any alleged infraction of the law.
>
> Those who have in their possession the evidence of gambling last fall in the world series should come forward with it and present it in a manner that may give assurance to the whole country that justice will be done in the case where the confidence of the people seems to have been so fragrantly violated.[9]

The Grand Jury

The Cook County grand jury met for the first time on September 22, 1920, to investigate the alleged conspiracy behind the 1919 World Series. White Sox owner Charles Comiskey had done some investigation into the matter and on September 20 had provided to presiding judge Charles McDonald the findings of his investigation. Comiskey would testify to the grand jury that he had investigated the 1919 World Series but found nothing which would indicate his players were involved.

As the grand jury dragged on, the players began to see that the evidence was mounting and pointed to them as the culprits. Giants pitcher Rube Benton and gambler Billy Maharg both testified before the grand jury. The *Philadelphia North American* published an interview with Maharg on September 27, 1920, in which he set forth all the details of the scheme and specifically named Eddie Cicotte as the mastermind behind the entire set-up. Maharg testified that Cicotte sold the idea to both gambler Bill "Sleepy" Burns and Maharg. Maharg said he paid Cicotte $10,000.

The grand jury issued indictments in late September 1920, and issued its final report on November 6, 1920:

> The jury is impressed with the fact that baseball is an index to our national genius and character, the American principle of merit and fair play must prevail, and it is all important that the game be clean, from the most humble player to the highest dignitary. Baseball enthusiasm and its hold upon the public interest must ultimately stand or fall upon its court.
>
> Baseball is more than a national game; it is an American institution, having its place prominently and significantly in the life of the people. In the deplorable absence of military training in this country, baseball and other games having "team play" spirit offer the American youth an agency for the development that would be entirely lacking were it relegated to the position to which horse racing and boxing have fallen. The national game promotes respect for proper authority, self-confidence, fairmindedness, quick judgment and self-control.[10]

Confessions

With pressure building, Eddie Cicotte was the first player to step forward and admit his wrongdoing in the 1919 World Series. Cicotte first went to the office of the club's attorney, Alfred Austrian. In the presence of Charles Comiskey, Sox manager Kid Gleason, and attorney Austrian, a sobbing Cicotte admitted he took money to fix the series. Cicotte was then taken to the criminal courts building where assistant state's attorney Hartley Replogle questioned Cicotte in front of Judge McDonald and the grand jury. Cicotte confessed his part in throwing the 1919 World Series, saying "I was a fool," as he exited the jury room.[11] The *New York Times* reported Cicotte's testimony as follows:

> "I've lived a thousand years in the last year."
>
> Describing how two games were thrown to Cincinnati, Ciccotte, according to court officials, said:
>
> "In the first game at Cincinnati I was knocked out of the box. I wasn't putting a thing on the ball. You could have read the trademark on it when I lobbed the ball up to the plate.
>
> "In the fourth game, played at Chicago, which I also lost, I deliberately intercepted a throw from the outfield to the plate which might have cut off a run. I muffed the ball on purpose.

"At another time in the same game I purposely made a wild throw. All the runs scored against me were due to my own deliberate errors. I did not try to win."[12]

...

"The day before I went to Cincinnati I put it up to them squarely for the last time, that they would be nothing doing unless I had the money.

"That night I found the money under my pillow. There was $10,000. I counted it. I don't know who put it there, but it was there. It was my price. I had sold out 'Commy.' I had sold out the other boys, sold them for $10,000 to pay off a mortgage on a farm, and for the wife and kids.

"If I had reasoned what that meant to me, the taking of that dirty crooked money — the hours of mental torture, the days and nights of living with an unclean mind, the weeks and months of going along with six of the seven crooked players and holding a guilty secret, and of going along with the boys who had stayed straight and clean and honest — boys who had nothing to trouble them — say, it was hell.

"I got the $10,000 cash in advance, that's all."[13]

Joe Jackson was next, confessing to his part in the scandal, testifying he was promised $20,000 but only got $5,000.[14] Jackson's story was a confirmation of Cicotte's.[15] He said he was given $5,000 by White Sox pitcher Lefty Williams while the club was in Chicago, and when he threatened to tell about it, White Sox players Chick Gandil, Lefty Williams, and Swede Risberg told him, "You poor simp, go ahead and squawk. Where do you get off if you do? We'll all say you're a liar, and every honest baseball player in the world will say you're a liar. You're out of luck. Some of the boys were promised a lot more than you, and got a lot less."[16] His story was summarized in the *Chicago Tribune*.

JACKSON'S STORY

Joe Jackson last night described his confession to the grand jury as follows:

"I heard I'd been indicted. I decided that these men couldn't put anything over on me. I called up Judge McDonald and told him I was an honest man, and that he ought to watch this thing. He said to me, 'I know you are not.' He hung up the receiver on me.

"I thought it over. I figured somebody had squawked. I got the idea that the place for me was the ground floor. I said 'I'll tell him what I know.'

"He said, 'Come on over and tell it to me.' I went over."[17]

At one point the *New York Times* reported that Jackson testified to the grand jury he either struck out or hit easy balls when hits would mean runs. Jackson never testified in such a manner. Following are the relevant parts of Jackson's testimony before the Cook County grand jury, Charles A. McDonald, Chief Justice of the Criminal Court, presiding, on September 28, 1920. Jackson was questioned by Hartley L. Replogle, Assistant State's Attorney.

Q: Mr. Jackson, you understand that any testimony you may give here can be used in evidence against you at any future trial; you know who I am, I am State's Attorney, and this is the Grand Jury, this is the foreman of the Grand Jury. Now, I will read this immunity waiver to you so you will know just what it is:

5. The Black Sox and Baseball's Most Famous Trial 81

"Chicago, Illinois, September 25, 1920. I, Joe Jackson, the undersigned, of my own free will make this my voluntary statement and be willing to testify and do testify before the Grand Jury with full knowledge of all the facts and of my legal rights, knowing full well that any testimony I may give might incriminate me, and might be used against me in any case of prosecution or connected with the subject matter of my testimony, and now having been fully advised as to my legal rights, I hereby with said full knowledge waive all immunity that I might claim by reason of my appearing before the Grand Jury and giving testimony concerning certain crimes of which I have knowledge.

(Whereupon the witness signed the foregoing document)

...

Q: You played in the World Series between the Chicago Americans Baseball Club and the Cincinnati Baseball Club, did you?
A: I did.

...

Q: Did anybody pay you any money to help throw that series in favor of Cincinnati?
A: They did.
Q: How much did they pay?
A: They promised me $20,000, and paid me five.
Q: Who promised you the twenty thousand?
A: "Chick" Gandil.
Q: Who is Chick Gandil?
A: He was their first baseman on the White Sox Club.
Q: Who paid you the $5,000?
A: Lefty Williams brought it in my room and threw it down.
Q: Who is Lefty Williams?
A: The pitcher on the White Sox Club.
Q: Where did he bring it, where is your room?
A: At that time I was staying at the Lexington Hotel, I believe it is.
Q: On 21st and Michigan?
A: 22nd and Michigan, yes.
Q: Who was at your room at that time?
A: Lefty and myself. I was in there, and he came in.
Q: Where was Mrs. Jackson?
A: Mrs. Jackson — let me see — I think she was in the bathroom. It was suite; yes, she was in the bathroom, I am pretty sure.
Q: Does she know that you got $5,000 for helping throw these games?
A: She did that night, yes.
Q: You say you told Mrs. Jackson that evening?
A: Did, yes.
Q: What did she said about it?
A: She said she thought it was an awful thing to do.

...

Q: Did you recall the fourth game that Cicotte pitched?
A: Yes, sir.
Q: Did you see any fake plays made by yourself or anybody on that game, that would help throw the game?
A: Only the wildness of Cicotte.
Q: What was that?

A: Hitting the batter, that is the only thing that told me they were going through with it.
Q: Did you make any intentional errors yourself that day?
A: No, sir, not during the whole series.
Q: Did you bat to win?
A: Yes.
Q: And run the bases to win?
A: Yes, sir.
Q: And fielded the balls at the outfield to win?
A: I did.
Q: Did you ever hear anyone accusing Cicotte of crossing the signals that were given to him by Schalk?
A: No, sir, I did not.

...

Q: Where did you put the $5,000, did you put it in the bank or keep in on your person?
A: I put it in my pocket.
Q: What denominations, in silver or bills?
A: In bills.
Q: How big were some of the bills?
A: Some hundreds, mostly fifties.

...

Q: Did you do anything to throw those games?
A: No, sir.
Q: Any game in the series?
A: Not a one. I didn't have an error or make no misplay.
Q: Supposing the White Sox would have won this series, the World's Series, what would you have done then with the $5,000?
A: I guess I would have kept it, that was all I could do. I tried to win all the time.

...

Q: Weren't you very much peeved that you only got $5,000 and you expected to get twenty?
A: No, I was ashamed of myself.

...

Q: Did you drink much, Mr. Jackson?
A: Now and then, I don't make no regular practice of it.
Q: Do you get drunk?
A: No, sir.
Q: Have you been drunk since you have been with the Chicago White Sox team?
A: Yes, Sir.
Q: Where?
A: Atlantic City.
Q: You were not playing?
A: Off days.
Q: Did Mr. Comiskey or Mr. Gleason know you were drunk at that time?
A: I don't judge they did, no, sir.
Q: Who was with you when you got drunk?
A: Claude Williams, John Fennier and myself.

5. The Black Sox and Baseball's Most Famous Trial

Q: That is some years ago, he played with the Chicago team, is that right?
A: I think it was '18.
Q: You haven't been drunk since you played with the Chicago team?
A: Not what you would call drunk, no.

...

Q: Had you ever played crooked baseball before this?
A: No, Sir, I never had.[18]
Q: Did anybody ever approach you to throw a game before this?
A: No, sir, never did.

...

Q: You think now Williams may have crossed you, too?
A: Well, dealing with crooks, you know, you get crooked every way. This is my first experience and last.

Joe Jackson. Jackson confessed his awareness of the Series fix in 1919 but swore he never did anything to lose (National Baseball Hall of Fame Library Cooperstown, New York).

Q: Where else did you talk to Williams, outside of the time you were out riding in his car?
A: Somewhere we were at, I believe in Washington.
Q: When was that?
A: That was this summer, I think.
Q: How long ago?
A: I think it was the second Eastern trip.
Q: What did you say to him at that time, and what did he say to you?
A: We just brought up the World's Series, I told him what a damned fool I thought I was, and he was of the same opinion, so we just let it go at that.[19]

After testifying for two hours, Jackson left the courthouse, saying, "I got a big load off my chest.... I'm feeling better."[20] Both Cicotte and Jackson were taken into custody by detectives of the state attorney's office.[21] Their detention was not in the nature of an arrest and both would be released later.[22]

Another White Sox player, pitcher Claude "Lefty" Williams would follow Cicotte and Jackson in confessing the "frame-up" of the 1919 series.[23] Significant portions of his statement, made under questioning by White Sox attorney Alfred Austrian, included:

Q: And how much did you receive after the fourth game?
A: $10,000.
Q: Did you keep the ten?
A: I did not.
Q: How much did you keep?
A: I kept $5,000 of it.
Q: $5,000 was for you, and $5,000 for Jackson?
A: That was what I was instructed.[24]

The *New York Times* reported the statement of White Sox outfielder Oscar "Happy" Felsch, another of the players to confess, as follows:

> "The whole deal seemed so easy when we fell for it — we were expert ball players and it would have been a snap for us to get away with it, they said. We fell. But you can't get away with it all the time — because while you can fool others you can't fool yourself.
>
> I got $5,000, I would have gotten that much on the level if the Sox had won. I'm out of baseball — thrown out because I was crooked. Have I gained anything? What I am going to do? I don't know — go to hell, I guess.
>
> We've sold ourselves and our jobs — the only jobs we knew anything about. We've gotten in return only a few dollars — while a lot of gamblers have gotten rich. Looks like the joke's on us, don't it?"[25]

White Sox owner and president Charles A. Comiskey immediately sent a letter to eight Sox players suspending them.

> You and each of you, are hereby notified of your indefinite suspension as a member of the Chicago American league baseball club [the White Sox].
> Your suspension is brought about by information which has just come to me

directly involving you and each of you in the baseball scandal [now being investigated by the grand jury of Cook County] resulting from the world's series of 1919.

If you are innocent of any wrongdoing you and each of you will be reinstated; if you are guilty you will be retired from organized baseball for the rest of your lives if I can accomplish it.

Until there is a finality to this investigation it is due to the public that I take this action, even though it costs Chicago the pennant.[26]

The Criminal Indictments

In late September 1920, eight White Sox players were indicted by the Cook County grand jury on the charge of "fixing" the 1919 World Series.[27] The *Chicago Tribune* reported the indicted octet of players as:

EDDIE CICOTTE, pitcher, admitted he received $10,000 from the agent of a gambling syndicate.
JOE JACKSON, outfielder, confessed $5,000 was paid to him.
FRED MCMULLIN, utility man.
OSCAR (HAPPY) FELSCH, center fielder.
CHARLES (SWEDE) RISBERG, shortstop.
CAUDE WILLIAMS, pitcher.
GEORGE (BUCK) WEAVER, third baseman.
ARNOLD (CHICK) GANDIL, former first baseman, who quit major league baseball at the beginning of the present season.[28]

The original indictments were quashed but the eight former White Sox would be reindicted by a Cook County grand jury in March 1921.[29]

In November 1920, Illinois elections resulted in a change in the Cook County State's Attorney's Office. The state's attorneys who had presented the case to the grand jury in September, Maclay Hoyne and Hartley Replogle, were out of office. A new state's attorney, Robert Crowe, inherited the case and discovered that the confessions of the players had gone missing. Just as any good lawyer would do upon discovering such a fact, he quickly assigned the case to assistant state's attorney George Gorman. Gorman appropriately went into a stall mode. Under Illinois law the state was required to file charges within 18 months of the alleged crime. On February 14, 1921, eight players were arraigned before Judge Dever but he dismissed the original indictments. On March 26, 1921, just a few days before the 18-month deadline was set to expire,[30] seven of the eight players were re-indicted. Fred McMullen was let off the hook.

In Illinois, in 1919, there was no law dealing with the "fixing" of a sporting event, so the state's prosecutors would have to be creative when filing charges against the players and gamblers. Even if it could be proven that the eight ballplayers had not done their best in the 1919 World Series, not doing their best was not a crime.[31] The state would have to prosecute the players and the gamblers on fraud and conspiracy charges, a much more difficult task.

The players were tried on twelve counts, but the state would voluntarily dismiss several counts before the case went to the jury. The remaining counts which went to the jury were:

1. Statutory conspiracy to obtain divers sums of money from divers persons by means and use of the confidence game.
2. Statutory conspiracy to obtain divers sums of money from divers persons by false pretenses and to cheat and defraud the same.
3. Common law conspiracy to injure the business and reputation of the American League Baseball Club.
4. Statutory conspiracy to obtain from the public generally and any individual whom the defendants might meet divers sums of money by means and use of the confidence game.
5. Statutory conspiracy to obtain from the public generally and any individual whom the defendants might meet divers sums of money by false pretenses.
6. Statutory conspiracy to obtain from the public generally and any individual whom the defendants might meet divers sums of money by false pretenses and to cheat and defraud the same.
7. Statutory conspiracy to obtain from the public generally and any individual whom the defendants might meet divers sums of money by means of the confidence game.
8. Common law conspiracy to cheat and defraud the American League Baseball Club of large sums of money by causing and indulging the players improperly and erroneously and not in accordance with their skill and ability to execute plays required of them.[32]

Bill of Particulars

Every trial has legal maneuvering by the lawyers and the Black Sox trial was no exception. In law school students take courses dealing with criminal procedure to learn how to make their way through the legal maze of the criminal courts. On February 14, 1921, Benedict Short, attorney for indicted players Joe Jackson and Claude Williams, and Nash & Ahern, representing Buck Weaver, filed a Petition for Bill of Particulars[33] asking the prosecutor to detail the charges on which the defendants were to be tried. This is a very common motion filed by criminal defense lawyers.[34] The players' 12-page petition was extensive and detailed.[35] The petition and the response by the state's attorney are instructive as to the legal positions of the parties.

5. The Black Sox and Baseball's Most Famous Trial

Relevant portions of the defendants' Petition for a Bill of Particulars included the following:

> And your petitioners further pray that the People be required to furnish to them any and all such further information and particulars as may enlighten your petitioners as to the nature of the several charges set forth in said first four counts of said indictment, so that they may have an opportunity of preparing a defense and of knowing the nature of the several offences with which they are charged.

Joe Jackson specifically pled the following with regard to "Sleepy" Bill Burns, Abe Attell, and Hal Chase.[36]

> [A]nd your petitioner, the said Joseph Jackson, says that he is acquainted with the said William Burns, mentioned in said indictment, and that he last saw the said William Burns in October of 1919 in the lobby of the Sinton Hotel at Cincinnati, Ohio, but that at that time he merely greeted him and that neither at that time nor at any other time has he had any business transactions or personal relations with the said William Burns; that he knows the said Hal Chase, but has not seen or hear [sic] from the said Hal Chase for a period of about five years and that during said time he has had no business transactions or personal relations with the said Hal Chase; ... and that he does not know and never saw and never had any business transactions or personal relations, either directly or indirectly with one Abe Attell....

With regard to how they played the series, the defendants stated:

> Your petitioners further say that they are not informed by said fifth count of said indictment in what particulars they and each of them and the other of their co-defendants baseball players intended to play unskillfully and not in accordance with their best skill and ability and they are not informed by said count in said indictment that said series of games was ever played, but that they know of their own knowledge that said series of games was played, but that they are uninformed as to what overt acts were done or committed by them in the playing of the games of said series in pursuance of said alleged conspiracy; that they are uninformed as to what particular games and what particular plays of each game were purposely and wilfully erroneously and improperly executed by them or any of them and that they are not informed by said indictment that the outcome of said games could or might have been any different in result than they actually were.

The players pled their innocence as well: "And your petitioners further allege and show to the court that they are entirely innocent of the charges...."

Buck Weaver, Joe Jackson, and Lefty Williams made their case and position very well known in their petition. They spent much of their petition detailing their statistics for the series:

> [T]hat your petitioner, the said Weaver, played the position of third baseman in said series and that he had a batting average of .324 and a fielding average of 1.000, while during the playing season of the year 1919 his batting average was .296 while his fielding average for said playing season at said position of third baseman was .963, and as contrast your petitioner shows that one Groh played the position of

third baseman for said Cincinnati Club and that during said series his batting average was .175 while his fielding average was .931 and that his batting average during his playing season for the year 1919 was .310 and his fielding average was .971, and your petitioner, the said Jackson, shows that during said series his batting average was .375 and that his fielding average was 1000 and that during the playing season of the year 1919 his batting average was .351 and his fielding average was .967, and as a contrast to said average during said periods his opponent on said Cincinnati Club was one Duncan, and that said Duncan during said series had a batting average of .269 and a fielding average of 1000 and that during the playing season of the year 1919 he had a batting average of .244 and a fielding average of .982, and your petitioner, Williams shows to the court that he is a pitcher on said American League Baseball Club of Chicago and that during said series he pitched three of the games of said series and that in two of said games he allowed but four hits to a game and that the average number of hits in the average baseball game is not less than eight hits and your petitioners show, as further contrast, to said averages, that there were certain other players who played with said Chicago Club during said series and during the playing season of the year 1919, who have not been indicted with your petitioners and who are not charged with conspiracy to execute plays unskillfully and that the averages of said players, are as follow: E. Collins, second baseman, batting average during said series .226, fielding average .963 and during the playing season for the year 1919, batting average .319 and fielding average .974; R. Shalk, catcher, batting average during said series .304, fielding average .978, batting average during the playing season for the year 1919 .282 and fielding average .981; J. Collins, right fielder, batting average during said series .250 and fielding average 1.000 and batting average during the season for the year 1919 .279 and fielding average .957; Ed Murphy, utility man and pinch-hitter, batting average during the said series .000 and batting average for the season of the year 1919 .486; Harry Liebold, right fielder, batting average for the series .056 and fielding average 1.000 and batting average for the season of 1919 .302 and fielding average .928.

Your petitioners, therefore show that on the whole their batting and fielding averages during said series were better and of a higher percentage than their batting and fielding averages during the playing season of 1919 and that such averages during such series were better than the averages of their opponents playing the same positions and that such averages on the whole were better and higher than the batting and fielding averages made by the members of the Chicago League Club who have not been indicted and who are not named as co-defendants with your petitioners.[37]

In response, the state offered the requested Bill of Particulars, stating among other things,

That the defendants participating in said games as players conspired, confederated and agreed together with the defendants not participating therein to so conduct themselves throughout the said games and so manipulate their playing in each of said games as to make certain in advance of the playing of said games the outcome thereof and the winner thereof, and so as to make certain in advance of the playing of all of the games of said series the outcome of the majority of the games of said series and the winner of the majority of said series of games; That, as a result of such false and fraudulent pretenses and by means of said confidence game, defendant

Edward Cicotte, procured the sum of $10,000.00; that the defendant Claude Williams, procured the sum of $5,000.00; the defendant, Joe Jackson, procured the sum of $5,000.00; that other of the defendants obtained divers other large sums of money, the exact total amounts of which is unknown.[38]

The Criminal Trial

Many criminal cases are settled without the necessity of a trial, but not this one. The Black Sox trial began on June 27, 1921, and ended on August 2, 1921, lasting just over a month and including eight days of jury selection. Judge Hugo Friend was assigned to hear the case. When the trial finally began, Judge Friend announced there would be no "balks" by either party because "these trials had been delayed long enough."[39] The defendants had nearly a dozen well-known lawyers representing them while the state assigned two lawyers to the case.[40] When the day of the trial came, all seven indicted ballplayers were present but the gamblers proved to be a little more difficult to apprehend. Abe Attell, Hal Chase, and Sport Sullivan were not present at the trial. Arnold Rothstein was never indicted.

The selection of a jury can be a tedious process, especially in a case involving celebrities. Six hundred men were questioned by the lawyers during voir dire.[41] After two weeks of voir dire and threats by Judge Friend that the court would begin to hold night sessions if a jury could not be selected, the jury was seated on July 15, 1924. The jurors and their occupations were as follows:

Stephen Shuben, Merchant
Herbert J. Jordan, Stationary Engineer
Paul E. Luebcke, Employee of Chicago Telephone Company
Joseph Vesely, Foreman for Air Motor Company
Harry Willis, Heater for Indian Steel Company
Andrew Jackson, Store Fixtures
Edward Linman, Clerk
William Harry, Hydraulic Press Operator
Paul J. Ziedke, Florist
Emil J. Groskopf, Clerk
William H. Deutcher, Automobile Mechanic
John Schoenhofer, Foreman for Darling & Co., Packers[42]

The fate of some of the most famous men in the country would now rest in the hands of everyday citizens of Chicago. There is little doubt that each one of the jurors would have heard of the well-publicized trial. That, however, would not disqualify them from serving as jurors.

It always helps when a charged defendant is willing to testify on behalf of the state. The prosecutors were anxious that the high profile ballplayers be found guilty, so they cut a deal with Bill Burns and Billy Maharg, providing them with immunity from all charges in exchange for their testimony. The success of the state's case now rested upon star witness Bill Burns, former White Sox pitcher.[43] Known to all as "Sleepy" Bill Burns when he played, Burns went 30–52 in five big league seasons with a lifetime ERA of 2.72. His last season in the majors was 1912.

The first witness called by the prosecution was Sox owner Charles Comiskey. Comiskey answered questions regarding the seating capacity of the grandstand and the amount of money paid to the orchestra during the World Series. The cross examination of Comiskey became heated when Attorney Ben Short began questioning Comiskey. The exchange was reported by the *Chicago Tribune*:

Denies He Was a "Jumper"

"It is a fact, is it not," queried Attorney Short, "that you jumped from the Brotherhood to the National league in the early 90's?"

"It is not," shouted the witness in the attorney's face. "I've never broken a contract. I haven't broken any or jumped any, you can't get away with that with me," he finished.

"Well, you jumped from one league to another," replied Attorney Short.

"I went to the National league but I never broke a contract. You can't belittle me."

"Well, you are trying to belittle the ball players on trial," put in the attorney.[44]

Before the prosecution's star witness Bill Burns testified, defense attorneys Berger and Nash asked the judge to exclude the jury so the attorneys could interview Burns before they began to question him. Attorney Nash said: "Your honor promised us an opportunity to interview Burns but when we attempted to see him Sunday in the State's Attorney's office he told us that he was under instructions not to say anything. This is clearly a violation of the court's orders."[45] The judge then turned to Burns and said: "Do you wish to talk to these gentlemen?"[46] Burns answered no and the jury was brought back in and Burns began to testify.

Bill Burns gave a dramatic account of the players and of the alleged "fix" of the 1919 World Series. On the first day of his testimony Burns testified that Cicotte said "he'd throw the first game if he had to throw the baseball clear out of the Cincinnati Park."[47] He testified about the inception of the plot beginning with gambler Abe Attell (former featherweight champion) and of the "double cross" between the players and gamblers.[48] Significant portions of Burns' testimony were reported in the *New York Times*[49]:

Q: During 1919 did you visit New York?
A: Yes, sometime in August. I went there to see about an oil lease.
Q: Did you meet any of the White Sox baseball players?
A: I met them all at their hotel.
Q: Did you have any conversations with any of them?
A: Yes, with Cicotte.
Q: Is he in the room now?
A: Yes. He's the man over there with the black tie.

Burns looked squarely at the former star pitcher, who leaped to his feet. Neither displayed any emotion.

"That's the man," said Burns.
Q: What did he say?

This was objected to by the Attorney Michael Ahearn for the defense on the grounds that the meeting was in New York City and also covered actions prior to the beginning of the alleged conspiracy. He was sustained by Judge Friend.

Q: When did you next meet Cicotte?
A: At the Hotel Ansonia on Sept. 18.
Q: Any one else there?
A: Yes, Chick Gandil and Maharg.
Q: Did you have any other meetings?
A: At another time I met Abe Attell, Hal Chase and Bennett.
Q: What did you do?
A: We had a talk, then we went to the Aqueduct race track to find Arnold Rothstein, but we did not find him.
Q: Had you met Attell previously?
A: Yes, I'd known him for seven years. He was formerly a prize fighter. I'd known all the fellows for several years. Maharg spent one year at my ranch in Texas.

Rothstein's Picture Introduced

A picture of Rothstein was then introduced in evidence after it had been identified by Burns, who told of several talks concerning the alleged conspiracy he had had with Rothstein. One meeting was in the grill room of a hotel in New York City.

Q: Who attended that meeting?
A: Rothstein, Maharg and I.
Q: When did you next meet the ball players?
A: At the Sinton Hotel in Cincinnati.
Q: Do you remember the number of the room?
A: I think it was room 708.
Q: Who was there?
A: There was Gandil, Fred McMullin, "Lefty" Williams, "Happy" Felsch, Eddie Cicotte, "Swede" Risberg and "Buck" Weaver.
Q: Was that all?
A: All I remember.
Q: How about Jackson?
A: I did not see him there.
Q: Did you have any conversation with them?
A: I told them I had the $100,000 to handle the throwing of the world's series. I also told them that I had the names of the men who were going to finance it. I told them they were waiting below.
Q: What did the players say?
A: They said to show them up.
Q: Who were the financers?
A: They were Rothstein, Attell and Bennett.
Q: What happened when the men were brought in?

A: Attell said he would give $100,000 to have the series thrown. They were to lose five games, after each game $20,000 was to be paid the players.
Q: Did the players agree to this?
A: Yes.

Attorney Ben Short for the defense objected that the reply was too vague.

Q: Who made most of the statements for the players?
A: Chick Gandil. He was supposed to be the ringleader.

"I object to what he supposes," interrupted Attorney Ahern.
"Confine yourself to what was actually said," ruled Judge Friend.

Q: Did the players make any objection to receiving the money in installments?
A: They did at first, demanding it in a lump sum. They finally agreed to take it after each game.
Q: Who was this man Bennett? You have not identified him?
A: He said he was acting as Rothstein's Lieutenant and that he was handling the money for him
Q: What did Attell say?
A: He said he was also working for Rothstein.
Q: Did the players say anything to that?
A: They wanted to know if Rothstein was a responsible man. Attell answered that he did not need to worry about Rothstein, that he was a walking bank.
Q: What was that $100,000 to be paid for?
A: To throw the games in the world's series.
Q: What series?
A: The series of 1919.
Q: What was said about the order of games to be thrown?
A: Attell said we did not have to follow any order — that they could throw the first three if they chose, or alternate.
Q: Did the players themselves make any statements concerning the order of the games to be thrown?
A: Gandil and Cicotte said the first two games should be thrown. He said, however, that it did not matter to the players. They would throw them in any order that the financers wished.
Q: Mr. Burns, state whether anything was said by any one of the players concerning the throwing of any particular games?
A: Cicotte said he'd throw the first game if he had to throw the baseball clear out of the Cincinnati Park.

A wave of laughter ran through the court room at the answer. Even the player defendants laughed. Cicotte appeared at first puzzled, then broke into a grin. Burns was wiping his face frequently, keeping his eyes steadfastly on the floor. He showed flashes of temper when attacked by attorneys for the ball players.

...

Told Money Was Out On Bets

Q: What was said by either Attell or yourself at that time?
A: He told me that all the money was out on bets and that the players would have to wait until it was collected.

5. The Black Sox and Baseball's Most Famous Trial 93

Q: Where did you go from there?
A: I went to the Sinton Hotel to meet the players. I told them that the money was out on bets and that they could not get it until the next day. I also arranged for a meeting between Williams and the financiers for the next day.
Q: Who was present besides yourself?
A: Maharg was with me when I met Attell, but I was alone when I talked to the players
Q: Was Jackson with the players?
A: No.
Q: What arrangements were made about the money?
A: I was to meet Gandil and Williams before the next game.
Q: Did you have the meeting with Williams?
A: Yes, we met on a side street near the Sinton Hotel that evening.
Q: Who was with you?
A: Attell and Bennett.
Q: Did you all go together?
A: No, we went first. The players followed later.
Q: What conversations followed?
A: They asked about the game for the next day. Williams agreed to throw it.
Q: Was anything said about the $20,000?
A: Attell said it would be paid the next morning.
Q: Was any place or time named?
A: It was to be paid at 10 o'clock.
Q: When did you next see Attell?
A: The next morning. He showed me a telegram from New York.
Q: Did you read it?
A: Yes.

Telegram Is Barred

Objection to reading the telegram was sustained. Burns then told of an unsuccessful attempt to locate the telegram at the telegraph office.

Q: Did you see the players at the hotel after that?
A: Yes.
Q: Who was there?
A: All except Jackson. I told them about the telegram. I said that Attell had a telegram for twenty grand, but had not received it.
Q: What did you understand by twenty grand?
A: $20,000.
Q: What arrangements were made then?
A: I told them I would get the money and then meet them on the side lines and pay them before the game on Friday.

A laugh went through the courtroom when Burns said the players objected to being paid on Friday because they were superstitious.

Q: Did Gandil say anything?
A: Yes, he wanted to know if they were being double crossed. I told him that I was not double crossing him.
Q: Did you offer them any security?
A: Yes. I told them I'd given them an oil lease.

The last was in such a low voice that Attorney Short demanded the answer read. The players and spectators laughed at the mention of the oil lease.

Q: Did you put it up?
A: No, Maharg advised me not to. He said Rothstein might double cross us, and then I would be out. The players wanted to put my lease in escrow, but I refused.
Q: What was the lease for?
A: I had 12,000 acres of Texas oil land.
Q: What did you tell the players?
A: I told them that it was all off; that I would not put up the lease.
Q: When did you next see Attell?
A: Immediately after the second game. Maharg was with me. We went to his room at the Sinton Hotel. Bennett was also there. (Italics added)

Significant portions of the cross examination of Burns by the defense team included the following:

Cross-examination of Bill Burns by Defense Attorney James "Ropes" O'Brien:

O'Brien: Mr. Burns, how much money did you receive from [American League President] Ban Johnson?
Gorman: Objection: [counsel is leading the witness].
Judge: Sustained.
O'Brien: Did you get five hundred dollars from Ban Johnson?
Burns: Yes, for my expenses for two months.
Q: How much of this went to your wife and how much did you keep?
A: I don't know.
Q: Had you any visible means of support during the last year other than Ban Johnson?

[Burns replied that he had worked in Mexico.]

Q: I suppose you went to work for Pancho Villa when you were there?
A: No, I wouldn't work for Villa. And I wouldn't work for you, either, Mr. Ahearn!...

[Burns explained his return in April to Del Rio, Texas.]

Q: What was your occupation then?
A: Well, fishing.
Q: What for — witnesses?

[No reply.]

Q: You knew you were coming under indictment when you came to Chicago?
A: Yes.
Q: Being under indictment didn't worry you, did it?
A: No....[50]

Cross-examination of Bill Burns by Defense Attorneys Michael Ahearn, Max Lusker, and Ben Short:

Ahearn: When you went to Cincinnati, you proposed the conspiracy to the players!
Burns: I did not.
Q: You talked of an offer of $100,000 made by Attell and Bennett.
A: That was the players' proposition!
Lusker: Mr. Burns, when did you see Bennett first?

5. The Black Sox and Baseball's Most Famous Trial   95

A: In the Ansonia Hotel in 1919.
Q: When last?
A: About a week ago, I saw his back in Chicago. He was about two hundred yards away.
Q: You have a good memory, have you? You are able to remember a man after two years' time?
A: I can remember faces.
Q: Backs, too, I suppose? [*Laughter.*]
A: I did, this man.
Q: By the way, where were you going to get your reward for fixing the Series?
A: The players, and also Attell.
Q: You were going to be paid by Attell?
A: Yes.
Q: You didn't think that was double-crossing, did you?
A: No.
Q: You were going to get a slice both ways, eh?
A: Sure.
Q: Did you tell the players?
A: No. It was none of their business.
Q: You were afraid you would lose it if you told them, weren't you?

   [No reply]...

Short: You told Gandil you would spill the beans if they didn't come through with your share, didn't you?
A: That's right.
Q: The players double-crossed you, didn't they?
A: Yes.
Q: Well, you double-crossed them.
A: Not until they crossed me.
Q: Is that a reason for testifying?
A: One of them.
Q: Then it is not for the purity of baseball?
A: Well, they double-crossed me and I would have been the fall guy for the whole outfit.
Q: If the players had really been crooked, you would have been satisfied! Do you think you are even with the boys now?
A: I am liable to be before I leave here! [*Laughter.*]
Q: You don't like me much, do you, Bill?
A: Sure I think you're a smart fellow, and I wish we had someone like you at the head of this deal; we'd all be rich, now....[51]

The Evidentiary Battle Over the Confessions

Any prosecutor would love to have a signed confession by a defendant. A signed, sealed, and delivered confession can make a defense lawyer's job very tough and frequently will induce a plea. The state was holding the proverbial "smoking gun," signed confessions by Jackson, Williams, and Cicotte. But somewhere during the legal process the confessions were "lost." There were multiple theories about how they became lost. The exclusion of this key price of evidence could potentially devastate the prosecution's case.

The parties knew an evidentiary battle was brewing. After the completion of Bill Burn's testimony, the prosecution attempted to enter into evidence the confessions of Cicotte, Jackson, and Williams. The prosecutor had unsigned copies of the confessions made from the stenographer's notes, but no signed wavers of immunity by the three players. Earlier in the trial, on July 20, Assistant State's Attorney George Gorman announced that the immunity wavers signed by Jackson. Williams and Cicotte had disappeared. When asked what happened to them he responded, "Ask Arnold Rothstein — perhaps he can tell you."[52] The state's attorney did have a ringer, however, Judge McDonald. The players had "confessed" in the presence of McDonald so he could testify about what was said by the players. Judge McDonald was called to the stand and, in an unusual moment, a judge testified in front of the court. Former State's Attorney Harly Replogle also testified about the confessions.[53]

The issue for the court to decide was whether the "confessions" were given voluntarily.[54] The jury was excused and not in the courtroom during the testimony relating to the confessions. Under questioning from Gorman, Judge McDonald testified that the players were never promised anything and that they had signed immunity waivers and that "they would be given no consideration by the state attorney."[55] The significant portions of Judge McDonald's testimony were as follows:

Q: Judge, I am going to ask you to tell the jury what Cicotte said to you when he made his confessions. I will ask, however, to leave out all names except the signer of the confession in giving your testimony.

A: He told me that the first meeting was held at the Ansonia Hotel in New York City in September, 1919. At that meeting he was asked what his price would be for throwing games in the world's series. He said he would have to have $10,000 cash. The next meeting, he said, was in the Warner Hotel in Chicago, three or four days before the series. At that time he demanded $10,000 cash. When he returned home he said the money was under his pillow. There were two or three $1,000 bills and the rest smaller. He started the first game, he told me, with the intention of walking the first man. Instead he hit him with a pitched ball. After that he said his conscience hurt him and he realized that he was doing wrong. He regretted his action, but did not return the money.

Denies Promise of Immunity

Q: Was anything said about immunity?

A: He at first did not want to go before the jury without a promise of immunity, but I told him that I could do nothing for him. I told him that I could make no bargain with him. Then he asked if he could go before the jurors without his teammates knowing. I took him the rear way. We met a George Wright, a reporter, on the way and he flashed the story to the newspapers.

Q: Did you have a talk with Joe Jackson?
A: He called me after Cicotte talked to the jury and said he wasn't implicated. I told him to tell that story to the jury when his name came up for trial. Fifteen minutes later he called up and said he wished to tell all.
Q: Tell us what he said.
A: He said he was approached by one man at the Ansonia Hotel. He was offered $5,000. He refused, so he told me, because he said that was not enough to influence a laborer to do a "dirty deal." He said he priced his co-operation at $20,000. He finally came to an agreement with the fixers that he was to get his $5,000 after each game.
Q: Did he get it?
A: He said that it was not until after the fourth game that he got anything at all. Then a man came in and tossed $5,000 on the bed and told him he could take or leave it — that it was all he could get. He said his wife cried after learning that he had accepted the tainted coin.
Q: Did he ask for protection?
A: He told me that he had heard that "Swede" Risberg (one of the defendants) had threatened to "bump him off." He asked for protection while he went to the Sox park for his automobile. I gave him two bailiffs.
Q: What conversation did you have with Williams?
A: He told me much the same story about the first two meetings and said he had received $10,000, which he had divided with Jackson. I had more sympathy for him and I made him more of a promise. I told him that if he came clean that I believed the trial court would make record of it.[56]

On cross examination Judge McDonald testified:

Q: You used every little stunt to get Cicotte to confess did you not?
A: We told him that, in the language of the street, Maharg had "spilled the beans."

There was a smile as the judge broke into slang.[57]

After Judge McDonald testified he walked over to Cicotte and Jackson and said, "Hello Eddie, I'm sorry, but I had to tell the truth."[58] Cicotte smiled and said, "Hello Judge."[59] Jackson said nothing to the judge and looked straight ahead.[60]

With Judge McDonald's testimony on the record it was now the players' turn to explain to the court why they had made the alleged confessions. Cicotte, Williams, and Jackson all testified about the proceedings before Judge McDonald. The significant part of Cicotte's testimony included:

Before the immunity waiver was read, did Replogle say to you, "Do you realize what you're saying may be used against you?" he was asked.
"No," he answered.
"Did Replogle make any explanation of the waivers?"
"Probably, but I did not pay any attention."
"What did Judge McDonald say to you?"
"He said, 'You have not told me all you know.' That I said, 'Yes, I have.'"
"The judge got peeved and said, 'Indict him, Mr. Replogle.'

"I said, 'Wait a minute Judge, Austrian and Replogle promised to take care of me.'"

"Did he explain to you what they meant by 'take care of you?'"

"Austrian said I would not have to go to the pen."[61]

Joe Jackson's trial testimony included:

Q: Did they say anything to you about immunity?
A: They told me I could tell my story and then go anywhere I liked. Judge McDonald suggested the Portuguese islands.
Q: Did you talk to Judge McDonald the next morning after you talked to the grand jury?
A: I was supposed to but I got on a big party and got drunk. I had the judge's two bailiffs with me.
Q: Now, Mr. Jackson, were you drunk when you went before the grand jury?
A: About half drunk, I guess I'd been drinking.
Q: Did Mr. Replogle tell you that you would have to sign an immunity waiver and that you would later be held responsible criminally for what you told the jurors?
A: He read a lot of stuff from a paper to me. I don't know what it was. He said it was a waiver or something.
Q: Didn't you read what you signed?
A: No; they had given me their promise. I'd signed my death warrant if they had asked me to.
Q: Did Judge McDonald give you any promise?
A: He told me that if I talked I wouldn't be indicted. I wouldn't have to go to jail, put up bonds or anything. All they wanted, they said, was my address.
Q: Did you leave town immediately after you were through at the state's attorney's office?
A: No, I got tee'd up again.[62]

It was reported that "Jackson's quaint dialect and humorous answers made it an entertaining morning for the spectators" and that "Jackson's testimony kept the court in an uproar of laughter when he told of repeated sprees about the time of the grand jury investigations and explained that he had gotten two court bailiffs drunk."[63]

After hearing all the witnesses and legal arguments, Judge Friend had a tough decision to make. Who should he believe: a colleague, a jurist and a former state's attorney, or the three players? The testimony of what they said had been transcribed, there was just no signature. The original copies of the confessions made by the players had disappeared as well.[64] Judge Friend's ruling was a major defeat for the defense. The confessions would be admitted as evidence and read to the jury.[65] Judge Friend ruled that the confessions could only be used as evidence against Williams, Cicotte, and Jackson.[66] After the lawyers spent some time editing the stenographic record of the confessions of Williams, Jackson, and Cicotte, the confessions were read to the jury.[67]

The prosecutors were now in the driver's seat. They had gotten the confessions into evidence and were headed for the home stretch. The state was set to close its case with the testimony of Billy Maharg.⁶⁸ Maharg confirmed the testimony of Bill Burns. His testimony was reported in the *New York Times* as follows:

> Maharg said he met Burns in New York before the series.
> "I was in conference with Burns, Cicotte and Gandil," said Maharg.
>
> **Cicotte Is Accommodating**
>
> "We discussed throwing the series at the Ansonia hotel in New York."
> "Cicotte said he would throw the series at the Ansonia hotel in New York if gamblers wanted."
> "I went to Philadelphia to raise $100,000 to buy the players. I couldn't raise it."
>
> Q: What conversation did you have with Burns at the Ansonia after Cicotte and Gandil left?
> A: Burns told me these boys had agreed to sell the series for $100,000 so gamblers would make a cleaning. Burns asked if I could raise the money. I told him I would try.⁶⁹

The case then shifted to the defense. White Sox manager Kid Gleason testified on behalf of the defense. The significant portions of his testimony stated:

Q: When did you arrive in Cincinnati at the 1919 world's series?
A: Tuesday morning the day before the first game.
Q: Did you go to the ball park for practice?
A: I did about 10 o'clock.
Q: How long did you stay?
A: For about an hour and a half.
Q: Then if "Bill" Burns said he saw these defendants in a room at the Sinton Hotel in the forenoon, he is not telling the truth?

> *An objection was sustained.*

Q: Well these defendants could not have been in a room at the Sinton Hotel during the hours between 10 and 12 o'clock that morning.
A: Not while they were practicing.
Q: I will ask you from your experience, have you an opinion as to whether or not these defendants executed the plays during the world's series to the best of their skill and ability?

> *An objection was sustained.*
>
> *Under cross-examination Manager Gleason admitted that he could not tell for certain just what time the players left the Sinton Hotel for morning practice. He thought it was about 10 o'clock.*⁷⁰

Many White Sox players also testified for the defense. None of the White Sox players who were called to testify showed any hostility towards the "Black Sox."⁷¹ In fact, most of them greeted the players as they made their way to the witness stand to testify.⁷² The players were asked on direct examination if they thought the World Series was played on the "square."⁷³ "Each witness was asked if, in his judgment, every play during the series was played to the best of the ability of the players."[74] The prosecutor objected to this line of questioning and Judge Friend sustained the objection.[75] Future Hall of Fame catcher Ray Schalk testified on behalf of the defense as follows:

Q: Do you remember when you arrived in Cincinnati at the time of the world's series in 1919?
A: Yes, on Tuesday morning.
Q: Did you practice that morning?
A: Yes, some time, between 10 and 12 o'clock.
Q: You know all the defendant ball players here, do you not?
A: Yes.
Q: Were they all there?
A: As far as I know.[76]

On cross examination Schalk's testimony was reported as:

Q: Did you recollect exactly when you went to the field the morning you arrived in Cincinnati?
A: Not exactly. We went to the park that morning.

Attorney Gorman then announced that he would question Schalk as a witness for the state.

Q: On the evening of the second game state whether you saw the defendants together in a room at the Sinton.
A: I did.
Q: That's all.

"Captain Collins and some of the other players were there, were they not?" asked Attorney Short.
"No." replied Schalk.[77]

White Sox players Collins, Kerr, and Wilkinson also testified for the defense and gave similar answers to manager Gleason.[78] The club trainer H.W. Stephenson was the last witness called for the defense and testified as follows:

Q: I'll ask you if you gave "Swede" Risberg any medicine on the evening before the first game?
A: Yes, I did. He complained of a cold in the chest.
Q: Did you see the morning practice the day before the series started?
A: No.
Q: Did you make any note of the time you visited Risberg's room?
A: Not exactly. It was somewhere around 8 o'clock.

Attorney Gorman cross-examined him.

Q: Was Risberg in bed?
A: Yes.
Q: Who was with him?
A: Eddie Cicotte and "Happy" Felsch.[79]

Part of the strategy of the defense throughout the case was to show that actually "fixing" the World Series was impossible.[80] Attorney Michael Aherm said in opening statement: "We will show ... that it would have been impossible for Eddie Cicotte, Joe Jackson, Claude Williams, or 'Chick,' Gandil to have fixed the games. Before we finish, the jury will be convinced that some of the games were thrown."[81]

The defense had anticipated taking several weeks to present its case but after a few witnesses offered testimony, the defense rested its case "abruptly" after a night session on July 29, 1921. The sudden closing of the case was a strategic move by the defense involving a surprise tactic.[82] The defense thought it had presented evidence which contradicted the state's main witness, Bill Burns. Burns had testified that the "details" of the fix had been worked out at the Sinton Hotel the morning of the first game. Manager Gleason, several of the White Sox players, and the club trainer all testified that all the players were at a two-hour practice at the Cincinnati park on the morning of the first game of the 1919 series.[83] The state said that the meeting could have been easily held before the practice because none of the witnesses were positive about the time the players left for the practice.[84] Happy Felsch had made a damaging statement to a newspaper reporter at the time of the investigation by the grand jury. The state had intended to cross examine Felsch about this statement, but he never took the witness stand, so the statement was never put into evidence.[85]

The defense also "wrote into the record" that the receipts of the White Sox had risen from $521,175.70 to $910,206.59 in 1919. They entered these figured into the record to prove that the alleged conspiracy had not in fact injured the business of Charles Comiskey as the indictment had charged.[86] 236,928 fans attended the 1919 World Series.[87] The receipts from the 1919 World Series were a record $722,414, with the winning share for the Reds at $5,207.01 and the White Sox losing share at $3,254.36.[88]

Closing Arguments

Many cases are won or lost in closing arguments. In his closing argument assistant state's attorney Edward Prindeville argued that the state did not have to convict the defendants because they had in fact convicted themselves.[89] In his closing argument, state's attorney George Gorman said, in his opinion, the state had put forth such a convincing case that a long closing argument was not necessary.[90] Prindeville argued:

> What more convincing proof do you want than the statements made by the players? Jackson, Cicotte and Williams sold out the American public for a paltry $20,000. They collected the money, but they could not keep quiet.
> Their conscience would not let them rest. When the scandal broke, they sought out the State's Attorney's office and made their confession voluntarily. Cicotte told his story to Chief Justice Charles A. McDonald. Then he told it to Grand Jury. He was followed to the Grand Jury room by Williams and Jackson.

> On evidence which they told the jurors, Bill Burns, the State's star witness in this case, was indicted. They have called Burns, who told his story to the jury, a squawker; but I tell you that he owes his connection in the case to what these defendant ball players confessed.
>
> This is an unusual case as it deals with a class of men, who are involved in great national game, which all red blooded men follow. This game, gentlemen, has been made the subject of a crime. The public, the club owners and even the small boy playing on the sand lots have been swindled. That is why these defendants are charged with conspiracy.
>
> This conspiracy started when Eddie Cicotte told Burns in New York City that if the White Sox won the pennant there was something on and he would let him in on it. The next step was when Chick Gandil and Cicotte told Burns that they would throw the series for $100,000.
>
> This is the statement of Burns. But we do not have to depend on Burn's statement. It is also the statement of Cicotte. In his signed statement he tells the Grand Jurors that he met Burns and framed the plot in the Ansonia Hotel, in New York.
>
> Burns told you that Cicotte said: "I will throw the first game if I have to throw the ball over the fence." Cicotte tells you the same thing. All the way through you will find Cicotte statements are corroborated by Burns, and vice versa.
>
> Cicotte was advised of his rights, yet he told his story. He told of the $10,000 he got under his pillow. He told of meeting his pals and talking over the conspiracy details. He told of watching while his companions filed one by one from the meeting place so as not to raise the suspicions of the honest players.
>
> Then what did this idol of the diamond do? He went home and took $10,000 from under his pillow. Of course he was uneasy.
>
> Then the gamblers met again on the morning before the world's series began. The gamblers accepted the players' terms. It was agreed that Cicotte should pitch the first game and lose.
>
> Of course he lost. With $10,000 in his pocket how could you expect him to keep his balance and win? The weight would bear him down.
>
> Gentlemen, you will find that Burns was also corroborated in his testimony by Jackson and Williams. Jackson tells you that he got $5,000 after the fourth game.
>
> "Swede" Risberg then tells you he had a cold. The only trouble with him was that he had an overdose of conspiracy in his hide. You recall the defendants said they could not win for Kerr because he was a busher. Abe Attell told them to win, and they won. There is no pitcher on God's green earth who could have won that ball game if the defendants had not backed him up.[91]

Prindeville "was particularly bitter in speaking of Cicotte."[92]

The prosecutor further argued:

> I say, gentleman, that the evidence shows that a swindle and con game has been worked on the American public. The crime in this case warrants the most severe punishment of the law. The crime strikes at the heart of every red blooded citizen and every kid who plays on a sand lot.
>
> This county is for sending criminals to the penitentiary whether they are idols of the baseball diamond or gangsters guilty of robbery with a gun. The state is asking in this case a verdict of five years in the penitentiary and a fine of $2,000 for each defendant.[93]

Attorney Ben Short argued for the players, stating:

> The State failed to establish criminal conspiracy. There may have been an agreement entered by the defendants to take the gambler's money, but it has not been shown the players had any intention of defrauding the public or of bringing the game into ill repute. They believe any arrangement they may have made was a secret one and would, therefore, reflect no discredit on the national pastime or injure the business of their employer as it would never be detected![94]

Jury Instructions

The closing arguments ended at 3 P.M. but the jury did not get the case until about 8 P.M. that night. After the closing arguments were made, the lawyers began arguing over jury instructions.[95] Much of the debate was over the issue of the "intent" of the ballplayers.[96] It was reported that Judge Friend spent most of the afternoon preparing the jury instructions.[97] After much debate, the judge gave instructions to the jury saying the state had to prove the ballplayers had the "specific intent" to defraud the public and the baseball owners. It was not enough for the state to prove the players merely threw the games for money.[98] The jury instructions was said to be one of the points that led to the not guilty verdict.[99]

Jury instructions can win or lose a case and in this situation the instructions given by Judge Friend virtually guaranteed the defendants an acquittal. Judge Friend stated that for the defendants to be found guilty, the jury must find that the defendants had the intent to defraud the public and injure their employer's business.

This may have been one of the jury instructions read to the jury on the day of the trial:

> As a matter of law unless you are convinced beyond all reasonable doubt that the defendants and each of them conspired with the specific and particular intent either
> 1. To injure and destroy the business and reputation of the American League Baseball Club of Chicago, a Corporation;
> 2. Or to cheat and defraud the American League Baseball Club of Chicago, a Corporation;
> 3. Or to cheat and defraud Ray W. Schalk;
> 4. Or to obtain money from the public generally by means and use of the confidence game;
> 5. Or to obtain money from the public generally by false pretenses;
>
> Then you should find the defendants and each of them not guilty.[100]

Another jury instruction which may have been given to the jury reads:

> Even though you believe beyond all reasonable doubt that the defendants and each of them conspired to throw the ball games or some one or more of them in question,

and even if you believe beyond all reasonable doubt that the natural and probable consequences of throwing the ball game or some one or more of them in question would be to injure and destroy the American League Base Ball Club of Chicago, nevertheless you should find the defendants and each of them not guilty under the sixth count of the indictment unless you also believe beyond all reasonable doubt that the said defendants actually had the intent to injure and destroy the business and reputation of the American League Base Ball Club.[101]

The jury instruction with regard to the confessions most likely stated:

A confession is a statement made by the defendant, which carries with it a suggestion of guilty as to the quality of his act, and a confession is admissible or inadmissible in evidence, depending upon whether or not it was voluntarily or involuntarily made, and where a defendant makes it spontaneously on request or otherwise, without being prompted by any menace or threat made, or fear instilled by any person in authority, and without being induced by any hope, expectation or belief caused or prompted by a person or persons in authority to the affect that the punishment due to crime charged and so confessed would be waived or mitigated by the giving of such confessions. A confession is involuntary where it is induced or obtained by menace or threat or fear, or by hope, expectations and belief aroused and encouraged in the defendant by some person or persons in authority, whereby the person making the confession is reasonably led to believe that the punishment due the crime charged or confessed would be waived or mitigated by the giving of the confession. If, therefore, you believe from the evidence that the defendants, Joseph Jackson, Claude Williams, and Edward Cicotte, made a confession implicating or involving themselves, as parties to the alleged crime charged in the indictment, and that a such confessions, if made by them, were voluntary on their part, as defined in these instructions, then you are at liberty to consider them like other evidence, in view of all the circumstances of the case, as disclosed by the evidence; if, on the other hand, you believe that the said defendants made the alleged confessions which have been introduced in evidence, and that such confessions, if any, were involuntary on their part, as defined in these instructions, then it would be your duty to exclude entirely from your minds such alleged confessions, and disregard them altogether, the same as though no mention whatever had been made of them, and as thought you had no knowledge whatever concerning them.[102]

Finally the court instructed the jury as follows: "Under your oaths you should not allow sympathy or prejudice to influence you in the least in finding your verdict in this case. In your deliberations you should not be influenced by anything other than the law and the evidence in the case."[103]

Jury Deliberations

The jury was left to their deliberations and it would not take long to decide the fate of the ballplayers. A jury is given a verdict form by the court to complete during the deliberations. The criminal court file of Cook County in the Black Sox case contained forty-five proposed forms of verdicts. The proposed verdicts were for the following defendants: Charles Risberg, George Weaver, Edward Cicotte, Claude Williams, Joe Jackson, Arnold Gandil, Oscar Felsch, Carl Zork, and David Zelser. One of the proposed verdict forms for Joe Jackson stated:

> We, the jury, find the defendant _Joe Jackson_ guilty of conspiracy in manner and form as charged in the indictment, and we fix his punishment at imprisonment in the penitentiary, and a fine of _____ ; and we further find, from the evidence, that the said defendant _Joe Jackson_ is now about the age of _____ years.[104]

Two hours and forty-seven minutes after they were given the case they returned a verdict finding all defendants not guilty on the first ballot! The jurors had voted in the jury room not to discuss the verdict.[105] Weaver said, "I'd know I'd be cleared and I'm glad the public stood by me until the trial was over."[106] Eddie Cicotte said, "All I want to do is to get to Detroit.... Talk, did you say? Not here. I talked once in this building never again."[107] Defense counsel Henry Berger said the verdict was a "complete vindication of the most mistreated ball players in history."[108] Three loud knocks were heard from the jury room and Judge Friend was summoned from the Cooper Carlton Hotel to call the court back into session. As the jury read each verdict, finding each defendant not guilty, cheers erupted in the courtroom. Judge Friend congratulated the jury and said he thought it was a just verdict.[109] Court bailiffs saw Judge Friend smiling and, as he exited for the chambers, they joined in the whistling and shouting.[110] Eddie Ciccotte was the first person to the jury box and grabbed the hand of the foreman William Harry and said, "Thanks, I'd knew you'd do it."[111] The jurors lifted Jackson and Williams on their shoulders; there was cheering and papers flying everywhere.[112] The crowd cheered, "Hooray for the clean sox."[113] Weaver and Risberg were the most excited over the verdict, Felsch and Williams merely smiled, while Joe Jackson remained very quiet.[114] Gandil shook hands with a few friends then slipped out.[115] Before leaving, Gandil (who was thought by many to be the leader of the Black Sox) said, "Boys, I want to give you a sailor's farewell.... Goodbye, good luck, and to hell with Ban Johnson."[116] After the verdict the players threw a party for themselves at a Chicago west side Italian restaurant "and made whoopie far into the night."[117]

Aftermath

With the not guilty verdict, the players now waited for another verdict, that of baseball's new commissioner. They would not have to wait long:

> Regardless of the verdict of juries, no player who throws a ballgame, no player that undertakes or promises to throw a ballgame, no player who sits in conference with

Joe Jackson's swing produced a .356 lifetime average, third all-time; but his involvement with the Black Sox has kept him out of the Hall of Fame (National Baseball Hall of Fame Library Cooperstown, New York).

a bunch of crooked players and gamblers where the ways and means of throwing a game are discussed and does not promptly tell his club about it, will ever play professional baseball.[118]

The Black Sox went their separate ways after banishment from the game. Buck Weaver protested his innocence until his death and asked for reinstatement to the game.[119] Twelve-thousand Chicagoans signed a petition in support of Weaver.[120] Weaver said while he did go to the meetings he took no part in throwing the series, took no money, and always played his best.[121] But Judge Landis denied Weaver's reinstatement, saying:

> Indictments were returned against certain members of the team, including Weaver. On the trial of the case, a witness for the prosecution gave what he claimed was a detailed account of his meeting with the indicted men and arranging with them for the throwing of the world's series games.
>
> The report showed that Weaver was present in court during the testimony of this witness, who most specifically stated that Weaver was present at the conference, and yet the case went to the jury without any denial from Weaver from the witness stand.
>
> If the incriminating evidence was false, the baseball public had a right to Weaver's denial under oath. Of course, it is true that a verdict of not guilty was rendered in Weaver's favor. It was also likewise true that the same jury returned the same verdict in favor of Cicotte, Claude Williams and Joe Jackson.
>
> Weaver denies he had anything to do with the conspiracy as alleged in the confessions, which were introduced at the trial. However, his own admissions forbid his reinstatement.[122]

Weaver would protest the verdict his entire life.[123] Buck Weaver sat apart from all the other indicted defendants at the trial.[124] Joe Jackson gave an interview to *SPORT Magazine* in October 1949.[125] In the interview he said, "I was an innocent man in the records."[126] The banned White Sox players did later play together on a semi-professional team playing under different names.[127]

Civil Lawsuits

Not satisfied with the victory in criminal court some of the players decided to try their hand in civil court, suing Charles Comiskey for the money he owed them on their contracts. After all, they were found not guilty in a criminal court by a standard of beyond a reasonable doubt and a plaintiff in a civil lawsuit has a lower hurdle to overcome to establish a burden of proof in a civil case. Happy Felsch, Swede Risberg, and Joe Jackson all sued their former club for breach of contract in 1922 because of Comiskey's failure to pay them what was due on their contract after the 1919 scandal.[128] Felsch and the club tried to settle the case before trial but the parties could not come to an agreement. The club mailed a check to Felsch and six months later they received a letter from

Felsch saying he never got the check.[129] They mailed him another check but Felsch sent it back.[130] Jackson sued for $20,000 which included back pay and a bonus.

Attorney James H. Shaw represented Jackson and, during his opening statement to the jury in the civil case, he said that a certain clause was "slipped into" Jackson's contract which Jackson was not aware of when he signed the contract.[131] A Milwaukee, Wisconsin, jury returned a verdict in Jackson's favor for $16,711. Not only did the jury determine that Charles Comiskey failed to pay money he promised for the 1917 season to Jackson,[132] it also determined that Harry Grabiner, the club secretary, misrepresented the contents of Jackson's contract to him. They found that the ten-day clause, which allowed the club to discharge the contract upon ten-day notice, was not removed from Jackson's contract and Jackson signed the contract believing it had been removed.[133] The trial judge, however, set aside the jury's verdict and dismissed the case, stating that it reeked of perjury. Jackson ended up spending one night in jail as a result of his perjured testimony.[134]

The Black Sox trial will continue to be written about and discussed for years to come. The most famous ballplayers in the country, not guilty on all counts, but they were still banished from baseball.

6

Rose v. Giamatti[1]
The All-Time Hit Leader Is Banned from the Game

I'd be willing to bet you, if I was a betting man, that I have never bet on baseball. — Pete Rose, 1989

The banishment for life of Pete Rose from baseball is the sad end of a story episode. One of the game's greatest players has engaged in a variety of acts which have stained the game, and he must now live with the consequences of those acts. — A. Bartlett Giamatti, Commissioner of Baseball[2]

I'm guilty of one thing in this whole mess. I was a horseshit selector of friends. — Pete Rose[3]

Four thousand two hundred and fifty-six hits. Two thousand two hundred runs. That's all I did.... I'm a Hall of Famer. — Pete Rose, 1989

The National League from its inception waged a relentless war against the gamblers and against all forms of practices which could cast a reflection on the respectability of the game. — Alfred H. Spink, *The National Game*, 2nd ed. (St. Louis, MO: Nat'l Game Pub. Co., 1911; Carbondale: Southern Illinois University Press, 2000).

Baseball is something more than a game to an American boy; it is his training field for life work.... Destroy his faith in its squareness and honesty and you have destroyed something more; you have planted suspicion of all things in his heart. — Judge Kenesaw Mountain Landis, Baseball Commissioner

Introduction

It seems as long as there has been baseball there has been gambling and gamblers.[4] Baseball grew in popularity after the Civil War and so did gambling in the national pastime.[5] Many famous names have been involved with or associated with gamblers throughout the history of baseball, including Joe Jackson, Tris Speaker,[6] Ty Cobb,[7] Leo Durocher,[8] and George Steinbrenner.[9] Throughout baseball history, many ballplayers have been suspended or disciplined for their involvement with gamblers. Baseball has always taken a tough stance on gambling and against gamblers.[10] Every player knows Major League Rule 21; it is posted in every major league clubhouse. It states in part:

> d) BETTING ON BALL GAMES. Any player, umpire, or club official or employee, who shall bet any sum whatsoever upon any baseball game in connection with which the bettor has no duty to perform shall be declared ineligible for one year.
>
> Any player, umpire, or club or league official or employee, who shall bet any sum whatsoever upon any baseball game in connection with which the bettor has a duty to perform shall be declared permanently ineligible.

Charlie Hustle[11]

Pete Rose was, and still is to many, a baseball icon. Loved by millions of fans for his blue collar hard work approach to the game, million of fans identified with Rose, even adored him, for how respectfully he played and loved the game of baseball. Rose embodied the American national pastime and fans loved to come to the park to see him play. His career exemplified the American ballplayer. He dominated baseball in the 60s, 70s, and even into the 1980s.

Rose's baseball achievements are too voluminous to list in their entirety, but naming even a few is sufficient to illustrate his great career in baseball. Rose is baseball's all-time leader in hits (4,256), games played, and at-bats.[12] He won three batting titles, two gold gloves, one Most Valuable Player Award, the Rookie of the Year Award, and three World Series rings. However, it was not his statistics or awards that made him a baseball star, but above all else the way he approached the game and played the game. When fans think of the Cincinnati Reds, they think of Pete Rose. Even his name conjures up an association with the Reds. Rose was destined to be a Cincinnati Red. He grew up in Cincinnati and, when he graduated from high school in 1960, he signed a $7,000 contract with the Reds. Rose made his major league debut in April 1963. He had a great rookie season with the Reds, with 170 hits, 101 runs scored, 25 doubles, 13 stolen bases, and a batting average of .273.[13]

One of the more famous episodes in Rose's career, which in some ways defined his persona, was his collision at home plate with Cleveland Indians catcher Ray Fosse in the 1970 All-Star game.[14] Rose ran over Fosse at home plate in the 12th inning to score the winning run for the National League. The collision with Rose permanently injured Fosse's shoulder.[15] Some questioned whether Rose's actions were necessary in the context of an all-star contest, but above all else, the incident showed Rose's competitive nature.[16]

Rose had clearly established himself as one of baseball's all-time greats, but events loomed that would cause Rose severe heartache and damage to the game of baseball itself. He would rise to the highest levels of the game he so dearly loved only to end up in prison by the end of his career. Pete Rose had a dark side that would, in the end, overcome his greatness and celebrity and lead to his permanent removal from the game he loved. His epic showdown with Major League Baseball Commissioner A. Bartlett Giamatti tested the legal limits of the powers of the commissioner's office and captivated the baseball world during the summer of 1989, as the two heavyweights battled through the Ohio courts and in the media. The Rose lawsuit was a challenge to the authority of the baseball commissioner. Rose would try to paint Giamatti as an outsider, an Ivy League intellectual who was relying upon the testimony of convicted felons to satisfy his personal vendetta against Rose. Rose waged a public relations battle he eventually lost. Rose's feud with Giamatti would become personal in nature and the two would battle throughout the summer in the courts and the press for legal dominance and public adoration.[17] The Rose/Giamatti legal tussle has elicited an innumerable amount of articles and discussion in the legal area.[18]

Rumors of Gambling

There had been rumors circulating for some time that Rose was a gambler and wagered on a variety of sports, including baseball.[19] These rumors eventually became the subject of much concern for the office of the commissioner of baseball. On February 23, 1989, the commissioner of baseball, Peter Ueberroth, retained the law firm of Akin, Gump, Hauer, & Field to investigate whether Rose, who at the time was the manager of the Cincinnati Reds, had bet on baseball games.[20] The firm, and specifically attorney John Dowd,[21] were retained to investigate allegations that Rose, while the manager of the Reds, had bet on baseball games, including games involving his own team.

On February 20, 1989, the Commissioner's Office asked Rose to meet with Peter Ueberroth and the incoming commissioner, A. Bartlett Giamatti.[22] Ueberroth said to Rose: "We have only one purpose here. We've heard rumors about your gambling. We don't want to hear about betting on basketball or football. Did you, or did you not, bet on baseball?"[23] Rose told Ueberroth that he had never bet on baseball. Later, when asked if it was unusual for him to be called to the Commissioner's Office, Rose said, "A lot of unusual things happen to me because I'm an unusual guy. It's unusual to have two commissioners there."[24] Rumors continued to swirl around Rose for the next month that he was a heavy gambler and that he had bet on baseball, even his own team. On March 20, 1989, the Commissioner's Office confirmed that it was investigating "serious allegations" that Rose was linked to gambling.[25] The Commissioner's Office issued a joint statement from Ueberroth and Giamatti saying:

> The office of the commissioner, which was founded to preserve the integrity of the game, has for several months been conducting a full inquiry into serious allegations involving Mr. Pete Rose. When the commissioner's office has completed its inquiry,

Pete Rose's hustling style of play was legendary, but so were his gambling habits (National Baseball Hall of Fame Library Cooperstown, New York).

the commissioner will consider the information presented and take whatever action is warranted by the facts consistent with the rules and procedures of major league baseball.[26]

Rose responded, "All I can say is that we're cooperating with the commissioner's office. We hope everything gets taken care of real fast before opening day so we can get down to business. Business is winning the National League West."[27]

Sports Illustrated published an article reporting Rose had bet on baseball. In the article, Ron Peters, who owned a café in Franklin, Ohio, was described as Rose's principal bookmaker.[28] Peters admitted in federal court that he was a bookmaker and cocaine distributor. He received an 18-month prison sentence.[29] Peters told federal authorities that Rose had placed bets with him, totaling more than $1 million over a two-year period.[30] Rose responded to the *Sports Illustrated* article saying, "They talked with four guys: two of them go to jail, the other says he's a bookie, and the other one's my friend; they didn't say anything about him."[31]

Rose was in serious need of a few friends because his old ones were telling tales about him that were not flattering. He was not getting any support from his ex-wife either. She gave an interview to *Gentlemen's Quarterly*, saying her former spouse once received a dead fish in the mail.[32] Rose responded: "I don't know about that article. All I know is that my wife's been dreaming about fish."[33] It was reported that Rose had sold the bat and ball he used when he broke Ty Cobb's hit record. He responded with "no comment."[34] Rose said the bat he used to break Cobb's hit record was being held by Steve Walter, his insurance agent.[35] After being backed into a corner, Rose eventually denied all the allegations made against him.

The Investigation

On March 27, 1989, attorney John Dowd said the Rose investigation was "complicated and time-consuming" and could take several more weeks to complete.[36] When opening day arrived, the Rose investigation was like the proverbial black cloud hanging over baseball. The question remained, how would fans react to Rose? Would they support him? When the Reds announcer identified him as the manager of the Reds, Rose hustled from the dugout like he had done so many times before and the 55,385 sold-out crowd gave him a standing ovation for a full minute.[37] Rose said about the response from the fans, "I got goose bumps. Anybody would be moved by that. I could stand here all day and describe what the fans of Cincinnati have meant to me. They treated me like a king. I feel like I'm playin' again. Everybody is pulling for me."[38] It must have brought back good memories for Rose. He had been standing on first base five years earlier after breaking Ty Cobb's hit record, basking in the adoration of the fans.

As the investigation continued and there was no report forthcoming, a rising tide of opinion grew that justice was being delayed and Rose was being treated unfairly by the Commissioner's Office. Former Players Association director Marvin Miller weighed in on the Rose issue. "Giamatti, I don't have to tell you, he comes from about the only institution in the country as right-wing and arrogant as the baseball owners — namely, academia, where notions of due process or just cause are completely foreign.... They know about as much about due process as the Hottentots." Giamatti responded to Miller: "With consummate deftness, Mr. Miller manages to insult or defame people of color, working women, teachers and intellectuals: that is, core constituencies of today's labor movement. He has not lost his sensitive, light touch."[39]

Rose began to feel pressure from another source, one not well known for its sympathetic stance or "light touch," the Internal Revenue Service. The IRS had turned its sights on Rose and began investigating him for tax evasion.[40] To make matters even worse, Rose's former teammate on the Big Red Machine, catcher Johnny Bench, saw the handwriting on the wall for Rose: "Too many things are pointed toward Pete Rose and as a result, baseball is starting to suffer."[41]

On April 12, 1989, it was reported that Rose had bet as much as $16,000 a day on the Reds to win[42] and that he had used his 1975 World Series ring to repay a gambling debt.[43] Rose denied the allegations, saying the ring had been duplicated and that he still had the original ring. In a surreal moment, Rose placed his three World Series rings on display at a bank in downtown Cincinnati to stop rumors that he had actually sold the championship rings.[44] He said he sold the bat he used to break Ty Cobb's hit record and a Corvette he received from Red's owner Marge Schott to his insurance agent for $175,000.[45] "At the time, I had a Rolls Royce, three Porsches and a Mercedes. What the hell did I need a Corvette for? If I want to see it, it's right down the street from where I live."[46]

Meanwhile, baseball's investigation of Rose continued. John Dowd was accumulating documents, talking to witnesses, and even getting help from the IRS who was putting additional pressure on Rose for payment of overdue taxes. Peter Ueberroth had stepped down from the commissioner's post and A. Bartlett Giamatti, who had taken his place, was now directing the Rose investigation. Dowd had not yet completed his report and would not do so for another three weeks. In the meantime, Giamatti's next move would create much controversy and provide some major legal hurdles for the Commissioner's Office to overcome in its case against Rose. On April 18, 1989, Giamatti sent a letter to United States District Judge Carl Rubin who was about to sentence Ron Peters, Rose's alleged bookie, on tax and drug charges. The Commissioner explained that Peters had been "candid, forthright and truthful" with the investigation by Major League Baseball and, furthermore, had "provided critical sworn testimony about Mr. Rose and his associates."[47] The letter would take some temporary momentum from the Commissioner's Office and would become a key legal point in a looming court battle between Rose and the commissioner. Giamatti had not specifically asked for special treatment for Peters but it was certainly implied in his message.[48] Giamatti politely requested that Judge Rubin keep the matter confidential but Judge Rubin was a Cincinnati judge and a lifetime Reds fans and he had absolutely no intention of doing so. Judge Rubin not only failed to honor the commissioner's request but, in addition, immediately sent a copy of the letter to Rose's lawyer, Reuven Katz. Judge Rubin also read the letter into the record at the criminal hearing for Peters.[49] Katz quickly jumped on the opportunity presented to him by Giamatti, stating, "We have to look at the commissioner, in Pete's case, as the judge. Now he is commenting favorably to a U.S. District Court judge about a man who is an admitted drug dealer. He has to be thinking about whether he has prejudiced himself in this case.... We have not asked him to step down. He needs to make that determination. I don't know what was in his mind when he wrote that letter."[50]

At his hearing, Ron Peters testified Rose bet more than $1 million but did not reveal if any of that money was bet on baseball.[51] Judge Rubin made his feelings known on the record and, in an unusual statement made during a pre-sentencing meeting in his chambers with the prosecuting attorney, he said: "I resent the baseball commissioner entering into what I think is — there's evidence here, in my opinion — a vendetta against Pete Rose."[52] Judge Rubin said he was annoyed at the commissioner and was offended by the letter he sent.[53] Attorney John Dowd came forward and said he wrote the letter at the request of the attorney for Peters. Assistant U.S. Attorney Robert C. Brichler, who was prosecuting the Peters criminal case, was questioned by Judge Rubin and Brichler and said a grand jury was investigating Rose on "tax matters."[54] It was now late April and the public was growing impatient over the Rose investigation and waiting anxiously for the Commissioner's Office to make a decision about Rose's situation.[55] Meanwhile, Judge Carl Rubin continued to inject himself and his personal opinions into the Rose case, even though he also said it was none of his business.

> I don't think that such a prolonged investigation can help either the manager or the team. Also, I think that the nature of it is such that the press has tried, convinced and executed Pete Rose and I think this thing was handleable in a different fashion. This could have been done differently. It could have been over and done with before the season started, I think.[56]

Judge Rubin eventually recused himself from the Peters case after coming under pressure for his comments.[57]

Rose gave a deposition to John Dowd on the evening of April 20 and the morning of the April 21.[58] At one point in the deposition, Rose told Dowd:

"See, what you have to realize, John, and you probably don't, the majority of bookmakers are crybabies. You know, they could have the biggest weekend in the world and they're always complaining about what they lose."[59] Meanwhile, the investigation of Rose dragged on.

The Dowd Report

On May 9, 1989, Dowd finally delivered his 225-page report to the commissioner. It consisted of the report itself and seven volumes of evidence supporting the report.[60] Dowd had talked to over 40 witnesses and taken sworn statements from Rose and the two main informants against him, Ron Peters and Paul Janszen. The evidence included betting sheets which handwritten experts said Rose had signed.[61] There were also records showing Rose had made calls to bookies immediately before games. The evidence showed that Rose had bet on his own team, although always to win. Dowd concluded in his report:

> Betting on baseball by a participant of the game is corrupt because it erodes and destroys the integrity of the game of baseball. Betting also exposes the game to the influence of forces who seek to control the game to their own ends. Betting on one's own team gives rise to the ultimate conflict of interest in which the individual player/bettor places his personal financial interest above the interests of the team.[62]

He also found that

> The evidence revealed that in order to protect his stature as one of the most famous baseball players in Major League history, Pete Rose employed middlemen to place bets for him with bookmakers and at the racetrack and to pay gambling losses and collect gambling winnings, thereby concealing his gambling activity.[63]

Giamatti immediately scheduled a hearing for Rose on May 25 and delivered the Dowd report, along with its numerous volumes of supporting evidence, to Rose's lawyers. Giamatti let it be known how he viewed the role of the Commissioner's Office:

> There has been a historic wisdom of the law in this country not to intrude upon private business, including baseball ... and [baseball's] pursuit of its internal administrative remedied is wise. This is what happens [when the courts intrude], and a county court in Cincinnati did. The result is to slow down and make vastly more complex and vastly more frustrating for millions a process which was otherwise very clearly, precisely laid out.[64]

Deputy Commissioner Fay Vincent announced that the purpose of the hearing "is to be sure Mr. Rose and his counsel have a full opportunity to provide the commissioner with their views."[65] Giamatti defended the length of time taken to prepare the report, noting, "The complexity, the amount of effort and the intensity of the investigation is reflected in the report and its accompanying materials. I am confident that the amount of time it took to complete the investigation and prepare the report was appropriate."[66] Rose's attorneys must have taken one look at Dowd's report and realized there was no way they would be ready to defend Rose at a hearing in two weeks on the charges alleged by the commissioner. They asked the commissioner for a postponement of the hearing to a later date. Giamatti willingly granted an extension and the hearing was rescheduled for June 26.[67]

As the parties began to prepare for the hearing, Rose's lawyers tried to interview Ron Peters, but Peters placed conditions upon the interview.[68] With the hearing only six days away, Rose and his lawyers were in a real dilemma and had limited options. Rose had asked Giamatti to recuse himself as the decision maker in the case, but it looked like that was not going to happen. Filing a lawsuit was not the best option either. Legal precedent was against Rose and he had little chance of prevailing in court against the Commissioner's Office. The law heavily favored the position of the commissioner. Baseball would most certainly argue that theirs was a private association and, absent a decision that was arbitrary or capricious, the decision of the commissioner should be upheld.

Hometown Court

Faced with little or no options, Rose filed a lawsuit in the Hamilton County Court of Common Pleas, in Cincinnati, arguing Giamatti was not an impartial decision maker and requesting the court to block the commissioner's hearing.[69] Rose's lawsuit was a legal long shot, but he was desperate and had to try something. Most legal pundits gave the Rose lawsuit very little chance of succeeding. The significant legal issue was whether a court could review or overturn a decision made by a private body, in this case the Commissioner's Office. Judge Norbert Nadel was assigned to the case and immediately scheduled a hearing for June 22 to consider Rose's request for a temporary restraining order to block the commissioner's hearing that had been scheduled for June 26.[70] It was clear Rose and his legal team had determined they would not address the evidence of Rose's gambling head on but instead would attack the process and the institution of the Commissioner's Office in hopes of staving off any pending discipline.[71]

The first hearing in the Rose matter took place before Judge Nadel in the Court of Common Pleas in Cincinnati. It would be the beginning of a civil procedural maze reminiscent of Col. John L. Rogers chasing Napoleon Lajoie through the Pennsylvania and Ohio courts in 1901.[72] Rose and Giamatti would battle in state and federal courts for the next two months, with Rose putting up a valiant legal fight but finally accepting the inevitable, entering into an agreement with Giamatti which would banish Rose from the game of baseball.

Rose's lawyer asked Judge Nadel for a temporary restraining order and preliminary injunction enjoining Giamatti, the Reds, and Major League Baseball from:

1. Further involvement in deciding whether Pete Rose should be disciplined, banned, suspended, expelled, or declared ineligible from participation in Baseball pending resolution of this action;
2. Terminating Pete Rose's employment as Field Manager of the Cincinnati Reds or taking any action to interfere with Rose's employment in that capacity....[73]

Rose's arguments set forth in his legal brief in support of his motion stated in summary[74]:

1. Giamatti was prejudiced against Rose and therefore could not make an impartial decision;
2. The investigation performed by the commissioner "did not comport with natural justice and fair play";
3. The procedures established by the commissioner were not judicial in nature.[75]

Rose's lawyers quickly pointed to the letter written by Giamatti to Judge Rubin on behalf of a "drug dealer," stating:

> Giamatti's letter to Judge Rubin, endorsing the cooperation and truthfulness of convicted drug dealer Peters, one of Pete Rose's primary accusers, and Giamatti's statement that he would rely on the Report in making his judgment show not only that Giamatti has not maintained an appearance of impartiality, but that he has actually prejudged the accusations against Pete Rose and has found the accusations and accuser credible before Pete Rose has ever had an opportunity to respond.[76]

They also argued the commissioner showed his bias by only spending two days reviewing a 225-page report, immediately scheduling the hearing for Rose two weeks after the report was delivered, by "permitting his agents to pronounce as truthful the testimony of convicted felons," and by giving credibility to the Dowd report, notwithstanding its numerous errors and hearsay.[77] Rose argued that the commissioner "is not bestowed with the unbridled power to investigate, hear and decide what conduct is not in the best interests of baseball."[78] Rose's lawyers argued that the Major League Agreement, the Major League Rules of Procedure, and Rose's contract provided that Rose was to receive a fair hearing before a neutral decision maker. Rose's lawyer quoted the Rules of Procedure: "Proceedings before the Commissioner shall be conducted in general like judicial proceedings and with due regard for of the principles of natural justice and fair play...."[79] They argued that the proceedings should be generally held

6. All-Time Hit Leader Banned from the Game 119

like a court of law, "which means, at a minimum, that the decisionmaker will be fair and impartial and not make a decision until he has heard all of the evidence."[80] They further argued that the entire investigation of Rose had been "grossly unfair."[81] Rose's lawyers continued their barrage against the commissioner by saying the Dowd Report was unreliable and based on hearsay evidence as well as unsecured recordings of telephone calls. They said it was not an investigative report as proclaimed by the commissioner, but rather a "closing argument of a frustrated and vindictive prosecutor."[82] Rose argued that baseball had failed to follow its own rules of procedure in dealing with his case. The rules stated in part that:

> "[t]he Commissioner will in general follow established rules of evidence," that any "[d]epositions ... will proceed substantially as if the testimony had been taken on an open commission in a judicial proceeding," and that "[i]n all claims and disputes submitted to the Commissioner the persons or organizations concerned shall be entitled to ... cross examine witnesses...."[83]

Rose also said he was entitled to a fair hearing under the law of private associations[84]:

> [P]rivate associations must provide their members due process consisting of (1) an absence of bad faith, (2) compliance with the constitution and bylaws of the association, and (3) natural justice.[85]

Rose's lawyers also objected to the fairness of Giamatti's proposed hearing. There was no right for Rose to confront and cross-examine his accusers. They argued the Commissioner had rejected a request that "the established rules of evidence for — testimony and documentary evidence — govern the hearing."[86]

Rose's lawyers closed by saying:

> Aside from a paltry extension of time during which the witnesses against Pete Rose have placed obstacles to fair discovery, Giamatti has done nothing to ensure fair procedures.[87]
>
> It is obvious that any further proceeding before Giamatti and based on the report will be futile. Thus, to prevent grave injustice to one of the greatest legends, living or deceased, of the game, this Court should require Giamatti to remove himself from these proceedings and ban use of the report in any further proceedings against Pete Rose.[88]

The hearing began in Judge Nadel's court on 10 A.M. on June 22, 1989. Both sides made opening statements. Baseball's lawyer, Louis Hoynes, said Rose had "bet large sums of money on Major League baseball games and specifically on games of the Cincinnati Reds."[89] John Dowd testified that nine people told him Rose bet on baseball or the Reds.[90] Rose's lawyers called Samuel Dash, former chief counsel to the Senate Watergate Committee, to testify. He called Dowd's report "faulty" and said if it had been presented to him during Watergate he would have fired whoever wrote it.

Rose's lawyers said the question was not whether Rose had bet on baseball but whether baseball would give him a fair hearing.

After three days of testimony, on June 26, Judge Nadel delivered his ruling.[91]

> [T]he Court finds that Pete Rose will suffer irreparable harm and absent the relief granted herein in that he will be subjected to disciplinary proceeding before a biased, unfair tribunal, on charges that he bet on Baseball, and that in permanent and irreparable damage will be done to his career and reputation.[92]

Judge Nadel was also quoted as stating that it "appears to this court at this point the commissioner of baseball has prejudged Peter Edward Rose."[93]

Judge Nadel issued a temporary restraining order in favor of Rose, preventing Giamatti, MLB, and the Reds from further involvement with Rose or from taking action to terminate him from the Reds.[94] The court's ruling stated in part:

> It is therefore ordered, adjudged and decreed that Defendants A. Bartlett Giamatti, Major League Baseball, the Cincinnati Reds ... are hereby restrained and enjoined ... from:
> 1. Further involvement in deciding whether plaintiff Pete Rose should be disciplined, banned, suspended, expelled, or declared ineligible from participation in baseball pending resolution of this action;
> 2. Terminating Plaintiff Pete Rose's employment as Field Manager of the Cincinnati Reds or taking any action to interfere with Pete Rose's employment in that capacity in response to any order, declaration, pronouncement, decree, edict, or decision from Defendants A. Bartlett Giamatti or Major League Baseball, or in response to Plaintiff Pete Rose having filed this action.[95]

Judge Nadel's ruling was unprecedented in the legal circles. Rose had successfully, albeit temporarily, stopped the commissioner from taking action against him.[96]

Rose's hearing that was scheduled for the next day was cancelled and the commissioner was ordered to take no action for at least 14 days. On the record in open court, Judge Nadel cancelled the Commissioner's hearing, saying it would be futile and illusory and the outcome a foregone conclusion.[97] Nadel's ruling constituted the first time in the history of the game that a commissioner's investigation was stopped by litigation and the first victory of its kind over a baseball commissioner's investigation into the wrongdoing of a player.[98] It looked as though Rose had the home field advantage over Giamatti and baseball, at least temporarily.[99]

The commissioner appealed Nadel's ruling to the Court of Appeals, 1st Judicial District, of Hamilton County, asking it to "suspend" the temporary restraining order issued by Judge Nadel, but the court denied the request. In the motion for suspension of the temporary restraining order, the commissioner argued that the law supported his position and that the lower court's order interfered with the right of a private association (the MLB) to govern itself.[100] The commissioner also argued that when a voluntary association has yet to render a decision a court should not intervene[101]:

> [T]he sport of baseball will be severely damaged if the Commissioner is barred from completing his investigation and taking the actions he sees as appropriate — steps consistent with his mandate to uphold the integrity of the game. The image of a sport no longer capable of policing itself in a matter as serious as a manager betting on his own team's games could only erode public confidence in and respect for the national pastime. The ability of the Commissioner to protect the integrity of baseball, the purpose for which his office was created, is at stake.[102]

On June 28, 1989, the court of appeals found in Rose's favor, saying it lacked jurisdiction to hear the case, once again preventing the commissioner from proceeding against Rose.[103] The baseball commissioner had now lost in two state courts in Ohio. It was clear that Pete Rose possessed substantial influence in the city of Cincinnati.[104] Giamatti must have been somewhat irritated at the way the proceedings had developed. Giamatti was conducting an investigation pursuant to the powers given to him by baseball's Major League Agreement and yet, there he was, in the office of the lawyer of a player giving a deposition about this investigation after losing twice in court.[105]

Changing the Playing Field

The commissioner clearly needed a new strategy. He sought a new playing field, one that might give him an advantage or at least get him away from Rose's influence. He decided to try to remove the case from Ohio state court to federal court in Columbus, Ohio. Columbus was a few hours from Cincinnati and maybe Giamatti could escape the influence Rose had in the Cincinnati area.

In yet another unprecedented battle, the lawyers for Rose and Giamatti met in U.S. Federal District Court with the Commissioner's Office seeking to have the case moved from Cincinnati while Rose's request for an injunction was still set for a hearing on July 6 in front of Judge Nadel. In a rather complicated legal opinion, the court framed the issue as follows:

> The critical question now before the Court is whether, in the controversy between Rose and Giamatti, there is "the necessary collision of interests" between Rose on the one hand and the Cincinnati Reds and Major League Baseball on the other hand so that the citizenship of these defendants may not be disregarded by the Court.[106]

The Federal District Court for the Southern District of Ohio, Eastern Division, took jurisdiction over the case. Ironically, Judge Rubin, who had criticized the commissioner's investigation and then removed himself, granted the request to transfer the case from the Western Division of the Southern District located in Cincinnati, to the Eastern Division, located in Columbus.[107] The case was assigned to Judge Holschuh. He would have to decide who had jurisdiction in the case. Would the matter continue in federal court or be transferred back to a state trial court in Cincinnati?[108] Rose's attorney submitted a 40-page brief, while the Commissioner countered with a 33-page brief. Arguments were held in Columbus on July 20, with each party presenting their side of the case for one hour and forty-five minutes about whether the case should remain in Columbus in federal court or be transferred back to Rose's hometown of Cincinnati. Baseball's lawyer stated at the outset of the hearing to Judge Holschuh:

> In the state court in Cincinnati I need not describe Mr. Rose's standing. He is a local hero, perhaps the first citizen of Cincinnati. And Commissioner Giamatti is viewed suspiciously as a foreigner from Mr. Rose. Your Honor, this is a textbook example of why diversity jurisdiction was created in the Federal Courts and why it exists to this very day.[109]

The judge told the parties he would have his decision to them no later than July 31. He kept his promise and, on that day, ruled that the case would stay in federal court in Columbus, where the commissioner wanted it. Judge Holschuh issued a detailed 47-page opinion with 20 footnotes.[110]

The court noted that this was "not a routine case."[111] The case could only be removed to federal court if the legal dispute was deemed to be a dispute between Commissioner Giamatti (a citizen of the state of New York) and Rose (a citizen of the state of Ohio). The commissioner needed to show that the dispute was only between Rose from Ohio and Giamatti from New York. The Cincinnati Reds was also a party to the lawsuit. Essentially, the commissioner's lawyers needed to get the Reds out of the case. If the club was considered "essential" to the conflict, then "complete diversity" would not be accomplished as required for federal jurisdiction, and the case could not be removed to federal court by the commissioner. The court found that only Rose and the commissioner were "real parties in interest" and therefore the case could be removed to federal court. "The court has examined the above authorities cited by Rose, as well as others, and concludes that none supports Rose's claims against Major League Baseball in this case. The controversy here, as stated, is between Rose and Commissioner Giamatti and not between Rose and the Cincinnati Reds or between Rose and Major League Baseball. Major League Baseball is, at best, a nominal party in this action. Therefore, the citizenship of Major League Baseball may be disregarded for diversity purposes."[112]

Judge Holschuh's ruling meant the Rose lawsuit would remain in federal court, unless Rose was successful on appeal. Rose wanted the case sent back to Hamilton County in front of Common Pleas Judge Nadel who had previously blocked Rose's scheduled hearing, but that would not happen. While

Rose's case was on appeal, one of his former friends, Paul Janszen, was holding a news conference at the offices of *Penthouse Magazine* in New York and pointing the finger at Rose for tax evasion.[113] On August 17, Rose's appeal was turned down by the United States Court of Appeals for the 6th Circuit.[114] Giamatti had boxed Rose in and he had nowhere to go. Rose's lawyer were successful only in postponing Rose's banishment from the game. His "filibuster" had come to an end.

The Suspension

On August 21, 1989, the Reds beat the Cubs at Wrigley Field, 6–5. At the end of the game, Rose hustled out of the Reds dugout and shook hands with his relief pitcher, John Franco. Rose was enjoying his last moments in Major League Baseball. He left the next morning to return to Cincinnati for the birth of his second child. Rose would never return to manage the Reds. On the afternoon of August 23, as the Reds played the Cubs, attorneys for Rose and baseball were putting the finishing touches on an agreement that would force Rose out of baseball.

Rose eventually accepted the ultimate penalty that could be given to him by baseball, a lifetime suspension. He could apply for reinstatement after one year. The five-page document signed by Rose and Giamatti was a total surrender by Rose. The Rose/Giamatti agreement stated in part:

a. Peter Edward Rose is hereby declared permanently ineligible in accordance with Major League Rule 21 and placed on the Ineligible List.
b. Nothing in this Agreement shall deprive Peter Edward Rose of the rights under Major League Rule 15(c) to apply for reinstatement. Peter Edward Rose agrees not to challenge, appeal or otherwise contest the decision of, or the procedure employed by, the Commissioner or any future Commissioner in the evaluation of any application for reinstatement.
c. Nothing in this agreement shall be deemed either an admission or a denial by Peter Edward Rose of the allegation that he bet on any Major League Baseball game.[115]

Rose agreed that "the commissioner has treated him fairly in this agreement and has acted in good faith throughout the course of the investigation and proceedings." That particular language in the agreement must have given Giamatti immense satisfaction. Giamatti and Rose would be allowed to talk about the agreement with the public, but any public statement made by either could not contradict the terms of the agreement between the parties. The matter had now been put to rest.

Giamatti and Rose would immediately hold dueling press conferences.

Rose held his on his own home turf, Riverfront Stadium. Rose stuck to his story and simply stated: "Regardless of what the Commissioner said today, I did not bet on baseball."[116] Giamatti gave his personal opinion that he thought Rose did in fact bet on baseball and on the Reds. Rose would later complain he was double-crossed by Giamatti. Rose said he was "dumbfounded" Giamatti would make such a statement based on the agreement they had entered into a mere 12 hours before.[117]

Death and Taxes

Tragically, one week after the agreement was signed, Commissioner Giamatti would pass away after serving only five months as baseball's commissioner.[118] He will long be remembered as an intellectual and a man of principle. Although his tenure as commissioner was short, he was well liked and had gained the respect of owners.[119] John Ward may have been baseball's Renaissance man in the nineteenth century, but Giamatti would easily fill that role in the twentieth.[120]

In April 1990, Pete Rose pled guilty to filing a false tax return.[121] He was sentenced to five months in prison and paid over $350,000 in restitution to the IRS. Rose began his sentence at a federal prison camp in Illinois[122] and was assigned to the prison machine shop where he made eleven cents a day. Rose was released from prison on January 7, 1991, upon which he began the second half of his sentence, 1,000 hours of community service in Cincinnati schools.[123] In September 1997, Rose applied for reinstatement to baseball but Commissioner Bud Selig refused to take any action on Rose's request.[124] On October 24, 1999, at a ceremony held at the World Series honoring baseball's all-century team, Bud Selig granted Rose permission to appear in the ballpark.[125] Rose received a great ovation from the Atlanta crowd when he appeared on the field. As Rose left the field, he was confronted by journalist Jim Gray of NBC. Gray was known to have a "hard-hitting" style of journalism and he presented Rose with some rather blunt questions. He asked Rose if he would like to apologize to the fans for betting on baseball. Rose attempted to shrug Gray off, saying he was very surprised at Gray's questions and that he was just there to enjoy his time. In November 2002, Rose met with Bud Selig in Milwaukee about possible reinstatement to baseball but no action was taken.[126] In 2004, Rose's tax troubles continued. The IRS filed a federal tax lien against Rose, alleging he owed almost $1 million in unpaid taxes from 1997 to 2002.[127]

In January 2004, Rose released his autobiography, *My Prison Without Bars*. In that book, Rose finally admitted that he did gamble on baseball games, including games in which he managed the Reds.[128] However, he said he always bet on his team to win.[129] Rose said when he did gamble as a manager he never took an "unfair advantage." He also said he never changed the way he bet based

6. All-Time Hit Leader Banned from the Game

on injuries or inside information, nor did he ever let his betting influence his baseball decisions.[130] He said it was not a mistake to confess earlier and when asked why he did it, he responded, "I didn't think I would get caught."[131] In his book, *My Prison Without Bars*, Rose said:

> I'm sure that I'm supposed to act all sorry or sad or guilty now that I've accepted that I've done something wrong. But you see, I'm just not built that way. Sure, there's probably some real emotion buried somewhere deep inside. And maybe I'd be a better person if I let that side of my personality come out. But it just doesn't surface too often. So let's leave it like this. I know I fucked up. All the shit that flowed from my bad decision hurts and hurts big time. I'm sorry it happened and I'm sorry for all the people, fans, and family that it hurt. Let's move on.[132]

There has been much debate about whether Rose should be allowed back in the game of baseball and eventually into the Baseball Hall of Fame.[133] Giamatti commented on Rose's possible reinstatement before his passing, saying, "The burden to show a redirected, reconfigured, rehabilitated life is entirely Pete Rose's."[134]

In 2003, Harvard Law School held a mock trial, "Pete Rose on Trial." The prosecuting attorney was Harvard Professor Alan Dershowitz and the defense lawyer was Johnnie Cochran. A cast of legal experts gathered to debate whether Rose should be admitted into the Baseball Hall of Fame. Witnesses included Lester Munson, *Sports Illustrated* investigative reporter; Jim Palmer, former Orioles pitcher, who gave his interpretation of Rule 21-D; Dr. Jon Grant, a professor of psychiatry and human behavior at Brown University, and an expert on compulsive gambling; Steve Garvey, former major leaguer; Dan Shaughnessy, *Boston Globe* columnist and author; Hank Aaron, who said Rose "deserves to have his plaque be put into Cooperstown" and that he's been punished enough; Bill James, baseball statistician and Boston Red Sox consultant; Bill "Spaceman" Lee, former Red Sox left-handed pitcher and two-time author; and Dave Parker, seven-time all-star, who played under Rose in Cincinnati from 1984–87. Cochran told the mock jury, "Fourteen years of banishment ... enough is enough. Now it's time to bring Pete Rose home — home to the Hall of Fame." Professor Dershowitz took a page from Johnnie Cochran's famous playbook in the O.J. Simpson murder trial and said: "If he bet on the game, there's no Hall of Fame."[135] The jury's verdict was, "Let him in."

Some baseball greats have stepped forward to support Rose's bid to be reinstated into baseball, including Hall of Famers Henry Aaron and Mike Schmidt,[136] but Rose remains on the outside looking in. Is it in the best interests of baseball to ban the all-time hit leader from the game and the Hall of Fame because as a manager he bet on his own team to win? There is a long list of "sinners" who played the national pastime and many of them are in the Hall of Fame. It seems the real jury is still out for Pete Rose.

7

The Arbitration Case of John Rocker[1]

John Rocker Speaks His Mind About Race Relations

John Rocker

If not for a *Sports Illustrated* interview, baseball reliever John Rocker might have gone into the annals of baseball as just another relatively successful baseball relief pitcher. Rocker was a fiery left-hander with a 100 m.p.h. fastball and a competitive attitude, and he quickly became a star closer for the Atlanta Braves in the 1999 season. Rocker appeared on the scene very quickly for the Braves and soon developed a "friendly" rivalry with New York Mets fans. The Mets were the chief rival of the Braves in the Eastern Division of the National League. Their fans jeered Rocker and he gave back as much as he got, sometimes working the crowd into a frenzy. His rivalry with Mets fans was well known throughout the league. Rocker was competitive and it showed in his playing style. New York fans are very enthusiastic and Rocker's antics would just spur them to greater enthusiasm. Mets fans developed an ongoing feud with Rocker for most of the 1999 season as the Mets and Braves battled for the National League Championship (NLCS) title. The Braves eventually prevailed in the NLCS over the Mets, 4 games to 2, with Rocker appearing in all six games, saving two, with a 0.00 ERA. The Braves were subsequently swept by the New York Yankees in the 1999 World Series, with Rocker making two relief appearances. Rocker completed the season with 38 saves, a 2.49 ERA, and 104 strikeouts in 72 innings. He had established himself as the Braves closer and also proved he could pitch well in post-season play.

The national pastime was in the books for the 20th century and sports fans began to turn their attention to football, basketball, and hockey. Ballplayers left to play golf and spend time with their families. John Rocker, like many other ballplayers, waited in anticipation for the next season to begin. Rocker was asked by *Sports Illustrated* writer Jeff Pearlman to give an interview and Rocker agreed, giving the interview as he drove around in his truck with Pearlman. Rocker was unaware of the impact the interview would have on his career, teammates, and the game of baseball. It would create a firestorm of controversy and initiate very public debate about race relations and prejudice in America. His actions would also cause the commissioner of baseball to take disciplinary action against him because of what he said in the interview.

The Rocker Interview

During the interview, Rocker gave uncensored answers to a variety of questions, sometimes diverting to subjects off the topic of baseball. In fairness to Rocker, some of his answers were supposed to be kept off the record, specifically his remarks concerning NBA player Latrell Sprewell.[2] The remarks that were published proved to be extremely controversial. He discussed a variety of "hot button" issues, some of which had little to do with baseball.

In response to a question about whether he would even play for a New York team, Rocker said:

> I would retire first. It's the most hectic, nerve-racking city. Imagine having to take the [Number] 7 train to the ballpark, looking like you're [riding through] Beirut next to some kid with purple hair next to some queer with AIDS right next to some dude who just got out of jail for the fourth time right next to some 20-year-old mom with four kids. It's depressing.[3]

Rocker also commented on the city of New York itself.

> The biggest thing I don't like about New York are the foreigners. I'm not a very big fan of foreigners. You can walk an entire block in Times Square and not hear anybody speaking English. Asians and Koreans and Vietnamese and Indians and Russians and Spanish people and everything up there. How the hell did they get in this country? ... I'm not a racist or prejudiced person, but certain people bother me.[4]

While driving in Atlanta as he answered questions from Pearlman, Rocker felt he needed to weigh in on the driving skills of his fellow Georgians:

> So many dumb asses don't know how to drive in this town. They turn from the wrong lane. They go 20 miles per hour. It makes me want to — Look! Look at this idiot! I guarantee you she's a Japanese woman. [A Beige Toyota is jerking from lane to lane. The woman at the wheel is white.] How bad are Asian women at driving?[5]

After the interview was published, talk radio stations were overwhelmed with calls debating Rocker's remarks. In fact, they were discussed in all forms of media. Some people were shocked, while others thought Rocker should be entitled to his opinion just like anyone else and it should not make any difference that he was a ballplayer. The Braves organization issued a statement disassociating the club from the viewpoints expressed by Rocker during the interview. The Atlanta City Council adopted a resolution condemning the remarks of Rocker and the resolution was signed by the mayor of Atlanta.[6] The most famous Brave of all time and one of the most decent people ever to don a baseball uniform, Henry Aaron, raised concerns about Rocker's place in baseball.[7] Rocker's teammates expressed concerns about his remarks.[8] Former Braves owner Ted Turner, who was known to have made a few choice remarks of his own, supported Rocker. In his defense, Rocker issued an apology after the interview:

> While I have evidenced strong competitive feelings about New York fans in the past, and take responsibility for things I have said publicly, including the *Sports Illustrated* article, I recognize that I have gone way too far in my competitive zeal. I want everybody to understand that my emotions fuel my competitive desire. They are a source of energy for me, however, I have let my emotions get the best of my judgment and have said things which, when read with cold, hard logic, are unacceptable to me and to my country. Even though it might appear otherwise from what I've said, I am not a racist. I should not have said what I did because it is not what I believe in my heart.
>
> I was angry and basically firing back at the people of New York. It is time to stop this process.
>
> I fully intend to learn from this experience. Everyone makes mistakes and I hope everyone can put this aside and begin with a fresh start in the 2000 season.
>
> I am contrite.[9]

Commissioner Bud Selig said he was "stunned" and "shocked" by Rocker's remarks. He said that he chose to discipline Rocker for several reasons, including that all those involved in Major League Baseball possess a social responsibility.[10] Rocker's suspension was the first of its kind in the history of baseball's arbitration procedures. Selig stated:

> Major League Baseball takes seriously its role as an American institution and the important social responsibility that goes with it. We will not dodge our responsibility. Mr. Rocker should understand that his remarks offended practically every element of society and brought dishonor to himself, the Atlanta Braves and Major League Baseball.
>
> The terrible example set by Mr. Rocker is not what our great game is about and, in fact, is a profound breach of the social compact we hold in such high regard.[11]

Rocker was immediately ordered by Selig to undergo psychiatric counseling.[12] The commissioner was now faced with the decision of whether to discipline Rocker for his statements. There were questions about whether the commissioner possessed the authority to discipline him for remarks made in the off-season and while out of uniform. Could the commissioner discipline a player for something he said in the off-season that could be viewed as his opinion on matters unrelated to baseball?

The Power of the Office of the Commissioner of Baseball

The Office of the Commissioner of Major League Baseball has been given broad authority to regulate the game of baseball and the individuals who play it. Commissioners have used their authority to regulate conduct both on and off the field in a variety of situations and with varying results since the creation of the office.[13] The "best interests" power of the commissioner emanates from Baseball's Major League Agreement and it has been used by the commissioner to curtail all types of conduct, both on and off the field.[14]

In the first year of the existence of the Commissioner's Office, Judge Landis wasted no time in banning New York Giants outfielder Benny Kauff for life when Kauff was merely charged with auto theft. Although Kauff was later acquitted of the crime, Judge Landis still refused to lift the lifetime suspension.[15] Kauff later contemplated suing the commissioner over the decision.[16]

Baseball has never tolerated gambling or gamblers and the Office of the Commissioner has taken action against those associated with gambling. William D. Cox, former owner of the Philadelphia Phillies, was forced to sell the club in 1943 for betting on his team.[17] Leo Durocher, manager of the Brooklyn Dodgers, was suspended for the entire 1947 season for his association with gamblers.[18] Baseball greats Mickey Mantle and Willie Mays were banned from the game while they worked for casinos, even though they were retired at the time. Pete Rose is still under a lifetime ban from baseball for gambling on baseball while he was the manager of the Cincinnati Reds. Yankees owner George Steinbrenner was suspended from baseball for associating with gamblers.

Numerous players have been suspended by the baseball commissioner for the use of drugs and alcohol. Commissioner Bowie Kuhn was faced with a unique situation involving Yankee players Fritz Peterson and Mike Kekich. The two players were teammates and evidently very close friends. They were so close they decided to exchange wives and children for one baseball season.[19] Commissioner Kuhn found no basis for taking any action against the players but did express concern over the players' conduct. "It is not possible for an administrator of sports to reach the private lives of people like these. But this isn't to say it is not a regrettable situation."[20] Yankees General Manager, Lee MacPhail, commented: "We may have to call off family day."[21] In the John Rocker case, the commissioner would use his authority in a rather unusual way to attempt to discipline a player for something he said in the off-season.

Free Speech Rights of Athletes

Rocker's comments presented new issues for the Commissioner's office. What free speech rights, if any, do players possess? Can players say whatever they want off the field and not be subject to discipline by the commissioner of the league? When are players allowed to express personal beliefs, if ever? To what extent can a commissioner act to curtail the speech of a player if the commissioner deems the speech not in the best interests of the sport?

The First Amendment to the U.S. Constitution states: "Congress shall make no law respecting an establishment of religion, or prohibiting the free exercise thereof; or abridging the freedom of speech, or of the press; or the right of the people peaceably to assemble, and to petition the Government for a redress of grievances."[22] The free speech protections under the First Amendment require "state action" and do not apply to the actions of private parties.[23] The First Amendment applies only to actions taken by the government. However, what happens when the actions of the government become "intertwined" with the private sector? There is a federal court decision dealing with this legal issue and the Office of the Commissioner of Baseball and the legal concept of "state action."[24] Linda Ludtke was a reporter for *Sports Illustrated* and sued baseball commissioner Bowie Kuhn over baseball's policy that excluded women reporters from baseball clubhouses. The court defined the legal issue as follows:

> The first legal question is whether New York City's involvement with Yankee Stadium and the lease arrangement with the Yankees is such as to make the Kuhn policy determination state action within the contemplation of the Fourteenth Amendment.[25]

The court held that Ludtke had pled enough facts to constitute "state action" on her constitutional claims for Equal Protection and Due Process violations by the defendants.[26] It would, however, be the unusual case where a plaintiff could prove "state action" when suing the office of the Baseball Commissioner. No arguments were made at the arbitration hearing that Rocker's First Amendment rights were violated. The arbitrator was not called upon to decide this legal issue but baseball still disciplined Rocker for what he said.

The commissioner did have some precedent upon which to rely to take action against Rocker for his off-season comments. There was one previous case in which the baseball commissioner disciplined a player merely for his speech.[27] New York Yankees left fielder Jake Powell was disciplined by Commissioner Landis in 1938 for comments Powell made while being interviewed on the radio.[28] Powell worked as a police officer in the off-season and when asked about his activities in that position he stated that "...he derived considerable fun out of his job 'cracking niggers over the head.'"[29] The commissioner took immediate action against Powell, suspending him for ten games for his comments.[30] Powell denied ever making the remarks saying: "To the best of my knowledge ... I said I was a member of the police force in Dayton during the winter months. And simply explained my beat was in the Negro section of the town."[31] There was no record of the interview so there was some dispute about what Powell actually said. When Powell returned after his ten-game suspension he was greeted in Washington with a shower of glass pop bottles in left field.[32] Powell's life tragically ended in 1948 when he committed suicide while in the custody of the Washington, D.C., police. He had been arrested for writing bad checks and was to be married the next day. Powell told his fiancé right before he killed himself "to hell with it — I'm going to end it all."[33]

Cincinnati Reds owner Marge Schott was known as a person who was not afraid to say whatever was on her mind.[34] The Commissioner of Baseball suspended Schott from the day-to-day operations of the Cincinnati Reds in February 1993 and fined her $25,000 for making racial and ethnic slurs. Schott was alleged to have said that Adolf Hitler "had the right idea" for the Jews "but went too far."[35] She also acknowledged she used the term "dirty Jews," the word "nigger" as a joke, and also used racial slurs on a regular basis while addressing club employees.[36]

Chicago White Sox manager Ozzie Guillen also is known for his colorful remarks on a variety of subjects. Guillen called *Chicago Sun-Times* columnist Jay Mariotti a "fag" in a profanity-laced tirade. He apologized later, saying: "I don't have anything against those people. In my country, you call someone something like that and it is not the same as it is in this country."[37] Guillen tried to make things better by saying he had gay friends, attended Women's National Basketball Association games, and had plans to attend the Gay Games when they came to Chicago. Guillen was fined and ordered to take sensitivity training by Commissioner Bud Selig.[38] Guillen also made some interesting comments on the controversial Arizona immigration law.

Charles Albert (Chief) Bender pitched for the Philadelphia Athletics from 1903 to 1917, with a 206–111 won-loss record for a .650 winning percentage. Bender was a full-blooded Chippewa Indian and fans would regularly ridicule him for his heritage. Bender's response was both intelligent and amusing:

> Hostile fans would howl in falsetto voice: "Whoop! Whoop!" at him like Indians in the movies all do. This would tickle Bender. When he returned from the field to the bench he would walk close to the stands and say:
> "Foreigners! Foreigners!"[39]

Commissioners in other sports have also disciplined individuals for speech which occurred off the field or court. NBA star Alan Iverson doubled as a rapper and one of his musical works contained the following lyrics:

> Come to me wit faggot tendencies
> You'll be sleepin where the maggots be
> Everybody stay fly get money kill and f__k bitches
> I'm hittin anything in plain view for my riches
> VA's finest fillin up ditches, when niggaz turn to bitches[40]

Evidently, NBA Commissioner David Stern failed to appreciate the artistic nature of Iverson's music, and he told Iverson that if he did not change the lyrics to his song he would be suspended. Stern called the lyrics "coarse, offensive and antisocial."[41] Iverson heeded the commissioner's warning and changed the lyrics to a more docile tune, avoiding the wrath of the NBA and certain suspension.[42]

NBA player Dennis Rodman has always been known for his outrageous behavior both on and off the court. After game three of the 1997 NBA finals, Rodman told a reporter that he thought Mormons were "assholes."[43] Rodman was fined $50,000 by the NBA for his comments. In typical Rodman-like fashion, he said: "If I knew it was a religious-type deal, I never would have said it."[44] Rodman's coach Phil Jackson came to his defense: "To Dennis, a Mormon may only be a nickname for people from Utah."[45] NBA Commissioner David Stern responded that insensitive and derogatory comments involving race or other classifications were unacceptable in the NBA. In a case involving speech conduct, Mahmoud Abdul-Rauf (born Chris Wayne Jackson) was suspended by the NBA for refusing to stand during the National Anthem, at the time a violation of league rules. Abdul-Rauf said standing for the National Anthem would conflict with his Islamic beliefs. A compromise was reached whereby he would stand during the playing of the National Anthem but would close his eyes, look downward, and silently say a Muslim prayer.

In the National Hockey League, Chris Simon used a racial slur against African American player Mike Grier.[46] Simon was suspended by the league for three games as a result of the incident. Sean Avery was suspended by NHL Commissioner Gary Bettman after the player gave a television interview in which he used crude and coarse language in describing his former girlfriend who was dating other hockey players.[47]

In an attempt to restrict a player's speech, the Cincinnati Bengals of the National Football League demanded players agree to a contract addendum that would permit the team to recoup a part or all of the player's signing bonus if a player made disparaging comments about management.[48] The clause has now been commonly referred to as the "Carl Pickens" clause.[49]

The Arbitration Case of John Rocker

Baseball Commissioner Bud Selig suspended Rocker with pay from both major and minor league spring training for 2000 and from the opening day of the season to May 1, 2000. He also required him to make a $20,000 contribution to the NAACP or a similar organization and to participate in a program for diversity training before he could return as an active player. Rocker was disciplined by the commissioner of the league, not his employer, the Atlanta Braves. The Braves could have taken action against Rocker as well but they chose not to do so.[50]

In the Rocker arbitration decision, the commissioner's authority to discipline was based on the "just cause" provision of Baseball's Basic Agreement.[51] After Commissioner Selig levied his discipline against Rocker, the Players Association filed a Notice of Grievance arguing the discipline was without just cause. An analysis of the just cause provision requires the examination of two questions:

1. What conduct warrants the discipline of the Commissioner?
2. What is the nature and severity of the discipline to be imposed?[52]

The Commissioner's Position

The commissioner asserted that the decision to discipline Rocker for "hate speech" should be given "great deference." He also maintained his powers were "exceedingly broad." The commissioner contended he had made a "fair and reasonable decision" because he was the individual responsible for protecting the best interests of baseball as well as the safety and security of its fans.[53] The commissioner set forth three reasons why the decision should be upheld:

1. Rocker's conduct violated paragraph 3(a) of the Uniform Player's Contract (UPC);
2. Rocker's actions were contrary to the best interests of baseball and in contravention of Major League Rule 21(f); and
3. Even if Rocker's conduct did not violate the UPC or the best interests provisions there was still "just cause" for the discipline imposed upon him.[54]

Paragraph 3(a) of the UPC requires a player conform his conduct to the "high standards of personal conduct, fair play and good sportsmanship."[55] The commissioner said that Rocker was under contract with the Braves at the time he made the statements and, while a player may no longer have any obligations to play baseball under the contract, other contract provisions imposed non-playing obligations on the part of the player which continue throughout the off-season.[56] The commissioner pointed out that three paragraphs of the UPC were still in force during the off-season even though the player was not playing baseball for the club. He cited paragraph 3(c) (requiring the player to make public appearances), paragraph 5 (requiring a player to refrain from engaging in certain sports in the off-season), and paragraph 10(a) (renewal). Furthermore, the commissioner noted that, traditionally, players in Rocker's position (with less than three years experience) have acted as though they were under contract to the club for which they were last employed. The commissioner argued Rocker was under contract with the club during the off-season, was bound by paragraph 3(a) of the contract, and violated that paragraph of the contract with his speech.

Alternatively, the commissioner said even if the arbitrator found Rocker was not bound by the UPC in the off-season, the commissioner could still act under the best interests clause of Baseball's Major League Agreement. The commissioner argued that Rocker was in violation of MLR 21(f), which was binding on Rocker through his UPC and through the Basic Agreement. MLR 21(f) states:

> OTHER MISCONDUCT. Nothing herein contained shall be construed as exclusively defining or otherwise limiting acts, transactions, practices or conduct not to be in the best interests of Baseball are prohibited and shall be subject to such penalties, including permanent ineligibility, as the facts in the particular case may warrant.[57]

In support of his decision to discipline Rocker under the best interests clause, the commissioner made seven arguments:

1. Rocker's hate speech offended a large group of individuals, including players, fans, citizens, and community and civic leaders;
2. His comments destroyed many years worth of goodwill and positive community relations of the club and MLB;
3. His comments minimized the efforts of MLB and the Atlanta Club to increase the hiring of minorities as well as MLB's attempts to build a diverse fan base;
4. His comments did economic damage to the Braves Organization and MLB;
5. His speech created security concerns for multiple parties, including Rocker himself, which caused the club and MLB to expend additional resources to provide for the safety of those on the field and in the stands at every major league park;
6. His comments damaged his relationships with his team and coaches; and
7. His speech "engendered needless controversy" when fans could have been focused on more positive aspects of the game.[58]

The commissioner argued that even if there was no violation by Rocker of the UPC or the best interests clause, there was still "just cause" for the discipline he had imposed. Article XII(a) of the Basic Agreement provided "a player may be subjected to disciplinary action for just cause ... by the commissioner." "It is firmly established that an employer properly may discipline an employee for inappropriate speech and, in particular, for speech that evidences bias, bigotry or insidious stereotyping."[59] The commissioner said Rocker's comments could not be considered "off duty" conduct because they were "work related" and increased his publicity as a ballplayer.[60] However, even if they were considered "off duty" comments, an employer can still discipline an employee under certain circumstances: if the off-duty misconduct has a close enough connection or "sufficient nexus" with the employer's business.[61] Generally speaking, unless an employer can provide a close enough connection between the employee's business and the employee's speech or conduct, the employee cannot be disciplined by the employer.[62] The commissioner argued that Rocker's off-duty comments had a sufficient nexus with his workplace for four reasons:

1. His actions harmed the reputation of his employer and MLB;
2. His actions created security and safety concerns for his employer;
3. His conduct damaged his employer's attempts to increase diversity in the workplace; and
4. His conduct interfered with his relationship with teammates and coaches.[63]

The commissioner then addressed the discipline portion of his decision. He said the discipline given to Rocker was within his discretion to protect the interests of baseball.[64] The commissioner cited to the suspension of Cincinnati Reds owner Marge Schott from baseball for one year for making racist and bigoted statements. He also noted that Rocker's suspension was more lenient than some of the drug suspensions administered by other commissioners. He noted that while drug-related misconduct certainly tarnished the game, it did not have the far reaching social and economic repercussions that Rocker's comments did. He pointed to previous arbitration cases which upheld suspensions up to 119 days. Lastly, the commissioner said it was necessary to remove Rocker from spring training to provide a "cooling off" period which was required because of heightened security risks created by Rocker's presence of spring training.

The Players Association Position

The Players Association filed a grievance on behalf of Rocker and sought to have the commissioner's decision rescinded. It argued that the commissioner had no authority to discipline Rocker under Major League Rule 21(f) because Rocker was not under contract with the Atlanta Club when the interview was given or published.[65] Alternatively, it argued even if the arbitrator found that

Rocker was under contract at the time he gave the interview, he could not be disciplined merely for speech. The Association noted that neither the Uniform Player's Contract nor Major League Rule 21(f) stated a penalty for a magazine interview.[66] The commissioner argued that Rocker's speech violated section 3(a) of the UPC and said that courts and arbitration decisions have found that "offensive speech" constitutes conduct.[67] The association pointed out that rule 21 was headed "misconduct" and did not mention speech. The Association did acknowledge that the First Amendment is not applicable to private employment disputes but argued there is still a distinction between speech and conduct.[68] It argued that if the clubs wanted to try to restrict a player's speech that would be a matter for collective bargaining between the parties. A team could not unilaterally impose a restriction on a player's speech.[69]

The Players Association cited other incidents of speech involving Ted Turner and former player Bob Knepper, neither of whom received discipline from the commissioner for their inappropriate comments. Knepper made several controversial remarks surrounding the league's potential employment of a female umpire, Pam Postema.[70] "This is not an occupation a woman should be in. In God's society, woman was created in a role of submission to the husband. It's not that woman is inferior but I don't believe women should be in a leadership role."[71] Astros management stated that it does not tell players what to think, but "obviously most people would reject Knepper's statements."[72] The Association pointed out that Knepper was never disciplined for his remarks by the Commissioner's Office. Similarly, the Association cited the remarks made by Atlanta Braves owner Ted Turner.[73] Turner compared his nemesis, Rupert Murdoch, to Adolph Hitler. He later apologized to Murdoch but not to Jewish groups.[74] The Commissioner's Office found the remarks by Turner to be offensive but took no action against him. The Association argued that because Turner and Knepper received no discipline for their remarks that Rocker also should not have been disciplined.

The Association stressed to the arbitrator that Rocker's comments were made in the off-season and out of uniform and were not addressed toward his employer or fellow employees. They said under these circumstances "just cause" principles required a showing of impact on the employer's business to justify discipline. The Association argued that legal precedent held that just because a business is "affected" by the employee's actions is not enough. The Braves and MLB had failed to prove any economic harm occurred because of Rocker's remarks.

The Association pointed the finger at the Commissioner's Office and the Atlanta Braves, saying they should accept blame for what happened because they failed to do anything to calm the feud between Rocker and rowdy Met fans that was ongoing during the season. Because of the inaction by the commissioner and the club, the Association argued that a more progressive discipline was in order.

The Association also argued the 73-day suspension "lack[ed] any semblance of fairness, consistency or proportionality."[75] It noted Rocker's suspension was twice as long as non-drug related suspension in the history of the game. It was longer than any challenged drug decision except that of Vida Blue's. The players in the Pittsburgh drug trials also received shorter suspensions than Rocker. The Association deemed the commissioner's reference to the UPC, rather than a playing rule or another written policy, "unique."[76] It said it was the first time a commissioner had used the best interests power of the Commissioner's Office without referring to a written policy or playing rule related to discipline.

The Arbitration Decision

Shyam Das,[77] chairman of the arbitration panel, issued an award on March 1, 2000, and a written opinion followed on November 30, 2000. After listening to the arguments of both parties, he found:

1. The decision to suspend Rocker was without "just cause";
2. The spring training suspension was to be rescinded;
3. Rocker's fine was to be reduced from $20,000 to $500.[78]

Das found that the commissioner had the authority to discipline Rocker for his speech, but that the suspension was too severe and without "just cause." The arbitrator found that Rocker was under contract with the Braves at the time he gave the interview so that issue need not be decided because the Association's act of filing the grievance was an acknowledgement that Rocker was subject to discipline for just cause by the commissioner. Furthermore, the arbitrator found that speech in and of itself has in fact been treated as "conduct" and that an employer may take disciplinary action against an employee for off-duty speech if it produces a negative impact on the employer's business.[79] The arbitrator agreed with the commissioner's position that Rocker's comments were "sexist, racist, homophobic and xenophobic."[80] He noted the remarks seriously offended many groups and although Rocker had been treated "rough" by Mets fans, his remarks were still unacceptable. He next turned to the fact that the interview was given in the off-season and out-of-uniform. He found that Rocker clearly knew his remarks were going to be made public and, with one exception, knew they would be published.

Arbitrator Das addressed the arguments made by the Players Association concerning the statements made by Bob Knepper and Ted Turner. He noted that Knepper's statements were considered by his team and National League President Bart Giamatti "as a permissible expression of his personal opinions."[81] He noted the remarks "were made more than ten years ago" and since that time Major League Baseball has taken great steps to promote diversity in management, its business operations, and its fans.[82] The arbitrator found that the lack of discipline of Knepper "does not establish a practice of condoning any type of speech by a player."[83] In addressing Ted Turner's remarks, arbitrator Das noted that although some of those remarks were made when Bud Selig was the commissioner, the commissioner did not discipline Turner because the remarks were inconsistent with Turner's philanthropic activities and the manner in which Turner and his organizations had promoted diversity.[84] Das wrote that although no action was taken against Ted Turner, Marge Schott was suspended for making racist and anti–Semitic remarks. Schott's suspension was, however, not subject to the just cause standard. He noted that he was not suggesting that Rocker's comments were not equal to Schott's; however, Rocker knew he was taking a chance when he made those statements to a national sports magazine and that they might offend people.

Notwithstanding, the arbitrator noted "the evidence, however, does not fully support the commissioner's claims as to the resulting harm."[85] There was no evidence to show that either Major League Baseball or the Braves would suffer a loss of attendance or loss of income because of the statements made by Rocker. Furthermore, "we are not prepared to hold that there was an irreparable breach between Rocker and his teammates...," nor will the team's performance suffer as a result of the statements. The arbitrator also agreed with the Players Association argument that a large portion of the general public believed Rocker should not be punished even though they might not agree with what he said.[86] The arbitrator summarized by writing, "The evidence is persuasive that all of this has been detrimental to some significant degree to the reputation of the Braves and Baseball."[87]

For these reasons, Das found the commissioner was correct in disciplining Rocker and just cause did exist for the discipline.[88] However, he warned that attempts to draw a "precise line beyond which off-field speech may justify discipline poses real difficulties."[89] The bar must be set high and the offensive content of the speech as well as the harm done must be considered in disciplining a player. The arbitrator said in Rocker's situation he had no difficulty in determining "the mark was definitely passed."[90]

He then turned to the legal concept of "just cause," stating it entails not only determining if discipline is proper under the circumstances, but also what penalty should be assessed for the conduct.[91] The arbitrator set forth the standard of review for just cause:

> As in any disciplinary matter, the burden of establishing just cause is on those imposing discipline. While the Commissioner has a "reasonable range of discretion" in such matters, the penalty he imposes in a particular case must be "reasonably commensurate with the offense" and "appropriate, given all the circumstances."[92]

He stated that in determining whether the penalty was proper; it should be noted that there was no specific rule or policy addressing the speech of players and since the initiation of the just cause standards in baseball, no player other than Rocker had been subject to discipline.

He called Rocker's suspension for 45 days of spring training and the first 28 days of the 2000 regular season a "very severe penalty."[93] It was twice as long as any previous suspension that was not drug related and there was no offer of a justifiable basis for the disparity.[94] The length of the suspension was too harsh and lacked just cause.[95] The arbitrator also found the arguments made by the Commissioner relating to spring training unconvincing considering that such a suspension would put Rocker at a competitive disadvantage.

In the end, the arbitrator reduced the suspension to 14 days (April 2 to April 17) and the fine from $20,000 to $500. The Major League Agreement capped the fine at $500. He did sustain the decision to have Rocker participate in diversity training during the off-season. Bud Selig responded to the decision by saying it "does not reflect any understanding or sensitivity to the important social responsibility that baseball ... has to the public."[96]

Aftermath

Although the 2000 season was a good one for both Rocker and the Braves, Rocker did have some bumps in the road. In June 2000, Rocker was demoted to the minor leagues one day after he verbally abused Jeff Pearlman, the writer of the *Sports Illustrated* article. On June 22, 2001, Rocker was traded to the Cleveland Indians along with a minor league prospect for Steve Karsay and Steve Reed. After completing the season with the Indians, in December 2001 he was traded to the Rangers. He was eventually signed as a free agent by the Tampa Bay Devil Rays on April 10, 2003, but was released in June 2003 after only pitching one inning for the Devil Rays. He left baseball at the age of 29, spending less than six years at the major league level. For his career, John Rocker appeared in 280 games, with a 13–22 record and a lifetime ERA of 3.42. He attempted a comeback in 2005 with the Long Island Ducks, but that failed.

John Rocker now operates a website where he advocates English as the official language of the United States. Rocker might have become one of the best closers in the game but for the interview he gave in December 1999.[97] He certainly had the required skills, but those skills diminished quickly under media scrutiny. John Rocker's baseball career will be overshadowed by his controversial remarks that created a national debate on race relations.

8

New York State Division of Human Rights v. New York–Pennsylvania Professional Baseball League[1]

Postema v. National League of Professional Baseball Clubs[2]

Bernice Gera and Pam Postema Try to Break Baseball's Glass Ceiling

> It's hard to accept. And I'll never understand why it's easier for a female to become an astronaut or cop or fire fighter or soldier or Supreme Court justice than it is to become a major league umpire. For Christ sakes, it's only baseball.—Pam Postema, *You've Got to Have Balls to Make It in This League* (New York: Simon & Schuster, 1992)
>
> Many baseball fans look upon an umpire as a sort of necessary evil to the luxury of baseball, like the odor that follows an automobile.—Christy Mathewson, Hall of Fame Pitcher
>
> They expect an umpire to be perfect on opening day and to improve as the season goes on.—Nestor Chylak, American League umpire

Introduction

Discrimination takes all forms in society including race, gender, national origin, sex, disability, age, and pregnancy. There are multiple federal and state statutes which make discrimination illegal and provide a remedy for those who have been discriminated against. Since its passage, the Federal Civil Rights Act of 1964 has become a major force in the area of employment discrimination law and has been used by many to remedy acts of discrimination in the workplace.

8. Gera and Postema Try to Break the Glass Ceiling

Discrimination has long been a societal problem in America. It also has been an issue in baseball and sports in general.[3] It is well known that Jackie Robinson was the first African American Major League baseball player when he broke baseball's color line in 1947.[4] Robinson was a standout athlete at UCLA and an Army officer in World War II. He was selected by Branch Rickey, a University of Michigan law graduate, to be the player who was to break baseball's color line. For many years there was a secret agreement among baseball owners to keep black players from playing in the major leagues. Many great players such as Satchel Paige and Josh Gibson spent their entire careers in the Negro Leagues, thus depriving baseball fans of seeing some of the greatest ballplayers ever to play the game.[5] Frank Robinson was the first African American manager in Major League history and the only player to win the Most Valuable Player award in both leagues. Emmett Ashford was the first African American Major League umpire.[6] Hank Greenberg was a standout slugger for the Detroit Tigers. He talked about how during his career he was ridiculed for his Jewish faith.[7]

This chapter focuses on two milestone cases which deal with gender discrimination in baseball.[8] Pam Postema and Bernice Gera both wanted desperately to become major league umpires but they were never able to realize those dreams, although it was not for lack of trying on their part. Both women worked hard to become the very best at their profession only to hit a "glass ceiling" preventing them from achieving their goal of umpiring in the major leagues. They both would be forced to file discrimination lawsuits based on gender discrimination and both cases presented unique legal issues. Although there has never been a woman umpire in the major leagues, Postema and Gera have provided a more level playing field for women in baseball through their tenacity, hard work, and dedication to the game. The game's first woman umpire will owe a debt of gratitude to both women.

The Umpire

Who would want to be a baseball umpire? It is certainly a thankless job. Umpires must make split-second decisions in front of crowds of 50,000 or more with an intricate knowledge of detailed rules. Even if umpires are right, they are wrong. Everyone knows better than the umpire, even though the umpire is only a foot away from the play and the fans are sitting four stories up in the air, in a large stadium with a beer in their hand. The umpire's ruling is also subject to intense scrutiny by millions of fans sitting at home as they review the umpire's decision many times over via replay in slow motion at multiple angles. No umpire's decision has suffered more scrutiny than that of Jim Joyce's first base call on June 2, 2010. With two outs in the bottom of the ninth inning, Armando Galarraga of the Detroit Tigers was pitching a perfect game against the Cleveland Indians. Jason Donald was batting for the Indians and hit a slow grounder to first, which Miguel Cabrera fielded and threw to Galarraga who was covering first base on the play. The ball clearly arrived at the bag before the runner and Galarraga had his foot on the bag. A perfect game? No, wait, Joyce calls the runner safe, saying he beat the play. It was clear Joyce had missed the call and cost Galarraga his perfect game and place in baseball history. It quickly became referred to as the worst call in the history of baseball.[9]

Despite the lack of popularity for the profession, however, many people continue to enroll in umpire school each year with the hope of fulfilling their dream to become a big league umpire. It is just as difficult for an umpire to make it to the major leagues as it is for a player. It is a rigorous, highly selective process, with only the elite rising to the top of the umpiring profession.

The baseball umpire is an icon of American life and has been the subject of numerous books, movies, and articles.[10] The umpire has been a staple in American life for over a hundred years.[11] Albert G. Spalding discussed the umpire in his early work on baseball:

> The umpire must be intelligent. And by intelligence I do not mean that he must have education or culture. The best umpire in the National League would not shine as a scholar in a gathering of college professors. But he could outclass the entire faculty of any university in America in promptly and quickly deciding the fine points of a game of Base Ball, and that because he has the peculiar quality of intelligence required for his duties. The rules in vogue for the government of our national pastime are not so numerous that one of ordinary acumen may not be able to acquire them. However, the acquisition of information and the ability to apply it are two very different things. One may have the capacity to commit the rules so thoroughly to memory that he can repeat them forward or backward, in the order of their setting or any other order, and such freakish accomplishments may only serve to unfit him for the duties of umpire, for they may overwhelm him with an "embarrassment of riches" along the line of multiplied rules which he has no talent to apply.[12]

There always seems to be a poem for every aspect of baseball and the umpire is no exception. The following from the *Chicago Tribune* in 1886 provides an outlook that many have had about the umpire:

> Mother, may I slug the umpire
> May I slug him right away?
> So he cannot be here, Mother
> When the clubs begin to play?
>
> Let me clasp his throat, dear mother,
> In a dear delightful grip
> With one hand and with the other
> Bat him several in the lip.

> Let me climb his frame, dear mother,
> While the happy people shout;
> I'll not kill him, dearest mother
> I will only knock him out.
>
> Let me mop the ground up, Mother,
> With this person, dearest do;
> If the ground can stand it, Mother
> I don't see why you can't too.
>
> Mother may I slug the umpire,
> Slug him right between the eyes?
> If you let me do it, Mother
> You shall have the champion prize.[13]

In a defamation action brought by an umpire against a baseball club owner, the court noted that Albert G. Spalding was reputed to have once said "that by harassing umpires fans were exerting their democratic right to oppose tyrants."[14] The umpire does always make the right call but they are well trained to take the verbal abuse they receive from fans, managers, coaches and even owners if others believe they fail to get it right. No one likes to be criticized and umpires certainly receive their share of criticism. Everyone has their boiling point and one umpire reached it and went on the offensive. Yankees owner George Steinbrenner did not particularly care for the umpiring skills of Dallas Parks and he let him know about it. The Yankees were playing the Toronto Blue Jays in a two-game series on August 27 and 28, 1982. Steinbrenner thought Park's umpiring of the two games were "below par." After the series was over, Steinbrenner issued a press release concerning the umpiring skills of Dallas Parks:

> Judging off his last two days' performance, my people tell me that he is not a capable umpire. He is a member of one of the finest crews umpiring in the American League today, but obviously he doesn't measure up.
>
> We are making no excuse for the team's play this season, but this weekend our team has had several key injuries and for umpire Dallas Parks to throw two of our players out of ballgames in two days on plays he misjudges is ludicrous.
>
> This man, in my opinion, has had it in for the Yankees ever since I labeled him and several of the umpires as "scabs" because they worked the American Leagues games in 1979 during the umpires' strike.
>
> Parks must learn that the word scab is a commonly used phrase. It is in no way meant as a personal insult. However, because he worked during the strike for baseball management does not mean he should be protected by them and annually given a job he is not capable of handling.[15]

In response to Steinbrenner comments, Parks filed a defamation lawsuit against Steinbrenner, alleging that he "falsely impugned his ability, competence, conduct and fairness as a baseball umpire."[16] The court ruled in favor of Steinbrenner, finding that the press release "constituted a constitutionally protected expression of pure opinion."[17] The Court concluded that "the press release in every respect falls within the orbit of an expression of 'pure opinion' which is constitutionally protected."[18]

The umpire is clearly a standard and mainstay of the game. The game could not function without the umpire.

The First Woman Umpire

The Baseball Hall of Fame recognizes Amanda Clement as the first woman to umpire a baseball game.[19] She umpired for six years at the semi-pro level, umpiring her first game in 1904 when she was only 16 years old. Clement was 5'10" and worked her way through Yankton College and the University of Nebraska earning $15 to $25 for umpiring games.[20]

Clement once said:

> If women were umpiring none of this [rowdyism] would happen. Do you suppose any ball player in the country would step up to a good-looking girl and say to her, "You color-bind, pickle-brained, cross-eyed idiot, if you don't stop throwing the soup into me I'll distribute your features all over your countenance!" Of course he wouldn't.[21]

Her well earned reputation spread and she became a big gate attraction.[22] It was reported she received more than 60 marriage offers from players, but she never married.[23] Clement was regarded as an umpire who was fair and knew the rules.[24] She was a multi-talented woman. She later worked as a justice of the peace, a newspaper reporter, a social worker, and an instructor at the University of Wyoming.[25]

Many women have made significant contributions to the game of baseball. The first woman in baseball was Lizzie Arlington. She pitched the last inning of a game for the Reading club in a victory over Allentown on July 5, 1889.[26] Jackie Mitchell was a fine pitcher. At the age of 17, she struck out Babe Ruth and Lou Gehrig with her slider.[27] And in response to the signing of 24-year-old Eleanor Engle by the Harrisburg Senators of the Class B Interstate League in 1952, George M. Trautman, President of the National Association of Professional Baseball Leagues, issued the following memorandum:

> Following press reports that the Harrisburg Club, of the Interstate League, had entered into a contract with a woman player, this office contacted that club regarding a woman player ever appear[ing] in a game of the Harrisburg Club.
>
> So as to remove any possible doubt as to the attitude of the National Association office toward any such contract, I am notifying all Minor League clubs that no such contract will be approved and that any club which undertakes to enter into such a contract, will be subject to severe disciplinary action. I have consulted Commissioner Frick on this matter and he has asked me to express his concurrence in the view

that it just is not in the best interests of professional baseball that such travesties be tolerated.[28]

In 2006, Effa Manley became the first woman ever elected to the Baseball Hall of Fame.[29] Ms. Manley was a co-owner of the Newark Eagles of the Negro National League. She ran the business operations of the team for more than a decade. Monte Irvin, Larry Doby, and Don Newcombe all played for her. Sherry Davis was the first woman public address announcer in major league baseball, announcing for the San Francisco Giants in their final years at Candlestick Park.[30] Davis was eventually replaced by other women, including Renel Brooks-Moon who became the first woman announcer for the World Series in 2002.[31] In July 2008, Jacqueline Parkes was named to a newly created position in MLB, Chief Marketing Officer.[32] Ria Cortesia, a graduate of Rice University, was the first female to umpire a major league exhibition game since Pam Postema.[33] She was released by the minor leagues in October 2007. She spent nine years in the minor leagues, the last five at the AA level.[34] The 2008 Racial and Gender Report Card produced by Dr. Richard Lapchick at the University of Central Florida gave MLB an "A-" for race and a "C+" for gender, for an overall grade of B.[35] Women held 19 percent of the general administrative positions in baseball and 29 percent of the professional administrative jobs in the big leagues. It is clear women are becoming more involved in all aspects of baseball at the major league level.

Some ballplayers have a bias against women being involved in the game of baseball. Following in the footsteps of Bob Knepper, in April 2006, Keith Hernandez, a Mets broadcaster at the time, made disparaging comments about a female member of the San Diego Padres training staff. After Mike Piazza hit a home run for the Padres in a game against the Mets, he gave a "high-five" in the dugout to Kelly Calabrese, the Padres full-time massage therapist. On seeing this Hernandez remarked:

> Who is the girl in the dugout, with the long hair? What's going on here? You have got to be kidding me. Only player personnel in the dugout. I won't say that women belong in the kitchen, but they don't belong in the dugout. You know I am only teasing. I love you gals out there. Always have.[36]

He later apologized for the remark saying he overreacted to the situation.[37]

So women have been owners, executives, trainers, and public address announcers, but there has never been a woman umpire at the major league level. There have been several women umpires who have tried, including Amanda Clement, Bernice Gera in the 1960–70s, Pam Postema in the 1980s and 1990s, as well as Theresa Cox.[38] Postema and Gera brought lawsuits against Major League Baseball for discrimination and both prevailed, although neither one ever umpired a major league game.

Pam Postema

Pam Postema always loved baseball and was intrigued with the position of umpire. She attended umpire school and graduated 17th in a class of 130 students.[39] Her first umpiring job was in the Gulf Coast League in 1977 and she worked there until she was moved to the single A Florida State League where she umpired for two years, from 1979 to 1980. She was promoted to the AA Texas League for 1981–82. Postema was the first woman ever to umpire a baseball game above the class A level. She was promoted to Triple-A and umpired at that level for six years. As a Triple-A umpire, Postema garnered several prime assignments. She worked behind the plate for the Hall-of-Fame Game in 1987 between the Yankees and the Braves and the following year umpired the Venezuelan All-Star Game. In 1988–89, she was the chief of her umpiring crew and also umpired MLB spring training games. She was the home plate umpire for the first ever Triple-A All-Star Game. She was requested to be a supervisor for umpires in the minor leagues in 1989. Many major league managers said she was an outstanding umpire, including Hal Lanier, Roger Craig, Chuck Tanner, and Tom Trebelhorn. It is uncontested that Postema received her share of accolades in her career as a minor league umpire. In 1988, she was pictured on the cover of *Sports Illustrated* ("The Lady is an Ump") and profiled in an article which said she had "a shot" at the majors.[40] She had fought her way through the minor leagues and paid her dues along the way.

Notwithstanding her accomplishments and despite her solid record of umpiring and professional demeanor in the minor leagues, she was forced to suffer through repeated acts of sexual harassment and gender discrimination.[41] She was spat on and told by both players and managers that she should be doing "woman's work" instead of umpiring. She was also repeatedly called a four-letter word on several occasions, one that begins with the letter "C" and refers to the female genitalia.[42] Chuck Tanner, manager of the Pittsburgh Pirates, asked if he could give her a kiss when he brought the lineup card out to start the game,[43] and in 1987 a manager of a minor league team actually kissed her on the lips when he handed her the lineup card.

One episode concerning Postema during the 1988 Spring Training created a national debate on the issue of gender equity in sports. Bob Knepper, a left-handed pitcher for the Houston Astros, stepped forward (without being asked) and decided he would give his opinion on the subject of women umpires and the Bible, an extremely lethal combination.[44] Knepper thought Postema, or all women for the matter, had no place in the game of baseball. He stated:

> I just don't think a woman should be an umpire. There are certain things a woman shouldn't be and an umpire is one of them. It's a physical thing. God created women to be feminine. I don't think they should be competing with men.
>
> It has nothing to do with her ability. I don't think women should be in any posi-

tion of leadership. I don't think they should be presidents or politicians. I think women were created not in an inferior position, but in a role of submission to men. You can be a woman umpire if you want, but that doesn't mean it's right. You can be a homosexual if you want, but that doesn't mean that's right either.

It's her choice what she wants to do with her life, and I'm not going to give her a hard time. I'll respect her more because she's a woman. I'm not going to condemn her. But if God is unhappy with her, she's going to have to deal with that later.[45]

Houston Astros manager Hall Lanier tried calling Postema several times after Knepper made his statements and could not reach her.[46] Much to his credit, he left her a note apologizing for Knepper's statements, saying he did not agree with Knepper: "I just want you to know that there is a place for good umpiring in the National League, and if I am asked, I certainly would recommend you."[47]

Postema also received a long letter from Knepper but said she could barely get through it because of all the biblical quotes asserting the superiority of man over woman.[48] She never wrote him back, saying it would have been a waste of time because "ability didn't matter to him."[49]

Postema's Lawsuit

Postema had made her way to Triple-A in 1989, one stop away from the major leagues. However, in 1988 and 1989 she began to see the handwriting on the wall and realized she would probably not become a major league umpire.

Postema was terminated from her position as a Triple-A umpire on November 6, 1989.[50] She alleged that the sole reason she lost her job and was unable to get a major league umpiring job was the "Defendants' malicious, wanton, willful, knowing, and intentional discrimination on the basis of gender."[51]

Postema brought a law-

Pam Postemas's lawsuit against baseball produced a settlement but not a major league umpire (National Baseball Hall of Fame Library Cooperstown, New York).

suit alleging employment discrimination in violation of Title VII of the Civil Rights Act of 1964, as well as violations of New York's Human Rights Law and illegal restraint of trade.[52] The defendants named in the lawsuit were the National and American Leagues, the Triple-A Alliance of Professional Baseball Clubs, and the Baseball Office of Umpire Development (BOUD). In her lawsuit, Postema alleged that she was fully qualified to be a major league umpire and male umpires who had less experience, less qualifications, and less abilities were promoted and hired by the American and National Leagues ahead of her.

Postema requested the court award her damages as well as make the defendants hire her as a major league umpire. The defendants believed that the case would never make it to a jury, anticipating that the court would dismiss Postema's lawsuit on their motion for summary judgment. If the court granted the motion, Postema could appeal, but appeals are always difficult, time-consuming, and the odds of a party winning an appeal are extremely low. If a plaintiff can survive a defendant's summary judgment motion, the plaintiff can then attempt to force the defendant to a trial or settle the case.

Postema pointed to specific times in 1988 and 1989 when "events came to a head."[53] Several statements by individuals involved in baseball indicated she would not make it to the major leagues as an umpire. In July 1987, Dick Butler, special assistant to the president of the American League and former supervisor of American League umpires, told *Newsday* the following with regard to Postema's chances of becoming a major league umpire: "She realizes that she has to be better than the fellow next to her. She's got to be better because of the fact that she's a girl. I'm not saying it's fair, but it exists and she's not going to change it."[54] None of the defendants named in the lawsuit did anything to contradict or retract the statements made by Butler.[55] Butler was not disciplined for his statements.[56]

Larry Napp, assistant supervisor of umpires for the American League, also stated to the *Richmond Times-Dispatch*: "She's a nice person, and she knows the rules. But the thing is, she's got to do the job twice as good as the guy, if he's a good one to get the job."[57] None of the defendants named in the lawsuit took action against Napp for his unusual statements about Postema. In 1989, Ed Vargo, the supervisor of National League umpires, required her to change her stance and technique "to resemble those used by him during his career."[58] No male umpires were required to change their technique or stance. These specific statements and requests indicated to Postema that there would be barriers for her in becoming a major league umpire.

During the 1989 season, Postema said the defendants "either ignored or criticized her." Of the nine minor league umpires invited to spring training in 1989, Postema and her partner, a male umpire, were the only two who were not given an opportunity to fill in when a major league umpire got sick or went on vacation.[59] Finally, at the end of the 1989 season, she received a negative written performance evaluation saying she had a "bad attitude" even though before 1989 she had never received a written performance evaluation.[60] Postema found out she was being sent down to the minors when she read it in the sports section of *USA Today* on March 24, 1989.[61] Baseball Commissioner Bart Giamatti called Postema and apologized, saying he had not made a decision yet[62] but Postema was eventually sent back to Triple-A.[63]

Court's Decision — Postema

The court summarized the plaintiff's claims against the American League as two separate claims under Title VII of the Civil Rights Act of 1964 as claims for wrongful termination and failure to hire or promote.[64]

The court first addressed the hiring and promotion claims of Postema. The defendants argued the plaintiff's claims were "time-barred," not filed by the dates required by law, and that the court should dismiss the lawsuit on that basis.[65] The court noted that under federal law an individual who brings a lawsuit under Title VII of the Civil Rights Act must first file a charge with the Equal Employment Opportunity Commission (EEOC) and they must do it within 180 days of the violation or "where the plaintiff first files with a state or local equal employment agreement, within 300 days of the violations."[66] A plaintiff must file a claim with the EEOC within the prescribed time limits to maintain a viable lawsuit.[67] Because Postema did not file a charge of discrimination within 300 days of the hiring of Joyce, the court dismissed "any claim ... [she] ... might have arising from the Joyce hiring...."[68]

The American League also argued that since it never hired or promoted any umpires during the 300-day period in which Postema had to file a claim with the EEOC, then "the absence of a vacancy for the position sought prevents Plaintiff from establishing her requisite prima facie case of employment discrimination."[69] The court also found this argument persuasive and dismissed Postema's claims for lack of hiring and promotion against the American League.

The court then turned its attention to Postema's wrongful termination claim under Title VII as well as her claim under New York Human Rights Law. Postema claimed in her complaint that the reason she was terminated was "that the American League and National League were not interested in considering her for employment as a major league umpire."[70]

In its defense the American League submitted the affidavit of Martin J. Springstead, the American League supervisor of umpires, who said that in October 1989 BOUD submitted to him a list of Triple-A umpires and wanted to know if he was interested in hiring any of those on the list. He said no because there were no vacancies for umpires at that time.

Postema responded that "the American League either understood that its expressed lack of interest in Plaintiff would cause her termination by Triple-A, or otherwise intended to encourage Triple-A to terminate Plaintiff."[71] Postema asked the court that she be given the opportunity to explore in more depth the detailed communication which occurred between the American League and BOUD in October 1989 to prove her claims of discrimination and the court agreed. Instead of granting the American League's motion for summary judgment for the plaintiff's wrongful termination claims they gave Postema an opportunity for further discovery to determine what role the American League played, if any, in her termination. The court did recognize that the American League was not Postema's employer but noted that if it did engage in any discriminatory action against Postema which caused her employer, Triple-A, to terminate her, then it could be liable for damages to Postema under Title VII.[72] "Where a third-party takes discriminatory action that causes an employer to terminate an employee, that third-party may be held liable under Title VII."[73]

Postema also brought claims under New York State Law for restraint of trade. The court disagreed with the argument of the defendants that baseball's exemption to antitrust challenges should apply in a case of baseball's employment relations with umpires.

> It is thus clear that although the baseball exemption does immunize baseball from antitrust challenges to its league structure and its reserve system, the exemption does not provide baseball with blanket immunity for anti-competitive behavior in every context in which it operates. The Court must therefore determine whether baseball's employment relations with its umpires are "central enough to baseball to be encompassed in the baseball exemption."[74]

The defendants were confident that the court would grant its motion for summary judgment in its entirety, but the court did not do so. Postema's case survived the defendants' motion for summary judgment. Her lawsuit could now move forward on a variety of claims for wrongful termination under Title VII. She had gotten past the first legal hurdle and could now pursue her lawsuit for discrimination.

A trial was on the horizon for the parties. Each would be ready to present their case but the case would never reach a jury. Trials are a gamble and good lawyers know that.[75] The parties understood that concept and instead entered into a confidential settlement agreement, the terms of which have never been disclosed.[76] A settlement of a lawsuit does not necessarily mean a party believes they are responsible but it might mean they believe the opposing party has a chance of winning the case in front of a jury. Postema had forced baseball to settle with her but she was finished as an umpire. The defendants could now take a sigh of relief and go back to business.

Pam Postema left baseball, never to return. She had umpired at the Triple-A level for many years but never got the chance to umpire in the big leagues. Postema has said:

Even though it hurts to do so I think about umpiring every day. I loved the freedom that came with my job, and I liked the theory — because that's all it ever turned out to be — that if you worked hard enough, you could advance to the big leagues. I can count on one hand the times I didn't give 100 percent on the field. Maybe if I had kissed ass I'd still be umpiring. But that's not the way I operate. The way I see it, I tried my best but got screwed by a system that wasn't built for women.[77]

After she left baseball in 1985, Postema said she doubted she would have anything else to do with baseball, notwithstanding her victory over baseball, because she always wanted to be a major league umpire.[78]

The current requirements to become a Major League umpire are set forth by the Professional Umpire Baseball Corporation of Major League Baseball.[79] They are:

- High school diploma or G.E.D.
- Reasonable body weight
- 20/20 vision (with or without corrective lenses)
- Good communication skills
- Quick reflexes, good coordination
- Some athletic ability
- Required preliminary training for the job (i.e., professional umpire school)[80]

Bernice Gera

If Pam Postema was a trendsetter, then Bernice Gera was the "original."[81] Gera was a Queens housewife who battled baseball executives and baseball players both in the courts and on the field. When she was eight years old living in Indiana, Pennsylvania, she discovered she was a better hitter than most boys[82] and baseball became her main interest.[83] She would later become a secretary but baseball remained a big part of her life. She dedicated evenings to teaching neighborhood kids about baseball. She also put on hitting exhibitions with Roger Maris and Sid Gordon.[84] When she met her future husband, "I wouldn't go out unless we went to Rockway Park where I could throw and hit baseballs at the concession stands."[85] She woke up one night at 2:30 A.M. in 1967 with the idea of being an umpire. After discussing it with her husband, she decided to enroll in a school for umpires in Florida. Gera was 5 feet 2 inches and 129 pounds when she applied for the Al Somers School for Umpires in 1967. She used "Bernie" as her first name, and did not state her gender since it was not required on the form.[86] She graduated with "high marks," notwithstanding the school's lack of facilities for women. They were so inadequate that Gera had to move to a local hotel.

Bernice Gera, professional baseball's first female umpire, makes a call on a Holy Family College player (photo archives of the New York *Daily News*).

After completing umpire school, in the summer of 1968 Gera wrote to Vincent McNamara, president of the New York–Pennsylvania League,[87] and requested an application to be an umpire. McNamara responded by sending a letter to Gera objecting to hiring a female umpire. "It is our professional opinion that it would be unwise to expose you or any other lady to situations such as those stated previously above."[88] Gera was certain she could perform the job of an umpire, saying, "I've been splattered with tobacco juice, I've been cursed, I've been pushed around. I am certain I can do the job as well as any man."[89]

Gera Lawsuit

After she was turned down, Gera filed a claim with the State Division of Human Rights for the State of New York, arguing she had been discriminated against based on her sex in violation of New York state law. She was represented by U.S. Congressman Mario Biaggi.

8. Gera and Postema Try to Break the Glass Ceiling

After filing the complaint with the Human Rights Division, McNamara sent Gera an umpire questionnaire to complete. She completed the application, listing her age, height, and weight and sent it back to McNamara. He in turn sent it to Phillip Piton, president of the National Association of Professional Baseball Leagues. Piton would have to approve Gera's application and any contract offered to her. McNamara forwarded the contract to Piton, stating that he did so "even though he did not consider complainant qualified, because of his having been importuned by the complainant and the Human Rights Commission."[90]

Piton failed to approve Gera's contract, citing the standard established by the umpire development program dealing with height, weight, and age.[91] He advised Gera he disapproved her umpire contract because she failed "to meet the physical requirements for admission to the Umpire Development Program and for employment by the National Association Leagues I have no alternative but to disapprove and invalidate your proposed contract."[92] Gera could have easily quit under the circumstances but she did not give up. She instead continued to pursue her case and her dream of being an umpire.

After reviewing her complaint, the State Division of Human Rights found that the league and its executives had barred Gera from employment as an umpire based on her sex in violation of Section 296 of the Executive Law of the State of New York:

1. It shall be an unlawful discriminatory practice:
   (a) For an employer, because of the age, race, creed, color, national origin or sex of any individual, to refuse to hire or employ or to bar or to discharge from employment such individual in compensation or in terms, condition or privileges of employment.
   ...
6. It shall be an unlawful discriminatory practice for any person to aid, abet, incite, compel or coerce the doing of any of the acts forbidden under this article or to attempt to do so.[93]

At Gera's hearing in the New York Human Rights Division, Bernard C. Deary, the administrator of professional baseball's umpire development program, testified that "[w]omen umpires would be welcome if they met age, height and weight standards."

The commissioner of the State Division of Human Rights entered an order requiring the league and its executives to "cease and desist" its unlawful discriminatory practices and to take steps to establish new physical standard for umpires which were not discriminatory. The commissioner noted the requirements should not discriminate against women or "other groups having smaller average stature than American men."[94] The commissioner also ordered the league to reconsider Gera's application with regard to the new standards that would be issued. In considering whether to reverse the commissioner's decision, the New York Supreme Court Appellate Division, stated: "Whatever policy organized baseball may conceive to be in its best interests must yield to a public policy established in the interests of the whole of society as evidenced by the statutory law of the State."[95]

The league refused to give in, seeking a reversal of the commissioner's ruling in a New York state court. Gera had won at an administrative level but now the case moved to a court of law. The court would affirm the decision of the Division of Human Rights in favor of Gera. The league and its executives argued to the court that there was an exemption under both state and federal law which supported their decision not to hire female umpires. They asserted that the "bona fide occupational qualification" under employment law was applicable and that it allowed the league to restrict its hiring to males.[96] The court succinctly responded to this argument by stating that "this contention is unsound."[97] The court noted that the league had the burden to prove its affirmative defense to plaintiff's lawsuit and found that they had not submitted any evidence to show "a factual basis for belief that women are not qualified for the job of a professional baseball umpire."[98]

The league argued that an umpire's job encompassed the requirements of physical strain, travel, and loss of weight as well as a possibility of physical injury. The court found this not to be enough for the league to meet its burden to establish its defense of bona fide occupational qualification.[99] The court noted that the guidelines issued by the Equal Employment Opportunity Commission (EEOC) rejected the idea that "an employer can refuse 'to hire an individual based on stereotyped characteristics of the sexes.'"[100] The court stated in conclusion: "In the light of the foregoing it would appear that it has not been established that being of the male sex is a bona fide occupational qualification for an umpire or that, as a matter of policy, hiring of umpires should be restricted to males."[101]

The court acknowledged that Gera failed to meet the physical standards set by the league. In fact, it noted less than one percent of women meet those requirements. Several witnesses testified on behalf of the league that the height and weight requirement for umpires was "born of the judgment of men with long experience in professional baseball."[102] They all testified that an umpire must command respect of "big men" and be ready if necessary to get into a confrontation with big athletes.[103] The court said while those are certainly considerations when setting the qualifications for an umpire, they do not justify a rigid standard requiring each umpire to be 5'10" and 170 pounds. The court also found that this standard had not been uniformly enforced in the past.[104] It concluded by stating:

> It would appear therefore, that the findings of the Commissioner were proper, and that the standards applied by the petitioners, inherently discriminatory against

8. Gera and Postema Try to Break the Glass Ceiling

women, have not been justified in the record. The finding of discrimination based upon sex was a logical conclusion and is supported by the record as a whole.[105]

The court confirmed the orders issued by the commissioner of the Human Rights Division and directed the league to comply with the orders.

Two justices filed separate dissenting opinions to the majority opinion of the court. Dissenting opinions have no precedent but can provide insight to the arguments of the parties and the legal issues presented. Dissenting Justice Gabrielli said he would not have upheld the ruling of the commissioner but instead found the evidence did not merit a finding of discrimination. He said the qualifications set forth by umpires have no relation to sex but were issued years before Gera made her application. He found that the standards were a reasonable relationship to the duties of an umpire.[106]

Gera had now beaten baseball twice and yet she still did not have a position as an umpire. The league and its executives would not give in to Gera, appealing one more time to the New York Court of Appeals the state's highest appellate court, hoping to keep Gera in her place. Gera was not to be denied. Approximately six months later, the court of appeals affirmed the lower court's ruling in Gera's favor and she was on her way to becoming an umpire. The legal arguments presented by the league and league officials had fallen short and seemed antiquated even for 1972. Gera had filed her complaint with the Human Rights Commissioner in 1968, battled her way through the New York court system, and won all three times a decision was made. She was now ready to pursue her dream.

With the litigation behind her, Gera took her position as a base umpire on June 24, 1972, in game one of a doubleheader between Geneva and Auburn of the New York–Pennsylvania Class A minor league. It was reported that Gera made several disputed calls during the game. When the game was over, Gera was through. She went to Geneva's manager and said, "I've just resigned from baseball. I'm sorry Joe."[107] She resigned after game one of a doubleheader, saying she had become disenchanted with the game when other umpires refused to cooperate with her on the field.[108] Bernice Gera had fought hard through the court system and chalked up three substantial legal victories but to no avail. Those court victories failed to change individual attitudes on the diamond. There was no place for women in baseball. Baseball was not yet ready for a female umpire even though Gera was clearly qualified.

In a letter to the editor of the *Chicago Tribune*, James M. Moran shed some light on the status of women umpires at the time:

> I see where Mrs. Bernice Gera, the female would-be umpire, said the National Association of Professional Baseball Leagues is discriminatory because of its rule that umpires must be at least 5 feet 10 inches tall and maybe 170 pounds or so, and Mrs. Gera is much smaller than that. I certainly do not advocate the hiring of female umpires, but I don't understand how the 5–10, 170 pounds rule could be

based on fact. I'm almost certain that Jocko Conlon was no more than about 5–6 and maybe 155 pounds or so, Jocko was a banty rooster type, but he took no guff from anybody including (or perhaps especially) Leo Durocher.[109]

Notwithstanding her lack of acceptance as an umpire, Bernice Gera stayed in the game she loved in other capacities, working for the New York Mets in community relations from 1974 to 1979. She passed away in 1992. Gera will be remembered as a woman who fought hard against baseball to realize her dream against long odds.

Other Significant Cases Involving Discrimination in Baseball

Postema and Gera are two milestone cases involving discrimination law and gender equity in baseball. There are a few other cases worth mentioning dealing with discrimination in baseball.

In *Ludtke v. Kuhn*,[110] Melissa Ludtke brought a civil rights lawsuit to prevent the New York Yankees from enforcing a policy of baseball commissioner Bowie Kuhn to prevent women from entering the clubhouse after the game. Ludtke worked for *Sports Illustrated* as a reporter and was assigned to cover the 1977 World Series between the Yankees and the Dodgers. Before the series began, the Dodgers told Ludtke she was free to enter the clubhouse after the game. However, Commissioner Kuhn told Ludtke she had to wait to enter the clubhouse even though her male counterparts could enter immediately after the game. The commissioner made no special arrangements for Ludtke to interview players after the game. Some ballplayers were offended by the policy and supported Ludtke, particularly Yankees slugger Reggie Jackson.

Ludtke brought a lawsuit alleging she had been discriminated against based on her sex under 42 U.S.C. 1983 on both Equal Protection and Due Process grounds. The federal district court found that the total exclusion of women sports reporters was in violation of the Equal Protection Clause of the Fourteenth Amendment[111] and also found the commissioner's policy "substantially and directly interferes with the right of plaintiff Ludtke to pursue her profession as a sports reporter."[112]

In *Schoeneck v. Chicago National League Ball Clubs*,[113] a ballgirl for the Cubs argued that her termination was actually a pretext for unlawful gender discrimination under Title VII of the Civil Rights Act of 1964. The court ruled in favor of the Cubs, finding no discrimination.

Sex under Section 1983 also is defined to mean sexual harassment. Lisa Kessner was a flight attendant on the private plane of the Detroit Tigers. She sued several entities alleging she had been the subject of sexual harassment on the team's private jet.[114] Her case made it to a jury and she was awarded $200,000 in damages.[115]

In a case involving an NBA woman referee, a jury found that the NBA discriminated against Sandra Ortiz-Del Valle when they failed to hire her as a referee.[116] In 1998, a jury awarded her $7.85 million after she had been passed over several times for an NBA referee position.[117] The jury awarded her $100,000 for loss wages, $750,000 in mental pain and emotional distress, and $7,000,000 million in punitive damages. A federal judge reduced the award to $350,000.[118]

The National Basketball Association took a giant step forward when they hired Dee Kantner and Violet Palmer as NBA referees in 1997. Palmer continued in the league as a referee and now is a league fixture. She said, "When I started my fourth season, I could kind of see the heads not turn anymore..., I could see players come up to me and just talk." Palmer has proven that she can referee at the highest level of the sport and is one of the best in the world at what she does.

Conclusion

Even though the NBA has had women referees since 1997, umpiring in the major leagues still seems off-limits to women who want to pursue their dreams to be an umpire. Whoever is the first will certainly owe a debt of gratitude to Pam Postema, Bernice Gera, Amanda Clement, and Theresa Cox. Those women have set the stage for the first woman umpire in the major leagues.[119]

9

Flood v. Kuhn[1]
Curt Flood Takes His Challenge Over Baseball's Reserve Clause to the U.S. Supreme Court

> I do not feel that I am a piece of property to be bought and sold irrespectively of my wishes. — Curt Flood, 1969

> You know what the real problem is? Baseball has become a corporate holding. There are too many men outside the game who make the most critical decisions. Baseball has become an industry for lawyers. — Curt Flood, 1994

> He made it possible for guys to get million-dollar contracts and $6 million contracts and $26 million contracts.... I'd like to think that most players, if you ask them who Curt Flood was, would say he was a fine outfielder for a number of years and that he was also involved in challenging the reserve system "way back when." — Dal Maxvill, Former Cardinals Shortstop, *The Sporting News*, 1997

> I am pleased that God make my skin black, I just wish He would have made it thicker. — Curt Flood, *The Way It Is* (1970)

U.S. antitrust laws have been the primary vehicle used to effect change in sports.[2] In 1890 Congress enacted the Sherman Antitrust Act which prohibited "any contract, combination or conspiracy in restraint of trade." The antitrust laws have been used by players, owners, franchises, and student athletes in attempts to strike down unreasonable restraints of trade.[3] Prior to the free-agency era in sports, professional athletes had very little "juice," or input, about where they practiced their profession. In the late nineteenth century, ballplayer John Montgomery Ward said players were essentially treated as chattel and had very little control over their careers.

Baseball's original reserve clause was instituted in 1879 by National League President William Hulbert. Ballplayers were essentially bound to their teams under some form of baseball's reserve clause until a labor arbitration decision dismantled it in the mid 1970s. John Ward first challenged the reserve clause using contract law but small claims by players under contract law would ultimately prove to be insufficient to permanently do away with the reserve clause.

The reserve system eliminated competition among teams for the services of players. It operated as a form of horizontal price fixing under the Sherman Antitrust Act. Athletes in other major sports challenged the reserve system on antitrust grounds and were eventually successful.[4] Baseball players, however, were unable to use U.S. antitrust laws to strike down player restraints because baseball was declared to be immune from U.S. antitrust laws in a series of decisions by the U.S. Supreme Court. In 1922, the Supreme Court held in *Federal Baseball v. National League of Professional Baseball Clubs*[5] that the "business of giving exhibitions" was "purely state affairs" and therefore not subject to the antitrust laws. In 1953, the Supreme Court heard *Toolson v. New York Yankees*[6] to determine whether baseball was subject to federal antitrust laws. In a one-paragraph opinion, the Court agreed with *Federal Baseball*, affirming baseball's antitrust exemption by a 7–2 decision. In 1970, another challenge was brought against baseball's reserve clause. Center fielder Curt Flood refused to be traded from the St. Louis Cardinals to the Philadelphia Phillies after the 1969 season. Instead of agreeing to the trade, he asked Commissioner Bowie Kuhn for his release from the Cardinals but his request was turned down. After contemplating his options, Flood sued baseball, challenging the reserve clause on antitrust grounds. Flood would lose in Federal District Court when the court agreed with the existing legal precedent. Flood would appeal his case all the way to the United States Supreme Court and lose. The court's decision would further cement baseball's exemption from federal antitrust laws.

Understanding Curt Flood

Curt Flood was one of the most influential people in the sports world in the twentieth century. Although he was a star center fielder for some of the best teams in baseball for several years, he is best known for his lawsuit against baseball. What would cause a ballplayer in his prime to give up his career and take on a corporate giant in the American court system with little or no chance of winning and very little support from the very people who would benefit if he was successful? The key to that question may be found in the background and person of Curt Flood.[7]

Flood was born in Texas but moved to Oakland, California, at an early age. He grew up in California and never had any experience with the American South. So when he entered minor league baseball in the South in the 1950s, Flood experienced discrimination firsthand for the first time as he played his way through the minor leagues. He began organized baseball just ten years

Curt Flood battled with Major League Baseball all the way to the United States Supreme Court (National Baseball Hall of Fame Library Cooperstown, New York).

after the integration of Major League Baseball by Jackie Robinson in 1947. When he reported to the minors in Florida, he was struck immediately by the separate drinking fountains for blacks and whites, something he had not seen before.[8] Flood was not able to stay in the hotel with white players, but instead had to stay at a local boarding house along with other African American players. When Flood played for Carolina, a Reds farm club, he was sometimes not able to eat at night because no place would serve him out of racial discrimination.[9]

He could not eat with white teammates or use the same restroom they did. He could go to a black bar or sit in the balcony at a movie theater but that was the extent of his social activities.[10]

Flood was eventually assigned to the Savannah minor league club for the 1957 season. He spent the season living in a dorm room at Savannah State College with roommate Leo Cardenas who spoke very little English.[11] Flood later talked about how fans would use racial and derogatory terms towards him and how fans would treat him poorly because of his race.[12]

One episode in the minor leagues stuck with Flood his entire life. After the first game of a doubleheader, he took off his uniform and put it in a pile with the white players' uniforms. The attendant pulled the uniform out with a stick that had a nail on it and sent it to be cleaned at a black laundry 20 minutes away. The uniform was not returned until the second game had started, so Flood could not play.[13]

Even after he became a star ballplayer in the major leagues, he would also be subjected to racism. Flood and his wife sought to buy a home in a white suburb of Oakland in 1964. Just prior to closing, the seller's boyfriend found out the buyers were black and was angry that a black couple was moving into the neighborhood. Rumors abounded that if the Floods moved into the neighborhood the man would take matters into his own hands with a shotgun.[14] The Floods were forced to file a lawsuit requesting a restraining order. Flood was a well-established ballplayer and a wealthy man but he still needed the assistance of a court to ensure he could safely move into a house in his own hometown. In another example of the racist treatment he received even after becoming a star, Flood was refused service at Musial and Biggie's, the restaurant co-owned by former Cardinal great Stan Musial.[15]

Everyone's life experiences shape their outlook and Flood was no exception. He was a proud African American man. He was intelligent, thoughtful, a very good artist, and an excellent ballplayer. Flood's life experiences would not allow him to sit idly by while others controlled his destiny. Flood said:

> I guess you really have to understand who that person, who that Curt Flood, was. I'm a child of the sixties, I'm a man of the 60's. During that period of time this country was coming apart at the seams. We were in Southeast Asia.... Good men were dying for America and for the Constitution. In the southern part of the United States we were marching for civil rights and Dr. King had been assassinated, and we lost the Kennedys. And to think that merely because I was professional baseball player, I could ignore what was going on outside the walls of Busch Stadium [was] truly hypocrisy and now I found that all of those rights that these great Americans were dying for I didn't have in my own profession.[16]

Flood's motivation may never be fully understood but his background certainly sheds some light on his decision to give up a lucrative baseball career to challenge baseball's reserve clause.

The Best Center Fielder in Baseball

Flood virtually played his entire career for the St. Louis Cardinals. He only batted 39 times in the major leagues for clubs other than the Cardinals. He debuted with the Cincinnati Reds in 1956, along with Frank Robinson, who won the 1956 National League Rookie of the Year award and was a well-respected African American player. Flood would get one hit for the Reds, a home run. In December 1957, he was traded to the Cardinals along with teammate Joe Taylor for Marty Kutyna, Ted Wieand, and Willard Schmidt. Kutyna would be out of baseball by 1962 and chalk up 14 career wins. Wieand would appear in six games for the Reds, with a lifetime record of 0–1,[17] and Schmidt would play two seasons for the Reds, compiling a 6–7 record and then be out of baseball. The player traded along with Flood to the Cardinals would never play for St. Louis, but end up with Baltimore, batting .156 for one season. Suffice it to say, the Cardinals got the better of the trade. Flood would become one of the National League's biggest stars and help lead the Cardinals to World Series titles in 1964 and 1967. The Cardinals would also make it to the series in 1968, losing a closely fought and very exciting series to the Detroit Tigers, four games to three.

Curt Flood was a very good hitter. He finished in the top ten in hitting in the National League five times, with a season high average of .335 in 1967. He led the league in singles three times, doubles once, at bats twice, and in hits once, 1965 with 211. He finished in the top ten in hits in the league five times. He was an all-star three times, 1964, 1966, and 1968. He completed his career with good offensive members: 1,861 hits, 271 doubles, 851 runs, and a lifetime batting average of .293. But it was his fielding skills that displayed his great athletic ability. He won seven straight Golden Glove awards for his work in center field (1963 to 1969). In 1968, Flood was called the best centerfielder in baseball by *Sports Illustrated* and featured on the cover. That was quite a compliment considering Willie Mays was still in the league with the San Francisco Giants. Flood still holds the record for the best fielding percentage for an outfielder in a season of 150 games or more, at .1000.[18] Many ballplayers never get the chance that Flood did to play alongside great players on championship teams. He played six seasons with Hall of Famer Stan Musial. He also played with such stars as Bob Gibson, Joe Torre, Orlando Cepeda, Lou Brock, Ken Boyer, Bill White, Roger Maris, Vada Pinson, Steve Calton, Curt Simmons, and Dick Groat.[19] Of those players, Flood was the only one who was in the starting lineup for the Cardinals for 12 straight years.

Flood was a staple in center field for the Cardinals from 1958 to 1969. He was a member of a great baseball organization that produced winning clubs and he became entrenched in St. Louis. He had business interests there and his family was well established in the community. He enjoyed his life and his baseball career. He had no intention of leaving St. Louis. However, the 1969 season was not the kind of season the Cardinals or its owner had become accustomed to. The Cardinals finished fourth in the newly structured National League Eastern Division at 87–75. Changes in the St. Louis lineup were imminent.

The Lawsuit

The 1969 season was over but Flood had no idea what was about to occur. On October 8, 1969, just a few days after the end of the season, Flood was informed by a person in the Cardinals organization that he had been traded to the Philadelphia Phillies. Flood would later write: "If I had been a foot-shuffling porter, they might have at least given me a pocket watch but all I got was a call from a middle-echelon coffee drinker in the front office."[20]

Flood had no desire to play in Philadelphia or for the Phillies. He was keenly aware of the problems that Phillies star player Richie Allen had experienced while in Philadelphia. Even though he was not perceived as being as contentious as Allen, Flood did not want to play in the city of brotherly love. He quickly issued a statement to the press declaring his retirement[21]:

> If I were younger I certainly would enjoy playing for Philadelphia. But under the circumstances, I have decided to retire from organized baseball, effective today, and remain in St. Louis where I can devote full time to my business interests. I hope all concerned will understand my feelings and reasons for making this decision.[22]

In contrast, Richie Allen's elated response to the trade showed he was ready to leave both the Phillies organization and the city of Philadelphia behind:

> I am going to go out to St. Louis and get myself settled down, not worry about anything but baseball. I'll get a place somewhere even if it's a room in the Y.M.C.A., and concentrate on baseball. I want to be on a pennant winner and this may be it. I thought they'd trade me out of the league, but I'm glad I'm going to have a chance to come back here. I'm thinking about that already. [I am] so glad to be out of here [Philadelphia]. Six years in this town is enough for anybody. I'm glad to be away from Quinn and all of them. They treat you like cattle.[23]

Some thought Flood's announced retirement might have been a ploy or merely a negotiation tool to garner a big raise from St. Louis. However, as time passed, it became clear Flood was serious about not playing for the Phillies and retiring from baseball. Flood was only 31 years old and in his last season with St. Louis he batted .285 in 606 at-bats, scoring 80 runs, with 31 doubles, and appeared in 153 games. Certainly not Flood's best season by any measure but not quite the statistics that would indicate a player was on the verge of retirement either. Flood had just won his seventh Golden Glove award for his outstanding play in center field and he still had a lot of baseball to play.

After refusing to go to Philadelphia, Flood traveled to Copenhagen, Denmark, where he was thinking about opening a restaurant. John Quinn, Phillies general manager, contacted him while he was overseas to try to persuade him to play in Philadelphia. Quinn eventually offered Flood a salary package of more than $100,000, more than he was earning with the Cardinals. Only ten players in baseball were making that much money at the time.[24] It was a good offer for Flood considering his age. Although he was a great fielder, Flood was essentially a singles hitter who did not steal many bases. The Phillies' offer would place him among the elite wage earners in baseball. If he was feigning retirement to increase the Phillies offer, he had achieved his goal. However, after much contemplation, Flood turned down the Phillies' offer.[25] It seemed no ballplayer would have made the decision Flood did. He was at the top of his profession and being paid a lot of money to play a game he loved. The only thing Flood disliked was that he could not play where he wanted to. Instead of playing baseball for the next two years, Flood made a decision that would cause him to deal with lawyers and judges, suffer intense pressure from the media, and eventually lose his case, as well as his career as a ballplayer.

Flood knew his first step in challenging the reserve clause was to talk to the head of the Major League Baseball Players Association, Marvin Miller. During their first meeting, Miller bluntly told Flood that his career in baseball would essentially be over if he sued, a prediction that sadly came to fruition.[26] The Players Association would provide Flood with the best possible counsel available, Arthur Goldberg, a former United States Supreme Court Justice. Flood was faced with a choice: take a job playing baseball, something he had done his entire life, for over $100,000, or essentially take on the barons of baseball in court with legal precedent against him. Flood understood that there were three Supreme Court decisions directly on point dealing with baseball's reserve clause and none of them were in his favor. The odds were clearly stacked against him. It is a wonder that Flood went forward with the lawsuit, instead of signing with Philadelphia, but he was a principled man and thought it was the right decision under the circumstances.

Miller proposed to Flood that the Players Association pay the legal fees and costs associated with the lawsuit. This would need to be approved by the Association. The Executive Committee of the Players Association held a meeting in Puerto Rico in early December 1969, at which Flood made a presentation to the player representatives. After two hours of "interrogation," Flood received unanimous approval to move forward with the lawsuit, and they also agreed to fund it.[27] The minutes of the executive board meeting showed a vote of 25–0 in support of Flood. Although Flood would receive a unanimous vote to proceed against baseball, later not one active major league player would attend the three-week federal court trial in New York City.

In an opening statement to the player representatives, Flood spent twenty minutes detailing his reasons for bringing the lawsuit. He was questioned about his motives, with some players wanting to ensure Flood was not bringing the lawsuit because of "racial issues." Tom Haller, catcher with the Los Angeles Dodgers, said to Flood, "This is a period of black militance. Do you feel that you're doing this as part of the movement? Because you're black?"[28] Flood confirmed that "the racial issue was not central to his objections, although being black perhaps made him more sensitive to issues of freedom and dignity."[29] His primary object "was to establish once and for all, that a player could set his value in an open market, as in other spheres of life."[30] The player representatives were veterans and superstars of the game who had a lot at stake if Flood were to prevail. It was a stellar group of ballplayers who had been around the game for many years.[31] Flood knew most of them because he had played baseball with them for years. They grilled him for two hours about his reasons for filing the lawsuit. The group before which Flood spoke included four future hall-of-famers, Brooks Robinson, Reggie Jackson, Jim Bunning, and Robert Clemente, three future general managers, two future big league managers, and one future U.S. Senator (Bunning). Flood was facing a tough line-up that day. His Cardinal teammate Joe Torre went on the record first in support of Flood and others quickly followed suit. Torre had just finished a great first season with the Cardinals, batting .289 and driving in 101 runs. Torre said, "I knew Curt didn't do something just for the sake of doing something, he did something because he felt strongly about it."[32] After the vote was taken, Flood signed a document promising to pay the Players Association's legal fees if he lost. The votes were in and Flood would now begin a long trek through the court system that would take him all the way to the U.S. Supreme Court.

Litigation is never pleasant. It is a long tedious process and all too often none of the parties are satisfied with the outcome. Flood would experience his share of unpleasantness as the litigation unfolded. Before filing his lawsuit, Flood made one last effort to avoid litigation. He wrote a letter to Commissioner Bowie Kuhn on December 24, 1969, telling him how he felt about being traded:

> After 12 years in the major leagues, I do not feel that I am a piece of property to be bought and sold irrespective of my wishes. I believe that any system that produces that result violates my basic rights as a citizen and is inconsistent with the laws of the United States and of the several states.
> It is my desire to play Baseball in 1970, and I am capable of playing. I have received a contract offer from the Philadelphia Club, but I believe I have the right to consider offers from other clubs before making any decision, I, therefore, request that you make known to all major league clubs my feelings in the matter and advise them of my availability for the 1970 season.[33]

Six days later Commissioner Kuhn responded:

> This will acknowledge your letter of Dec. 24, which I found on returning to my office yesterday.
>
> I certainly agree with you that you, as a human being, are not a piece of property to be bought and sold. That is fundamental in our society and I think obvious. However, I cannot see its applicability to the situation at hand.
>
> You are entered into a current playing contract with the St. Louis Club, which has the same assignment provision as those in your annual major league contracts since 1956. Your present contract has been assigned in accordance with its provisions by the St. Louis Club to the Philadelphia Club. The provisions of the playing contract have been negotiated over the years between the clubs and the players, most recently when the present Basic Agreement was negotiated two years ago between the clubs and the Players Association.
>
> If you have any specific objection to the propriety of the assignment, I would appreciate your specifying the objection. Under the circumstances and pending any further information from you, I do not see what action I can take and cannot comply with the request contained in the second paragraph of your letter.
>
> I am pleased to see your statement that you desire to play baseball in the 1970. I take it this puts to rest any thought, as reported earlier in the press, that you were considering retirement.[34]

On January 3, 1970, Flood taped an interview with noted sportscaster and lawyer Howard Cosell for the popular television show *ABC's Wide World of Sports*. Marvin Miller appeared alongside Flood during the interview. Flood would make some controversial remarks during the interview. He was asked by Cosell:

> It's been written, Curt, that you're a man who makes $90,000 a year, which isn't exactly slave wages. What's your retort to that?

Flood responded:

> A well-paid slave is nonetheless a slave.[35]

Flood was not the first ballplayer to compare the reserve clause to slavery. John Montgomery Ward also referred to the reserve clause in terms of slavery during the establishment of the Brotherhood in 1885.[36]

At the time Flood initiated his lawsuit in early 1970, the U.S. was still in the midst of civil unrest. The assassination of Dr. Martin Luther King had occurred on April 4, 1968. Tommie Smith and John Carlos made their now famous "black power" gesture while receiving their medals in Mexico at the 1968 Olympic Games. At the same time Flood was bringing his lawsuit, Muhammad's Ali lawsuit regarding his conscientious objector status for the Vietnam War was still in the courts.[37] Tennis great Arthur Ashe was also seeking to become the first black athlete to compete individually against whites in South Africa.[38] Black athletes were becoming more notable as corporate spokespersons and receiving more exposure in the media. Although Flood's lawsuit was based on a violation of antitrust law, some perceived it as having racial overtones.[39] These were clearly tumultuous times and Flood was risking his career and reputation by filing the lawsuit.

On January 16, 1970, Flood's lawyers filed his complaint in Federal District Court in New York.[40] It stated in part: "The baseball establishment maintains a lifetime grip on any player who wishes to play professional baseball in the United States."[41] The lawsuit named Commissioner Kuhn, both league presidents, and all 24 major league teams as defendants. Flood argued that the reserve clause violated both federal and state antitrust laws and common law as well.[42] He asked for $1 million in damages. Most associated with the case knew Flood would never receive any damages and Flood said he did not care about the money but only about striking down the reserve clause.

At the same time he filed the complaint, Flood filed a motion for preliminary injunction, requesting the court nullify his trade to the Phillies. Even before the case had its first court hearing, some major league players began to grumble about the lawsuit. Carl Yastrzemski ("Yaz") was a baseball superstar in 1970. In 1967 he won the baseball's triple crown in the American League and in 1969 he was fresh off a 40-home run season.[43] Yaz was one of baseball's superstars.[44] Owners must have been overjoyed when they saw the remarks Yaz made about the Flood lawsuit:

> Personally I am against what Curt Flood is trying to do because it would ruin the game. I want every player to vote on this thing. It's our right. We were never consulted and should have been. I've talked with many players, both active and inactive, and all of them say they were shocked to hear the association backed him without taking a vote of the full membership.[45]

It became clear to Flood, Marvin Miller, and Flood's lawyers that they would have to not only fight baseball but also convince some of the current players that a lawsuit was the proper course of action under the circumstances. While Yaz's comments were enough to cast a cloud over Flood's lawsuit, other current players thought it necessary to weigh in as well.[46] Twins great Harmon Killebrew said, "As far as I'm concerned, the reserve clause is something all of us knew about when we came into baseball."[47] Slugger Frank Howard chimed in, "I can't speak for Curt Flood, but if he believes in what he's doing, God bless him, I don't agree with him."[48] Other current players like Ron Santo, White Sox player Pete Ward, and Cubs great Billy Williams also were less than complimentary about the filing of the lawsuit.[49] Even retired ballplayers like former Red Sox great Ted Williams would call the lawsuit "ill-advised."[50] One notable player who came to Flood's defense was Sandy Koufax. Koufax could lend automatic credibility to any position and his support would go far in combating negative comments by other players. Koufax was a class individual and well-respected in the game. He said, "I have to give Curt the greatest amount of credit for believing in what he's doing. At the salary he's making that's the kind of money which he's never going to get back."[51]

February 3, 1970, was the day the court set for the preliminary injunction hearing requested by Flood.[52] The hearing would last for two hours with Flood's lawyer Arthur Goldberg arguing: "The ancient Romans had high-priced slaves, some with access to the king's treasury — but they were still slaves. The basic concepts here are the morality and the legality of the situation."[53]

A little over a month later, on March 4, 1970, Judge Cooper rendered his decision rejecting Flood's request for a preliminary injunction. In a detailed 55-page opinion with 71 footnotes, Judge Cooper found that the probability of Flood's success at trial in overturning baseball's exemption to federal antitrust laws was not likely and denied his request for an injunction.[54] Judge Cooper's ruling only denied Flood's request for an injunction; it was not a trial on the merits of the case. It was now settled: Curt Flood would not play baseball in 1970. On April 7, 1970, Flood was placed on the Phillies' restricted list for failure to report. The trial was set for May 18 and would actually begin on May 19. The parties began to scramble to get ready. Two and a half months would be totally inadequate for preparation time for such a significant case.

Civil lawsuits allow parties to engage in discovery procedures to obtain documents from the opposing party and to take testimony by way of depositions of witnesses who may testify at trial. The purpose of the discovery process is to prevent any surprises at the trial. Parties are supposed to put all their cards on the table to encourage settlement. Discovery in a case like Flood's could normally take up to two years, but the lawyers would have to do the best they could in a very short period of time. No depositions would be taken prior to trial and very little documentation would be exchanged before the trial.[55]

The lawyers were frantically preparing for the case when Flood received some disappointing news. His lawyer, Arthur Goldberg, announced he was running for governor of the State of New York.[56] Goldberg would have little time to prepare for the trial and it would show.[57] As the trial date grew closer, Commissioner Kuhn sent a telegram to Flood on April 2, 1970, which read:

> Am disappointed you declined my invitation for a personal conference in Los Angeles on Friday. I desire an opportunity to discuss with you personally your baseball career without prejudice to the basic issues involved in the pending litigation. My counsel has ascertained from your counsel that the latter had no objections to such conference with the explicit condition that he has not recommended that you assent or decline. This is to advise you that if you reconsider I will continue to be available.
> Bowie Kuhn[58]

Flood declined the commissioner's offer and the matter would proceed to a trial.

The Trial

The trial would be a bench trial. A judge would decide the case, not a jury. The trial began on May 19 only one day after it was scheduled. Flood testified on the first day of the trial.[59] By all reports he did poorly. On direct examination, Goldberg attempted to lead him through some general questions about his playing career and his decision to file the lawsuit. Flood was visibly nervous and had troubling answering basic questions from his own lawyer. Judge Cooper interjected himself into the fray:

"You're not finding this is as easy as getting up to bat."
"No sir," Flood replied.
"Well, you see, other people have their problems, too."[60]

Flood's salaries for his 14 years in baseball were entered into evidence. This information was practically never released during Flood's era.[61] While testifying, Flood had trouble remembering his salary in his early years in baseball and he also could not recall some of his batting averages.[62] In a surreal moment, one of his lawyers, Jay Topkins, gave Flood his own baseball card that Topkins kept in his wallet. Flood used the card while he was on the witness stand to help him refresh his memory. What a sight that must have been. A seven-time Golden Glove winner testifying about his batting averages in federal court using his own baseball card. The judge had to ask Flood to keep his voice up several times during the trial. Flood was asked the following on cross-examination:

"And if Mr. Miller succeeded in inducing the clubs to modify the reserve clause, would you drop this lawsuit?"
"Yes, I would."[63]

Marvin Miller was called to the stand after Flood and was, of course, a masterful witness. Flood and Marvin Miller would be the only two witnesses called by Goldberg on the first day of trial.[64] The trial resumed on May 21 with a surprise star witness, Jackie Robinson. Who else better to testify on Flood's behalf than Jackie Robinson, the man who had broken baseball's color barrier 23 years before? Robinson certainly must have known what Flood was up against and what it meant to fight against the odds. Robinson testified in part:

As the matter stands now, it is in favor of the owners and the reserve system should be modified so the players have some control over their destiny. Unless there's some change in the reserve system, I can see nothing else but that the players go on strike.[65]

Following Robinson was another former baseball great, Detroit Tiger star Hank Greenberg. He testified that the "reserve clause should be eliminated entirely, thereby creating a new image for baseball."[66]

After Flood presented his evidence, the defense began to call its witnesses and present evidence. The witnesses included, among others, Pro Football Commissioner Pete Rozelle, Baseball Commissioner Bowie Kuhn, the president of the National League, and several other executives and economists. The defense's last witness testified on June 8. In a trial, a party is allowed to have rebuttal witnesses and Flood presented a "ringer" as the plaintiff's last witness on rebuttal. Former baseball owner Bill Veeck was known as baseball's innovator and never as a conventional baseball man.[67] He testified in part: "Everyone at least once in his career should be able to determine his own future and not be held in perpetuity."[68]

All the witnesses who testified for Flood were essentially baseball outsiders, Robinson, Greenberg, and Veeck. The trial ended on the afternoon of June 11. It lasted over three weeks, produced over 2,000 pages of court transcripts in 15 separate sessions,[69] and included 21 witnesses testifying. The decision concerning baseball's reserve system was now in the hands of the court. Would Judge Cooper, a Federal District Judge, overturn baseball's reserve clause in the face of Supreme Court decisions upholding the clause?

Flood seemed to lose interest in the trial proceedings somewhere along the way. He was not present when Bill Veeck testified or for the lawyers' closing arguments. In fact, one day Flood left the trial to watch his friend Bob Gibson pitch in a Cardinals win at Shea Stadium against the Mets. It is highly unusual for a client in a trial not to be present for his lawyer's closing argument. The closing argument is a culmination of the trial and many cases are lost or won during it. One of the most glaring items about the trial was that not one active player attended the trial held in New York. The Cardinals played the Mets on May 26 and 27 in New York and no Cardinal teammate came to federal court in New York to show support for Flood. Of course, many of the players were afraid of the consequences if they attended the trial. Joe Torre later stated: "I can't give you a good reason why we weren't there."[70] Flood must have certainly felt alone in his quest. He was criticized by former and present players and his own teammates failed to lend support to his cause, even though the case affected all major league players. In hindsight, Flood clearly should have received more support from current players. Marvin Miller would later say that not encouraging such players to come to the trial was one of his biggest tactical mistakes. Miller said he would have liked to see players show up at the trial and support Flood.[71] He called this a failure of leadership on his part.[72]

About one month later, on August 12, 1970, Judge Cooper delivered his decision. This time it was a 47-page opinion and, although Flood and his lawyer hoped Cooper's ruling would be in their favor, it came as no surprise when he ruled in favor of baseball. Judge Cooper declined to overrule *Toolson* and once again upheld baseball's antitrust exemption.[73] Judge Cooper stated:

For the first time in almost fifty years opponents and proponents of the baseball reserve system have had to make their case on the merits and support it with proof in a court of law. As a long line of litigation and congressional inquiry attests, this system has often been a center of controversy and a source of friction between player and club. Existing and, as we see it, controlling law renders unnecessary any determination as to the fairness or reasonableness of this reserve system. We are bound by the law as we find it and by our obligation to "call it as we see it."[74]

Bowie Kuhn issued a statement in response to the court's ruling: "I am particularly pleased that the court has recognized the need for a reserve system and has recognized further that baseball has not disregarded the extremely important position the player occupies."[75] John Quinn even indicated that the Phillies would be glad to have Flood play for the Phillies,[76] but Flood turned down the offer. Flood would learn about the court's decision when he read it in the local paper in Copenhagen. All parties knew an appeal was forthcoming and that the case would most likely make its way to the U.S. Supreme Court.

The Federal Court of Appeals

In August 1970, Flood appealed his case to the Federal Court of Appeals. Three judges would now be called upon to review Judge Cooper's decision. On appeal, judges review a trial court's proceedings to determine if there was reversible error made by the lower court.[77] However, before the Court of Appeals could rule, the case took a little twist. The Washington Senators[78] acquired the rights to Flood and made him a contract offer. Flood had turned down the Phillies after he lost in Federal District Court, but after conferring with his lawyer and Marvin Miller, Flood agreed to a contract with the Senators for the 1971 season for a salary of $110,000.[79] Flood really needed the money because he was in a financial bind. There was discussion about whether the reserve clause would appear in the contract. It was decided the contract would contain the reserve clause but the parties agreed that it would have no legal effect on the pending litigation. Curt Flood was back in baseball. However, the litigation would march forward.

The Court of Appeals followed U.S. Supreme Court precedent, ruling in favor of baseball against Flood. Flood was still playing baseball for the Senators and, though it would take a while, the case was headed to the U.S. Supreme Court.[80] However, the pressure proved to be too much for Flood. He had not regained the form he had with the Cardinals and became dejected and depressed. In his defense, Flood only played 13 games. He quit the Senators on April 28; he was 7 for 35 at the plate at the time he left the club. He decided to go overseas. On his way to Spain, Flood sent a telegram from Kennedy Airport to Robert Short, President of the American League: "I tried. A year and one-half is too much. Very serious personal problems mounting. Thanks for your confidence and understanding. Flood."[81]

Flood was on his way to Madrid where no one would notice him, where he could get away from lawyers, courts, and judges. Joe Reichler, a personal friend of Flood's and the assistant to the baseball commissioner, learned of Flood's whereabouts and rushed to the airport to try to catch him before he boarded the airplane.[82] Reicher found Flood at the airport and said Flood told him he was going to Washington. When Reichler responded, "by way of Barcelona," Flood knew he had been had.[83] The two men talked for twenty minutes. Reichler said at one point he almost convinced Flood to stay, explaining the fans did not expect him to hit .400 in his comeback. Flood responded: "No, no. I'm not going to do it. I've reached the end, I'll go crazy if I don't get out, I'll go crazy, if I don't get out."[84]

Flood boarded the plane to Spain and never played major league baseball again.

The Supreme Court of the United States

In July 1971, Flood's lawyers appealed his case to the U.S. Supreme Court. The Supreme Court was not under any obligation to take the case, but in October 1972, the court agreed to hear it.[85] On the same morning, the court declined 82 cases and agreed to hear only two, one of which was Curt Flood's. The court would hear oral arguments on Flood's case on March 20, 1972. Each side had 30 minutes for oral argument. Flood was not present at the Supreme Court hearing. His lawyer, former Supreme Court Justice Arthur J. Goldberg, argued in part: "This is a hard core violation of antitrust law. It is a boycott and a blacklist. Mr. Flood was the victim of a reserve system that violated all antitrust laws."[86]

Paul Porter and Lou Hoynes argued on behalf of baseball that the case was essentially a labor dispute and that the real plaintiff in the case was the Players Association.[87] They argued the matter should be resolved at the collective bargaining table and not the courts. Approximately three months later, on June 19, 1972, the Supreme Court rendered its decision. "Reserve Clause Upheld by Court," the headlines read.[88] Flood had lost in three courts, including the United States Supreme Court. He had taken on baseball and lost. The case was now over.

Flood v. Kuhn, 407 U.S. 258 (1972)

In *Flood v. Kuhn*, the U.S. Supreme Court was asked to decide the application of federal antitrust law to baseball within the context of the reserve clause.[89] Before it was faced with *Flood*, however, the Supreme Court had essentially tied its own hands with its prior decisions in *Federal Baseball* and *Toolson*. In *Flood*, the Supreme Court affirmed the Federal Court of Appeals decision, 5–3. The justices were deadlocked at 4–4 when Chief Justice Burger changed his vote in favor of major league baseball. Justice Powell abstained because he owned stock in Anheuser-Busch, Inc. In its decision, the Supreme Court finally acknowledged that baseball did engage in interstate commerce but found that congressional inaction to repeal baseball's exemption implied a continued approval of baseball's exemption to the antitrust laws. It also noted the "anomaly" of baseball having such an exemption from antitrust laws, while football, basketball, and hockey were subject to antitrust laws. The court disagreed with the rationale for the exemption stated in *Federal Baseball* but ruled against Flood on the basis of *stare decisis*.

Justice Blackmun was a well-known baseball fan and wrote the majority opinion at the request of the Chief Justice Burger. The court's decision in *Flood* is more than 20 pages long, but only four pages of the opinion actually discuss the rationale behind the court's ruling. The court's opinion was neatly divided in five sections.

In Section I, Justice Blackmun provides a list of 88 players as well as giving a brief history of the game of baseball.[90] He quoted "Casey at the Bat," and the famous double play combination of Tinker to Evers to Chance. His list of ballplayers has become fodder for scholars and baseball fans alike. How did he complete the list? What criteria did he use in compiling the list? Why would he begin one of the most significant legal opinions of the United States Supreme Court with an "ode to baseball" that essentially had no bearing on the ultimate decision of the court? Of the 88 players named on the list, 67 have been inducted to the Baseball Hall of Fame. There has been some debate about the inclusion of Jackie Robinson, Satchel Paige, and Roy Campanella on Blackmun's list. Bob Woodward and Scott Armstrong, authors of *The Brethren*, indicated that the three African American players were only included at the request of Justice Marshall.[91] Blackmun later took umbrage with this statement.[92]

Section II of the court's opinion is entitled "The Petitioner," referring to Flood. It outlines Flood's career and his salary history. It discusses the proposed trade to the Phillies and Flood's filing of the lawsuit.

Section III, "The Present Litigation," is a summary of the entire Flood case from the day of the filing of the lawsuit until it reached the Supreme Court.

In Section IV, the court discusses the legal precedent it relied upon in arriving at its decision. The court first addressed *Federal Baseball Club v National League of Professional Baseball Clubs*.[93] In that case, the Baltimore Club of the Federal League filed an antitrust action against the National and

American Leagues as well as others. The plaintiff argued that the business of baseball affected commerce and that baseball was more than a sport. Justice Holmes stated in *Federal Baseball*:

> The business is giving exhibitions of base ball, which are purely state affairs.... But the fact that in order to give the exhibitions the Leagues must induce free persons to cross state lines and must arrange and pay for their doing so is not enough to change the character of the business.[94]

The Supreme Court said that although baseball has been the subject of antitrust attacks, it still rejected the challenge based on the *Federal Baseball* decision. "For the most part, ... the Holmes opinion was generally and necessarily accepted as controlling authority."[95]

Section V of the court's opinion in *Flood* contains the rationale of the court. The court made eight specific findings[96]:

1. "Professional baseball is a business and it is engaged in interstate commerce."
2. Baseball's exemption from antitrust laws is an "anomaly."
3. Although baseball's exemption may be seen as illogical, "the aberration that has been with us now for half a century [is] one heretofore deemed fully entitled to the benefit of *stare decisis,* and one that has survived the Court's expanding concept of interstate commerce. It rests on a recognition and an acceptance of baseball's unique characteristics and needs."
4. Other sports are not exempt from antitrust laws.
5. The increased exposure of baseball by radio and television since *Federal Baseball* and *Toolson* has not caused them to be overruled.
6. Historically, baseball has been left alone to expand "unhindered by federal legislative action.... The Court, accordingly, has concluded that Congress as yet has had no intention to subject baseball's reserve system to the reach of the antitrust statutes. This, obviously, has been deemed to be something other than mere congressional silence and passivity."
7. Overruling *Federal Baseball* would cause problems. If a change is to be made it must come from "legislative action."
8. And, citing to *Radovich*, the court said "the slate with respect to baseball is not clean."

The court concluded:

> We continue to be loath, 50 years after *Federal Baseball* and almost two decades after *Toolson,* to overturn those cases judicially when Congress, by its positive inaction, has allowed those decisions to stand for so long and, far beyond mere inference and implication, has clearly evinced a desire not to disapprove them legislatively.[97]

The court affirmed the previous court's holdings in *Federal Baseball* and *Toolson*: "If there is any inconsistency or illogic in all this, it is an inconsistency and illogic of long standing that is to be remedied by the Congress and not by this Court."[98]

Justices White and Burger both concurred in the majority's opinion. White wrote a very short concurring opinion indicating he agreed with the majority opinion, except for Section I, "Blackmun's List." White was a former All-American football star at the University of Colorado and thought it was demeaning to the court to include Section I in the court's opinion. Burger also concurred with the majority, excepting Section I as well. Burger also stated that he agreed with Justice Douglas about having "grave reservations as to the correctness of Toolson...."[99] Douglas had joined in the decision in *Toolson* but "lived to regret it."[100] Burger further agreed with Douglas that Congress should resolve the problems, and not the courts.[101]

There were two separate dissenting opinions filed, one by Justice Douglas with Justice Brennan concurring, and one by Justice Marshall with Justice Brennan again concurring. In his now famous dissent Justice Douglas wrote:

> This Court's decision in *Federal Baseball Club v. National League*, made in 1922, is a derelict in the stream of the law that we, its creator, should remove. Only a romantic view of a rather dismal business account over the last 50 years would keep that derelict in midstream.[102]

Douglas had also joined the court's opinion in *Toolson* but indicated in a footnote in the *Flood* opinion that he had lived to regret it. He completed his dissent by writing that "[t]he unbroken silence of Congress should not prevent us from correcting our own mistakes."[103]

Justice Marshall wrote a lengthy dissent to Blackmun's majority opinion. Attacking the rationale behind the opinion, Marshall said Flood posed a very difficult decision because the court was faced with the dilemma of relying upon *Federal Baseball* and *Toolson* on the basis of *stare decisis* even though those cases were "at odds with more recent and better reasoned cases."[104] Marshall said the court was faced with the choice of following court precedent by refusing to reexamine *Federal Baseball* and *Toolson* or proceeding with the reexamination and "let[ting] the chips fall where they may."[105] The most famous part of the Marshall's dissent stated:

> The importance of the antitrust laws to every citizen must not be minimized. They are as important to baseball players as they are to football players, lawyers, doctors, or members of any other class of workers. Baseball players cannot be denied the benefits of competition merely because club owners view other economic interests as being more important, unless Congress says so.[106]

Marshall said he would have overruled both *Federal Baseball Club* and *Toolson* and reversed the decision of the Federal Court of Appeals. Marshall cautioned that this would not mean that Flood would be the winner in the lower court. Marshall said that the Flood case really dealt with the "interrelationship between antitrust laws and labor laws" and that he would have remanded the case to the District Court "for consideration of whether petitioner can state a claim under the antitrust laws despite the collective-bargaining agreement, and, if so, for a determination of whether there has been an antitrust violation in this case."[107]

All three cases, *Federal Baseball, Toolson* and *Flood,* failed to actually tackle the question of whether the reserve system violated the Sherman Act, but merely focused on the issue of baseball's immunity to antitrust law.

The Legacy of Curt Flood

The Players Association did learn something from the loss in the *Flood* litigation. They knew they had to unite in order to beat the owners. John Ward had had the right idea when he had organized the Brotherhood eighty years before. The Players Association knew if it was going to get what it wanted, the players would need to band together and present themselves as one. This had not happened in the *Flood* case. Flood had sat in federal court without the support of any current major leaguers. Just three years after *Flood,* the players would turn to the labor arbitration process and through collective bargaining get what they were unable to achieve at the United States Supreme Court. Although *Flood* failed to eradicate the reserve clause, the court made it very clear it was only ruling in favor of the defendant based on the doctrine of *stare decisis.* The trilogy of *Federal Baseball, Toolson,* and *Flood* showed the difficulty the Supreme Court had in dealing with the legal issues of the national pastime. Although Flood's lawsuit was ultimately unsuccessful, his willingness to take on baseball's behemoths contributed to the eventual demise of the reserve system in baseball.

Flood would encounter personal difficulties after leaving baseball. He settled in Spain, and he already knew how to speak Spanish. One of his biggest supporters was sportscaster Howard Cosell, who sent him recordings of boxing matches to play in the bar Flood owned. He later gave up the bar, working as a carpet layer for awhile. When Flood did return to the U.S. four years after the Supreme Court decision, the players had won their freedom in the Messersmith/McNally arbitration decision. Flood did not personally gain from that decision although he obviously had a hand in its success. Time passed and Flood began to fade from the limelight, popping up occasionally as a footnote to the players' new found freedom and huge salary increases. In the summer of 1976, Flood fell down some stairs after having "a couple of beers too many" and suffered severe injuries.[108] He had no job, no money was coming in, and he was living in an apartment next to his mother in Oakland. He reminisced about the six weeks he spent in a New York courtroom with little or no support from other players.

9. Curt Flood Challenges Baseball's Reserve Clause

[A]nd not one player came to see what was going on. All right, I had all the news media there; that was cool. There were ex-baseball players who came and said how they got ripped off. But not one baseball player who was playing at the time came just to see — I didn't want him to testify — just to see what was going on because it involved them so dramatically. But no one came just to sit and say hey, this is pretty important.[109]

He was still happy that the players were getting their due: "These guys are getting what they're worth and that's cool." Flood still desired to get back in the game he loved but knew that would be difficult because of the lawsuit. In 1978, Flood was hired as an announcer for Oakland A's games but that career would not last long.[110] In the 1980s, Flood landed a job with the little league in Oakland that he really enjoyed. Ironically, he also served as the baseball commissioner of a short-lived senior league.

Players have begun to realize the impact that Flood had on the game and their salaries. When Rod Carew signed a $4 million contract with the Angels in 1979, he said, "All today's baseball players should thank Curt Flood, who got the whole thing started." In 1994 Donald Fehr, head of the Players Association, invited Flood to a meeting of the MLBPA. This occurred during a season that resulted in a strike that cancelled the World Series. When Flood entered the meeting, player representatives gave him a standing ovation. It was not until 1993 that Flood would receive his final Golden Glove award.[111] He never received the award from baseball after he refused to report to the Phillies.

Curt Flood's personal convictions led him to file a lawsuit against the baseball commissioner, all twenty-four Major League teams, and the president of both leagues. He knew when he filed the lawsuit he would probably not win, receive no damages, and never play baseball again. He turned down a raise in the prime of his career to pursue a lawsuit that legal precedent said he would not win and, sadly, he received no support from his fellow players who, in the end, benefitted from his action. Flood may have not directly caused the demise of the reserve clause but he did create a seam for others to exploit.

10

Andy Messersmith / Dave McNally Arbitration Case[1]

Players Win Their Freedom in Arbitration

> There was no doubt in my mind that the game's integrity and public confidence were at stake in the potential destruction of the reserve system.[2] — Bowie Kuhn, Baseball Commissioner, 1969–1984

> I had never made a secret of my contention from the beginning, that Paragraph 10(a) in the Uniform Player's Contract clearly stated that the owners had a right to renew an unsigned player for one year, and one only.[3] — Marvin Miller, Executive Director of MLBPA, 1966–1982

> Great! What do I do next? — Andy Messersmith, Dodgers Pitcher, 1975[4]

Introduction

After Curt Flood lost his U.S. Supreme Court case, baseball club owners believed they were in the proverbial driver's seat once again. Flood's three-year court battle against the owners had failed to dismantle baseball's reserve clause. After the hard fought victory through the courts, the owners believed that they were once again invincible. Their fears of financial ruin of the game could now be put to rest, or could they? While the Flood case was proceeding through the courts, Players Association Executive Director Marvin Miller was chipping away at free agency for players, gaining concessions from the owners, one piece at a time. Miller was merely looking for the right opportunity and the appropriate avenue to strike down the reserve clause, or at least to modify it in some fashion. The first players' strike in Major League Baseball had occurred in 1972, lasting 13 days and costing the season 86 games. The season resumed after the owners agreed to an increase in pension fund payments to the players. The strike sent a message to the owners that the players were not afraid to face off with the owners and that the Players Association was gaining strength. Meanwhile, there was trouble brewing with one of baseball's most colorful owners.

James "Catfish" Hunter, Baseball's First "Real" Free Agent

When asked, many fans would quickly say that Andy Messersmith was baseball's first free agent. That distinction actually goes to Oakland Athletics Hall of Fame pitcher James "Catfish" Hunter. Hunter grabbed the title when he signed a five-year contract with the New York Yankees in 1974.[5] Hunter had a contract to play for the A's for the 1974 and 1975 seasons at $100,000 each season. A special covenant in the contract stated: "[T]he said Club will pay to any person, firm or corporation designated by said Player, the sum of Fifty Thousand ($50,000) Dollars, per year, for the duration of this contract to be deferred compensation, same to be paid during the season as earned."[6] When requested, A's owner Charles Finley refused to make the deferred compensation payment as required in the contract,[7] Hunter's attorney asked Finley to state in writing his refusal to make the deferred compensation payment, but Finley refused. On October 4, the general counsel for the MLBPA telegraphed Finley, telling him he had breached the contract and giving him an opportunity to cure his breach within 10 days. Finley did not respond to the letter. In late October, the Players Association filed a grievance on behalf of Hunter, seeking free agency on his behalf as well as the $50,000 deferred compensation payment Hunter was promised. After a hearing, the arbitration panel found in favor of Hunter.[8] The award of the panel stated: "Mr. Hunter's contract for services no longer binds him and he is a free agent. The Club shall compensate Mr. Hunter in the amount deducted from his salary during the 1974 season, as deferred compensation, with interest...."[9] The Oakland Club appealed the award but lost.[10] The arbitrator who declared Hunter a free agent was Peter Seitz, the same arbitrator who would be called upon to make the decision in the Messersmith/McNally arbitration case.

Catfish Hunter was now free to negotiate with any team he wanted because the A's had breached his contract. He eventually signed with the Yankees for $3.5 million, the largest contract signed by a major league player at that time.[11] The Yankees would get their money's worth. Hunter won 23 games for the Yankees in his first season with the club, tying Jim Palmer for the league lead in wins. He also led the American League in complete games with 30 and innings pitched with 328. Notwithstanding his great season, Hunter's former club, the A's, won their division while the Yankees finished third.

Hunter's arbitration case involved a relatively straightforward breach of contract by a club. Baseball owners had breached player contracts in the past, but in Hunter's case it inured to his benefit in the form of a lucrative contract with another club.[12] Marvin Miller was involved in the Hunter contract dispute and understood what a great victory it was for the Players Association, even though it did not involve the reserve clause.[13] Miller credited the victory to a combination of Finley's arrogance and Seitz's fairness in interpreting the contract.[14] The Hunter case had shown that the owners had money to pay the players much larger salaries than they had been receiving. With the Hunter case complete, another legal skirmish was on the horizon. This one would be far more complicated than Hunter's and would involve all the owners — all 24 clubs and both leagues. The decision would forever change the economic structure of the game.

Andy Messersmith and Dave McNally

With the fight over Catfish Hunter resolved, all eyes turned to the dispute growing between all-star pitcher Andy Messersmith and the Los Angeles Dodgers. Messersmith was a solid major leaguer, throwing 2,230 innings with the Angels, Dodgers, Braves, and Yankees. He had a lifetime record of 130–99 and a sparking 2.86 career ERA.[15] He was a three-time all-star and won two gold gloves fielding his position. Nevertheless, he probably would have gone into the baseball annals as just another very good right-handed pitcher but for the somewhat reluctant role he would play in the players' century-long battle for contract freedom from the owners.

Andy Messersmith had a great 1974 season. He led the National League with 20 victories, tying knuckleballer Phil Nierko. He also had the league's best winning percentage at .769, was second in innings pitched with 292, second in opponents batting average at .212, and fifth in ERA at 2.59.[16] Messersmith finished second in the Cy Young voting behind Dodger teammate Mike Marshall. The Dodgers won a league leading 102 games, easily besting the Pittsburgh Pirates in the NLCS. However, they did lose the World Series to the Oakland A's in five games. Still, Messersmith was a star pitcher on the National League's best club.

After his phenomenal 1974 season, Messersmith wanted a raise but he also wanted to stay in Los Angeles. Messersmith asked Dodgers owner Walter O'Malley for a no-trade clause in his contract, the first of its kind in baseball negotiations.[17] O'Malley dismissed the request from Messersmith, asserting that the National League prevented him from negotiating such an arrangement with a player.[18] During the negotiations the Dodgers were willing to increase Messersmith's salary, but would not budge on the requested no-trade clause.[19] Messersmith was not satisfied with the response he got from the Dodgers and refused to sign a contract for the 1975 season. Six players had actually begun

10. Players Win Their Freedom in Arbitration

the 1975 season without a contract, but Messersmith remained the only player still unsigned in August 1975.[20] Subsequently, the Dodgers unilaterally renewed Messersmith's contract from the previous year. In 1975, Messersmith pitched like a man on a mission and produced another outstanding season for the Dodgers. He was third in the league in strikeouts (213), first in games started (40) and complete games (19), gave up the fewest hits per game (6.83), first in innings pitched (321) and opponent's batting average (.213, tied with teammate Don Sutton), first in shutouts, and second in ERA (2.29) and wins (19).[21] After another stellar season in 1975, Messersmith once again requested a no-trade clause be placed in his contract but O'Malley once again refused.[22] Messersmith was in a quandary. He really wanted to stay in Los Angeles but he also felt strongly about the no-trade clause. Curt Flood had challenged the owners head on in the U.S. Supreme Court even though binding legal precedent was against him. Andy Messersmith merely sought a no-trade clause in his contract. He did not see himself as a leader or hero in the players' battle against the reserve clause. He just wanted a simple no-trade clause from the Dodgers, but instead he became the player who would clear the way for free agency and financial success for future ballplayers for years to come.

Marvin Miller and Messersmith met and discussed Messersmith's contract situation. They considered whether or not to file a grievance under the Basic Agreement.[23] Messersmith did not want to sign a contract unless O'Malley met his no-trade demand.[24] The salary offer was satisfactory and Messersmith apologetically told Miller that if the Dodgers met his no-trade demand he would sign the contract.[25] But the Dodgers still refused to budge on Messersmith's no-trade demand.

Miller saw Messersmith as the test case in arbitration to once again attempt to strike down or at least modify the reserve clause. However, if Messersmith signed with the Dodgers, Miller would need a back-up plan. That plan involved another all-star pitcher but this one was retired. Miller found only one other unsigned player for the 1975 season, former Orioles pitcher Dave McNally. After the 1974 season, McNally had been traded by the Orioles to the Montreal Expos. He was not satisfied with the offer from the Expos and so he did not sign a contract for the 1975 season. McNally started poorly for the Expos, winning only three games while losing six. Losing the desire to play, McNally quit baseball on June 8, walking away from an $85,000 contract for the 1975 season.[26] Miller located McNally working as a Ford dealer in McNally's hometown of Billings, Montana. Miller considered him the perfect player to challenge the reserve rule.[27] He had been a player representative while on the Baltimore Club and Miller considered him a good union man[28] and, because he had no intention of playing baseball again, McNally was safe from retaliation from the owners.

Meanwhile, the owners were busy behind the scenes trying to fend off the looming arbitration case. Montreal Expos president John McHale just happened to be passing through Billings, Montana, in mid–November 1975 and decided to pay McNally a visit.[29] He offered McNally $25,000 just for showing up to spring training and $125,000 if he made the club.[30] Not a bad offer for a 33-year-old retired pitcher with significant arm problems. Many players would have jumped at the chance to play, not to mention a $25,000 appearance bonus. However, McNally stayed true to his union roots and turned down the offer. He said McHale had not been honest with him in the past and he was not going to trust him now. He said he was tempted to show up and take the $25,000, but it would not have been right.[31] The stage was now set. The man who ruled that Charles Finley had breached his contract with Catfish Hunter, making the pitcher a free agent, would now decide baseball's future economic structure.

The Messersmith/McNally Arbitration Case

Under labor law, management and labor can agree to resolve disputes through binding arbitration instead of litigating every dispute that may arise between the parties. Arbitration is a form of dispute resolution that can be much cheaper, and certainly much quicker, than litigation. The rules of evidence do not usually apply to arbitration hearings and there is no jury to decide the case. Litigation can drag on for years but an arbitration case frequently can be decided in a matter of months. If a player has a dispute with a team, whether it be for an injury, salary, or another matter, it can be much quicker to arbitrate the claim with the club than to go through years of litigation. Arbitration has become the preferred method by which professional athletes resolve disputes with their clubs.[32] Arbitration provisions now appear in all major sports collective bargaining agreements. Some arbitration cases have only one arbitrator who decides a case, but the parties can agree to more if they choose to do so. Major League Baseball's Basic Agreement had determined a panel of three arbitrators was appropriate to resolve disputes. Marvin Miller was the players' arbitrator, John Gaherin was named the arbitrator for the clubs, and Peter Seitz was the neutral arbitrator agreed to by both parties.

With the Dodgers and Messersmith at a stalemate, the Players Association filed two grievances in early October 1975 on behalf of Messersmith and McNally. Immediately after the filing of the arbitration claims, Marvin Miller made the position of the Association perfectly clear. "Under the contract a club can renew it [the contract] by itself for one year. That one year is over."[33] Historically, U.S. Courts had always been favorable to baseball owners. Therefore, instead of going forward with the arbitration hearing, the owners filed a lawsuit in Federal District Court in Kansas City, attempting to have the arbitration case dismissed.[34] They sought an injunction to prevent the arbitration hearing from moving forward, arguing that the issues set forth in the players' grievances were outside the scope of arbitration as previously agreed to by the parties in the Basic Agreement. The clubs argued that the arbitrator had no jurisdiction to hear the case. The Players Association argued the owners were required by law to recognize the arbitration panel's authority and subsequent award as set forth in the Basic Agreement and that the court should dismiss the owners' lawsuit. After hearing arguments from both parties, the court denied the owners' request for an injunction; however, the parties agreed the owners could return to court to challenge issues relating to the jurisdiction of the arbitrator. The matter would now be heard by the arbitrator. The hearing would be held over a three-day period, November 21, 25, and December 1 in New York City.[35] When the hearings were complete, all eyes turned to arbitrator Seitz as the parties anxiously awaited his opinion. They would have not to wait long.

The Arbitration Decision

On December 23, 1975, Seitz issued his ruling, making the two all-star pitchers free agents.[36] Within minutes after he signed the arbitration decision, Seitz was fired by the owners.[37] Seitz had anticipated this action by the owners. Commissioner Bowie Kuhn said he was "enormously disturbed" by the ruling and that it should be reviewed by the courts. Kuhn considered the arbitration decision as merely serving the financial interests of the players and nothing more. While the reserve clause had placed an artificial restraint on player salaries in the past, he was extremely leery because of the financial madness that had set in after the Catfish Hunter arbitration case.[38]

The arbitration opinion was 65 pages long with numerous footnotes and essentially divided into two parts. The first section dealt with the question of jurisdiction. Parties to a labor agreement can exclude certain issues from arbitration and can limit the scope of the issues they want to be heard in arbitration. This was one of the major legal issues in the Messersmith/McNally arbitration. The clubs wanted a more limited interpretation of the Basic Agreement, while the players desired a broader interpretation to include the reserve clause. The issue was whether the arbitrator even had the power to hear the grievance.

It was the position of the clubs that Article XV of the 1973 Basic Agreement clearly stated that the Basic Agreement did not deal with the reserve clause. Article XV stated: "Except as adjusted or hereby modified, this agreement does not deal with the reserve system." That seemed very straightforward and not subject to interpretation. The clubs said the arbitrator had no authority to rule on the grievances based on this provision. Notwithstanding Article XV, however, the Basic Agreement contained numerous provisions that referred to the reserve system. The Major League Rules, a part of the Basic Agreement, contained provisions for reserved lists of players and ones prohibiting clubs from tampering with reserved players. The Uniform Player Contract also contained the essence of the reserve system, the option clause, as well as requiring all players to abide by the Major League Rules. All these documents were intertwined and contained, or referred to, in the Basic Agreement.

The Players Association stated at the hearing that the original impetus for including Article XV in the Basic Agreement in 1970 was to respond to Curt Flood's pending antitrust lawsuit against baseball. Essentially, it was a "cease-fire" resolution on the reserve clause at the time.

Arbitrator Seitz found it odd that the labor agreement would state it did not deal with the reserve system, but would contain provisions of two documents, the Uniform Player Contract and the Major Leagues Rules, which both clearly addressed the reserve system. Seitz concluded that the owners could not have it both ways and ruled in favor of the Players Association, finding that the parties did not intend to exclude the reserve clause from arbitration. Seitz concluded by saying his review of the evidence showed nothing in the Basic Agreement (or any other documents for that matter) which excluded a dispute about the interpretation or application of section 10(a) of the Uniform Player Contract from the arbitration procedure described in the Basic Agreement.

The second issue before the panel was whether the contracts of Messersmith and McNally had expired, thereby allowing the players to declare themselves free agents.[39] The disputed contractual provision from the Uniform Player Contract, section 10(a) stated:

> 10(a) On or before December 20 ... in the year of the last playing season covered by this contract, the Club may tender to the Player a contract for the term of that year.... If prior to March 1 next succeeding said December 20, the Player and the Club have both agreed upon the terms of such contracts then on or before 10 days after said March 1, the club shall have the right by written notice to the Player ... to renew this contract for the period of one year on the same terms, except that the amount payable to the player shall be such as the same terms, except that the amount payable to the player shall be such as the Club shall fix in said notice; provided, however, that said amount ... shall be an amount not less than 80 percent of the rate stipulated for the next preceding year and at a rate not less than 70 percent of the rate stipulated for the year immediately prior to the next preceding year.[40]

The Players Association claimed that Messersmith had completed his "renewal year" on September 29, 1975, and was no longer under contract with the Dodgers after that date.[41] The players had long asserted that section 10(a) gave the clubs the right to renew the contract for one year and nothing more. It was the club's position that it could reserve a player based on the language in section 10(a) and that the club "may renew this contract for the period of one year on the same terms on a perpetual basis."[42]

Seitz would agree with the players' interpretation of Section 10(a), finding the provision was merely a one-year option and not a perpetual option as claimed by the clubs. Seitz noted that there was nothing in contract law to prevent parties from renewing their contract, even in perpetuity, if the intent of the parties was clear and the right of subsequent renewals did not have to be implied from the contract.[43] In his opinion, Seitz compared baseball contracts to the renewal of real estate leases.[44] He found there was nothing in section 10(a) which explicitly stated that the contract could be renewed for any period beyond the first renewal year.[45] He further stated that he would have expected a more explicit expression of intention by the parties for a contract dealing with personal services and he found no explicit statement that the contract was perpetual in nature.[46] Seitz compared baseball's Uniform Player Contract to several cases involving professional basketball players dealing with the same contractual issue.[47] He noted that the renewal clause in basketball contracts did not "differ materially or significantly from Section 10(a) in the baseball Players Contract...."[48] In interpreting the basketball player contracts, he said the courts found the renewal clause meant only one year and not successive renewals.[49] Seitz concluded his analysis by stating:

> In these circumstances I find that Section 10(a) falls short of reserving to a Club the right to renew a contract at the end of the renewal year. Accordingly, I find that Messersmith was not under contract when his renewal year came to an end.[50]

After delivering his interpretation of paragraph 10(a) of the Uniform Player Contract, Seitz next had to decide whether a club could reserve a player who was not under contract, or in other words, a player whose contract had expired. To do so, Seitz turned to a discussion of the Major League Rules and their applicability.[51] The clubs claimed they still had the exclusive reservation of a player's services under MLR 4-A(a), notwithstanding a lack of a contractual relationship between the parties.[52] The clubs said they had the ability to control a player and that control was not dependent solely upon the renewal clause found in the Uniform Player Contract. The clubs and leagues asserted that because they had sent their reserve list to the appropriate officials on November 17, 1975, they had reserved Messersmith for another year, even if there was no signed contract between the club and player.[53] The Players Association argued that the Dodgers' placement of Messersmith on the reserve list was futile because Messersmith's renewal year had expired in September 1975. Major League Rule 4-A(a) established club reserve lists and stated:

> (a) FILING. On or before November 20 in each year, each Major League Club shall transmit to the Commissioner and to its League President a list of not exceeding forty (40) active and eligible players, whom the club desires to reserve for the ensuing season.... On or before November 30 the League President shall transmit all of such lists to the Secretary-Treasurer of the Executive Council, who shall thereupon promulgate same, and thereafter no player on any list shall be eligible to play for or nego-

tiate with any other club until his contract has been assigned or he has been released....[54]

Rule 4-A(a) seemed to indicate that a player could be placed on a reserve list only if he was under contract to a club. However, Major League Rule 3(g) seemed to state the opposite. That rule prohibited tampering with players and indicated a club had protection for any reserved player, even if he was not under contract to the club. To assist in the interpretation of these seemingly contradictory rules, Seitz examined the 1903 Cincinnati Peace Compact of the National and American Leagues.[55] Seitz deemed this document "probably the most important step in the evolution and development of the present Reserve System."[56] Seitz noted the Peace Compact showed that clubs believed a player had to be under contract to be reserved. Seitz summarized his findings with regard to the Major League Rules by stating:

> I reach the conclusion that, absent a contractual connection between Messersmith and the Los Angeles Club after September 28, 1975, the Club's action in reserving his services for the ensuing year by placing him on its reserve list was unavailing and ineffectual in prohibiting him from dealing with other clubs in the league and to prohibit such clubs from dealing with him.[57]

Seitz had made his decision. The players' grievances had been upheld and they were now free to negotiate with other clubs. The clubs accused Seitz of distributing his own brand of justice, but Seitz had attempted several times to get the parties to settle their differences without the need of an arbitration decision.

After rendering his decision, Seitz stated the rationale for his decision and also discussed the repercussions of his ruling upon the future of the game. He asserted that his opinion should not be read to indicate that he opposed the reserve system and that he saw his job as an arbitrator as only deciding the legal issues presented before him and nothing more. He stated it was not his job to determine the "scope and effect of a reserve system," that the task was best left to the parties themselves. He said his charge was merely to interpret and apply the provisions dealing with the various agreements between the parties. "To go beyond this would be an act of quasi-judicial arrogance."[58] He referred to Curt Flood's lawsuit against baseball and said that his ruling did not free players from "involuntary servitude" as was alleged by the Flood lawsuit.[59] He said his opinion made no judgment concerning the reserve clause on either constitutional or moral grounds.[60] Seitz noted that it was his understanding that neither Messersmith and McNally opposed the reserve system; however, the Players Association had stated that the reserve system should be modified in some respects.[61] Seitz quoted from a memorandum sent by Marvin Miller to all major league players on December 26, 1969:

10. Players Win Their Freedom in Arbitration

The players and the Players Association never have proposed to abolish the reserve rules. Rather, we seek to make appropriate amendments which will enhance the players position but which will not do harm to the game.[62]

Seitz spent the last four pages of his opinion addressing collective bargaining issues between the players and clubs. He wrote that the presidents of both the National and American leagues had told him that if he sustained the players' grievances he would do irreparable damage to the national pastime.[63] He was also told that a decision in favor of the players would destroy the competitive balance between the clubs, and the clubs with the most money would sign all the available top free agents.[64] Finally, they said a decision in favor of the players would increase the high costs of training young players and that those costs would be lost to the clubs if players could become free agents at the end of the renewal year.[65] The owners further argued that free agency would cause a bidding war between the owners and put severe financial strain on many franchises that were already having difficulty. It was even stated to Seitz that the "integrity of the sport" would be at risk if he ruled in favor of the players. Seitz did not address any of these concerns on the merits in his written opinion, saying they were all based on speculation. He said some of the fears may have been exaggerated and some may have been real. They were being posed by experienced baseball executives so they did deserve attention, but it was not his job to determine if something was good or bad for the reserve system, only to make a ruling on the legal issues. He believed if there was any damage to the reserve clause it could be ameliorated through collective bargaining. "This decision is not the end of the line by any means."[66] He said the parties could feel free to disregard his ruling and modify the reserve system however they believed would best serve their interests. Seitz strongly believed that the parties should resolve their disputes through collective bargaining rather than through the courts or arbitration. He closed by stating: "The clubs and the players have a mutual interest in the health and integrity of the sport and in its financial returns. With a will to do so, they are competent to fashion a reserve system to suit their requirements."[67]

The Players Association had now achieved something players had tried to do for over one hundred years: gain their freedom from baseball owners by striking down the reserve system. The die was now cast; the players had finally won their long sought freedom from the onerous reserve clause. Not through a court ruling as had been attempted several times before, but through the decision of one person, a labor arbitrator. Labor law had done for the players what antitrust law was never able to do, free them from the reserve clause. The owners would hustle back to the courts to attempt to have the ruling vacated, but Marvin Miller was confident the arbitration ruling would remain intact, notwithstanding the owners' penchant for the courts.[68]

United States District Court, Kansas City

Defeated in arbitration, the owners would turn once again to the courts to challenge the arbitration award, going back to federal district court in front of Judge John W. Oliver.[69] After the first court hearing, before the arbitration hearing had taken place, the parties had agreed to go forward with the arbitration with an agreement in place that issues regarding jurisdiction of the arbitrator could still be decided by the courts.[70] The owners asked the court to vacate the arbitrator's decision, but this time the court would be of no assistance to club owners.

The court was called upon to review Seitz's decision. Just as legal precedent was against Flood when he sued baseball over the reserve clause, legal precedent was against the owners this time around. The U.S. Supreme Court, in a line of cases called the *Steelworkers Trilogy*,[71] had ruled that courts had very limited power to overrule an arbitrator's decision. A court's review of the arbitration decision was limited merely to an inquiry of whether the arbitration award "drew its essence" from the labor agreement. Essentially, if the arbitrator's ruling was based on an analysis of the labor contract, the court was prohibited from vacating the award, even if the court would have decided the case differently. The owners were arguing that the arbitration decision was wrong, that Seitz had made an error in his interpretation of the contract. However, that would not be enough for the court to vacate the arbitration award. Judge Oliver noted that the *Steelworkers Trilogy*, "enunciated what is now an established presumption of arbitrability of all labor disputes and grievances which can be said to be within the coverage of a particular arbitration clause...."[72] The presumption meant that courts will generally find arbitration is in order when a dispute between the parties is even "arguably" intended by the parties to be resolved through the arbitration process.[73] The court concluded the grievances filed by Messersmith and McNally were intended by the parties to be within the scope and coverage of the arbitration clause of the 1973 Basic Agreement.[74] The court further stated: "Application of established principles of federal labor law requires that we find and conclude that the parties were under obligation to submit the Messersmith and McNally grievances to arbitration...."[75] The court said it was compelled by legal precedent to conclude that the "presumption of arbitrability is applicable" to this case and that the grievances were covered by the 1973 Basic Agreement.[76] On appeal, the issue of jurisdiction was resolved in favor of the players.

The second legal issue addressed by the federal district court was whether the Players Association was entitled to an order enforcing the arbitration panel's award.[77] The owners argued that the arbitrator dispersed "his own brand of industrial justice" in ruling in favor of the players.[78] The court said it did not consider whether it would have interpreted the UPC and the Basic Agreement similar to the panel.[79] It noted the court had no business overruling an arbitration decision based on the arbitrator's interpretation of a labor contract. The court found that the panel had not exceeded the jurisdiction given to it by the parties through their labor agreement and that, in this case, the panel "drew its essence" from the Basic Agreement.[80]

Federal Court of Appeals, Eighth Circuit

Down 2–0, the owners tried one last appeal to the Eighth Circuit Federal Court of Appeals. The owners would be shut out, with the court of appeals affirming the district court ruling by a two to one vote. The court of appeals held the arbitration panel had jurisdiction to resolve the dispute. It also found the arbitrator's award drew its essence from the collective bargaining agreement. The owners contemplated taking their case to the United States Supreme Court, but chose not to do so. The owners had little option now other than to face off with the players at the negotiation table.

1976 Labor Negotiations

After losing in arbitration and two federal courts, most of the owners knew they were beaten and would now be forced to negotiate with the players. While the clubs' appeal to the Eighth Federal Circuit Court of Appeals was pending, Marvin Miller was busy scheduling meetings with John Gaherin, director of the owners' Player Relations Committee. The Basic Agreement had expired on December 31, 1975, and the parties were bound by federal labor law to continue to negotiate in good faith to try to strike a deal.[81] The owners knew they were in a tough negotiating position. They also clearly understood that the players were serious about challenging them over their piece of the economic pie. The stage was now set. The parties would begin a continuous bargaining war over baseball's economic structure that would last for the next 35 years.

Gaherin come to the negotiations with an offer in hand, but Miller deemed it "preposterous."[82] The offer from the owners called for a player to be eligible for free agency after nine years in the major leagues. The tenth year would be the player's option year and, if no deal could be reached with the club in the tenth year, the player could then declare for free agency. Even then, the club could still retain the player's services if they offered him a contract of at least $30,000.[83] If that was not onerous enough, the club that signed the free agent would be required to compensate the player's former team with cash.[84] Miller proclaimed this offer ridiculous in light of the arbitration decision which had just granted free agency to all players without reservations or conditions.[85] But Miller knew that having all major league players available every year as free agents would actually have the effect of depressing the free agent market and driving salaries down, so he sought to make a compromise.

In response to the Eighth Circuit Court of Appeals decision, the owners decided not to open spring training camps to the players and locked them out.[86] However, the owners' concerted activity lasted only until mid–March.[87] The parties continued to negotiate and finally, after months of negotiations, on the eve of the all-star break, July 12, 1976, the parties reached an agreement.[88] Free agency would be granted to every eligible player at the end of the 1976 and 1977 seasons, notwithstanding their length of service in the major leagues. This constituted almost half of the major leaguers at that time. Free agency for future major leaguers would begin at the end of their sixth playing year.[89] A player with at least five seasons could demand a trade and submit a list of the teams he could not be traded to. He could then become a free agent if the demanded trade did not occur by March 15.[90] With the free agency rules in place, the stage was now set for a major escalation in player salaries and that is exactly what happened over the next nine years.

Messersmith and McNally Aftermath

After prevailing at the arbitration table, Andy Messersmith would never again enjoy the success on the field that he once had with the Dodgers. He would, however, be wealthy after signing a three-year, one-million dollar contract with Ted Turner, owner of the Atlanta Braves.[91] Messersmith's contract with the Atlanta Club gave the Braves a right of first refusal at the expiration of his contract.[92] Messersmith gave back to Atlanta the very thing he fought so hard to win at arbitration, free agency.[93] Marvin Miller understood this issue clearly and, when he learned about Messersmith's contract, he took immediate action. Miller called Chub Feeney, President of the National League, and requested the clause be removed from the Messersmith contract and Feeney agreed. He pointed out to Feeney that a player could not give back, through negotiations with a team, what the Players Association had gained through the collective bargaining process.[94]

With their new superstar on the mound, the Braves were now ready to make a move in the standings and possibly a run at the National League pennant. In 1975, the Braves had won a league-worst 67 games and finished 40½ games out of first in a six team division.[95] With Messersmith on the mound, hopes were high, but the Braves could only manage three more wins in 1976, still finishing last in their division. In his first season with the Braves, Messersmith became a .500 pitcher at 11-11, albeit with a very respectable 3.04 ERA.

The 1977 version of the Braves would win a meager 61 games while losing 101, the worst record in the National League. Messersmith went 5–4 with a 4.40 ERA. After two seasons with the Braves and a cumulative record of 15–14, Messersmith left to join the Yankees for the 1978 season. He fared no better in New York, failing to post a win, at 0–3 with a 5.64 ERA. Messersmith had one more season in him and, ironically, he pitched his last season for the Dodgers in 1979, going 2–4 with a 4.91 ERA. Messersmith had proved a player could negotiate a large contract, but he also proved that a player who signs a large contract may not always perform as expected by the signing club. In the four seasons after signing the contract, Messersmith posted an 18–22 record. Unlike Catfish Hunter, Messersmith performed poorly after signing a huge contract. Ironically, Messersmith's case probably would have never become an arbitration grievance had the Dodgers simply agreed to a no-trade clause. However, it was clear that free agency was inevitable.

When Dave McNally left the Montreal Expos in the middle of the 1975 season, he knew was never going to play baseball again. The arbitration ruling did not change that. McNally retired from baseball with a lifetime record of 184–119 and a 3.24 ERA. He was an outstanding pitcher and the only pitcher ever to hit a grand slam in World Series play.[96] He also won 17 straight games, a record which was later broken by Roger Clemens. McNally died at the age of 60 of lung cancer in 2002.[97]

Conclusion

In the 1970s major league players made great strides towards leveling the playing field with the owners. Notwithstanding Curt Flood's loss in the U.S. Supreme Court in the early 1970s, the players won their free agency rights, not through antitrust law but through labor law and collective bargaining. One of the more significant concessions Marvin Miller was able to get from the owners in 1970 was the use of impartial arbitration procedures for grievances. Without this vehicle in the Basic Agreement, the players would have had little recourse against the owners.[98] The players won the right to salary arbitration in 1973.[99] The Messersmith/McNally decision, which was handed down in late 1975, and the 1976 Basic Agreement, gave the players significant economic gains.[100] Before Marvin Miller arrived on the scene, there was no free agency, no salary arbitration, no grievance arbitration, no multi-year contracts, and the minimum salary was $6,000.[101] In just ten years the winds of change had swept through and the players were in a much better bargaining position in 1976. Beginning with the 1977 season, the owners were now forced to bid for the services of major league veterans who had at least six years of big league experience.[102] The average player's salary rose from $29,000 in 1970 to $146,000 in 1980.[103]

Andy Messersmith. Messersmith was a good pitcher for the Dodgers but, ironically, was not as good after gaining his hard-won free agency status (National Baseball Hall of Fame Library Cooperstown, New York).

In 1976, total major league baseball payrolls were $32 million; ten years later they were $284 million.[104]

Andy Messersmith is certainly the name that people associate with baseball free agency. However, others placed chinks in the armor of the owners along

10. Players Win Their Freedom in Arbitration   193

the way, including John Ward, Napoleon Lajoie, Hal Chase, Sandy Koufax, Don Drysdale, Curt Flood, Bobby Tolan,[105] and Catfish Hunter, with Andy Messersmith and Dave McNally striking the final blow. The players' revolt had finally come to fruition. Baseball owners would now have to open their wallets to the players, which they did. Player salaries would skyrocket for almost a decade until the owners would shut their wallets again during the collusion years, after they "agreed" they were paying too much money to the players.

11

Baseball's Collusion Cases
Free Agents Take On the Owner

> The owners got together and rigged the game. — Donald Fehr, Executive Director, MLBPA, 1986[1]
>
> Man, I did love this game. I'd have played for food money. — Ray Liotta as Joe Jackson, *Field of Dreams*, 1988
>
> You can't get 26 owners to agree on anything. — Peter Ueberroth, Baseball Commissioner
>
> No one is going to tell George Steinbrenner he can't sign a free agent, and no one is going to tell him he must sign one.[2] — George Steinbrenner

1976–1985

Curt Flood, Catfish Hunter, Dave McNally, and Andy Messersmith all made some headway against baseball and the owners in the players' struggle to even the labor playing field. Each had taken a shot at the owners and major league baseball, with varying success.[3] Curt Flood had taken the biggest chance and essentially ended his baseball career with his challenge of the reserve clause that ended at the U.S. Supreme Court in a victory for the owners. Hunter received a big contract as a result of his arbitration victory, exposing the owners and showing his fellow ballplayers there was money to be had. With Flood and Hunter leading the way, Andy Messersmith and Dave McNally (along with Marvin Miller) forged ahead and claimed a victory for the players in arbitration. The players were now ready to reap the benefits of their hard-earned victories.

The owners challenged the Messersmith arbitration decision through the courts, a traditional bastion of immunity for the owners, but lost. They were left with no other option but to negotiate with the players yet they still refused to do so, locking the players out of spring training in 1976. The owners and players eventually agreed to a new Basic Agreement that summer. Although players could claim free agency as a result of the Messersmith arbitration decision, Marvin Miller knew free agency for every player, every year, was not a good idea and could actually have the ultimate effect of driving player salaries down. Therefore, Miller agreed to a free agency system which allowed players to declare for free agency after six years of major league service. Players with less than six but at least two years of service at the major league level could go through salary arbitration with their club.[4] Clubs still held the exclusive rights for players who were not eligible for arbitration but would have to pay a minimum salary to those players under the Basic Agreement. The final result? Baseball players' salaries skyrocketed! In 1975, the average salary in baseball was approximately $51,501.[5] It rose to $76,066 in 1976 and by 1980 was a whopping $143,756.[6] Average major league salaries from 1979 to 1988 were as follows[7]:

Major League Average Salaries
1979–1988

Year	Salary	Change
1979	$113,558	—
1980	$143,756	+26.6%
1981	$185,651	+29.1%
1982	$241,497	+30.1%
1983	$289,194	+19.8%
1984	$329,408	+13.9%
1985	$371,175	+12.7%
1986	$412,520	+11.1
1987	$412,454	*
1988	$438,729	+6.4%

Less than one percent.

The 1980 Basic Agreement made a few minor changes to the new player compensation system but helped move salaries from $143,756 to $371,157 in 1985, an increase of 158 percent.[8] In six years the average player salary had virtually tripled. A fifty-day mid-season strike occurred in 1981, resulting in 719 cancelled games.

Baseball labor talks in 1985 were, like previous negotiations, hotly contested. Clubs wanted to impose a salary cap. They also sought to limit the raises that could be awarded in arbitration and to move the salary eligible standard from 2 to 3 years.[9] The clubs argued they could no longer afford to pay the players' escalating salaries and agreed to release their financial records to the Players Association to prove their case. Professor Roger Noll, a Stanford economist, analyzed the owners' financial records on behalf of the players and determined that the clubs collectively had earned a profit of $25 million in 1984. The clubs had claimed a loss of $41 million. The sixth work stoppage in baseball history occurred in 1985 but lasted only two days.[10]

The 1985 negotiations also created changes in the free agency system that were expected to create more competition in the marketplace for players.[11] One significant change increased eligibility for salary arbitration from 2 to 3 years.[12] The player compensation system and the free agent draft, which had restricted the ability of clubs to bid on free agents, were done away with. December 7 was established as a deadline date for a player's former club to sign him to a contract. Before December 7, the former club was required to offer salary arbitration to the player or it would lose negotiating rights to that player until May 1 of the next year. The player had until December 19 to accept the club's offer. If an offer for salary arbitration was not accepted or the player was not signed by January 8, the club lost its negotiating rights to sign the player prior to the May 1 deadline.

Owners complained about multi-year contracts that players received from 1976 to 1980. Over 200 players who were not yet eligible for free agency signed multi-year contracts in late 1976.[13] Between 1977 and 1980 over 200 players with less than six years of major league service signed multi-year contracts.[14]

Shortly after the 1985 season was over, player agents began to sense something was wrong. It now seemed agents that had to beg for a meeting with a general manager. Noted baseball agent Randy Hendricks described the environment: "It was a casual indifference. It was: 'You've got nothing to sell.'"[15] Legal counsel for the Players Relation Committee (PRC) Barry Rona attributed the players' return to their 1985 club as merely a trend "over the years" toward players remaining with the same club.[16]

The players refused to sit back and let the owners take back the gains they had worked so hard for. With the 1985 Basic Agreement in place, the stage was now set for a labor war which would result in several major victories for the players and cause the owners to dig deep in their pockets to pay for their illegal behavior.

Collusion I, Grievance No, 86–2 Panel Decision 76 (September 21, 1987)[17]

The first collusion case was filed by the Players Association on February 3, 1986, after the 1985 season.[18] It alleged that the 26 major league clubs "have been acting in concert with each other with respect to individuals who became free agents under article XVIII after the 1985 season."[19] The dispute centered around paragraph H of article XVIII of the Basic Agreement, which stated:

> The utilization or non-utilization of rights under this Article XVIII is an individual matter to be determined solely by each Player and each Club for his or its own benefit. Players shall not act in concert with other Players and Clubs shall not act in concert with other Clubs.

Ironically, paragraph H, the clause which became the center of the collusion cases, was originally proposed by the clubs during the 1976 labor negotiations. The clubs did not want the players to "band together" under their new free agency rights. Owners were leery the players might engage in a joint holdout similar to that of Los Angeles Dodgers star pitchers Sandy Koufax and Don Drysdale, when they banded together in 1966 to negotiate for higher salaries.[20] The Players Association agreed to the inclusion of the paragraph, but also insisted the clubs be subject to the same provision, never anticipating that paragraph H would later become the basis of multiple arbitration awards in favor of the players.

The arbitration decision for the Collision I grievance was handed down in September 1987. Tom Roberts wrote the arbitration decision for Collusion I.[21] He began his opinion by noting that following the 1984 season, 16 of the 26 major league clubs had signed free agents who had been with other clubs but that "the winter of 1985–1986 was entirely different...."[22] In the off-season following the 1985 season only one of 27 players, Carlton Fisk, received a bona fide offer from a club other than his current employer. Twenty-nine of the re-entry free agents signed with their former clubs. Arbitrator Roberts noted that "the clubs showed no interest in the available free agents at any price until such time as their former club declared the player no longer fit into their plans."[23]

The Players Association argued the 26 clubs "participated with an intent to destroy free agency"[24] and further that they had this specific goal since the Messersmith/McNally labor arbitration decision in December 1975. The clubs asserted that the circumstances following the 1985 season were "nothing more than the culmination of a predictable evolution to a more sober and rational free agency market from that present to the 1970s."[25] They argued that each club had made its own individual decisions about players and the employment of free agents and that those decisions were based on "legitimate baseball, business management and financial decisions."[26] The clubs said the lack of movement in the free agency market was due to several factors, none of which they had any control over. These factors included general economic conditions, changes in the basic agreement, and a lack of available "quality" free agents.[27] The lack of movement "was simply the culmination of a ten year trend rather than the sudden result of a conspiracy...."[28] The Players Relations Committee (PRC) had produced a memorandum and circulated it to the owners after the 1985 season. The memo said players who signed contracts of three or more years usually spent more time on the disabled list and were less productive after signing a long-term contract. The owners' research showed that in the first year after signing a new deal a player's output declined to 124 games, 11 home runs, 56 RBI, and a batting average of .273. In the year prior to signing the contract, the player's average performance was 133 games, 13 home runs, 63 RBI, and a batting average of .280.[29]

Arbitrator Roberts said in his opinion that "in the context of the present inquiry any agreement or plan involving two or more of the clubs and governing the manner in which they will or will not deal with free agents is contractually forbidden."[30] The arbitrator said the agreement to collude did not have to be in writing or even be a formal contract. All that was necessary was a "common scheme or plan," and that would be enough to constitute a violation of the Basic Agreement. Clubs were free to exchange information with each other, but "what is prohibited is a common scheme involving two or more clubs and/or two or more players undertaken for the purpose of a common interest as opposed to their individual benefit."[31]

Commissioner Ueberroth testified during the arbitration proceedings for Collusion I:

> I wanted them to know the economics. I wanted them to understand — If somebody is going to make a multimillion dollar transaction in something as simply structured as a baseball team, they ought to know what that is. They ought to know the impact. They ought to know short range, long range. They have to know how it impacts the rest of the players, impacts their budgets, impacts their planning process, impacts their policy, and I hammered on that and I — If that is wrong, I did it, you know, that is clear.[32]

At a meeting of the owners on October 22, 1985, during the World Series, the retiring director of the PRC, Lee MacPhail, distributed a memorandum to all owners. The memorandum discouraged owners from signing players to long-term contracts. MacPhail said:

> We must stop day dreaming that one free agent signing will bring a pennant. Somehow we must get our operations back to the point where a normal year for the average team at least results in a break even situation, so that Clubs are not led to make rash moves in the vain hope that they might bring a pennant and a resulting change in their financial position. This requires resistance to fans and media pressure and is not easy.[33]

At the general managers' meeting on November 6, 1985, Commissioner Ueberroth said: "It is not smart to sign long-term contracts."[34]

Arbitrator Roberts found the following:

> The distillation of the message of these meetings resulted in every major league club abstaining from the free agency market during that winter until an available free agent was "released" by his former club upon the announcement that the former club was no longer interested in his services. That result was obtained through the conduct of the clubs uniformly established and maintained. The right of the clubs to participate in the free agency provisions of the Basic Agreement no longer remained an individual matter to be determined solely for the benefit of each club. The contemplated benefit of a common goal was substituted. This action constituted a violation of the prohibition against concerted conduct found in Article XVIII(H) and Grievance No. 86-2 is therefore sustained.[35]

> Only a common understanding that no club will bid on the services of a free agent until and unless his former club no longer desires to sign the free agent will accomplish such a universal affect. In the case at hand, just such a result obtained. This, in itself, constitutes a strong indication of concerted action.[36]

The result of all of this was a preemption of free agency negotiating rights by the former club, a result that could only be obtained through common consent in violation of Article XVIII(II).[37]

Each and every free agent had the same experience, i.e., no offers until their former clubs stated they were no longer interested. This is precisely the result forbidden by Article XVIII(H).[38]

It is reasonable to anticipate that interest in the services of at least some of them will be expressed by a team other than the club by whom they were employed at the time they elect free agency, they surely had a value at some price and yet no offers were advanced.[39]

AWARD

1. The Clubs violated Article XVIII(H) of the Basic Agreement following the completion of the 1985 championship season by acting in concert with regard to the free agency provisions of the said Article XVIII.[40]

Collusion I, New Look Free Agents

The Collusion I ruling found the owners colluded in violation of the Basic Agreement. It was now up to Arbitrator Roberts to determine the legal remedy to compensate the players for the illegal actions of the owners. On January 22, 1988, Arbitrator Thomas Roberts ruled that seven players were "new look" free agents, the most notable being Detroit Tigers outfielder Kirk Gibson. Roberts stated: "This award specifically addresses the MLBPA's request for a "new look" for 1985 free agents.[41] The MLBPA had requested that Roberts rule on their claims for both monetary damages and "new look" free agency. However, Roberts only ruled upon the "new look" issue, saying other "remedy issues would be decided in a subsequent arbitration ruling."[42]

Roberts noted that players Juan Beniquez, Kirk Gibson, Donnie Moore, Joe Niekro, Butch Wynegar, Tom Brookens, and Carlton Fisk "were deprived of the opportunity to negotiate with more than one club" because of the owner's conduct.[43] He ruled:

> It is hereby ordered that the 1985 free agents identified in Paragraph I hereof be provided the opportunity to seek employment, free from the Clubs' violation of the Basic Agreement, in addition to any other remedies to which they may be entitled in the present proceeding.[44]

Collusion I, Damages

Liability had been found against the owners and "new look" free agency had been granted to several players in January 1988. In a trial, a jury is asked to determine both liability and damages. They first make a determination of whether or not the defendant is legally responsible or liable under the law as claimed by the plaintiff. If a jury finds liability, the question then turns to the remedy to grant to the prevailing party. "New look" free agents had already been given their freedom; it was now time to determine the amount of money damages sustained by the players as a result of the conduct established in the Collusion I decision.

The first collusion case was filed in early 1986 and the first arbitration ruling in favor of the players was issued on February 20, 1987. The damages portion of the Collusion I ruling would not be issued until August 31, 1989, over two years after the owners were found to have colluded after the 1985 season. Arbitrator Tom Roberts framed the issue as follows:

> At the suggestion of the parties, the framing of the remedial award begins with this effort to determine, with the highest degree of precision permitted by the operative circumstances, the aggregate impact, if any, of the Club's violation of Article XVIII(H) on the 1986 salaries of affected players.[45]
>
> The Arbitration Panel is now asked to determine whether or not this conspiratorial conduct depressed the level of salaries negotiated on and after November 1, 1985.[46]

Roberts cited to a case decided by the United States Supreme Court in determining the standard for evaluating the players' claims for damages: "While damages may not be determined by mere speculation or guess, it will be enough if the evidence shows the extent of the damages as a matter of just and reasonable inference, although the result be only approximate."[47]

The Players Association argued that players not only had been damaged by the amount of the salaries they were able to negotiate, but that they had sustained other damage as well, including:

- the effect collusion had on the length of guaranteed player contracts;
- the frequency and size of player performance bonuses in player contracts;
- the decrease of signing and award bonuses in player contracts; and
- the effect collusion had on the number of contracts which contained special covenants such as trade restrictions for players and option clauses in contracts.[48]

The Players Association filed 139 individual claims on behalf of players, based on illegal acts by the owners that occurred after the 1985 season, with claims totaling $16,662,000.[49] The players argued that the total amount of damages was yet to be determined with "absolute minimal precision" but that the best the arbitrator would be able to do was establish a "range of total monetary injuries."[50]

The clubs argued that 1986 salaries were actually consistent with what players had received in previous years and that "there was no significant salary shortfall."[51]

The arbitrator categorized each element of the players' damages, but spent the majority of his time discussing "the salary shortfall." The Players Association presented three models showing salary shortfalls for the 1986 seasons: $13,033,562, $11,285,402.50, and $7,265,295.63.⁵² The panel eventually adopted the average of the three figures, settling at $10,258,086.71 as the salary shortfall for the players "as a consequence of the violation of Article XVIII(H) of the basic agreement...."⁵³

The arbitrator next turned to specific areas of damage claimed by the Players Association in addition to the salary shortfalls. The clubs argued that any shortfall in special covenants should have been included as a part of the aggregate damages, while the Association argued that loss of special covenants (if found) would be in addition to the aggregate salary shortfall of $10,528,086.71.

Length of Multi-Year Contracts

The arbitrator noted: "In the earlier years of free agency the risk of player injury or non-performance fell primarily upon the clubs."⁵⁴ There was, however, a gradual decline in both the "number and length of multi-year contracts."⁵⁵ He found that the change that took place in 1986, however, was "precipitous and directly attributable to the violation of Article XVIII (H)." The fact that a large number of players with over six years of service were not able to negotiate multi-year contracts during the winter of 1985–1986 could not be dismissed.

Option Buyouts

The arbitrator next turned to option buyouts in player contracts as an element of damage in collusion. He defined option buyouts as "contract provisions under which a Club is able to either continue a player on its roster at a guaranteed salary for an additional year or terminate the contract upon the payment of a lesser amount."⁵⁶ He noted that the option buyout could constitute an additional sum of guaranteed money for a player. Although it would be expected that the number of option buyouts would be more common as clubs reduced the number of long-term guaranteed contracts, that was not the case. In fact, the "number and contract price for the option buyout dipped significantly in 1986."⁵⁷ The arbitrator found:

> An impact of this magnitude upon both the number and value of option buyout clauses established a need to consider the individual claims of players asserting money damages flowing from an absence or diminution of an option buyout affixed to a contract signed for 1986.⁵⁸

Performance Bonuses

The next area of damages addressed by the arbitrator was that of performance bonuses in player contracts. Many player contracts contained clauses that paid the player for achieving a specified level of performance, such as the number of plate appearances, innings pitched, or number of games played. These types of bonuses also decreased in quantity and in the amount of the bonuses during collusion.[59] The arbitrator ruled that individual players who could show injury by the absence of a performance bonus or a bonus below market value could make a claim for damages.

Award Bonuses

Bonuses for receiving an award also could be included in a player's contract. Awards could include being named to the all-star team or receiving a most valuable player award. In 1985, players' contracts with six or more years of major league service had a potential value for award bonuses of $215,362. In 1986, the value of players' potential award bonuses had decreased to $91,458.[60] The arbitrator ruled once again that if a player could show a loss then he could make a damages claim for the loss of award bonuses in the contracts.[61] "The only permissible conclusion permitted by the record is to attach the cause to the contract violation."[62]

Signing Bonuses

Signing bonuses for players had decreased during collusion as well. In 1985, all players with at least six years of experience had negotiated a signing bonus.[63] In 1986, the number of signing bonuses decreased to 30.[64] In the eight years prior to Collusion I, signing bonuses ranged from 47 to 88 players. The arbitrator ruled that players who had a claim for loss of a signing bonus in 1986 were entitled to an opportunity to establish their claim.

No Trade Clauses

Many players were able to negotiate a "no-trade" clause in their contract. The arbitrator noted that a contract provision that "limited or remov[ed] the ability of a club to trade a player without his consent" may have some value. In 1985, 37 players had contracts that contained no-trade clauses. That number fell to only 17 for the 1986 season.

Other Forms of Bonuses or Pay

The arbitrator further noted that as many as 139 players may have had additional unique clauses in their contracts that provided additional compensation to the player. These included payment to the player if certain attendance levels were reached, payment for maintaining a certain weight, or even a payment made to the player's favorite charity. These forms of bonuses could also provide additional compensation to the player. If players could prove damage as a result of the loss of these contractual provisions, they could make a claim within the collusion settlement framework.[65]

Arbitration Award

The arbitrator issued his final ruling for damages in Collusion I for events occurring after the 1985 season, stating:

Interim Award

1. The concerted actions of the Clubs in violation of Article XVIII(H) of the Basic Agreement following the completion of the 1985 championship season resulted in an aggregate salary shortfall for 1986 in the amount of $10,528,086.71.
2. That same violation of Article XVIII(H) of the Basic Agreement resulted in a decline in the number and value of multi-year contracts and had an adverse impact upon bonus provisions and other special covenant contract clauses negotiated for new player contracts commencing in 1986.
3. The 139 players on behalf of whom the Players Association has submitted individual claims in this proceeding are entitled to an opportunity to advance those claims in further proceedings before the Arbitration Panel....[66]

Collusion II: In the Matter of the Arbitration Between Major League Baseball Players Association and the 26 Major League Clubs

The 1986 season was one of the best baseball had ever seen. The Mets beat the Astros in one of the greatest NLCS's ever played.[67] The World Series was one for the books as well, with the Mets beating the Red Sox and the error by Bill Buckner adding fuel to the fire for the Curse of the Bambino.[68] Notwithstanding those great moments, it was back to business as usual with free agents facing the same difficulties in 1986 as they did in 1985. The first collusion case had not been decided yet when the players filed a second collusion case on February 20, 1987, for actions taken by the owners after the 1986 season. The 1987 season was in the books and the 1988 season was well underway when arbitrator George Nicolau issued his opinion on August 31, 1988, finding the owners also had colluded after the 1986 season against players.

Following the 1986 season there were 79 re-entry free agents.[69] Of these, 27 were offered salary arbitration by their former club on or prior to the December 7 deadline. Some players who declined salary arbitration did not reach an agreement with their former club by January 8. Therefore, those clubs were not permitted to sign that player until May 1. Andre Dawson, Tim Raines, Lance Parrish, Doyle Alexander, Bob Hunter, Bob Boone, Ron Guidry, and Rich Gedman failed to reach an agreement by January 8. Raines, Alexander, Boone, Guidry, and Gedman signed new contracts with their former clubs on or after May 1. Andre Dawson, who was coming off a good season with the Montreal Expos, signed a contract with the Chicago Cubs during spring training.[70] Dawson allowed the Cubs to unilaterally set his salary. Parrish signed a one-year deal with the Phillies during spring training of 1987. Horner received no offers and eventually played baseball in Japan.

It was the position of the Players Association that 1986 was just like 1985. The Association said it was clear: no re-entry free agent had received offers from any other clubs (other than his former club) "unless and until his [former] club had declared its lack of interest or became ineligible to sign the player or negotiate with the player" after the January 8 deadline.[71] They also said, with one possible exception, that no free agent had even had two or more offers from two or more clubs.[72]

The Association further argued that it was not required to show an agreement between the clubs to violate the Basic Agreement: "proofs of acts in furtherance of a 'common benefit' is all that is needed."[73] The clubs said no such agreement existed, citing to the Minnesota Twins contract negotiations with pitcher Jack Morris and the Yankees contract negotiations with Gary Ward.[74] They also said there was both interest and offers to players before their former clubs declared their lack of interest. They noted that Ward, Dawson, and Parrish switched clubs and that Morris, Gedman, and Raines received offers from other clubs before they signed with their former club. The clubs said these actions showed "significant market activity," especially with the most prominent free agents. The clubs also pointed out that the Basic Agreement did not mandate a certain level of free agent activity.

The clubs said various factors contributed to a lack of activity with "certain" free agents. They also pointed to the "continuing bitter litigation between the parties," as well as the actions of certain player agents whose purpose was to create "evidence for use by the association" which had a "dampening effect" on the market and created a "fear of entrapment."[75] The clubs pointed a finger at the players, saying Alexander, Morris, and Horner had limited their own opportunities by either listing the teams they would play for or by adopting "no-negotiation" postures on certain issues.[76] Finally, the clubs said no collusion or "imagined conspiracy" existed as the players alleged but it wags rather

> an economic contest waged within the rules, featuring, at least on the owners' side, the independent, uncoerced pursuit of self-interest made up of "unilateral, non-consensual responses to similar competitive conditions." Though those independent judgments were largely known among those who made them and resulted in essentially similar behavior, this, standing alone, the Clubs say, is proof of nothing.[77]

In his ruling, Arbitrator Nicolau began by stating that the events of 1986 should not be viewed in isolation but had to be viewed within the context of the 1985 season because certain events were set in motion in 1985 that had continued during 1986. He noted that just because the clubs acted in concert in 1985 did not mean they did so in 1986, but that he still must consider 1985. Nicolau agreed with Tom Roberts, the arbitrator in Collusion I, that a mere exchange of information would not be a violation of the basic agreement.[78] He further stated,

> the existence of a common scheme, plan or understanding need not rest on absolute uniformity of action or a finding that its adherents are bound to it by some stated cluster of penalties for failure to conform. Consensual undertakings are not ordinarily of that nature. Deviations may negate the existence of a common understanding, but not necessarily. If there are deviations, they must be examined and considered. Nevertheless, it is not one piece of evidence, but the evidence taken as a whole that tells us whether a common understanding exists.[79]

He summarized his findings:

> I have concluded, based on the evidence, that there was such a common understanding in 1986; that it was an unbroken continuation of the understanding of 1985; and that the meager free-agent activity subsequent to January 8, examined herein, is simply insufficient to justify any other determination.[80]

The arbitrator divided his opinion into the events that occurred before January 8 and after.

Jack Morris Tries to Go Home

In 1986, Jack Morris was coming off another great season for the Detroit Tigers.[81] Morris had led the Tigers to the World Series in 1984 and was known as one of the league's fiercest competitors.[82] Morris and the Tigers could not consummate a deal. Faced with no other options, Morris declared free agency on November 12, 1986.[83] After Morris turned down the Tigers offer, his agent, Dick Moss, went to work. Moss contacted the Angels, Expos, and Cubs on behalf of Morris. They all had the same response: "Give us an offer and we will say 'yes' or 'no.'"[84] Moss wrote Mike Port, vice-president of the Angels, and asked for a meeting during the December winter meetings but Port never responded. On December 7, the day before the meetings began, the Tigers offered Morris salary arbitration.[85] Morris had no other offers and had until December 19 to accept the Tigers offer. But Dick Moss had a strategy. On December 7, he told the press he would make a series of proposals to four clubs (Twins, Yankees, Phillies, and Angels). If the first club said yes to his proposal, a deal would be struck. He would go to each club in turn and would not use one club against another in negotiations.

On December 12, Morris selected the Twins as his first choice. Morris and Moss could not meet with the Twins until December 16, just three days before he had to accept the Tigers offer. Twins general manager Andy MacPhail would later testify that the Twins did make Morris an offer that day. The offer was not in dollars but MacPhail said the Twins told Morris they would make him the "highest paid Twin." Arbitrator Nicolau detailed the negotiations with the Twins in his opinion to show the lack of authenticity of the Twins offer to Morris.

Moss called the Twins on Friday, December 12, and asked for a meeting on Monday the 15th. Twins General Manager MacPhail testified that before he got Morris's call he had "little use for ranking free agents on his club and did not really want to meet with Morris,"[86] and deliberately put the meeting off until Tuesday. He said he did not need a starting pitcher and that he "would not have pursued Morris as a free agent" if Morris had been "a regular re-entry free agent and had not come into Minnesota on the circus road show...."[87] The only reason he met Morris and his agent was because of the public pressure they brought to bear.[88] MacPhail further testified that although this was his viewpoint, he still intended to listen on the 16th to Moss and Morris and that he had actually recommended to the Twins five-person executive council that the Twins make an offer to Morris for $2.3 million for two years and deem it a "counter-offer."[89] However, MacPhail also told the Twins executive council that previously negotiated multi-million dollar contracts had damaged the club.[90] MacPhail testified he told the Twins council the Tigers were at $1.2 or $1.25 million for each of two years and in his estimate the team would go up to $1.4 million in salary arbitration.[91] The Twins council told MacPhail to set the counter offer at $2.5 million with a two-year maximum of $3 million.[92] A Tuesday meeting was set.[93] Moss then proceeded to make a contract proposal for two years at $1.85 and $2.05 million[94] or three years at $1.8 million and four years at $1.7 million.[95] He also offered an alternative for salary arbitration for each proposal. MacPhail testified Moss said that the timetable was "tight" and that he was not going to accept any counter proposals, although he would listen to a revision of one of his own offers. MacPhail said Moss offered no counter proposal and that the meeting ended with the Twins Executive Council saying the Twins owner Pohlad would want to "sleep" on Moss's proposal, and Moss saying that would be a discouraging sign.[96] After reporting back to the council, the Twins decided not to accept any of the proposals made by Moss based on two studies.[97] After further discussion it was determined that instead of "talking" dollars with Moss and Morris, the Twins would offer to make him the "highest paid Twin."[98] Pohlad did attend a meeting that afternoon and MacPhail testified that Pohlad told Morris "how highly he thought of him," but could not meet his demands in the Twins market and, if the Morris offer was "take it or leave it," he would have to "leave it."[99] MacPhail also said Pohlad told Morris he would continue to negotiate if Morris wanted to come back and that he would make Morris the highest paid Twin.[100] MacPhail said Morris did show some signs of "flexibility" relating to the arbitration offers. MacPhail perceived that Moss was saying he would put up $1.85 million and $2.05 million as Morris's two-year arbitration figures.[101] Pohlad then declared the meeting "over." In a short club meeting after the negotiations, Pohlad said, "That's it, you tell them we have reviewed the proposals and we are not going to do it."[102] MacPhail went back into the room and told Moss: "This was your show.... We are left under your instruction. We say yes or no. Our answer is no, we can't accept any of these."[103]

Steve Fehr, an associate of Moss's, testified during the arbitration proceedings that no Twins club representative made an offer stating Morris would be "the highest paid Twin" and no offer was ever made in terms of dollars.[104] Fehr said after the club "caucus" of about 30 minutes (in which he was assuming they were discussing a counter-offer), the meeting resumed with MacPhail saying there was nothing more to discuss.[105]

Dick Moss held a press conference after the "negotiations." MacPhail later held a press conference and, speaking from prepared notes, "express[ed] regrets at not being able to sign Morris."[106] He then spoke of the poor performance of the past six free agents and the good performance of the six draft choices they had to give up to sign the free agents. He also noted the market size for the Twins, the impact the type of contract Morris was seeking would have on other Twins players, and MacPhail's lack of faith in the arbitration process. He also noted he was given a "take it or leave it" situation by Morris's agent.[107] MacPhail testified that the club had "offered" to make Morris "the highest paid Twin."[108] However, Arbitrator Nicolau said the "words of [MacPhail's] carefully-structured written outline — prepared to make him the highest paid Twin" — were by no means emphatic or direct.[109] The clubs argued that the Minnesota Twins had made Morris a contract offer at a time when a Detroit salary arbitration offer was still outstanding to Morris.[110] Notwithstanding, Arbitrator Nicolau found the Twins offer was made merely for "public relations" purposes and was not a legitimate offer.[111]

Nicolau framed the issue surrounding the Morris situation by stating:

> The issue here is not Detroit's interest, but whether, as the Clubs assert, Minnesota made an offer to Morris on December 16, between the time the Tigers made their offer and Morris accepted it, thus establishing, at least in this one instance, a deviation from the pattern of 1985.[112]

He concluded:

> The club may have been "prepared" to make Morris the highest paid Twin at some point in time, but this detailed examination of the evidence dispels the notion, at least in my estimation, that the Twins actually made such an offer to Morris on December 16, or even "entered into serious negotiations" with him on that day. Rather, the Record establishes that the club's strategy was to appear to have made an offer so as to explain his non-signing to the press.[113]

Nicolau noted that MacPhail's own testimony said the "offer" was mentioned only once and that it was done in course of a speech as opposed to a "back and forth" negotiation.[114] MacPhail said the reason why the offer was never explained or reiterated (at two meetings) was because Club officials and the owners felt "intimidated" by Moss.[115] Nicolau commented on this position:

> This, in my view, is the least convincing of explanations. If they were in fact intimidated by the alleged "take it or leave it" approach, why, as MacPhail testified, was a great deal of time spent between the first and second meetings determining whether to counter and how? Intimidation would have foreclosed such a debate, if debate there was.[116]

Nicolau said the reason why so much time was taken between the two meetings "was not to make a serious proposition to Morris, but to fashion a means of avoiding that, while establishing, if they could, a defensible position to the press and their fans."[117] Nicolau said if the Twins had been serious in their offers they "would not have made an offer in such an off-handed, 'flash card' way or cloaked their asserted proffer in a shroud of ambiguity." They would have unambiguously put their proposition to Morris so he could say "yes or no."[118]

The arbitrator found the following:

> In my judgment, the Twins made no offer on December 16. Nor, in meeting with Morris and his representatives, did they intend to engage in serious negotiations. While, as MacPhail said, no love was lost between Minnesota and the Tigers, that did not translate into competitive bidding for Morris' services.[119]

After the Twins unsuccessful "negotiation," Morris received no other offers. On December 17 Moss made a new proposal to the Yankees and George Steinbrenner: arbitration for a one-year contract. This was the same offer the

Tigers had made but with one important distinction. If Morris accepted the Tigers offer, he could once again declare free agency after the expiration of the one-year contract. If the Yankees were to accept the one-year offer, they would have the right to Morris's services for four additional years, either through negotiations or salary arbitrations. George Steinbrenner did not testify during the collision hearings, but Moss said that the Steinbrenner indicated that while he found the offer intriguing, he believed it would have been "unfair" to current Yankees players Ron Guidry and Willie Randolph.[120] Moss made the same offer to the Phillies and Angels. Both clubs turned him down without a counter-offer. With no where else to go, Moss reluctantly went back to the Twins. He called MacPhail back and made him a one-year repeater rights proposal, which had not been part of the original offer to the Twins. MacPhail turned the offer down.

Jack Morris, one of baseball's best pitchers in the 1980s, was faced with no offers from other clubs. Convinced that none would be forthcoming, he accepted Detroit's offer to arbitrate his 1987 salary. The Tigers filed their arbitration number at $1.35 million[121] and Morris filed at $1.85 million. At the February arbitration hearing, the arbitrator selected Morris's number and he was once again pitching for the Tigers in 1987, with an increase in salary.[122]

Arbitrator George Nicolau summarized:

> Things in 1986 were as they had been in 1985. As Chairman Roberts was to find in September 1987, there was no rush in 1985, as there had been in previous years, to sign players about to became free agents or to buy-out upcoming free-agency years. The same pattern prevailed in 1986. Like '85, clubs had no fear of losing "their" players to another.[123]

The Cubs Get "The Hawk" on the Cheap

The arbitrator next looked at those free agents who had not reached an agreement with their club prior to the January 8 deadline. In 1985, all players who refused salary arbitration eventually signed with their former clubs. The eight players who remained unsigned after January 8 were in a unique situation. The previous offers could not be accepted until May 1, but other clubs could sign the players without restriction. The clubs argued that the 112 days between January 8 and May 1 was clear evidence of a free market. They cited to Lance Parrish and Andre Dawson as examples of players who signed with other clubs.[124] Andre Dawson's case was well publicized and unique in its contract negotiations.

The Cubs signed Andre Dawson but never had to bid for his services.[125] The contract "negotiations" between Dawson and the Cubs were unusual to say the least. Dallas Green, the general manager of the Cubs, was under a mandate from the Cubs corporate owners not to sign any high profile free agents.[126] Andre Dawson wanted to get away from the hard surface of Montreal to play on natural grass and so his agent made a contract offer to the Cubs on March 2. The Expos had offered Dawson a two-year deal worth $2.4 million but Dawson turned them down.[127] Without any offer from other clubs, Dawson's agent, Dick Moss (also Jack Morris's agent), asked Dallas Green, "Why not let Dawson report to the Cubs camp without a contract?" Green said he would check into it and called Moss back in 30 minutes. He told Moss, "If we get Andre over here, it's going to raise everybody's hopes, and if somehow it doesn't work out, everybody on the team is going to be depressed about it. So we'd better not do it."[128]

Moss told Dawson, "Why don't we just walk into camp? Stir something up."[129] That is exactly what they did. In mid-March, Moss and Dawson walked into Green's office in Mesa, Arizona, but were told that Green would be out all week.[130] Moss left an envelope containing a contract for Dawson and attached a note inviting Green to fill in the salary portion of Dawson's contract. Moss immediately told the press what he had done. The next day the Chicago papers reported Andre Dawson was going to be a Cub! The president of the Cubs was furious for being put on the spot by Moss.[131]

Moss negotiated with a Tribune Company lawyer who asked, "Does this really mean what it says? ... Can we put anything we want in paragraph two?"[132] The next day the club lawyer and Dallas Green called Moss and said they would fill in the blank with $500,000, plus $200,000 in incentives. It was half of what Dawson made in 1986.[133] Moss said: "Well, I am a little disappointed. We gave you a blank check, but I thought your definition of fairness would be a little more generous than this, but that was our offer and that's our deal."[134] Green responded: "Well, you know I thought you were going to try some way to wiggle out of it, but you're going to live up to your deal."[135]

The Cubs eventually got Dawson for $650,000 with $500,000 guaranteed.[136] In his six years at Montreal, he made $5.38 million.[137] The Cubs would get their money's worth from Dawson. In 1987, he had an outstanding season in his first season in Chicago. Dawson was voted an all-star, won the silver slugger award, a golden glove, and was the National League MVP. He led the league in home runs (49), RBI's (137), and total bases (353).

Arbitrator Nicolau found that the Club's basis for refusing to negotiate was unpersuasive:

> Article XVIII (H) does not guarantee any particular level of market activity and it may well be, as the Clubs assert, that a growing awareness of the economics of the game and the "learning curve" of free-agent performance would lead to fewer offers, perhaps at lower prices. But the period at issue was not one of "declining activity"; The Record demonstrates that there was literally no market; no bid, save one: that of the former club. Those players who only received that one bid "surely had a value

[to other clubs] at some price," in Chairman Roberts' words, yet there were no other bidders "at any price." Only when the former club no longer wanted "its" player, did other clubs "feel free" to bid.[138]

He also stated:

In light of this Record, the Clubs' assertion that "the 1986 free-agent market was marked by the existence of significant bidding activity for a number of free agents," either before or after January 8, and that all club were proceeding "according to their own lights," is contrary to the evidence and insupportable.[139]

In my judgment, the evidence as a whole convincingly establishes that everyone knew there was to be no bidding before January 8 for free agents coveted by their former clubs. It was also known that "other clubs" were not expected to sign such a free agents after January 8.[140]

When Jerry Reinsdorf, a co-owner of the White-Sox, informed Dick Moss that he would not bid for Jack Morris' services, "courtesy" and the virtues of communication cannot explain his sending a blind copy of his letter to the Commissioner and Campbell of the Tigers.[141]

In my opinion, their conduct with respect to the 1986 free agents was in deliberate contravention of Club obligations as embodied in Article XVIII(H), for which an appropriate remedy is fully justified.[142]

The final award stated:

AWARD

The Clubs violated Article XVIII(H) of the Basic Agreement following the 1986 season by acting in concert with respect to the utilization or non-utilization of rights under said Article.[143]

Collusion II Award; "New Look" Free Agents; Grievance 87–3, Opinion of the Chairman (October 24, 1988) (Nicolau)[144]

Grievance 87–3 was the remedial award for the owners' illegal conduct under Collusion II. The Players Association had requested that "new look" free agency status not just be confirmed to those players under contract, but that the arbitration also provide relief to fifteen 1986 re-entry or non-tender free agents who also became or were eligible to become free agents after 1987 and who had signed new contracts at that time. The arbitrator declined to adopt that position.[145] The remedial award found that each player affected by the award could negotiate and enter into a new uniform player's contract with any club "without restrictions or qualifications." If a player had not entered into a new contract before December 16, 1988, he was to notify his current club whether he would continue to negotiate with them.

Collusion III; Panel Decision No. 83, Grievance 88–1 (July 18, 1990)

The 1987 season was now in the books and it seemed things were much the same. Fresh off their victory, the players filed a third grievance on January 19, 1988, stating the clubs, "acted in concert" to "retrain, restrict, limit, interfere with and/or destroy ... free agency rights."[146] At the time of the filing of the third grievance, the Players Association was not aware that the PRC had established an "information bank" in the fall of 1987 to deal with free agents. Through that bank, "clubs could, if they chose, advise the PRC of salary offers they were making to free agents and also learn, whether they 'deposited' bidding information or not, what offers were being made by other clubs."[147] The Players Association argued that the purpose of the bank was to control prices (players' contracts and the lengths of those contracts) and to further depress the free agent market. The players further argued the information bank was a violation of Article XVIII(H) of the Basic Agreement. They argued "that the Clubs acted to help each other; that they expected reciprocity and that the purpose of the Bank was to pay players' particular club."[148] The clubs asserted the bank was there merely to "stimulate competition while eliminating club-to-club discussions to which the Association had historically objected."[149]

The clubs argued that the bank was created to "foster competition and it was in place to protect clubs from the 'wily agent' who has a tendency to inflate offers for players they represent." The clubs contended that it was just an "information exchange" and that a violation could only be found "if it is determined that the bank's purpose or effect was to improperly interfere with or influence the exercise of free agency."[150]

In his ruling, the arbitrator said the case was really a matter of contract interpretation when looking at the contractual provision at issue. The arbitrator said Article XVIII(H) did not permit the player or the club to "act in concert," i.e., to act together, in the utilization or non-utilization of free agency rights.[151] The arbitrator noted: "Here, the PRC, the labor relations representative of the 26 owners, established an undisclosed mechanism through which all major league clubs could transmit, receive, share and act upon free-agent bids."[152]

Although it was voluntary, the bank was still an example of clubs acting in concert about free agency rights.[153] The arbitrator also stated:

> Participating clubs were acting together so that information to which only one was privy — offers it had made to particular players — could be shared, used and acted upon by others for their own benefit to the possible detriment of the club supplying that intelligence.[154]

The arbitrator concluded:

There can be little question that the Information Bank was intended to affect free agent salaries and intrude on the free-agency process. It does so by its very nature. And despite its presently advanced pro-competitive justifications, it is evident that the Bank was not established to offer free agents more money than achievable without a Bank, but in an effort to keep bidding within bounds.[155]

That individualized bargaining system, with its built-in advantages and disadvantages for both sides, is the system the parties adopted and recently agreed to continue in their latest Basic Agreement. The unilaterally adopted and undisclosed 1987 Information Bank was an improper intrusion on that system and violated Article XVIII(H).[156]

AWARD

The clubs violated Article XVIII(H) of the Basic Agreement following the 1987 unilaterally establishing and maintaining the Information Bank during the 1987–88 free-agent market.[157]

Collusion III, Damage Awards for Collusion after the 1987 and 1988 Seasons; Panel Decision No. 83A, Grievance 87–3 (September 17, 1990)

Once again it was time to determine damages for collusion by the owners. This time the owners would feel the blow. Arbitrator Nicolau ordered the owners to pay aggregate salary shortfalls as follows:

1987 Season	$ 38,000,000
1988 Season	$ 64,500,000
Total	$102,500,000!

Players Objections to the Proposed Collusion Framework; In the Matter of Objections to the Proposed Framework for the Evaluation of Individual Claims Required by the Agreement in the Settlement of Grievances No. 86–2, 87–3 and 88–1 (Roberts, Nicolau) (September 11, 1991)

After all grievances had been settled, the difficult process of deciding how to distribute the awards began. It would not be an easy task. How would it be determined which players would receive the biggest awards? Eight-hundred forty-three players filed 3,713 claims for collusion totaling $1,321,948,295.[158] Many players claimed they had lost contract opportunities and were damaged as a result of the owners' illegal actions.

The stated purpose of the proposed framework was to: "Establish an appropriate process for evaluation and determination of individual claims given the violations previously found by the Panels."[159] The framework was to

> set forth the principles to be applied and the procedures to be utilized by the MLBPA in its consideration of individual claims as well as the procedures and criteria to be utilized by the Arbitration Panel in its independent determination of individual claims and objections.[160]

In February 1991, copies of the proposed framework were sent to players and players' agents to review.[161] Players could object to the framework on the following basis:

1. The association's conclusions regarding loss job claims;
2. The method the association used to evaluate individual salary awards; and
3. The association's decision not to allocate sums of money for distribution to those groups of players who were not eligible for salary arbitrations during the years of collusion.[162]

The arbitrator was called upon to determine if the proposed framework was fair. He denied virtually all of the players' objections. The arbitrator concluded: "Except for the suggested threshold applicable to lost jobs claimants, we have denied all of the objections advanced so that the terms of the Proposed Framework to which those objections were directed are found to be appropriate and thereby approved."[163]

Collusion Settlement and Aftermath

The collusion settlement provided for a total payout of $280 million. An amount of $242,731,061 was to be divided by season among players eligible for free salary arbitration as follows:

1. $10,038,997 for 1986
2. $37,558,653 for 1987
3. $66,335,366 for 1988
4. $72,311,186 for 1989
5. $38,620,859 for 1990
6. $17,866,021 for 1991 and later seasons
7. $27,268,939 to be allocated for interest[164]

The 26 clubs were to pay the MLBPA $120 million on January 2, 1992, and four payments of $40 million plus interest on July 15, September 15, November 15, 1991, and April 15, 1992.[165] Bob Horner garnered the biggest award at $7,034,112, which included interest.[166] Other awards were given to

Lance Parrish for $5,866,599; Jack Clark, $4,406,238; Doyle Alexander, $4,068,115; Kirk Gibson, $3,710,398; Doug DeCinces, $3,709,504; Jack Morris, $3,124,618; and Andre Dawson, $3,287,146.[167] Rod Carew received $782,035.71 for damages for the 1986 season.[168] Butch Wynegar was the only player to receive an award for emotional distress damages.[169] Dave Kingman was awarded $648,000 for the 1987 season and, after adding interest, his total award came to $829,849.54.[170]

With collusion now settled, the players witnessed significant salary increases. Prior to 1988, the highest annual salary in baseball was approximately $2 million.[171] In 1990, the first $3 million salary was paid. In 1993, Barry Bonds signed a six-year contract with an average annual salary of $7.24 million.[172] Between 1989 and 1992, the average major league player's salary doubled.[173] Baseball's average salary went from $597,537 in 1990, to $1,119,981 in 1996.[174] The average MLB player salary for the opening day roster for 2010 was $3,340,133.[175]

Baseball's collusion cases may be the most expensive labor battle ever fought. The players' union felt somewhat vindicated but Marvin Miller believed the settlement amount was still not enough. Miller said that all the $280 million settlement did was make a profit for the owners. He said the payment of $280 million only made the players "whole" and did not in any way penalize the owners.[176] He also said since the $280 million was a negotiated settlement, the actual loss to the players was greater. Some owners believed they did nothing wrong and their actions were within the bounds of the law. No action was ever taken by the commissioner's office against the owners for collusion, with Commissioner Fay Vincent saying any further penalty against them would constitute "double jeopardy."[177]

Collusion Time Line

February 3, 1986 (Collusion I Grievance)
    The MLBPA files first grievance based on owners' actions following the 1985 season.
February 20, 1987 (Collusion II Grievance)
    The MLBPA files a second grievance claiming the owners' illegal actions continued after the 1985 season into the 1986 season.
September 21, 1987 (Collusion I Decision)
    Arbitrator Thomas Roberts issues a ruling that clubs colluded to destroy the free agent market after the 1985 season.
January 19, 1988 (Collusion III)
    The MLBPA files a third grievance claiming the illegal activity continued following the 1987 season and that management operated a free agent "Information Bank" in violation of the basic agreement.

January 22, 1988 (Collusion I — New Look Free Agents)
   Arbitrator Thomas Roberts grants free agency to seven players, deeming them "new look" free agents: Kirk Gibson, Carlton Fisk, Juan Beniquez, Tom Brookens, Donnie Moore, Joe Niekro, and Butch Wynegar.

August 31, 1988 (Collusion II Decision)
   Arbitrator George Nicolau rules the clubs illegally conspired against free agents.

October 24, 1988 (Collusion II — New Look Free Agents)
   Arbitrator George Nicolau makes 12 players from the second collusion case "new look" free agents.

August 31, 1989 (Collusion I Damages)
   Arbitrator Thomas Roberts awards damages against the owners in the amount of $10.5 million for damages sustained by the players during the 1986 season.

July 18, 1990 (Collusion III Decision)
   Arbitrator George Nicolau rules against the owners in Collusion III, saying that following the 1987 season owners conspired against free agents by establishing an information bank in violation of the basic agreement.

September 17, 1990 (Collusion II, III Damages)
   Arbitrator George Nicolau rules the owners must pay $102.5 million in damages for illegal behavior during the 1987 and 1988 season.

October 26, 1990 (Collusion Settlement)
   The players and management agree to settle all their claims dealing with collusion for a total sum of $280 million.

12

Schentzel v. Philadelphia Baseball Club[1]

Benejam v. Detroit Tigers, Inc.[2]

A Day at the Ballpark Isn't Always a Can of Corn[3]

> The chance to apprehend a misdirected baseball is as much a part of the game as the seventh inning stretch or peanuts and Cracker Jack.—Michigan Court of Appeals, 2001

> Head-hunting while blurs coveted by fans who risk life and limb and often times beer trying to catch them.—A foul ball[4]

The Simple Foul Ball

Steve Evans was born in Cleveland, Ohio, in 1885, and played eight years of professional baseball, including two seasons in the Federal League. He finished with 32 career home runs, 963 hits, and a respectable .287 lifetime batting average.[5] He batted .348 his first year in the Federal League.[6] Notwithstanding those stellar statistics, Evans, much like any other ballplayer, would now and then be the subject of ridicule by a "bug."[7] A "bug" infested the St. Louis National League Park one day in 1914 and devoted the majority of his time to calling Evans names like "wooden head" and "bore head."[8] Evans was waiting in the on-deck circle when a teammate struck a high foul ball. The ball was headed in the direction of the "bug," also occasionally referred to as a "knocker"[9] in classic baseball parlance. The "bug" saw it coming and tried to dodge the ball but he misjudged it and "just before the ball struck him on the head the knocker grabbed off his hat and let the sphere land solidly on an absolutely bald dome."[10] Evans observed this series of events with much satisfaction and, as soon as the crowed laughter died down, Evans said in a voice loud enough for everyone to hear, "that's the gink that has been calling me a bonehead."[11] Fellow "bugs" at the game were "sore" at the "knocker," and "roared and kept up a running fire of comments, which drove the victim from the stands."[12]

A foul ball is a common occurrence at a baseball game. Even the most casual baseball fan understands what a foul ball is. Hitting a round ball with a round bat is not always going to produce a ball hit on a straight line. A pitcher can throw a ball close to 100 mph and, if a batter merely gets a piece of the ball, it can be sent into the stands directly at spectators at a high rate of speed. Thousands of baseballs are hit into the stands over the course of a major league season. Some balls drift over the crowd hanging in suspension, while other balls may be hit into the stands like a rocket as fans quickly duck or run for cover, hoping to avoid injury. Many fans treat a foul ball like gold, ruining expensive suits in an attempt to take home a souvenir. Many others position themselves like Bill Russell going for a rebound in hope of grabbing one.[13] A foul ball hit into the stands may seem like such a simple proposition, yet throughout baseball history, foul balls have created an array of human emotions in fans, ranging from greed, hate, love, amusement, frivolity, to sadly, tragedy. Foul balls have caused injuries, deaths, marriages, and even led to an arrest or two.

There have been many famous home runs hit in baseball but have there been famous foul balls as well? No one has taken on the task of categorizing famous foul balls but a recent one might receive a lot of votes, at least if Cubs fans were doing the voting. If the monetary value of a ball is the gauge of the most famous foul ball in baseball history, then a foul ball which occurred in the 2003 National League Championship Series (NLCS) would garner the top spot. In that NLCS, the Chicago Cubs were five outs away from their first World Series since 1945. With the Cubs leading the Marlins 3–2 in the eighth inning, a foul ball was headed for the seats at Wrigley Field. Cubs outfielder Moises Alou attempted to make a play on the ball but before he could make the catch, Cubs fan Steve Bartman tried to grab the ball.[14] Bartman missed the ball as did Alou.[15] Alou was furious. The Cubs then went on to lose the game, as the Marlins rallied for eight runs in the eighth inning. The Cubs lost game seven to the Marlins who would beat the Yankees in the World Series.[16]

Grant DePorter, managing partner of Harry Caray's Restaurant Group, purchased the ball at auction for $106,600 in 2003.[17] Many Cubs fans blamed Bartman for the Cubs' hard luck, while others took their vengeance out on the ball itself.[18] The most famous, or infamous depending on a fan's perspective, foul ball met its demise in an extravagant ceremony on February 26, 2004, that was intended to break the curse on the Cubs.[19] The ball was exploded as millions of people watched a live telecast of the event on MSNBC in an attempt to put the Cubs back on track to the World Series.

12. A Day at the Ballpark Isn't Always a Can of Corn

Foul balls have a way of creating a variety of emotions among baseball fans.[20] William J. Barbeau was a third baseman for the Columbus ball club and was very popular for his "brilliant playings" during his career.[21] Nona C. Fitzgerald was attending a game on ladies day at the park in Milwaukee in 1908 but could not find a seat in the grandstands so she sat in the bleachers. Cupid would be on her side that day. A foul ball made its way into the stands and eventually right into Ms. Fitzgerald's lap. Third baseman Barbeau went into the bleachers after the foul ball and ran into Ms. Fitzgerald. One thing led to another and the two eventually married; the simple foul ball struck that day had brought the two together. In 1913, Carl Franklin Keener was playing baseball for the College of Pharmacy when he fouled off a pitch while playing in Philadelphia. The foul ball struck spectator Marie Gibble in the ankle, seriously injuring her.[22] After the game, Keener wanted to apologize for the injury he had caused so he called a friend and asked him to introduce him to the girl he hit with the foul ball. Several months later the two became engaged and eventually married.[23] However, foul balls don't always bring people together. In fact, it can drive a wedge between couples, especially if you dive out of the way of the ball and let it strike your girlfriend.[24] Jay Gibbons of the Baltimore Orioles was already married when he was batting in the ninth inning of a game against the Twins in September 2006. He fouled off a pitch that landed in the rib cage of his biggest fan, his wife.[25] What are the odds of that? Fortunately, she was not seriously injured and by all accounts it did not affect their relationship. It seems romance has always been present at the ballpark, and owners understand a marketing opportunity when they see one. Couples can now arrange for a wedding at the ballpark and many fans become engaged or get married at the ballpark.[26]

There is no doubt Richie Ashburn was a great ballplayer and hitter. He had a lifetime batting average of .308 and was considered the ultimate lead off hitter of his generation. On August 17, 1957, in a game against the Giants, Ashburn struck a foul ball that broke the nose of Alice Roth.[27] As they were placing her on the stretcher, Ashburn continued his barrage against Ms. Roth, striking her once again with another foul ball while she was incapacitated on the stretcher. Notwithstanding his unintended boorish behavior, Ashburn and Roth would actually strike up a friendship lasting for many years.[28]

Many fans who go to a baseball game hope to bring home a foul ball. However, keeping a foul ball that has been hit into the stands has not always been a privilege given to the spectator. In fact, in June 1905, Samuel Stott was arrested for hiding a ball in his hat that was hit into the stands in Chicago.[29] Stott was sitting in Box AA among 200 "charmed" fans who enjoyed "Hart's roof garden view," evidently at some rather steep prices. The roof garden seats were named after Jim Hart, president and owner of the Cubs until 1905.[30] When the foul ball made its way into the stands, Stott stopped the ball with his hand and then quickly hid it under his hat.[31] Stott was sitting in a box right next to Hart, who, as president of the Cubs, had paid for the ball. Hart was sitting with President Pulliam of the National League. An usher dutifully raced over to Stott and asked him for the ball, but Stott refused to hand it over. The usher then grabbed Stott and marched him out of the stadium. A police paddy wagon from the Chicago Warren Station was called and two detectives put Stott into the wagon and took him away to jail. He was booked on a charge of larceny brought by complainant James A. Hart, president of the Chicago National League Club![32]

Tort Law and Baseball

No book on baseball and the legal system would be complete without a discussion of tort law. There have been cases in baseball dealing with a range of torts including defamation, assault and battery, false imprisonment, intentional infliction of emotional distress, trespass, and negligence. But the foul ball has lead to more tort litigation than all the other torts combined in the baseball arena. Torts is one of the oldest areas of common law. Negligence has been the tort action of sports participants and fans. Negligence is conduct that falls below the reasonable person standard. The burden of proof is on the plaintiff to show that a negligent act or omission occurred on the part of the defendant and that the defendant's conduct was the proximate case of plaintiff's injury. To win a case of negligence, the plaintiff must show a duty of care, a breach of that duty, a proximate cause between defendant's actions and the injury, as well as damages.

A basketball or football that makes its way into the crowd during a game is not likely to do as much damage to a fan as a baseball or a hockey puck.[33] Whereas baseball fans are encouraged to keep balls that go into the stands,[34] it is customary in the National Basketball Association that courtside fans merely hand the ball back to the referee. The National Football League prevents footballs from going into the stands by the use of nets in the end zone. The National Hockey League allows fans to keep pucks that go into the stands.

Going to a ballgame can be an exciting adventure but it can also be very dangerous. Club owners understand the legal issues dealing with foul balls and projectiles making their way into the grandstands. Notwithstanding the pastoral nature of the game, many tragedies have occurred at the ballpark.[35] A recent survey shows approximately 35 spectators are injured from foul balls at major league games for every one-million visitors.[36] About 300 people a year are hospitalized by foul balls at major and minor league parks.[37] Stadium owners are premises owners under the law and have substantial liability concerns every time the gates open and 45,000 excited fans pour into their stadium, cheering, booing, drinking, and eating. Just like the owner of a department store or restaurant, a stadium owner owes its patrons a duty of care when they enter onto the premises of the ballpark. Stadium owners are not the insurers of the safety of their patrons, but the law dictates that they do have duty of care to their patrons to exercise ordinary care while they are on the premises. Notwithstanding, a stadium owner does not owe a duty of care to spectators to warn them of "open and obvious" dangers, and that includes foul balls that go into the stands. Owners have attempted to distance themselves from liability through written warnings on the back of the ticket,[38] posting signs in the stadium, making announcements during the game, and posting scoreboard messages. All these actions taken by the owner are meant to protect against spectator lawsuits. Stadium owners deal with unusual and sometimes hazardous scenarios for fans. Ballparks can be crowded, with limited lighting in certain areas and fans drinking alcohol. There can be steps and inclines to traverse, escalators, kids running through the park, not to mention the projectiles going into the stands, some at a very high rate of speed. If that is not enough, owners try everything they can to add to fan excitement. Some of these events can distract the fan from the game itself. Fireworks, "bring your dog to the park" night,[39] beach day,[40] extravagant promotional giveaways, and other events have all become a part of the fan's experience at the ballpark. Although they may not be "traditional" baseball events, they do bring people to the park. The owner must be keenly aware of liability issues as fans file through the turnstiles. During a game, projectiles will go into the crowd both during the playing of the game and between innings. It could be a ball, a bat (in one piece or shattered pieces), a player's glove, a t-shirt, or even a player.

The legal question presented in most spectator lawsuits is what is the stadium owner's liability for bats, balls, and other objects that make their way into the stands and injure spectators? Furthermore, do spectators assume the risk when they enter the ballpark that they may be struck by a foul ball, a bat, or some other flying object that goes into the stands? These questions have been debated and analyzed by courts for over a hundred years. In fact, it is such a common occurrence that courts have developed a special baseball rule called the "limited duty rule" which sets the parameters of a baseball stadium owner's tort liability.[41] The limited duty rule has been recognized by the U.S. courts since 1915.[42]

The Deadly Foul Ball

Foul balls at a baseball game can cause serious injuries and have even resulted in the death of spectators.[43] Safety at the ballpark is not a new issue for owners and fans. From the early days of baseball, foul balls were seen as a danger to spectators, umpires, and players alike.[44] There are numerous instances of injury and death from foul balls throughout the history of baseball. In August 1897, umpire Tim Hurst suffered a brain hemorrhage after he was struck by a foul ball in the head.[45] In May 1899, catcher Edward Connor was killed after being struck over the heart with a foul ball.[46] Also, in 1889, 14-year-old Edgar Howard was batting in a baseball game on the playground when a pitched ball hit him in the stomach.[47] In this tragic moment, an explosion occurred and Edgar was enveloped in a cloud of smoke. The boy had been at a railroad construction site before the game and he had forgotten that he had been given a dynamite cap which he had placed in his pocket before the game. The pitched ball struck the cap, exploding it, injuring the boy.[48] One of the best players in Massachusetts, a former Holy Cross ballplayer, was killed by a foul ball in 1900.[49] In a highly unusual and tragic case, Thomas Walker was killed by a foul ball on October 28, 1902, while sitting on a fence with some friends and watching a baseball game.[50] One of the boys sitting with Thomas asked another boy for a knife to keep the score of the game. As the knife was being passed by Thomas, he was struck by a foul ball in the hand which drove the knife blade into his side. The knife severed an artery, causing almost instant death to the boy.[51] On September 5, 1904, a 12-year-old boy was tragically killed after being hit by a foul ball in the temple.[52] Grove Thomas was a catcher for the Babcock baseball team of Johnstown, Pennsylvania, in 1904.[53] While catching, a foul ball struck Thomas over the heart.[54] It was reported that he turned to his wife in the grandstands and smiled, and then fell on his face and died 20 minutes later.[55] A nine-year-old boy, John Coffey, was killed by a foul ball in 1909.[56] He went to the Manhattan field on September 12, 1909, to see a game between the Giants and the Yonkers Field Club.[57] The game with the Giants was called off so two new teams took the field. In the ninth inning a foul ball struck the young boy in the temple, killing him. His mother held him until an ambulance came, but the boy tragically passed away. In 1911, a foul ball hit a 15-year-old girl in the forehead and knocked her unconscious.[58] She was revived by a physician at the park but insisted upon staying at the game.[59] After the game, she went out with friends and was the life of the party.[60] Five hours later, she "dropped dead" as she entered her home as she was saying goodnight to her friends.[61] Twenty-year-old Grace Ribey was killed at a game in Kansas in 1912 after being hit behind the left ear with a foul ball.[62] Major League outfielder Manny Mota had hit many foul balls into the stands in his baseball career but it was the one he hit in May 1970 that changed his life.[63] On that particular day in the third inning of a game against the Giants, he lined a foul ball into the seats down the first base line. The ball struck a 14-year-old boy in the head just above the ear. Five days later the boy died. Mota was devastated by the event and still has bad memories of the day it happened. After learning of the boy's death, Mota rushed to the hospital to see the boy but was prevented from entering the boy's room when he got there.[64] In 2008, a seven-year-old Illinois boy was placed in a medically-induced coma after being hit by a foul ball that fractured his skull. He later recovered.[65] In June 2010, a three-year-old girl suffered a fractured skull during Dodgers batting practice when Russell Martin hit a line drive into the stands. The girl had surgery and did recover. Martin was very upset by the accident and offered to pay all medical expenses for the young girl.

The Deadly Baseball Bat

Not only must fans be aware of balls coming into the stands, they also must watch for bats flying into the stands and the bats do not always arrive in one piece. Broken bats are common at baseball games. A batter may strike a ball and the bat may shatter into pieces and fly onto the playing field or in the stands. In August 2005, a Marlins fan suffered a ruptured spleen after being hit by a bat that was accidentally thrown into the stands. She was sitting behind the first-base line at a game between the Dodgers and Marlins with her husband and children when the bat of Dodgers outfielder Shawn Green sailed into the stands striking her in the side and injuring her.[66] Spectator Susan Rhodes suffered two fractures to the jaw at Dodger Stadium when a bat from Todd Helton "exploded" and struck her while she was seated in the stands.[67] Fan James Falzon filed a lawsuit against the New York Mets after being hit with parts of a shattered bat.[68] He suffered a split palate, facial fractures and some broken teeth as a result of the bat striking him.[69]

Major League Baseball has recently become concerned about the issue of fan safety from broken and shattered bats. From July to September 2008, there were 2,232 bats broken during major league games and 756 of those shattered into multiple pieces.[70] In 2009, MLB and the Players Association adopted nine recommendations made by the Safety and Health Advisory Committee of MLB which had investigated broken bat incidents.[71] The nine recommendations were adopted to reduce the frequency of bat failure.[72] Additionally, the Office of the Commissioner increased insurance limits from $5 million to $10 million for authorized bat suppliers of Major League Baseball.[73]

The Foul Ball and the Courts

Foul ball litigation has a long history in baseball as it seems spectators have always been litigious. For whatever reason, law professors and lawyers have had a fascination with the foul ball, penning numerous academic articles addressing foul ball litigation.[74] Odd facts make unique lawsuits and the foul ball has created its share of unusual legal decisions. Although it is the general rule that spectators assume the risk of batted and thrown balls and bats at baseball games, fans have still sued and some have prevailed, but most have not. In one of the earliest known baseball lawsuits in 1890, A.H. Potts sued a ball club after he was hit by a foul ball which broke his nose.[75] Potts was on his way to his seat when he was struck by the ball. Colonel Cook represented the club and argued that the "foul tip" had been made by a visiting batter. However, under intense questioning by Justice Cox, Colonel Cook confessed that the ball that hit the plaintiff Potts had actually been thrown by the pitcher of the home club.

In 1905, spectator Edward Velhmeyer sued the Washington Ball Club and its manager Malachi Kittridge after Velhmeyer had been struck by a foul ball off the bat of Kittridge.[76] Velhmeyer sustained severe injuries from the ball including a dislocated jaw. He sued for $300, arguing he lost two months of wages as well as damages for pain and suffering.[77] On November 14, 1905, Justice Gould in Criminal Court No. 2 ruled in favor of the defendants "upon the ground that a person attending games takes the risk of injury from being hit by baseballs which might fly from the field into the stands, unless the patron purchases a seat behind the wire screens."[78] The court's decision was deemed "a ruling of considerable importance to both baseball clubs and fans."[79] On January 31, 1913, Annie Dobkin filed a lawsuit against the Chicago National League Club, seeking $25,000 after being injured by a foul ball. A baseball sailed over the fence from West Side Park through the window of her home, striking her in the head where she was sitting in a chair.[80] The ball knocked her off her chair and caused partial paralysis, with her injuries lasting several months.[81] In February 1917, Ms. Magda Decker was injured when a foul ball struck her in the nose while she was attending a game at Browns Park.[82] She sued the St. Louis American League Club for $5,000.[83] On January 5, 1912, Miss Ruby Florsheim sued the Chicago Cubs for $10,000 after she was hit on the head by a foul ball when she attended a game during the 1911 season.[84] Mrs. Julie Fletcher was hit in the right eye by a foul ball on August 29, 1910, in the grandstands during a game in St. Louis.[85] She sued the club for $20,000.[86] She alleged she suffered permanent disfigurement as a result of the injury.[87]

There have been a line of cases where a spectator has been able to recover from a club. Spectator Charles Edling won a verdict against the Kansas City Club for $3,500 in May 1913 for injuries he suffered after he was hit by a foul ball.[88] He alleged that he suffered a broken nose and lost his eyesight as a result of the accident.[89] Then again, Mr. Edling was an attorney so maybe he had some insight other plaintiffs did not. Edling's ticket allowed him to sit anywhere in the park and he chose to sit behind the catcher so he could see the pitcher "curve the ball."[90] Edling purchased a ticket for 50 cents and sat behind the "catcher's box."[91] The area where he was seated was protected by chicken netting. The evidence at trial showed the ball went though a large hole in the netting, striking Edling in the face and breaking his nose. The hole the ball passed through was about a square foot in area.[92] The court estimated that about 700 balls are pitched in a game, with an average of ten percent of the balls "fouled off" by batters.[93]

The court of appeals found the club failed to keep the netting in good repair and upheld the verdict of the jury.[94] The club had argued that Mr. Edling was negligent for failing to dodge or catch the ball. Edling had said he was watching the game but failed to see the ball that hit him. In addressing the issue of whether his client was negligent, the lawyer for Mr. Edling stated: "If the Kansas City Blues had kept their eyes on the ball with the accuracy defendant says plaintiff should have displayed, they would have attained a higher place in the race for the pennant."[95]

In October 1925, Isabel McIntyre sued the Rochester Baseball Club for $5,000 when a foul ball broke her nose.[96] Ms. McIntyre was outside of the stadium waiting for a car when a foul ball sailed over the fence and injured her. It was reported as the first case of its kind on the record. Mildred Saxton was enjoying herself at a game at Sportsman Park in St. Louis in August 1937 when she was struck by a foul ball. However, an usher attempted to catch the ball first and was unsuccessful. The ball was deflected and struck Mrs. Saxton.[97] She sued the club and a jury returned a verdict in the favor of $4,500 against the St. Louis National Baseball Club.[98] In *Grimes v. American League Baseball Co.*,[99] another case at Sportsman Park, the plaintiff was struck in the eye by a batted ball. The matter went to trial in circuit court in St. Louis and a ten-member jury returned a verdict of $5,000 in favor of the spectator.[100] The plaintiff was injured on the last day of the regular season. At the time she was injured there were temporary boxes built in front of the grandstands to make room for the overflow crowds anticipated for the upcoming World Series set to begin in three days between the Cardinals and Philadelphia Athletics. She suffered injuries when a batted ball hit the railing of the temporary stands, deflecting the ball from its course and striking her in the eye.[101] The court of appeals upheld the jury's verdict, finding that because the plaintiff was only an occasional woman patron she was not fully aware of the risk of foul balls.

Spectators are not the only ones who may be injured at the ballpark by flying objects from the playing field. In *Cohen v. Sterling Mets, L.P.*,[102] the plaintiff was a concession vendor at Shea Stadium when he was struck by an enthusiastic fan who was diving for a shirt that had been "shot" into the stands between innings. The plaintiff argued he did not assume the risk of his injuries because "he was subject to an inherent compulsion to work despite misgivings about the safety of the t-shirt launch."[103] The court disagreed with the plaintiff and dismissed his case, ruling in favor of the Mets.

With so many foul ball lawsuits to choose from, it was a difficult task to select a representative case which best displayed liability issues for stadium owners. The *Schentzel* and *Benejam* cases both dealt with foul ball litigation which explored the legal issues of stadium owners. *Schentzel* dealt with a woman attending her first baseball game who was struck by a foul ball, while the *Benejam* case dealt with a four-year-old girl who suffered injuries after being hit by the shattered bat of Jose Canseco.

Schentzel v. Philadelphia National League Club[104]

On Sunday afternoon, June 5, 1949, Reba Schentzel and her husband traveled from Allentown, Pennsylvania, to historic Shibe Park in Philadelphia with great excitement to watch a baseball game. Mrs. Schentzel was about to attend her first two baseball games, a doubleheader between the Chicago Cubs and the Philadelphia Phillies. She did not see the second game of the doubleheader and would only see part of the first game. Unbeknownst to her, her first visit to the ballpark would result in a lawsuit and a subsequent Pennsylvania Superior Court decision which would provide lawyers with binding legal authority and became fodder for law students for many years to follow.

The doubleheader involved two struggling teams. It was still early in the season but the Cubs already were 16–25, in next to last place, 8 games off the lead, while the Phillies were hoping to break .500 with a win.[105] They were mired at 22–22, 3½ out of first place. Upon arriving at the park, the Schentzels saw a "tremendous crowd"[106] of fans at the ticket windows, all hoping for a beautiful day for the Sunday doubleheader. Mr. Schentzel got in the long line for tickets.[107] When he finally reached the ticket window, he purchased two tickets and was assured by the ticket clerk that the seats were "pretty good" and they were "back of the screen," as Mr. Schentzel requested.[108] As they made their way to their seats, the Schentzels must have thought the ticket seller was mistaken about the location of the seats. The seats were actually located in the upper stands on the first base side and were approximately 15 to 20 feet from the protective screening.[109] When they did finally reach their seats, it was about the sixth or seventh inning of the first game of the doubleheader. When Mr. Schentzel saw they were not in the protected area, he left to try to return the tickets. When he saw it would be impossible to do so because of the crowd, he quickly returned to his seat.[110] A minute or two after he returned to his seat, his wife was struck by a foul ball, causing her injuries.[111]

Mrs. Schentzel was 47 years old and had never been to a baseball game before the Cubs-Phillies doubleheader. She testified at the trial that she had seen games on television but had never seen a ball go into the stands and "knew nothing about it."[112] Alternatively, Mr. Schentzel was clearly aware of hazards of a baseball game, testifying on cross examination at the trial "there are a million foul balls, maybe three or four or five in an inning, [that go] into the stands."[113] The Schentzels filed a lawsuit against the Philadelphia Club for "trespass to personal injuries."[114] Mrs. Schentzel claimed damages for pain and suffering for the ball striking her in the head, and her husband sought damages for expenses that were incurred because of his wife's injuries as well as his own loss of consortium.[115] Mrs. Schentzel stated in her lawsuit that the club owed her a legal duty to provide for her safety, which also included taking "exceptional precautions" for women patrons.[116] She said this was necessary because many women were unaware of the hazards presented by the game. Therefore, the club should take exceptional precautions because many women are enticed to the ballpark by special invitation where they are admitted free to the game.[117] She said exceptional precautions would include extending the screening behind the catcher, while still leaving "a few sections" for spectators who would like to watch the game without looking through a screen.[118]

The case went to trial and, after presentation of all the evidence, the jury sided with the Schentzels, awarding them $500.[119] The club appealed the jury's verdict to the Pennsylvania Superior Court, which serves as an intermediate appellate court which hears appeals from Common Pleas Courts.[120]

The Superior Court called the lawsuit a case of "first impression" in Pennsylvania. Faced with a new legal issue, the court examined case law from other jurisdictions in arriving at its opinion.[121] The court noted the general duty of a premises liability owner:

> One who maintains a "place of amusement for which admissions is charged," is not an insurer, but must use reasonable care in the construction, maintenance, and management of it, having regard to the character of the exhibitions given and the customary conduct of patrons invited.[122]

The Superior Court found the jury's verdict to be "mere conjecture" and reversed in favor of the club. In overturning the jury's verdict, the court stated that "we think that as a matter of law plaintiff has failed to prove negligence on the part of the defendant, and that she must be charged with an implied assumption of the normal and ordinary risks incident to attendance at a baseball game."[123] The court said the plaintiff had presented no proof that screening a wider area of the park would have resulted in her sitting behind the screened area.[124] They also noted that plaintiff had failed to produce any evidence at trial to show the club's screening of the grandstands was different than the custom at other baseball parks.[125] The court stated that if a plaintiff fails to show that a defendant's conduct deviated from this ordinary standard, then the question of negligence should be dismissed and never heard by a jury.[126] The Pennsylvania Superior Court dismissed plaintiffs' arguments, stating if they adopted the plaintiffs' reasoning, the club would be required to always have a seat available behind the screen when a spectator requested one.[127]

The plaintiffs never claimed the screen was defective, only that it failed to extend far enough to prevent her injuries. The screen at Shibe Park on the day of Mrs. Schentzel's injuries protected almost all the seats in five sections of the upper stands and the lower stands as well.[128] The court found there was no evidence to show how many seats were behind the protected screen. Jury members were given very little evidence about proper screening by the plaintiff and were left to set their own standard for negligence, which they could not do under Pennsylvania law. The Superior Court noted that there were several other cases in which evidence had been presented dealing with the measures of screening and the number of seats behind the screen, but the Schentzels had failed to present such evidence and this was one of the failings of the lawsuit.[129]

The club argued that not only had the plaintiff failed to prove a negligence case against the club, but as a spectator she had also assumed the risk of being hit by balls that came into the stands. The court noted that while Mrs. Schentzel did not "expressly consent" to accept the hazards presented at the ballpark, consent could be implied from her conduct under the circumstances.[130] Because it was her first baseball game, Mrs. Schentzel argued she could not be deemed to have assumed the dangers presented at the ballpark.[131] The court did not agree with Mrs. Schentzel and said there was no indication she was of "inferior intelligence," had "subnormal perception," or that she had led a "cloistered life."[132] Therefore, she was presumed to have the "neighborhood knowledge" with which individuals living in an organized society are normally equipped[133]:

> We think the frequency with which foul balls go astray, alight in the grandstand or field, and are sometimes caught and retained by onlookers at baseball games is a matter of such common everyday practical knowledge as to be a subject of juridical notice. It strains our collective imagination to visualize the situation of the wife of a man obviously interested in the game, whose children view the games on the home television set, and who lives in a metropolitan community, so far removed from that knowledge as not to be chargeable with it.[134]

Facing certain defeat, Mrs. Schentzel stressed to the court that her husband had requested tickets for seats behind the screen but was prevented from exchanging them because of the crowded aisles at the ballpark.[135] The court said this fact may have been relevant if she had sued for breach of contract, but she had not pleaded that cause of action. The jury's verdict was overturned and the court entered judgment for the club.[136]

The Schentzels had no idea when they passed through the gates of Shibe Park in Philadelphia that beautiful Sunday afternoon of the events that would take place. A day at the ballpark was certainly no can of corn for the Schentzels of Allentown. The *Schentzel* case has continued to be cited numerous times by lawyers and courts as binding legal precedent.[137] The case also continues to be used by legal scholars to teach premises liability law at the ballpark.[138]

Benejam v. Detroit Tigers, Inc.[139]

Over fifty years after Mrs. Schentzel attended her first game, four-year-old Alyssa Benejam went to see her first baseball game in Tiger Stadium in Detroit. Alyssa, along with her family and some friends, was seated along the third-base line for a game against the Texas Rangers. Tiger Stadium, like all baseball stadiums, had a net behind home plate which extended part of the way down the first and third-base foul lines.[140] Alyssa was sitting behind the net, seemingly protected by flying objects coming from the field. A 56-foot wide net was protecting the area.[141] Alyssa was only 68 feet away from the plate.[142] During the game she was struck in the hand by a fragment of a bat that curved around the net.[143] The batter was Jose Canseco. Alyssa suffered crushed fingers and multiple injuries as a result of the accident. After the injury, Alyssa's left middle finger stopped growing and her ring finger began to grow at a 45-degree angle.

Alyssa and her parents sued the Detroit Club, arguing that the net behind home plate was not long enough and that the warnings that had been given by the Detroit Club on the day of the game were inadequate.[144] After the lawsuit was filed, the Tigers filed a motion for summary disposition to have the case dismissed before trial but the motion was denied by the court.[145] The parties attempted to settle the case but were unsuccessful. Just as the *Schentzel* case had done over fifty years before, the *Benejam* case went in front of a jury. The matter proceeded to trial in Wayne County Circuit Court in Detroit.[146] After deliberating, the jury returned a verdict of $914,000, the award including $56,700 for loss of earnings capacity and $35,000 for past and future medical expenses.[147] This verdict was a substantial victory for any plaintiff and under any circumstances was a major legal victory for a spectator. Just as the Schentzels had, the Benejam won their case in front of a jury. The club then appealed the jury's verdict.

On July 10, 2001, the Michigan Court of Appeals issued its opinion reversing the jury's verdict.[148] No Michigan case had ever addressed the specific legal issue presented to the court of appeals. The court framed the legal issue in the case as "[w]hether we should adopt, as a matter of Michigan law, the 'limited duty' rule that other jurisdictions have applied with respect to spectator injuries at baseball games."[149] The case was reduced to whether the court would adopt baseball's special limited duty rule which some other jurisdictions had adopted as their state law.

The court noted that under the limited duty rule a baseball stadium owner cannot be held liable for injuries suffered by spectators that occur from projectiles leaving the field of play "if safety screening has been provided behind home plate and there are a sufficient number of protected seats to meet ordinary demand."[150] The plaintiffs argued to the court that the traditional principles of premises liability law should apply, or, in other words, negligence law should be used to determine the liability of the defendant club. The plaintiffs said baseball should not have a special rule dealing with owner liability and urged the court against adopting the limited duty rule for baseball owners. They argued on appeal that the jury's verdict was supported by the evidence because the club had "failed to fulfill [its] duty because it did not provide a screen extending long enough along the third (and first) base lines."[151]

The Michigan Court of Appeals noted that many jurisdictions had adopted the limited duty rule.[152] The court found the logic behind the limited duty rule convincing, that spectators should understand there is an inherit danger of objects leaving the playing field when they attend a baseball game.[153] They also noted that fans want to see the game in an "intimate way" and some even come to the game hoping to catch a souvenir.[154] The court said spectators know about the risk of being in the stands and even welcome that risk.[155] However, the area behind home plate is especially dangerous and fans who desire a protected seat should be able to find them in this area. The court found that many courts have adopted the limited duty rule, which states no liability exists for the stadium owner if there are enough protected seats behind home plate to "meet the ordinary demand for that kind of seating. If that seating is provided, the baseball stadium owner has fulfilled its duty and there can be no liability for spectators who are injured by a projectile from the field."[156]

The court said the limited duty rule did not do away with the well-established principles of premises liability law but merely "identifie[d] the duty of baseball stadium proprietors with greater specificity than the usual 'ordinary care/reasonably safe' standard provides."[157] The stadium owner would still be bound to exercise reasonable care to protect its patrons against injuries. The limited duty rule merely establishes the "outer limits" of liability for a stadium owner.[158] The court also stated: "By providing greater specificity with regard to the duty imposed on stadium owners, the rule prevents burgeoning litigation that might signal the demise or substantial alteration of the game of baseball as a spectator sport."[159] The court noted that the limited duty rule relieves the owner of liability and frees it to accommodate those fans who want to see the game unobstructed.[160] If the court were to merely apply "invitor-invitee" principles, much more screening would be required.[161]

The court found there must be a balance between the interests of both the stadium owner and the spectators and that the limited duty rule struck that balance.[162] The court ruled:

> Specifically, we hold that a baseball stadium owner that provides screening behind home plate sufficient to meet ordinary demand for protected seating has fulfilled its duty with respect to screening and cannot be subjected to liability for injuries resulting to a spectator by an object leaving the playing field.[163]

The court then applied the rule to the facts in *Benejam* and said the plaintiff had failed to prove any liability on the part of the club.[164] There was a screen behind home plate and there was no proof presented that fans who wanted to sit behind the screened area could not have been accommodated.[165] The court found the screening to be adequate under the limited duty rule.[166]

The court next turned to the plaintiff's claim that the defendants failed to provide adequate warnings that objects may come flying into the stands. The court of appeals quickly dismissed this claim, saying defendant had no duty to warn of a "well known risk." The court said it would be inconsistent to impose a duty upon the stadium owner to warn of well known risk when in fact the idea of a spectator understanding the full nature of the risk was the basis of the limited duty rule.[167]

The plaintiffs appealed the court of appeals ruling to the Michigan Supreme Court but it was under no legal obligation to hear the case and declined to do so. After the ruling, the plaintiffs' attorney, James Elliott, commented that the Michigan Court of Appeals had adopted a new standard in its ruling that had no basis whatsoever in Michigan law and was inconsistent with the testimony at trial.[168]

The *Benejam* decision is a well-recognized legal opinion which has been cited numerous times by courts, parties, and lawyers across multiple jurisdictions.[169] Just as with *Schentzel*, *Benejam* became a seminal case exploring the liability of the baseball stadium owner. The case has also become a topic for academics exploring the relationship of tort law and the foul ball.[170]

The *Benejam* case has been followed by many jurisdictions; however, a recent case in Connecticut distinguished the case by carving out an exception to the *Benejam* decision. In *Mantovani v. Yale University*,[171] the plaintiff was struck by a batted ball on July 29, 2003, while participating in a cookout in the right-field pavilion at a minor league game. The ball hit the plaintiff in the eye and he suffered substantial injuries. The defendants sought to have the claim dismissed based on the limited duty rule. The court denied the defendant's motion to have the case dismissed, holding that the limited duty rule applied only to injuries occurring in the stands.[172] Because the plaintiff was in a place in the stadium operated by the club that encouraged fans to engage "in activities inconsistent with paying close attention to the action on the field," the court found the limited duty rule inapplicable under the circumstances.[173]

Conclusion

Baseball's ubiquitous foul ball has led to both triumph and tragedy. From a legal standpoint it is very difficult to win a lawsuit against a stadium owner for injuries caused by a foul ball. There have been some recoveries for injuries but those cases usually have involved exceptional circumstances. The general rule of law states that fans assume all risks associated with the playing of the game and that includes a foul ball. Baseball is a pastime. Fans are not necessarily intensely watching the action on the field at all times, although they should. Owners have created numerous diversions at the ballpark over the last few years for fans ranging from pesky mascots, exploding scoreboards (thanks mainly to Bill Veeck), the always annoying "t-shirt cannon," fan giveaways, televisions in the seats, and much more! Stadium owners are instructed by legal counsel not to distract the fans from the play on the field. If they do, legal liability may result. Some good legal and practical advice for the baseball fan may be to keep your eye on the ball!

13

C.B.C. Distribution and Marketing v. Major League Baseball Advanced Media[1]
Baseball's Battle for the Box Score: A Constitutional Question

> JANE AUBREY: Do you lose very much?
> BILLY CHAPEL: I lose. I've lost 134 times.
> JANE AUBREY: You count them?
> BILLY CHAPEL: We count everything.[2] — *For Love of the Game* (1999)

> Statistics are kept on every aspect of the game imaginable. — Court of Appeals of California, 2001

> Some people could do without the games as long as they got the box scores. — John M. Culkin, *New York Times,* 1976

> They both (statistics and bikinis) show a lot, but not everything. — Toby Harrah, infielder

Introduction

It's the bottom of the eighth inning in a game late in September between the Padres and Pirates and both teams are well out of the pennant race. Some 7,000 fans are left from the 13,000 or so that originally filed in to watch two teams with sub-par records go at it. A Pirates batter drills a single to center, scoring his teammate from second base and drawing the Pirates closer at 9–4. A few fans give a forced cheer to the activities yet thousands of others not present at the game give collective groans as the runner scores because the ERA of the Braves pitcher just went up. Such is the life of the fantasy baseball manager.

Baseball's Love for the Numbers

When Henry Chadwick invented the box score in the 1850s, it is probably safe to say that he did not envision that the statistical data contained in a box score would become the subject of a constitutional debate over 150 years later — but it did.³ The box score tells a story of every game. The statistics compiled in the box score reveal the performance of each player, the attendance of the game, the umpires, who played and at what position, how long the game took to play, and a myriad of other interesting facts. Baseball's box score has appeared in America's newspapers since the 1860s.⁴ One wonders if Chadwick would recognize the modern box score or what he would think about statistics such as WHIP,⁵ the HOLD,⁶ and BABIP.⁷ The baseball fan has always had a fascination for the baseball statistic. No other sport worships statistics and numbers like baseball. Numerous books have been written on baseball statistics and the use of statistics in the game.⁸ In no other sport do fans memorize and regurgitate statistics like baseball.⁹ In baseball, there is the 3,000 hit club, the .300 hitter, the 300 win club, and the 500 home run club. Players are categorized as a "30–30" or "40–40" player. Baseball has a long history of famous numbers. Some have become part of baseball culture and mystique. Baseball aficionados know of Ted Williams's .406 batting average, Joe DiMaggio's 56-game hitting streak, Bob Gibson's 1.12 ERA, Cal Ripken's 2,131 consecutive game streak, and Babe Ruth's lifetime home run total of 714. Baseball statistics provide fans with endless material for debate over the details of the game. Ty Cobb's lifetime average has been the subject of debate.¹⁰ Hack Wilson's single season record for RBIs was changed from 190 to 191 in 1999, 69 years after he set the record in 1930.¹¹ You might say who cares. Suffice it to say, many people do. Baseball is also the only sport where player positions are designated as a number for the official scorer, such as is in 6–4–3 double-play. Fans have kept score at baseball games for over one hundred years. Fans scoring the game are unique to baseball. Scorecards are still given out in programs at the game for the hardcore fan who wants to keep the score of the game and many fans still keep score of games broadcast over the radio as well.

"Sabermetrics"¹² is a way of looking at baseball statistics that has challenged the traditional way of examining baseball statistics. Sabermetrics created new statistical tools and developed new ways of thinking about batting, fielding, and many other categories of baseball performance.¹³ Bill James is considered to be the founder of sabermetrics and also seen by many as baseball's preeminent statistical scholar. James took a revolutionary approach to the use of statistics in baseball, analyzing and studying them in an effort to determine why clubs win or lose. In 2006, *Time Magazine* named him one of the 100 most influential people in the world. When he first began writing about baseball, James's articles were a little esoteric even for the hard-core baseball fan, so he published his own 80-page book, *The Bill James Baseball Abstract*.[14] The book was his analysis of box scores from the preceding season. James's evaluation of baseball statistics reinvented the game for many players and managers. James is now a senior advisor of baseball operations for the Boston Red Sox.

The History of Playing Baseball Games

Since the origin of baseball it seems that people have always been interested in playing baseball games. Baseball's preoccupation with statistics and data led naturally to baseball board games or table-top games. Baseball games long have involved cards, dice, spinners, charts, and miniature bats and balls, and finally, evolved to computer games. Some of the baseball games invented have detailed rules of strategy for the players while other games are governed by just plain luck. Early baseball saw its share of games, including *Home Baseball Game* produced by the McLoughlin Brothers (1886).[15] The Baseball Hall of Fame had a 2008 exhibit dedicated to antique baseball games, entitled "Home Games: A Century of Baseball Games from the Collection of Dr. Mark Cooper."[16] One of the items in the exhibit was a game which is considered to be the oldest existing baseball game, *The New Parlor Game of Base Ball* from 1869.[17] Also on display was *League Parlor Base Ball* of 1884, which was the first game to use dice in the playing of the game. The renowned board game maker, Parker Brothers, produced its first baseball game in 1890, *The Champion Game of Base Ball*, which featured Hall of Fame players John Clarkson[18] and Dan Brouthers.[19] Other games include *Zimmer's Base Ball Game* (1893) and *Major League Indoor Base Ball* (1912), which used a spinner as part of the game. *National Pastime* (1930) was the first game to use player statistics in a game. Players could simulate the playing of a baseball game by using actual statistics on cards that represented MLB players. The game allowed participants to choose line-ups from actual major league games and with the use of dice and a spinner make baseball game decisions similar to big league managers. Two of the best known games in the 1950s were *APBA Baseball* (1951)[20] and *Strat-o-Matic* (1961).[21] These games were more sophisticated than their predecessors, allowing trades, all-star teams, and game participants to play alone or against others. These games, as well as many others, including *Negamco Major League Baseball* and *Big League Manager,* allowed participants to calculate their own statistics.[22]

Baseball games proved early on that the name of a player had value. Many famous players throughout history have had a baseball game associated with their name. Parker Brothers had a baseball game for Napoleon Lajoie (1913). Other famous players who had baseball games named after them included Christy Mattewson (1922), Ty Cobb (1924), Lou Gehrig with *Lou Gehrig's Official Playball* (1932), Jimmie Foxx with the *Jimmie Foxx Baseball Game*,[23]

Carl Hubbell,[24] Dizzy and Daffy Dean with the *Official Dizzy and Daffy Dean Nok-Out Baseball Game*,[25] Jackie Robinson with the *Jackie Robinson Baseball Game* (1948),[26] Roger Maris with *Roger Maris Action Baseball* (1962),[27] Denny McLain with the *Official Denny McLain Electric Baseball*,[28] Rocky Colavito with *Rocky Colavito's Own Baseball Dart Game*,[29] Willie Mays with *Willie Mays "Say Hey" Baseball Game*,[30] Johnny Bench with *Johnny Bench Electric Baseball Game*,[31] and Jose Canseco with *Jose Canseco's Perfect Baseball Game*.[32]

The Business of Fantasy Sports

Fantasy sports games are games where fantasy "owners" build a team through a draft or trades, and then compete with other fantasy owners in either "head to head" competition or in a rotisserie league. In fantasy sports the owner has the ability to trade, cut, and sign players to a roster similar to a real club owner. The results of the competition are based on the actual statistics that are generated by the players over the course of the season. Statistical performance of the players is calculated using the categories agreed to by league members and whoever has the most points at the end of the competition is the victor. Many leagues have a "commissioner" who performs the calculations and other "commissioner-like" duties in running the league. Of course, since it is a competition, there will be the inevitable rhubarb between owners. However, the good news is there are companies that will resolve fantasy league disputes for a small fee.[33]

Baseball is the longest running form of fantasy sports and also the most time intensive due to the 162-game schedule played by each major league team, although some fantasy leagues play shorter seasons. Baseball is not the only fantasy sport available to the fan. There are a myriad of fantasy games people can play depending on their interests. The four major sports are available—baseball, football (American), basketball, and hockey—but other fantasy sports include football (soccer), NASCAR, golf, fishing, wrestling,[34] major league lacrosse, Australian Rules Football, tennis, cricket, boxing, skiing (snow and water), fantasy Olympics, and yes, even fantasy badminton.[35] The fantasy league concept has also expanded outside the realm of sport. There are now fantasy leagues for celebrities, an American Idol fantasy league, a fantasy parliament league where participants create their own party and enter the electoral system, and Fantasy Congress.[36] In Fantasy Congress the players are called "citizens" and draft members of the U.S. House of Representatives and Senate, keeping track of their participation in Congress.

The first fantasy baseball game may have begun in the spring of 1960 when sociologist William Gamson introduced his new game to colleagues at the Harvard School of Public Health.[37] He called the game *Baseball Seminar*. The participants bid on players through a mail auction and at the end of the season declared a winner based on players' performance statistics.[38] Gamson left the Ivy League for the University of Michigan, bringing his game along with him.[39] The fantasy league at Michigan was called the "Assistant Professors League" or, for those with lesser status, "The Untenured Faculty League."[40] One of the professors in the league was Bob Sklar, who had a student, Daniel Okrent, who fell in love with the game.[41] Okrent is now widely recognized as the inventor of rotisserie baseball, now primarily referred to as fantasy baseball.[42] Okrent became a writer for *Sports Illustrated* and in the early 1980s ate regularly with friends at a La Rotisserie franchise in Manhattan. He and nine friends started the Rotisserie League Baseball Association.[43] Many of the original league participants were members of the New York media so the idea of the game spread quickly. Okrent was retained as an expert witness in *C.B.C. Distribution and Marketing, Inc. v. Major League Baseball Advanced Media, L.P.* and under oath stated: "I am widely recognized as the inventor of the first well-known fantasy baseball league, called Rotisserie League Baseball. I first wrote down the idea on a scratch piece of paper while on an airplane flight to Austin, Texas, during the 1979–1980 off-season."[44] Many famous people began to play rotisserie baseball. One of the most famous was former President Richard Nixon who was a big baseball fan. His son-in-law, David Eisenhower, was the "owner" and President Nixon was the "general manager" of their rotisserie team.[45] Another famous fantasy player was noted author Jack Kerouac, who played his own version of fantasy baseball in the 1960s.[46]

Fantasy sports have become a worldwide multi-million dollar industry. The Fantasy Trade Sports Association (FTSA), which deems itself "the voice of the fantasy sports industry," estimates twenty-seven million adults play fantasy sports.[47] With an economic impact of almost $2 billion a year and the average fan spending $150 a year to participate, fantasy sports is clearly a burgeoning industry and professional sports leagues understand that as well.[48] Fantasy baseball's estimated revenues are $1.5 billion.[49] With that figure in mind it is easy to see how the Players Association was interested in retrieving as much revenue from the fantasy industry for its players as possible. Fantasy baseball has grown to be a huge industry and, with the advance of the Internet, has gained astounding popularity among fans of all ages. Throughout the 1990s and into the 2000s, the fantasy sports industry saw phenomenal growth in the number of websites offering fantasy services, the number of participants, and revenue.[50] Many Internet sites, including ESPN.com, CBS Sportsline, and Yahoo! Sports, provided full scale services to fantasy fans, including online drafts and statistical calculations. The Internet was able to immediately provide the fantasy addict with up-to-date statistics instead of having to wait for the next day's newspaper.[51] The growing fantasy industry in baseball caught the eye of the Players Association which continued to see it as a great licensing opportunity for major league players.

The Right of Publicity

The right of publicity is the "inherent right of every human being to control the commercial use or his or her identity."[52] The right of publicity is derived from the right of privacy.[53] Entertainers, celebrities, and athletes are paid millions of dollars from companies who want them to endorse their products and that identity must be protected so it is not diluted and continues to be valuable. The right of publicity is infringed upon when a party, without consent, uses the commercial value of another's identity. The right of privacy is a creation of state law and has now been adopted as law by over one-half of the states. The right of publicity protects athletes and entertainers as well as others whose identity has been exploited for commercial value.[54] The first case to recognize the right of publicity was a case dealing with baseball players. In *Haelan Laboratories, Inc. v. Topps Chewing Gum, Inc.*,[55] the federal second circuit court of appeals held that professional baseball players had a "right of publicity" in their photographs that were used on baseball cards.[56] The U.S. Supreme Court has addressed the right of publicity in only one case, *Zacchini v. Scripps-Howard Broadcasting Co.*[57] In that case a performer brought a lawsuit when his act, the "human cannonball," was shown on television. The court held in Zacchini's favor, stating that the right of publicity protects an individual's interest to "reap the rewards of his endeavors."[58]

The Players Association and the Right to Publicity

The Players Association has an obligation to its members to maximize and explore new avenues for revenues for players. The Association was formed in 1953 and in 1965 they appointed their first full-time executive director, Wisconsin Circuit Court Judge Robert C. Cannon. Marvin Miller and Hall of Fame pitcher Bob Feller also applied for the job but Cannon was selected. However, Cannon would never take the post, declining the position once he realized he would have to surrender his judgeship, so Marvin Miller was finally selected.

Through the leadership of Miller, the Players Association struck its first licensing deal with Coca-Cola, who purchased the right to place the players' pictures under its bottle caps. After the agreement with Coca Cola was in place, the players entered into an agreement with Topps, a baseball card company. Topps would typically have individual ball players sign long-term contracts for a flat fee, allowing Topps to use the image of a player on a baseball card. The Players Association sought to maximize revenues for players by identifying the entities that were using the pictures and names of MLB players without the consent of the Association and seeking a licensing agreement with the entity. Until 1967, players' names, statistics, and likenesses had been used in games without having to pay the players. In January 1967, the Players Association sent letters to the leading manufacturers of simulation baseball games stating the manufacturer was infringing upon the property rights of players and offering to license the names and images of the players.[59]

The Right of Publicity — Baseball Cases

The right of publicity doctrine has been explored in conjunction with baseball players in several different cases that involve some of the greatest names in baseball. A quick overview of some cases shows the evolutionary process of the right of publicity dealing with baseball players.

In *Pirone v. MacMillan Inc.*,[60] the daughters of Babe Ruth filed a lawsuit against the publisher of a baseball calendar based on several legal theories, including the infringement of Ruth's common law right of privacy. The calendar included three photos relating to Ruth. One showed Ruth helping a young boy with his batting grip, another picture showed Ruth saluting General John J. Pershing, and the final photograph was of a baseball autographed by Ruth. The court dismissed the daughters' lawsuit on behalf of their famous father because New York law limited the right of publicity protection to "any living person."[61]

In *Newcombe v. Adolf Coors Company*,[62] former major league great Don Newcombe filed a lawsuit against Coors for violation of his right of publicity under California law.[63] Killian's Irish Red Beer, owned by Coors, published an advertisement in the 1994 *Sports Illustrated* swimsuit issue that featured the drawing of an old-time baseball game. The drawing appeared on the left side of the page while the right side had some text and a picture of a glass of beer. The advertisement showed a baseball scene with a pitcher in the windup position and the background of the picture showed one fielder and an old-fashioned outfield fence. The players' uniform did not indicate a team nor did the picture indicate the location of the game. However, Newcombe, along with his former teammates, family, and friends, immediately recognized the pitcher in the advertisement as himself. Newcombe was incensed by the advertisement because he was a recovering alcoholic and had devoted many hours to speaking about the dangers of alcohol.[64] Coors admitted that the drawing was based on a 1949 newspaper photograph of Newcombe pitching in the 1949 World Series. The only major difference between the newspaper photograph and the advertisement was that the pitcher's number had been changed from 36 to 39 and the bill of the hat was a different color from the rest of the cap.[65] Otherwise, the advertisement was identical to the newspaper photograph.

The legal question before the court was to what degree did the plaintiff

(Newcombe) have to be "identifiable" from the alleged likeness (in this case the advertisement in *Sports Illustrated*) for the court to rule the plaintiff's "identity" was taken? The standard the court used was that a photograph must be "readily identifiable" as the plaintiff to recover under a right of publicity claim. The court said this standard was specified by the California statute: "when one who views the photograph with the naked eye can reasonably determine that the person depicted in the photograph is the same person who is complaining of its unauthorized use."[66] In essence, would people think Don Newcombe was the pitcher in the advertisement?

Defendant Coors argued that a player's stance alone could not meet the "readily identifiable" standard but the court disagreed. The court noted that Newcombe was the only player with the particular stance depicted in the advertisement. Interestingly, the defendant had at one time thought of using Giants pitcher Juan Marichal in the advertisement because he had such a distinctive windup. Marichal had one of the most distinctive windups of any major league pitcher in the history of the game with his "patented" high leg kick. Coors eventually chose not to use Marichal because his windup would have easily identified him. The court said this operated as an admission by the defendant that a pitcher's windup could be in fact be "distinctive." The court also said that in addition to the stance, Newcombe was also identifiable because the pitcher's skin in the advertisement was "moderately dark," which they said was "quite similar to Newcombe's skin color." Even though his facial features were not entirely visible, the court said a jury could rationally determine the advertisement was indeed Newcombe.

In *Gionfriddo v. Major League Baseball*,[67] the four plaintiffs were Albert Gionfriddo,[68] Adolph L. Camilli,[69] Frankie R. Crosetti,[70] and Peter J. Coscarat.[71] The plaintiffs had appeared in their share of all-star games and World Series. Because of their many accomplishments, MLB had included their names and statistics along with other former players in All-Star game and World Series programs for many years as well as producing the information on its website, mlbworldseries.com. Their names appeared in lists of player awards and their pictures in video and photographs. The plaintiffs asserted these uses by MLB were unauthorized and violated their right of publicity and claimed damages from the use of their likenesses. In its ruling, the court said: "The First Amendment requires that the right to be protected from unauthorized publicity 'be balanced against the public interest in the dissemination of news and information consistent with the democratic processes under the constitutional guaranties of freedom of speech and of the press.'"[72] The court noted that the precise information being conveyed by MLB was factual data dealing with the players, their performance statistics, and verbal and video descriptions of their play. The court categorized this information as "mere bits of baseball history,"[73] identifying it as names of players included on All-Star and World Series rosters; descriptions of memorable performances from former games included within All-Star and World Series game programs created for the benefit of the media and the enjoyment of the fans; photographs and video clips taken of plaintiffs when they were playing the game themselves, and made available to the public through Web sites, home videos, and other programs presenting historic events from long ago. In short, they are fragments from baseball's mosaic.[74]

The court in ruling for MLB stated baseball was followed by millions of people on a daily basis and that baseball fans "have an abiding interest in the history of the game." They further noted that the viewing public has a fascination with records set by former players and that "[s]tatistics are kept on every aspect of the game imaginable."[75] The records and statistics are a major interest to public because they allow fans "to better appreciate (or deprecate) today's performances."[76] A history of professional baseball is integral to a fan's full understanding and enjoyment of the current game and its players. The court said that MLB was merely using historical facts that were available to the general public through game programs, websites, and video clips. The court found that there was a "substantial public interest" in the athletic performance of baseball players. It ruled that the league's use of players' names, voices, signatures, photographs, and likenesses on websites and in game day programs was protected by the First Amendment, and so the court dismissed the players' lawsuit.

In *Cardtoons, L.C. v. MLBPA*,[77] Cardtoons produced and marketed trading cards that were a parody of active Major League Baseball players. The trading cards parodied players with a variety of humorous and insightful themes. One of the most notable cards depicted baseball's all-time stolen base leader Rickey Henderson as "Egotisticky Henderson." The card featured a caricature of Henderson raising his finger in a "number one" sign while simultaneously patting himself on the back.[78] Cardtoons sued the MLBPA[79] seeking a court ruling that they had not violated the MLBPA's publicity rights. The 10th Circuit Court of Appeals held in favor of Cardtoons, finding that the players' rights of publicity were outweighed by the First Amendment right in producing the information.

In another right of publicity case, *Brooks v. The Topps Company*,[80] the daughter of James Thomas Bell, aka James "Cool Papa" Bell, sued the Topps Card Company, claiming it had used Bell's "name, likeness, signature, intellectual property rights and publicity rights"[81] without consent. She also sued Topps for defamation.[82] Bell was a famous player in the Negro Leagues and was well known for his blazing speed. His good friend Satchel Paige once remarked that Bell was so fast he could turn out the lights and be in bed before it was dark.[83] In 2001 and 2004, without authorization from Brooks, Topps released seven baseball cards depicting Bell. The court dismissed Brooks's lawsuit under the right of publicity statute because she failed to file the case within the one-year statute of limitations required under New York law. The parties later settled the litigation for an undisclosed amount.

The Battle Over Fantasy Games

The Major League Baseball Players Association represents the interests of major league baseball players, including the highly lucrative areas of sponsorships and licensing. With the explosion of the Internet in 2000, the owners of several major league teams created Major League Baseball Media, L.P. (Advanced Media) to provide interactive media for Major League Baseball and to operate its website, MLB.com. Advanced Media offered licenses for online fantasy providers. In January 2005, MLBPA and Advanced Media entered into a five-year, $50 million exclusive agreement which allowed Advanced Media to market the personal identities of MLB players through interactive media.[84] The agreement gave them "a license to use rights and trademarks for exploitation via all interactive media."[85] The agreement gave Advanced Media the exclusive rights to use and sublicense to other entities the rights of major league players for online games and all wireless applications, including games for all cell phones. By entering into this agreement, MLBPA was attempting to capitalize on the increasing interest in fantasy games and hopefully create more revenue and marketing opportunities for MLB players. After they entered into the 2005 agreement, Advanced Media sent a request for proposals to prospective providers to enter into a licensing agreement with Advanced Media which would allow providers to participate in Advanced Media's fantasy baseball licensing program. Before MLBPA had given Advanced Media an exclusive license to market the identities of MLB players, there had been more than one hundred fantasy providers. Advanced Media increased the minimum licensing fee from $25,000 to $2 million. This exorbitant increase in the licensing fee essentially priced almost all providers out of the market except for the top three: CBS Sportsline, ESPN, and Yahoo! Advanced Media did offer to provide sublicenses to smaller companies who sold fantasy products but they would have to agree to limit their membership to 5,000 members.

CBC Distribution and Marketing sold fantasy sports products including fantasy baseball via the Internet. CBC had entered into licensing agreements with the MLBPA from July 1, 1995, to December 2004 for the use of the "Players Rights." A second agreement was entered into in 2002 extending the license to 2004. The agreement stated that upon termination, CBC would have no further rights to "player rights" and should discontinue their use after the agreement. On February 4, 2005, Advanced Media offered CBC a license to promote fantasy games on the CBC website, under the umbrella of Advanced Media, for a percentage of the revenue generated by the games.⁸⁶ CBC did not waste any time, filing a lawsuit just three days later on February 7, 2005, against Advanced Media.⁸⁷ CBC sought a declaratory judgment, alleging it had a "reasonable apprehension" of being sued by Advanced Media because CBC intended to continue operating fantasy games on its website using player names and statistics. Advanced Media filed a counterclaim against CBC alleging a breach of the 2002 licensing agreement between the parties and further asserting that CBC had violated the players' right of publicity.⁸⁸ The parties had stated their legal positions and the court's legal decision was much anticipated.

The U.S. Federal District Court of Missouri summarized the legal issues they were called upon to decide as

> whether the players have a right of publicity in their names and playing records as used in CBC's fantasy games; whether, if the players have such a right, CBC has, and is, violating the players' claimed right of publicity; whether, if the players have a right of publicity and if this right has been violated by CBC, such a violation is preempted by copyright law; whether, if the players have a right of publicity which has been violated by CBC, the First Amendment applies and, if so, whether it takes precedence over the players' claimed right of publicity; and whether CBC has breached the 2002 Licensing Agreement.⁸⁹

Although the issues may have seemed convoluted they were relatively simple: Who owned professional performance statistics in Major League Baseball?⁹⁰ Although the right of publicity and First Amendment arguments were the primary issues presented to the court, other interesting legal issues of copyright law and breach of contract were also analyzed and would be addressed by the Federal District Court as well as the Federal Court of Appeals.

Federal District Court, CBC Distribution and Marketing v. Advanced Media⁹¹

Before the case ever made it to a jury, it was brought before the Federal District Court on a motion for summary judgment by CBC. CBC hoped the judge would rule in its favor without the necessity of a trial and decide that CBC could use players' names and statistics in its fantasy games. The court did find in favor of CBC, granting a declaratory judgment in its favor. The court found that Advanced Media failed to prove its right of publicity claim and therefore the players' rights of publicity were not violated.

The court noted that Missouri law did recognize the right of publicity. The court said the elements of a right of publicity claim are "(1) that defendant used plaintiff's name as a symbol of his identity (2) without consent (3) and with the intent to obtain a commercial advantage."⁹² The court first discussed whether the use of the players' names was a "symbol of their identity." The court said it was significant to examine exactly how the players' names were used rather than the mere fact that the names were used.[93] The court said not all uses of another person's name are considered tortious, but to prevail in a right of publicity action "the name must be used as a symbol of the plaintiff's identity."[94] The district court compared the use of the players' names in the fantasy games to a case of a hockey player, a well-known National Hockey League enforcer, Tony Twist. In *Doe v. TCI Cablevision*,[95] a character in the Spawn comic book series was named after NHL tough man Tony Twist. Todd McFarlane created a "mob-like" character named Antonio "Tony Twist" Twistelli who McFarlane later acknowledged he named after Twist. A Missouri court found in favor of Twist after examining the "nature and extent of the identifying characteristics used by the defendant...."[96] The Missouri Court of Appeals upheld a $15 million jury verdict in favor of Twist.[97] In contrast to the Tony Twist case, the court in *CBC* found that the fantasy owners' use of players' names in conjunction with their playing statistics did not violate the players' rights of publicity. It said the use of the players' names did not involve the "character, personality, reputation or physical appearance of the players" as it had in the Twist case, but merely used "historical facts" about the players like "batting averages, home runs, doubles, triples, etc."[98] The use did not involve "the persona or identity of any player."[99] The Players Association had failed to establish the first element of their claim for the violation of their right of publicity. The second element of their claim was met because it was agreed that CBC used the information without the consent of Advanced Media.

The court then turned to the third element of the players' right of publicity claim, whether the use of the players' names constituted a "commercial use." In examining the "commercial element" of the right of publicity claim, the court said that using a plaintiff's name "to attract attention to a product" was clear evidence that the defendant was in fact obtaining a commercial advantage through the use of the plaintiff's name. However, the court found in favor of the fantasy owners on the third element of the right of publicity claim as well, stating "there is nothing about CBC's fantasy games which suggests that any Major League baseball player is associated with CBC's games or that any player endorses or sponsors the games in any way."[100]

The court said the use of the names by CBC was not intended to attract customers from other fantasy games because all fantasy games use MLB players' names and statistics. Furthermore, there was no reason to think that customers would believe that the players endorsed CBC's fantasy baseball game. Advanced Media argued they should have prevailed under the analysis of *Palmer v. Schonhorn Enterprises*.[101] That case dealt with golfing great Arnold Palmer and other golfers whose names, pictures, and playing records were used in a board game without a licensing agreement. The defendant sold a game called *Pro-AM Golf* which included short biographies of 23 golfers. Each profile contained facts about the career of the golfer. The defendant claimed the information contained in the game was easily obtained public data available to all and they were free to use such data. The court found in favor of Palmer and the other golfers, stating: "It is unfair that one should be permitted to commercialize or exploit or capitalize upon another's name, reputation or accomplishments merely because the owner's accomplishments have been highly publicized."[102]

Advanced Media and the Players Association also relied upon *Uhlaender v. Henricksen*[103] in arguing they should prevail on their right of publicity claim. In that case, the defendants sold a game, *Negamco's Major League Baseball*. The game used eight player statistics such as batting average, ERA, and other statistical averages of 500 to 700 major league players.[104] The players were identified by team, uniform number, and the players' position.[105] At the time of the *Uhlaender* lawsuit, the MLBPA had 27 agreements for group licenses, including four or five which called for payments of 5 percent of gross sales with a minimum royalty of $2,500 per year. The licensing agreements earned in excess of $400,000 income in 1969.[106] James (Jim) Katt and James (Jim) Perry both testified at the trial they believed their names had financial value and that they never consented to the use of their name or likeness by Negamco.[107] The MLBPA wrote a letter informing the defendant that it was violating a property right of the players and offering to enter into a licensing agreement with Negamco.[108] The defendant's legal position in *Uhlaender* was the same as that asserted by the defendants in *Palmer*: that the data in the board game was readily available to everyone and was published extensively in newspapers and the media. The court in *Uhlaender* relied upon *Palmer* in finding in favor of the MLB players. The court found that a celebrity has a legitimate proprietary interest in his or her public personality regardless of whether the information is readily available to all through the media.[109] The district court entered an injunction against the owners of Negamco, but it continued to manufacture the game with some minor changes. The next year Negamco's player cards contained only statistics from the previous year and did not have player names on the cards. The cards had short blank lines, one for each of the player's first and last names. "Owners" could easily identify the players by their previous year statistics and merely fill in the player's name in the blanks on the card. Notwithstanding the creativity of Negamco's owners, the Players Association took no further action against Negamco.

Advanced Media had presented to the court what it believed were two cases that were binding legal precedent, both of which had found in favor of the players. Although the players had won legal victories in *Palmer* and *Uhlaender,* the district court in *CBC* found the plaintiff's reliance on these cases to be unpersuasive. The court acknowledged that while *Palmer* had some similarities to the fantasy games case before it, in *Palmer* the defendant had used the golfers' pictures, while the fantasy leagues had merely used the statistics produced by the players. Furthermore, the court said *Palmer* was decided in 1967 and was "inconsistent" with the most recent case dealing with the right of publicity, *Zacchini v. Scripps-Howard Broadcasting Co.* It found *Palmer* was "not controlling" because it did not "accurately reflect" the current state of the law of the right of publicity. The court also noted that *Uhlaender* was decided in the early stages of development of the doctrine of right of publicity and was therefore unpersuasive as well.

The court also addressed whether the defendant's use of players' names was in violation of the policy considerations behind the right of publicity.[110] The court actually said that CBC's use of players' names and statistics increased the marketability of players.[111] Former President Richard Nixon would have been a great expert witness for the fantasy owners on this issue. His son-in law, David Eisenhower, said when he and the former president went to see the Yankees play the Angels they did not really care who won but were more concerned about the players on their rotisserie teams so they could move up in the standings.[112]

The case would never reach a jury. The United States District Court for the Eastern District of Missouri granted summary judgment to CBC.[113] The court found that CBC had not violated the players' right of publicity under Missouri common law. The court also found that CBC had a First Amendment right to use the names and statistics of MLB players and that this right trumped the players' rights of publicity. Even though the district court found the players had not established a violation of their right of publicity, it chose to consider other legal issues presented to it.[114] First, whether the First Amendment would defeat the players' claimed rights of publicity (assuming the players proved a right of publicity claim), and second, whether federal copyright law preempted the players' right of publicity claim as CBC had argued.[115]

With regard to the first issue, the district court found that CBC's use of players' names and statistics was entitled to First Amendment protection. The court found that player names and statistics were historical facts covered by the First Amendment and just because CBC was making a profit on fantasy games did not preclude it from First Amendment protection. It found that although CBC's use of players' names and statistics on a website was a "less traditional" form of expression, it was still entitled to First Amendment protection. It also found that the First Amendment applied to speech that was "entertaining" [116] and interactive.[117] Advanced Media argued that because the "speech" was of a commercial nature the First Amendment was inapplicable. The court found the speech was not "commercial speech" because it did not use the players' names and statistics to advertise a product or service.

After determining that the First Amendment was applicable, the court next engaged in "Balancing CBC's First Amendment Right of Freedom of Expression with the Players' Right of Publicity."[118] The district court found

13. Baseball's Battle for the Box Score

that if in fact the players did have a right of publicity, it would have been defeated by CBC's First Amendment Right to freedom of expression. Part of the rationale supporting a claim for right of publicity is to give performers, ballplayers in this case, an incentive to perform well. The court found the incentive argument uncompelling, saying that ballplayers had an incentive to perform based on their player contract, not whether they profited from their use of their names or statistics in fantasy games. The court relied upon *Gionfriddo*, stating that the public has a substantial interest in the names, playing records, and history of baseball.

The district court also addressed the copyright argument advanced by CBC even though it was unnecessary in light of its ruling on the plaintiff's right of publicity claims. The court's discussion of copyright law shed light on the intellectual property treatment of player performance statistics. CBC had argued that if Advanced Media was able to prove a right of publicity, federal copyright law would preempt that claim. Where state law conflicts with federal law, federal law preempts and the state law must give way to federal law.[119] The district court rejected CBC's argument, that federal copyright law pre-empted the players' state law right of publicity claim. It found that players' names and records were arguably within the subject matter of copyright but stated that baseball statistics were not copyrightable because they lacked the requirement of originality under copyright law. Thus, copyright preemption would not apply.

It is a rudimentary statement that facts are not protected under copyright law.[120] Facts identify persons, places, and events, and are not protected under copyright law. The first person to report and find a fact did not create the fact but merely discovered its existence.[121] The essence of copyright law is originality.[122] To be original, the work must be independently created as opposed to being copied by others. There must be some minimal degree of creativity to qualify for copyright protection,[123] but the level of creativity is extremely low.[124] Although a single fact cannot be a subject of copyright, a compilation of facts may obtain copyright protection.[125] A factual compilation can be copyrightable "if it features an original selection on arrangement of facts, but the copyright is limited to the particular selection or arrangement."[126]

The court said the records of MLB players as used by CBC in fantasy games were not copyrightable. The names and records of MLB players, including the box scores found in the newspaper, is factual information available in the public domain. Box scores include statistics such as hits, doubles, triples, and other data used by CBC in their games. Any person attending a baseball game could also get the same information contained in the box score. The players' names and statistics lacked the essential quality of copyright protection: originality. The court said that CBC was not using the broadcasts of games, as some other cases had addressed, but merely the factual data from the underlying games themselves.

There have been several cases addressing the issue of copyright law and sporting events.[127] In *National Basketball Ass'n v. Motorola*,[128] Motorola had a device known as the Sports Trax that displayed up-to-date information on 1.5 inch by 1.5 inch screen. Every few minutes Motorola would update current scores of games, allowing the fan to track his or her favorite team's game. Motorola relied upon information provided to it by the Sports Team Analysis and Tracing System (STATS) Company, which monitored the games by television or radio. The NBA sued Motorola, asserting Sports Trax violated federal copyright law. The Federal Court of Appeals held that the NBA had no copyright protection in the actual scores of games.

In *Kregos v. Associated Press*,[129] the Second Circuit Court of Appeals indicated that there might be copyright protection for a compilation of baseball statistics. The plaintiff had developed a pitching form which contained statistical data relating to the past performance of the pitchers scheduled to start in each day's game. Many forms of this sort were available before Kregos developed his but each used different information and arranged it in a different manner. Kregos's form had nine columns for three different pitching categories. In 1984, the Associated Press produced its own pitching form that mirrored the one created by Kregos. The Federal District Court found in favor of Associated Press but the Court of Appeals reversed a part of the lower's court ruling dealing with the copyright issue. It said the validity of Kregos's copyright could not be rejected as a matter of law for lack of originality and that he might have some protection in his form.[130]

The court in CBC also addressed the 2002 license agreement between the parties. The court found the provisions preventing CBC from using players' names and statistics after the expiration of the agreement were enforceable on public policy grounds.

Eighth Circuit Court of Appeals

The Federal District Court issued its opinion on August 8, 2006, and Advanced Media wasted no time in filing an appeal.[131] The oral arguments took less than an hour.[132] The three-judge panel seemed skeptical of the claims of the players from the start. Judge Morris Arnold stated: "Major League Baseball is like a public religion, it's like a civic religion in the United States, isn't it? Everybody knows their names, what they look like, what their averages are, they talk about it all the time. This is just part of being an American, isn't it?"[133] Attorney Virginia Seitz represented MLB players and argued to the three-judge panel that fantasy games were no different than board games that use players' identities.[134] She argued that placing names on fantasy games was no different than putting players' names on coffee cups or posters.

The Eighth Circuit Court of Appeals rendered its decision on October 16, 2007. The court affirmed the district court's ruling but disagreed with its analysis in arriving at its decision. The eighth circuit was more succinct in disposing of the case than the district court. The players now had two strikes on them. Advanced Media appealed the case to the U.S. Supreme Court but were turned down, resulting in strike three.[135]

Unlike the district court, the court of appeals held that the players did in fact have a valid right of publicity claim under Missouri Law. It also found, contrary to the district court, that CBC's use of the names and statistics in its fantasy baseball production was in fact for a commercial purpose and did infringe upon the players' right of publicity. It first disagreed with the lower court's analysis of whether the players' names were used as a symbol of identity. The court of appeals had "no doubt" that the players' names used by CBC referred to actual Major League players. It said that the district court failed to understand when a name alone is enough to establish identity.[136] The court of appeals found the Players Association had indeed met the first element necessary to establish a claim for a violation of the right of publicity. It next addressed the "commercial advantage" element of the right of publicity claim. It once again disagreed with the lower court's analysis because it was clear that CBC had used players' identities in its fantasy products for the purposes of profit; thus, the court found their identities were being used for commercial advantage. The court of appeals ruled the players had in fact established a case for a violation of their publicity rights under Missouri law.

The court then analyzed whether the First Amendment trumped the players' right of publicity claim. It agreed with the holding of the lower court, finding that "CBC's first amendment rights in offering its fantasy baseball products superseded the players' right of publicity."[137] It gave several reasons for ruling in favor of CBC. First, as indicated by the district court, the information used in fantasy baseball games "is readily available in public domain." It noted it would be a "strange law" to not allow a person a First Amendment right to use information that is available to everyone. The court of appeals also recognized the unique public value of information relating to the game of baseball and its players, referring to it as the "national pastime." It quoted from *Gionfriddo*: "Major League baseball is followed by millions of people across this country on a daily basis.... The public has an enduring fascination in the records set by former players and in memorable moments from previous games.... The records and statistics remain of interest to the public because they provide context that allows fans to better appreciate (or deprecate) today's performances."[138] The court said there was "substantial public interest" in baseball statistics. The court of appeals also addressed the economic incentive argument that the district court had analyzed. It said MLB players are handsomely awarded for playing baseball games and can also earn additional sums from endorsement and sponsorship, therefore, the policy reasons behind the right of publicity was not in favor of the players.

The court of appeals did not address the federal copyright issue because its ruling on the First Amendment disposed of plaintiffs' claims. The court of appeals had ruled against the players based on a different rationale. Regardless, a loss is a loss and the players' legal claims were denied.

Conclusion

Who owns a home run was never thought of as a constitutional question but baseball fans and constitutional scholars can now rest easy; the crisis is over, it has now been resolved.[139] The million of fans who pour over fantasy statistics nightly in hopes of making the trade that will produce a first division club can do so now without the fear of legal action against them. They are legally entitled to use the information. It might have been interesting to try to measure the "good will" the players would have lost if they had won their lawsuit, prohibiting million of fans from playing fantasy baseball unless they paid a fee. Was the CBC case decided correctly? Some think players should have a right to receive compensation for the use of their names because the fantasy games would have no appeal to the baseball fan without their use. However, two federal courts disagreed. It is now settled that baseball has become so engrained as the national pastime that the discussion of players' names and statistics is a part of American culture and falls under the umbrella of the First Amendment to U.S. Constitution. It is safe to say Henry Chadwick would agree with the court's rationale.

14

The Arbitration Case of Steve Howe[1]
Testing Baseball's Patience

> I've been severely wounded by drugs, but my health is good. I still have my family, and I have no criminal record of drug-related offenses. I've fallen down often, but thanks to all the loving people who didn't give up on me, I've been able to let God guide me in the right direction. He's already recorded the most important save of all — my life. — Steve Howe, *Between the Lines,* 1989

> A seven-time offender convicted of a Federal drug violation should not be permitted to remain in baseball. — Fay Vincent, Baseball Commissioner

The Story of Steve Howe

There was no doubt Steve Howe could play baseball. There was also little doubt that he was haunted by personal demons which caused him severe heartache both on and off the diamond throughout his life. He was a two-time all Big Ten selection at the University of Michigan and was selected in the first round of the 1979 baseball draft by the Los Angeles Dodgers. He paid immediate dividends for the Dodgers, winning the National League Rookie of the Year award in 1980.[2] He saved a rookie-record 17 games in 1980 and gave up only one home run in 85 innings. In October of 1981, he won game four and saved game six of the World Series as the Dodgers beat the Yankees to win the championship. In 1982, he was selected to the National League All-Star Team and led the Dodgers in appearances, saves, and ERA. At 24 years old, Steve Howe was a baseball star. He had won awards, been an all-star, and pitched in a world series. His career was on the rise but serious trouble was on the horizon. Howe would shuffle in and out of the game of baseball for the next 14 years, at times pitching well and at others battling personal problems. He would be given multiple chances to redeem himself while trying to shed the personal demons that hounded him throughout his life and baseball career.[3]

Howe later admitted that he used cocaine in an effort to control his nervousness and excitement at the 1981 ceremony for the Rookie of the Year honors.[4] His use of cocaine increased and would continue throughout his entire baseball career.[5] The 1981 baseball season was a strike-shortened season. According to Howe, he snorted "significant quantities" of cocaine in the second half of the season, but still managed to pitch pretty well because he had a "system."[6] Beginning in 1982, Howe began to use cocaine during the season.[7] Between the years 1982 and 1988, Howe was hospitalized six times for treatment of cocaine use.[8] During the 1983 season, he was suspended twice by the Dodgers, fined $54,000, and placed on three years probation.[9] On May 28, 1983, he was suspended after admitting to drug use and placed in a treatment center until June 29. He was suspended again for one game on July 16, 1983, after arriving late to a game. Howe pitched from July to September 22, 1983, but missed a team flight and refused to take a urine test, and was suspended the rest of the season. In 1983, Howe had a win-loss record of 4–7, appearing in 46 games, striking out 52 batters in 68 innings, and posting a stellar 1.44 ERA. In December 1983, Dodgers Vice-President Al Campanis showed support for Howe saying, "He's not a problem man. He's a young man with a problem. We consider him a part of the family and we're not going to desert him."[10] Howe and the Dodgers were scheduled for a salary arbitration hearing in February 1984, but they settled the case prior to the hearing.[11] Howe had submitted a proposed salary figure of $790,000 while the Dodgers submitted one of $325,000. The parties eventually agreed to a figure of $325,000. It was same salary Howe had with the Dodgers in 1983.[12]

Howe was suspended by Commissioner Bowie Kuhn for the entire 1984 season after he tested positive for cocaine during the off-season.[13] Howe agreed not to play the 1984 season and to continue his probation and treatment for alcohol and drugs.[14] In turn, Commissioner Kuhn removed Howe from baseball's suspended list to an inactive status.[15] The Commissioner's Office issued a statement saying: "Steve continues in treatment, and there is unanimity of feeling among us, including Steve's medical advisers, that a return to baseball this season would not be appropriate. The most important thing for this young man is his long-range recovery."[16] The Dodgers agreed to forego the $54,000 the team was asking Howe to pay back.[17] The Dodgers request for repayment would most likely have been an exercise in futility because Howe had recently filed for bankruptcy.[18] Howe stated that one of the reasons he was forced to file for bankruptcy was his $1,500 a week cocaine habit.[19] The Dodgers did agree to loan Howe $10,000 a month for the remainder of the 1984 season as an advance of his 1985 salary.[20]

He returned to the Dodgers for the 1985 season with great enthusiasm.

Steve Howe, a promising pitcher in the early 1980s, fought both baseball and his inner demons for many years (National Baseball Hall of Fame Library Cooperstown, New York).

Although he was no longer using cocaine, he was now drinking heavily.[21] After Howe reported late to a game on June 30, 1985, the Dodgers took immediate action, giving him his unconditional release on July 3, 1985.[22] For the 1985 season, Howe appeared in 19 games for the Dodgers with a 4.91 ERA. Notwithstanding Howe's personal troubles, the Minnesota Twins signed him to a contract on August 12, 1985. He went 2–3 with the Twins, with a 6.16 ERA, appearing in 13 games. Howe did not last long with the Twins either. He once again relapsed into cocaine use, and on September 20, 1985, he entered the chemical dependency unit of St. Mary's Hospital in Minneapolis.[23] Reluctantly, Howe asked for his release from the Twins.

The future did not look bright for Steve Howe. Failing to sign on with a major league club at the beginning of the 1986 season and still wanting to play baseball, he signed a contract with the San Jose Bees of the class A California League.[24] At 28 years old, Howe, once a National League Rookie of the Year and Major League All-Star, was playing single-A baseball. While with the Bees, Howe was suspended for what was deemed a "drug test discrepancy," but was reinstated by the club in June 1986.[25] He admitted to using cocaine a few weeks later and was suspended for the remainder of the season. As a result of the suspension, Howe's name was placed on baseball's voluntarily retired list.[26] Howe was seemingly on the bottom, having now been suspended from single-A baseball.

As the 1987 season began, Howe once again got the urge to play baseball. He started the 1987 season playing in Mexico and was surprised and eager when he was picked up by the Texas Rangers in July 1987.[27] However, the Rangers had signed Howe without notifying the Commissioner's office. When Commissioner Peter Ueberroth learned of the signing, he ordered Howe to play in the minor leagues before playing for the Rangers.

An addendum to Howe's contract with the Rangers contained special provisions dealing with termination for drug use:

> (e) The player and the Club ratify, adopt and incorporate herein ... all of the terms and conditions of that certain "Texas Rangers After Care Program for Steve Howe" and in the event of a breach, violation, or transgression of any of the covenants contained in the Program, the remedies set out in the Program (including but not limited to suspension and/or termination of this contract) shall be fully enforceable in all respects in accordance with their terms and supersede any and all other covenants or remedies contained in this Contract that relate to the subject matter of the Program.

Howe once again went back down to the minor leagues but was called up by the Rangers on August 6 and compiled a 3–3 record in 24 appearances, registering one save with a 4.31 ERA for the 1987 season. Former Cleveland Indians great Sam McDowell, a certified alcohol counselor employed by the Rangers, counseled Howe when he pitched for Texas.[28] At the end of the 1987 season, Howe signed a two-year contract with the Rangers, which was to pay him $425,000 for 1988 and $500,000 for 1989, with the opportunity to earn more money through performance bonuses.[29] Notwithstanding the proposed incentives, Howe's demons would get the best of him once again. He tested positive for amphetamines in January 1988, and was given his unconditional release by the Rangers. From 1985 to 1987, Howe pitched for three teams and produced mediocre results. He was now 30 years old and a known drug user in baseball circles. It seemed like Steve Howe had worn out his baseball welcome.

He did not play organized baseball in 1988 or 1989 but still had a burning desire to return to the game he loved. He wrote a letter to the commissioner on December 12, 1989, asking if he could return to baseball. The commissioner did not respond to the letter so the Players Association filed a grievance on Howe's behalf, seeking reinstatement.[30] After some negotiations, the parties agreed to have Howe meet with the commissioner and two doctors, Dr. George DeLeon, a psychologist chosen by the Players Association, and Dr. Riordan, a psychiatrist chosen by the Commissioner's Office. After meeting with Howe, Dr. DeLeon made several observations about Howe, saying he was aware his recovery was a "lifetime process" and that a return to the game would "not constitute an unacceptable risk to relapse."[31] Dr. Riordan disagreed with Dr. DeLeon, stating there would be a "high" risk that Howe would turn to substance abuse with therapy alone.[32] He suggested a "very rigid" testing program, saying it was the only guarantee that Howe would not relapse into his previous bad habits. Dr. Riordan reported to Commissioner Vincent:

> We talked about the possibility of Steve giving a supervised urine every other day of his life as long as he may remain involved with organized baseball at any level, player, coach or manager. He acknowledged that he felt that this would be a reasonable strategy. I must emphasize that if this course were chosen and if he had a year or two of success, I would suspect that very likely Steve would come back demanding that this strategy be altered. It is my judgment that any altering of such a strategy, especially if it were successful, would be doomed to clinical failure. I believe that such a strategy must be linked to an absolute statement that single dirty urine will mean his removal from organized baseball.[33]

After hearing all the evidence, Commissioner Vincent decided to give Howe one more "last chance." The commissioner's decision on March 10, 1990 to allow Howe to return to the game stated in part:

> Howe will be placed on probation, but permitted to return to Major League Baseball for the 1991 season if he agrees to participate in an aftercare program approved by the Commissioner's Office which includes drug testing, possibly as often as every other day if necessary, through the remainder of his career in Baseball. Howe may sign a Major League contract in the meantime, but he may play only in the minor leagues prior to the 1991 season. This result will afford Howe an opportunity to determine the effects a return to the game will have on his continued sobriety and could lead to a return to the major leagues. As Dr. Riordan recommended, Howe will be immediately removed from Baseball in the event of a positive drug test.[34]

The interpretation of what "one last chance" meant would later become a major issue in arbitration.

Due to Howe's admitted past lies about his drug use, the commissioner decided Howe could play one year in the minor leagues and then have a chance to return to Major League baseball with very stringent requirements for drug testing. It was back down to class "A" ball where Howe played for Salinas in the Independent California League in 1990, compiling a 0–1 win-loss record with a 2.12 ERA. To the surprise of many, Howe appeared in the New York Yankees spring training camp in 1991 and asked the club for a tryout. He impressed the Yankees so much that they signed him to a contract. Howe pitched for the Yankees from early May until August 10, when he injured his elbow, but when he pitched he was superb. He went 3–1, appearing in 37 games, saving three with a 1.68 ERA in 1991.[35] Steve Howe was back. He had fought his way through the Mexican League, single-A baseball twice, and several years where he never even played organized baseball. It seemed he had finally overcome his personal demons. At the end of the 1991 season, Howe left for his home in Whitefish, Montana, to enjoy the great outdoors and to revel in his return to the game he loved. He had just completed a successful season with a good club. On November 7, 1991, Howe signed a new contract with the Yankees for a salary of $600,000 plus incentives that could pay him as much as $2.3 million.[36] Howe's return to baseball was a great comeback story and things were looking positive for Howe; however, once again, his success would be short-lived.

Howe's new contract required that he subject himself to drug testing and if he tested positive he could be terminated by the club. Howe's last drug test at the season's end was October 6, 1991. He was contacted by the president of Comprehensive Drug Testing (CDT), the firm that arranged drug testing of Major League players, on October 30 to arrange for some off-season testing. Howe said he wanted to talk to the Players Association before he agreed to be tested.[37] When CDT did not hear back from Howe, the president of CDT called him on November 22, 1991, attempting to arrange for testing. Howe told her that his in-laws were in town and asked if the testing could be postponed again and it was. He was finally tested on December 4, 6, 12, 13, 17, and 18.

On December 19, 1991, Howe was arrested for attempted possession of cocaine.[38] Howe was charged with two federal misdemeanor counts for attempted possession of one gram of cocaine on one occasion and possession of two grams of cocaine on another.[39] He pled not guilty to both charges.[40] On November 23, the day after he agreed with CDT that testing would begin on December 4, Howe had made arrangements to buy cocaine. When Commissioner Vincent heard the news about Howe, he stated: "I'm heartbroken. This is terrible news. I'm totally surprised and shocked. It's really disturbing if it's true. If it's true, it's a great tragedy." Eventually, Howe would plead guilty to attempted possession of cocaine and would receive three years probation. He would also be required to perform 100 hours of community service and attend a substance abuse program.[41]

Howe had paid for two grams of cocaine but never received it because the man he gave the money to, "J.J." (Jones), dropped the packet of cocaine in a pile of melting slush at the time of the "transaction." Howe later went back to J.J.'s house on several occasions to get the cocaine but discovered J.J. had been arrested. J.J. had told Howe if he was not around, Howe could try to contact Steve Boyd, an employee at a local used car dealership. Howe contacted Boyd about buying cocaine and they met the next day at a car dealership. What Howe did not know was that Boyd was a government informant and was wearing a "wire." They agreed on a price of $100 a gram and Boyd told Howe to come back later in the day to complete the deal. When Howe returned that same day Boyd told him the cocaine was located in the visor of a pickup truck in the car lot. Howe went to the truck and, when he reached for the cocaine in the visor, he was surrounded by law enforcement agents and arrested. There was no evidence Howe ever used cocaine, only that he was trying to purchase it. Notwithstanding pending criminal charges, Howe started the 1992 season with the Yankees. On June 8, 1992, he entered a plea of guilty to the criminal charges and on that same day was suspended indefinitely from baseball by Commissioner Fay Vincent.

Baseball's Drug Policy

The arbitrator in Howe's case gave a short history of baseball's drug policy as background to the arbitration decision. In October 1983, although there was no formal agreement between the Players Association and Major League Baseball concerning drug use, the commissioner's rules, as promulgated by then Commissioner Bowie Kuhn, banned the use and possession of drugs. In serious cases, the commissioner's discipline could merit "suspension or dismissal and termination of contract guarantees."[42] On May 24, 1984, the Major League clubs, represented by its Player Relations Committee (PRC), and the Players Association agreed to a Joint Drug Agreement (JDA).[43] In September 1985, Commissioner Ueberroth sought voluntarily participation of the players for testing but no players agreed to be tested. On October 22, 1985, the clubs terminated the JDA. After the Pittsburgh drug trials, Commissioner Ueberroth brought all testing within the jurisdiction of the Commissioner's Office. At the end of the 1986 season, Ueberroth issued a memorandum, "Baseball's Drug Abuse Program." The Players Association never agreed to the policy. George Nicolau, arbitrator in the Howe case, cited to baseball's present drug policy, the policy he would reference in deciding Howe's case. It stated the "possession, sale or use of any legal drug ... is strictly prohibited" and those "involved in ... possession, sale or use ... risk permanent expulsion from the game."[44] The policy further stated:

> Baseball will attempt to treat and rehabilitate individuals with a drug problem through a Club's Employee Assistance Program (EAP) or through resources identified by the Commissioner's Office. Baseball will approach its treatment and rehabilitation efforts with the welfare of both the individual and the game foremost in mind. However, Baseball will not hesitate to permanently remove from the game those players and personnel who, despite our efforts to treat and rehabilitate, refuse to accept responsibility for the problem and continue to use illegal drugs.[45]

Fay Vincent's Other Challenges

In 1992, Commissioner Vincent had a lot on his plate. Not only was he having to address the Steve Howe situation and the subsequent arbitration grievance filed by the Players Association, but he was also being sued by the Chicago Cubs and dealing with New York Yankees owner George Steinbrenner's suspension as well. On July 7, 1992, Vincent had ordered realignment of the National League's Eastern Division by sending the Atlanta Braves and Cincinnati Reds to the Eastern Division and the Chicago Cubs and St. Louis Cardinals to the Western Division.[46] The Cubs refused to "move west" and the U.S. Federal District Court in Chicago granted a temporary injunction preventing the enforcement of Vincent's decision.[47] Also in July 1992, Vincent allowed George Steinbrenner back in baseball after a two-year suspension. Steinbrenner had been suspended for his relationship with Howard Spira, a known gambler.[48]

In July 1992, the Players Association filed a grievance against Vincent for summoning three New York Yankees officials to his office because of statements they made during the Steve Howe arbitration hearing.[49] Buck Showalter, Gene Michael, and Jack Lawn were requested to come to the Commissioner's Office to discuss statements they made about baseball's drug policy during their testimony in the Howe arbitration case.[50] The commissioner believed their testimony displayed their unwillingness to support baseball's drug policy and enforce the rules.[51] Four weeks later, the Players Association filed a grievance "to protect the integrity" of future hearings.[52] The commissioner eventually cancelled the meeting at the request of George Nicolau, the chairman of the Howe arbitration panel.[53] The Players Association settled the grievance by getting Vincent to promise he would never again "consciously or unconsciously" try to intimidate witnesses.[54] In the midst of all this turmoil, Vincent sent a letter to the owners telling them he would never resign his position as baseball commissioner.[55] However, Vincent was losing the confidence of the owners and on September 3, 1992, the owners voted 18–9 in favor of requesting he submit his resignation.[56] Four days later on September 7, 1992, Fay Vincent resigned as baseball commissioner. It would be another two months before Vincent would know if his decision concerning Howe would be upheld.

The Commissioner's Decision

On June 8, 1992, Baseball Commissioner Fay Vincent announced the indefinite suspension of Steve Howe. Commissioner Vincent wrote a letter to Howe referencing his guilty plea to a charge of attempted possession of cocaine and "other evidence" that Howe had violated baseball's drug policy. The commissioner also relied on the fact that Howe said he wanted to "party" one more time before spring training. The commissioner said that he had made the suspension indefinite so he and Howe could meet and the "appropriate duration" of the suspension could be determined.[57] The Players Association filed a grievance challenging the commissioner's decision, stating a suspension of an indefinite length was in violation of baseball's Basic Agreement.[58] A hearing was held on June 16, 1992, concerning the commissioner's indefinite suspension of Howe.[59] After the hearing, the parties attempted to agree on the structure of a meeting between Howe and Commissioner Vincent but negotiations failed and no meeting ever took place. Commissioner Vincent then banned Howe from baseball for life on July 24, 1992. Howe was already pitching for the Yankees in the 1992 season when the suspension was announced. He was 3–0 with six saves in 20 appearances with a 2.45 ERA at the time he was suspended. Commissioner Vincent stated a lifetime ban was necessary to "maintain a meaningful deterrent" to drug use in baseball and that "the best interests of baseball [would] be served by holding that Steve Howe [had] finally extinguished his opportunity to play...."[60] He said baseball had done all it could for Howe but he also had to consider baseball's institutional interests and the concerns people had for the continued integrity of the game. Vincent said he had no other alternative but to suspend Howe.[61]

The Standard of Review for Commissioner's Decision

Before rendering his opinion, Arbitrator Nicolau set forth the guidelines the commissioner should have used in arriving at his decision. He said the commissioner has a reasonable range of discretion and any penalty imposed must be commensurate with the offense and appropriate, considering all the circumstances.[62] A penalty must be carefully fashioned and must be responsive, consistent, and fair.[63] The commissioner should give careful thought to the individual circumstances and particular facts relevant to each case.[64] The arbitrator noted that because of the severe nature of the penalty imposed by the commissioner in this particular case, the decision would be severely scrutinized. He said the Commissioner's burden was greater than that of an "ordinary employer" who fired an employee. An "ordinary" employee could go elsewhere and work but, in the Howe case, the Commissioner's decision had essentially prevented Howe from working in his chosen profession because of the lifetime ban.[65] It was clear the bar was set high for the commissioner. The arbitrator made it known that he would examine the commissioner's decision to suspend Howe from baseball for life with a very keen eye. Would the arbitrator uphold the commissioner's decision? After all, how many chances should any player get? Didn't the commissioner make it clear to Howe that he only had "one more" chance? If baseball was going to seriously address the issue of drug use, would letting Howe back into baseball damage the reputation of the game and send the wrong message?

The Commissioner's Position at Arbitration

The first argument made by the commissioner to support his decision to suspend Howe was that the post-hearing medical evidence of Steve Howe was irrelevant and should have not been considered by the arbitrator in arriving at his decision. He argued that it would place an unfair burden on the commissioner to be required to go back through the player's entire medical history before imposing discipline. He said Howe had been treated at very good institutions and had been given multiple opportunities for rehabilitation.

The commissioner argued that Howe was not the individual the Players Association presented but rather a "conscious, manipulative drug user" who clearly understood the consequences of his actions and should he held accountable for those actions. This was clearly shown by Howe's statement to authorities after his arrest that he wanted to "party" one last time as well as his manipulating several drug testing dates so he could buy cocaine. He was given every possible opportunity to rehabilitate himself but squandered multiple "second chance" opportunities. The commissioner said that Howe refused to take responsibility for his own actions and instead chose to always blame others for his behavior, including the Dodgers, his physicians, the Texas Ranger's drug advisors, the government, the Commissioner's Office, and anyone else other than himself. The commissioner argued that failure to uphold the lifetime ban would only perpetuate Howe's tendency to blame others and would never force him to change his ways. The commissioner stated that although Howe had a good support group, he never made any efforts to rely on it when he got the urge to buy drugs. He noted that Howe had failed to reach out to his teammates, friends, pastor, or counselor about his desire to purchase drugs and essentially made no effort to help himself. He further argued that Howe's intentions were clear when he changed the date of his drug test and made a decision to buy cocaine. The commissioner stated that Howe's plea of guilty to a federal drug charge was enough evidence by itself to support a permanent suspension. The commissioner noted Howe asked for "one more chance" in 1990 and had been given that chance. He also said that Howe knew it was his last chance but still decided to buy cocaine.[66] The commissioner further argued that arbitration decisions generally support the right of the employer to fire employees who use drugs and are convicted of crimes. This was especially true when an employee had been given multiple chances to redeem themselves but failed. Finally, the commissioner argued that baseball would lose substantial credibility if it did not take severe action against Howe because of his drug use. The commissioner stated that his decision was "unprecedented" because Howe's drug use in baseball was "unprecedented."[67]

The Players Association's Position at Arbitration

The association argued that the commissioner had failed to understand that Steve Howe actually lived two separate and distinct lives. One life they deemed as Howe's "lost years" from 1982 to 1988. The association said his second life started in 1989 when he regained control of his life to a large extent and changed his behavior. Furthermore, the commissioner should have known that Howe's chemical dependency had never really been treated based on the 1990s reports of Dr. DeLeon and Dr. Riordan. The association contended that the commissioner was to blame for Howe's relapse because Baseball failed to maintain a rigorous, year-round testing program, something that Dr. Riordan deemed as essential to Howe's success.[68] The commissioner had set as a condition that testing occur every other day, but had failed to follow through and thus he should be held responsible as well. It argued that once baseball assumed the responsibility of testing Howe and for Howe's after care, they should have followed up but they failed in that regard. The association agreed that Howe was not free from fault and believed that he understood that what happened was an unacceptable failure on his part.[69]

The association then turned to the discipline portion of the commissioner's decision. It pointed out that none of the players implicated in the Pittsburgh drug trials were suspended for even a day and that the longest drug suspension ever assessed before Howe was 100 days. Howe's penalty was just too severe. It believed any penalty in excess of 90 days would be excessive.[70] Howe was a changed man and no longer "out of control." The association further noted the support that had been given to Howe from his teammates and Yankees management. In conclusion, it argued that mitigating factors and precedent called for the commissioner's decision to be rescinded and Howe reinstated.

Medical Evidence Concerning Howe's Condition

Howe had been in and out of rehabilitation many times and there was substantial medical evidence concerning his condition. Two well-known psychiatrists, both experts in the field of drug and alcohol abuse, testified at the Howe arbitration hearing: Dr. Robert Millman, a psychiatrist who was the overseer of baseball's drug program, and Dr. Joel Solomon, a psychiatrist who periodically advised the Players Association on drug testing issues. Dr. Solomon interviewed Howe before the arbitration began. Based on this interview and other observations he made of Howe, Dr. Solomon thought Howe might suffer from Attention Deficit Hyperactive Disorder (ADHD).[71] He said if Howe had ADHD he would not be able to recover from substance abuse unless he had the appropriate medical treatment.[72] He also said that there was an adult version (ADHD-Residual Type) and if Howe was suffering from that disorder, he could take medication which might assist him in his treatment. Dr. Millman did not personally examine Howe and could not determine if he did have residual ADHD. However, Dr. Millman did testify that it would not be uncommon for a drug abuser to have another psychiatric disorder and that both disorders could be addressed in a good treatment program.

After hearing the testimony of Dr. Millman and Dr. Solomon, arbitrator Nicolau requested the two doctors nominate a psychiatrist who could perform "an in-depth clinical evaluation" of Howe. The arbitrator stated that what he wanted was:

1. [An] evaluation and diagnosis of Mr. Howe.
2. [An] opinion as to the adequacy of his prior diagnoses and the quality and appropriateness of the medical and psychiatric care he previously received.
3. [A] recommendation for treatment.[73]

Two psychiatrists were eventually selected to evaluate Howe: Dr. Paul Wender from the University of Utah, a well-known expert on ADHD; and Dr. Herbert Kleber from Columbia University. Both interviewed Howe and his wife and reviewed all of Howe's medical records. After his evaluation, Dr. Wender found that Steve Howe did in fact have the psychiatric disorder, ADHD. He noted that Howe had had "clear-cut" symptoms as a child which continued to his adult life. Dr. Wender said that anyone with Howe's childhood experiences would be at great risk for substance abuse. Dr. Wender believed Howe had a "comparative small risk" of further involvement with drugs but still warned that psychiatric predictions can be inaccurate.

Dr. Kleber submitted a 26-page, single-spaced report in which he fully agreed with Dr. Wender's diagnosis of ADHD. However, he thought that Howe would have a greater chance to relapse than Dr. Wender did. Dr. Kleber made several recommendations for treatment:

1. continued involvement with Alcoholics Anonymous and religious groups;
2. psychotherapy to make Howe aware of the role ADHD had played in his life;
3. formal relapse prevention training;
4. appropriate trials of certain medications during the off-season;
5. strict urine testing with no chance of alteration of the sample; a missed test would be deemed to be a positive test.

Dr. Kebler was aware that Howe had a tendency to blame others for his problems but believed that a comprehensive treatment program would give him the tools he needed to be successful. Dr. Solomon met with Howe and his wife once more after their initial meeting. He determined that Steve Howe's treatment was "incomplete since he had never had a formal diagnosis of ADHD." He recommended treatment for Howe addressing the disorder combined with dictating the consequences to Howe in case of relapse. He suggested that any new program for Howe be put in the form of a contract.

The Arbitration Award/Opinion

On November 12, 1992, the arbitration award was issued and the written opinion supporting the award quickly followed on November 19, 1992. After the arbitration hearing on June 29, 30, and July 3, 1992, arbitrator Nicolau ordered additional medical evaluations of Steve Howe.[74] The results of the evaluations were made available to the parties to the arbitration on a confidential basis.[75] First, Nicolau concluded that Commissioner Vincent's decision to ban Howe from baseball permanently was without just cause. Second, he rescinded the lifetime suspension, sustaining a suspension from June 8, 1992, to the end of the 1992 season. Third, he required Howe, the Commissioner's Office, and the Players Association to meet with medical personnel and agree to a treatment and aftercare program for Howe. The treatment and aftercare program was to be included in any player contract signed by Howe.[76] The program would then be submitted to the arbitration panel for approval. Nicolau set the minimum requirements for Howe's program as follows:

1. Year-round drug testing, every other day. A missed test would be considered to be Howe's fault. A positive test would result in his permanent suspension of the game[77];

2. Year round aftercare program. He would be required to attend both Alcoholics Anonymous and Narcotics Anonymous or other similar groups[78];
3. Professional psychiatric care for ADHD-RT;
4. Formal relapse prevention training.[79]

Arbitrator George Nicolau's opinion was a detailed 54 pages in which he stated his rationale for overturning the lifetime suspension of Steve Howe and sustaining a suspension only through the end of the 1992 season. He first framed the issue in a disciplinary hearing involving the just cause standard.[80] He noted two questions must be posed: "whether the individual involved committed the act or acts alleged and, if so, whether the penalty imposed for that conduct was appropriate."[81] He said because Howe had pled guilty to possessing cocaine, the only issue was whether a lifetime ban was warranted under the circumstances.

The arbitrator first examined the "nature" of the chance that Howe was given by the commissioner. The arbitrator disagreed with the commissioner's characterization of the decision which had allowed Howe to re-enter baseball in 1990. The commissioner had deemed Howe's acceptance of his 1990 decision as a "last chance agreement" in which Howe promised he would no longer be involved with drugs. The arbitrator said that what Howe had actually agreed to was immediate expulsion from baseball "in the event of a positive drug test." But that specific event never occurred. Howe had only attempted to purchase cocaine, he had never tested positive for drug use. That action could not operate as an automatic forfeiture of the "last chance" the commissioner had given to him. Although the arbitrator did express concern for Baseball's effort to keep the workplace free from drugs, he believed Baseball's conduct, as well as Howe's, should be reviewed. The arbitrator pointed the finger at Baseball, saying that it should accept some of the blame for Howe's behavior as well. Although the commissioner argued that Baseball did everything it could have done for Howe, the arbitrator disagreed. The arbitrator said that the commissioner had failed to grasp the reality of the situation. He also said that it was now known that Howe did in fact have a psychiatric disorder that had never been diagnosed or treated. He further found that Howe's condition was a contributing factor to his drug use and, when it went untreated, he was susceptible to a relapse. The arbitrator noted that in 1990, the commissioner's medical advisor warned that Howe should not be allowed to return to baseball unless he was tested for drugs every other day. Baseball failed to implement this testing notwithstanding the Commissioner's suggestion in 1990 that every other day testing for Howe be imposed.[82] The arbitrator found that because the suggested testing was never implemented, Howe was "unfortunately set on a course without the strategic safeguard" that Dr. Riordan had stated was essential to Howe's recovery. If this safeguard had been put into place, it is unlikely that Howe would ever even have attempted to buy cocaine. The arbitrator concluded by saying:

While Howe can certainly be faulted for seeking to delay testing at a time of his admittedly increasing sense of vulnerability, the office of the commissioner cannot escape its measure of responsibility for what took place in 1991. Based on medical advice the commissioner had solicited, the need for continuous testing was obvious. To give Howe "yet another chance" of returning to the game without implementing those conditions was not, in my judgment, a fair shot at success.[83]

One of the major legal issues in the case was post-hearing medical evidence. The arbitrator said that "after acquired" medical evidence should be considered in any decision.[84] The arbitrator also said that the Commissioner had paid very little attention to Howe's medical records and had made no effort to probe "beneath the surface" to determine if Howe had been properly diagnosed or treated. The arbitrator stated it was not unfair to expect an "exceptionally scrupulous review of the record" when the case involved a potential lifetime ban of a player. He emphasized that because the commissioner could prevent the employment of a player regardless of how many potential employers there were, any decision he made was subject to a higher standard. Nicolau's opinion said that because the commissioner's power is exercised unilaterally and not the result of collective bargaining, it must be scrutinized. He also said that the commissioner's failure to look at the circumstances of Howe's case, "irrespective of the cause," was inconsistent with the responsibility of the Commissioner's Office.

Nicolau also addressed the commissioner's argument that anything less than a lifetime suspension would send the wrong message to the players. He said drug use in baseball had actually declined and "steady progress towards a drug free environment is likely to continue." He noted that while deterrence is a good objective, it cannot be achieved "at the expense of fairness." In ruling on the merits, Nicolau stated:

> What was considered vital to Howe's sobriety at this point in his life should have been implemented. Moreover, the Office of the Commissioner should have looked closely at all the circumstances in order to ascertain and evaluate his condition and the adequacy of his treatment before deciding what discipline to impose. These failings lead me to conclude that the Commissioner's action in imposing a lifetime ban was without just cause.

Nicolau found that in light of the commissioner's failure to examine all the circumstances, a lifetime ban from baseball was not warranted. He said that the interest of "deterrence and fairness as well as punishment ... would be met if the penalty imposed by the former commissioner was reduced to time served." Howe's suspension lasted 119 days, costing him $400,000 in salary and lost opportunities to earn $1.5 million under his contract. The arbitrator said that Howe's penalty would operate as a clear warning that drug use will be treated severely by baseball. Nicolau concluded by saying:

> As is evident from these proceedings, no one can predict whether Howe will succeed even with the treatment and safeguards provided for in the Award. It is not at all certain, as the impartial medical evaluations reflects, that he is quite ready to accept full responsibility for his actions or that he fully understands, even at this juncture, the complex reasons for his behavior. While fundamental fairness requires that his permanent expulsion be set aside, only with his understanding and acceptance of responsibility will his future truly be secure.[85]

Fay Vincent was out of office by the time the award was rendered, but in response to the ruling, he stated:

> We're fortunate that Mr. Nicolau doesn't review the criminal convictions of most felons. Otherwise we'd have them all out on the streets. No one would be in jail. If you pushed these medical, psychological reasons, you'd have no justice system. No one would be guilty. It's psychology run wild.[86]

Conclusion

The Steve Howe arbitration decision tested the limits of the baseball commissioners' authority to discipline players who use drugs. Steve Howe had tested the limits of baseball's drug policy as well as its goodwill and patience. Essentially, arbitrator George Nicolau cited to inconsistencies in baseball's drug testing of Howe as well as Howe's undiagnosed hyperactive condition that could have led to drug use by Howe in support of his decision.[87] The arbitration decision of Steve Howe provides interesting insight into baseball's drug policy from the 1980s to 1990s and is controversial because of Howe's continuing violation of that policy. Unbelievably, Howe was still pitching in the major leagues despite being suspended multiple times by Major League Baseball for the use and possession of drugs. Howe received numerous chances to return to baseball and stay clean and yet he had major difficulties in overcoming his addiction. He drifted in and out of baseball from 1985 to 1991, attempting to overcome his substance abuse problem. When Howe returned to baseball in 1991, he said he was clean and ready to start over. Was Steve Howe treated fairly by baseball? Commissioner Fay Vincent was adamant that his decision was fair under all the circumstances. Maybe the arbitrator would have agreed with the commissioner's ruling had he ensured that Howe was tested every other day as first suggested.

Howe returned to the Yankees after the arbitrator's ruling and performed under the terms of the arbitration award. He saved 32 games for the Yankees from 1993 to 1996.[88] He earned $700,000 in 1992, $2.5 million in 1993, $2.1 million in 1994, and $2.3 million in 1995.[89] Steve Howe was eventually released by the Yankees on June 24, 1996. Two days later, he was arrested at New York's Kennedy airport for carrying a .357 Magnum in his luggage.[90] He pled guilty to gun possession charges and received three years probation.

Howe's father and mother were members of the United Auto Workers Union in Michigan.[91] Howe was very supportive of the union, saying, "My parents explained to me unions are for rights in a free America."[92] Notwithstanding, Howe later became the first striking major league player to cross over into a replacement spring training camp in 1995.[93] Howe said that one of the reasons he did so was to comply with his probation requirement of employment in a "structured environment."[94] In 1995, during a baseball work stoppage, Howe actually went to work for management in the Yankees ticket office. He earned $772 a week selling tickets. It was quite an odd situation. A player who at one time had been suspended by baseball for life was working for management selling tickets to replacement games during a player's strike. A labor law brain teaser, if there ever was one.

In 1996, Howe sued the New York Post Company for defamation and intentional infliction of emotional distress.[95] On August 16, 1993, the *New York Post* had printed the following article:

> The off-Broadway smash "Tony 'n Tina's Wedding"—recently starring ex–Met Lee Mazzilli—re-creates an Italian wedding. Part of the show has the cast and audience/guests going from the somber ceremony to the raucous reception afterwards. At a recent performance, as the group made its way down Christopher Street from the church to the catering hall, one person lit up a marijuana cigarette, took a few puffs, and good-naturedly handed it to the guy behind him—who promptly went ballistic. "Get that f---ing thing away from me. You're trying to entrap me, you bastard." Turns out it was Yankee hurler Steve Howe, a seven-time drug offender, on his last chance with the Bombers.[96]

The story was reprinted in several newspapers, including the *New York Daily News* and the *Forth Worth Star Telegram*. Howe sued, saying that he had never attended the play and the entire incident never happened. He also said that he was forced to take an extra urinalysis test by his probation officer because of the newspaper articles and that the whole matter caused him severe emotional distress which required him to have "psychiatric assistance."[97] Howe demanded a retraction but one never came. The court eventually dismissed Howe's lawsuit.

> The article does not accuse Howe of violating the terms of his probation. Nor does it "give the impression that [Howe] is once again involved in drug use" or that he "frequents" or deliberately placed himself in a location where drugs are available. Moreover, the article does not ridicule his efforts at rehabilitation. To the contrary, the story depicts Howe's ardent refusal of an offer of drugs. For the average reader, such conduct is worthy of praise.

And in dismissing his claim for intentional infliction of emotional distress, the court said:

> Although Howe alleges that he suffered severe emotional distress (public humiliation, wounded feelings, embarrassment, and psychological injury), this cause of action

does not withstand scrutiny because the *Post* has not engaged in "extreme and outrageous conduct."[98]

Howe tried a comeback with the Sioux Fall Canaries in the Independent League in 1997,[99] but a motorcycle accident cut his comeback short.[100] He lived in Montana until his tragic death on April 29, 2006.[101] Howe was killed when his truck rolled over in the early morning hours in Coachella, California. Tests performed after the accident showed methamphetamines in Howe's bloodstream, although the amount was not disclosed.[102]

Steve Howe was a good ballplayer. He ended his playing career with a 47–41 won-loss record, 91 saves, and an ERA of 3.03. He attended an outstanding university where he was an All-American ballplayer, won baseball awards, played in a World Series, was an all-star, and appeared in 497 major league games with the New York Yankees, Los Angeles Dodgers, Texas Rangers, and Minnesota Twins. Howe lived a life many dream of but his personal problems haunted him. It has been said that baseball mirrors society in many respects, including having its share of people with personal troubles. Steve Howe was one of these individuals. After his death, the Yankees honored Howe in a moment of silence at Yankee Stadium.

Chapter Notes

Preface

1. *Confirmation Hearing on the Nomination of John G. Roberts, Jr. to be Chief Justice of the United States: Hearing Before the Comm. on the Judiciary*, S. Hrg. 109–158, 109th Cong., 1st Sess., 2005 (statement of Judge John G. Roberts, Jr.). For further study, see Ross E. Davies and Craig D. Rust, "Supreme Court Sluggers: Behind the Numbers," *Green Bag 2d* 13 (2010): 213–226; Aaron Zelinsky, "The Justice as Commissioner: Benching the Judge-Umpire Analogy," *Yale Law Journal Online* 119 (2010): 113–125; Earl Warren, "A Majority Opinion by the Chief Justice of the U.S.," *Sports Illustrated*, April 9, 1956, 23.

2. Robin Finn, "Giamatti Playing Position Strictly by the Book," *New York Times*, 21 May 1989, S1.

3. Many books have been written about the Office of the Commissioner of Baseball and its occupants. A few examples include Bowie Kuhn, *Hardball: The Education of a Baseball Commissioner* (New York: Times Books, 1987); David Pietrusza, *Judge and Jury: The Life and Times of Judge Kenesaw Mountain Landis* (South Bend, IN: Diamond Communications, 1998); Fay Vincent, *The Last Commissioner: A Baseball Valentine* (New York: Simon & Schuster, 2002); Andrew Zimbalist, *In The Best Interests of Baseball? The Revolutionary Reign of Bud Selig* (Hoboken, NJ: Wiley, 2006); Peter Ueberroth, *Made in America: His Own Story* (New York: William Morrow, 1988).

Chapter 1

1. No. 400545, 2002 WL 31833731 (Cal Super. Ct. Dec. 18, 2002).

2. Springer's knuckleball was clocked at 50 miles per hour. Matt Bean, "A Slugger, Two Fans and a $1 Million Baseball," *www.courttvnews.com*, 12 June 2007. The 2002 season would be Springer's last. He finished his major league career at 24–48 with a 5.18 ERA.

3. *Popov v. Hayashi* is now used in many law schools throughout the U.S. to teach property law. Many legal scholars are using the case in textbooks to explain the acquisition and ownership rights of personal property. *See* James C. Smith et al., *Property: Cases & Materials* (New York: Aspen, 2008); Bruce H. Ziff et al., *A Property Law Reader: Cases, Questions, and Commentary* (Toronto, Ont.: Thomson Carswell, 2008).

4. Who ever thought a fly ball into the right field stands would create an endless series of law review articles by legal scholars? But it has. For starters, see Steven Semeraro, "An Essay on Property Rights in Milestone Home Run Baseballs," *SMU Law Review* 56 (2003): 2281; Peter Adomeit, "The Barry Bonds Baseball Case–An Empirical Approach – Is Fleeting Possession Five Tenths of the Ball?" *Saint Louis University Law Journal* 48 (2004): 475; Jason Cieslik, "There's a Drive ... Way Back ... It Might Be ... It Could Be ... Another Lawsuit: *Popov v. Hayashi*," *Thomas M. Cooley Law Review* 20 (2003): 605; Patrick Stoklas, "*Popov v. Hayashi*, A Modern Day *Pierson v. Post*: A Comment on What the Court Should Have Done With the Seventy-Third Home Run Baseball Hit by Barry Bonds," *Loyola University Chicago Law Review* 34 (2003): 901; Michael Pastrick, "When a Day at the Ballpark Turns a "Can of Corn" Into a Can of Worms: *Popov v. Hayashi*," *Buffalo Law Review* 51 (2003): 905; Paul Finkelman, "Fugitive Baseballs and Abandoned Property: Who Owns the Home Run Ball?" *Cardozo Law Review* 23 (2002): 1610.

5. Daniel Paisner, *The Ball: Mark McGwire's Home Run Ball and the Marketing of the American Dream* (New York: Viking, 1999). Carton Fisk's home run ball off the foul pole in game 6 of the 1975 World Series sold for $113, 273. "Eddie Murray's 500th Home Run Ball Garnered $500,000.00. Ball to Museum," *New York Times*, 2 November 1996. The infamous ball that traveled through the legs of Bill Bucker was bought by actor Charlie Sheen for $93,500. Sheen put the ball on the auction block in 2000 and it was sold for approximately $60,000. Joe Concha, "Top Five Sports Memorabilia of all Time," *NBCSports.com*, 25 February 2004.

6. "McFarlane Buys Bonds' Historic Home Run Ball," *CBC Sports*, 25 June 2003.

7. The attendance of the park that day was more than 41,000. At Wrigley Field, fans have the habit of throwing an opposing player's ball back after a home run. Would a fan have enough gumption to throw back a valuable ball? Lee Jenkins, "At Wrigley, Fans Debate What to Do with a Ball," *New York Times*, 18 July 2007. Some major league parks actually prohibit fans from throwing balls back onto the field.

8. To assist fans in their quest for the ball, the Giants website provided fans with a map showing where Bonds had hit all of his home runs during the 2001 season.

9. The official name for the cove is "China Basin." McCovey Cove was named by two writers, Mark Purdy and Leonard Koppett. Purdy first suggested McCovey Channel or Stream. Koppett later suggested Cove. Mark Purdy, "Honoring Him Wouldn't Take a Stretch," *San Jose Mercury News*, 9 May 1999.

10. See Gene Wojciechowski, "McCovey Cove Regulars Await Chance to Paddle for History," *ESPN.com*, 23 May 2007.

11. Popov ended up face down on the pavement under several layers of people. He was "grabbed, hit and kicked." *Popov*, 2002 WL 31833731, 2.

12. Ibid.

13. Ibid. Keppel filmed the event and much of what he recorded was used as evidence in the lawsuit. A movie was eventually made from the events that happened at Pac Bell Park that day. *Up for Grabs* (2004).

14. *Popov*, 2002 WL 31833731, at 2.

15. Ibid.

16. Declaration of Kathy Sorensen in Support of Issuance of Temporary Restraining Order and OSC Re Preliminary Injunction, para 7, *Popov v. Hayashi*, 2002 WL 31833731 (Cal. Super. Ct. Dec. 18, 2002) (No. 400545), *available at* 2001 WL 34131854.

17. Declaration of Kevin Griffin, *Popov v. Hayashi*, 2002 WL 31833731 (Cal. Super. Ct. Dec. 18, 2002) (No. 400545).

18. Ibid.

19. *Popov*, 2002 WL 31833731, at 2.

20. Ibid.

21. Ibid.

22. Ibid.

23. Ibid.

24. Ibid.

25. Ibid.

26. Ibid. Mr. Hayashi's lawyer argued that Popov's movement after he got up off the ground indicated Mr. Popov was actually attempting to give Mr. Hayashi a "high five" for getting the ball. Later, Judge McCarthy described this argument as one "only a true advocate could embrace."

27. Declaration of Jeff Hacker, *Popov v. Hayashi*, 2002 WL 31833731 (Cal. Super. Ct. Dec. 18, 2002) (No. 400545). Hacker can also be heard on the Keppel film making the statement.

28. There was some speculation that Popov actually brought the "Sucker-Ball" to the game but he denied it. Would the "Sucker-Ball" have had some value on e-Bay?

29. Several fans who were at the game and on the arcade that day filed declarations stating Popov caught the ball. They said:

"I saw the ball fly directly into POPOV's glove." Declaration of Stephen Kowalski, November 27, 2001.

"I saw the ball coming down on the Arcade walkway where I saw Alex Popov (hereinafter POPOV) catch the baseball cleanly in the air. I saw the ball fly directly into his glove." Declaration of Bill King, November 27, 2001.

"I saw POPOV catch the Baseball cleanly in his mitt."

"I saw POPOV go down to the Arcade floor with the Baseball." Declaration of Jeremy Putoff, November 20, 2001.

"I clearly saw POPOV catch the Baseball in his mitt. I did not see a loose ball." Declaration of Russ Reynolds, November 20, 2001.

"I watched the baseball go into POPOV's glove."

"I watched Mr. POPOV secure the baseball with both hands as he was knocked to the ground."

"I saw no loose ball." Declaration of Maurie Bennett, November 20, 2001.

"POPOV fielded the ball cleanly from the air, and I saw the ball fly directly into his glove."

"I saw POPOV come down with the baseball in his glove as he went to the floes of the Arcade."

"There was no loose ball." Declaration of Evan Knight, November 20, 2001.

"I saw the Baseball descending at a very steep angle as it flew over my head and directly into POPOV's glove. POPOV's glove was the one glove that went up for the ball. I heard the sound of the ball hit the leather of the mitt. POPOV caught the ball firmly in his glove before being knocked to the ground by the crowd. There was no loose ball." Declaration of John Creek, November 20, 2001.

"Within seconds after catching the ball, POPOV was attacked, assaulted and battered by no less than six and as many fifteen individuals, including Defendant Patrick Hayashi (hereinafter HAYASHI). Many of these individuals knocked POPOV to the cement ground and piled on top of him. POPOV landed on the cement ground with his head located neat my feet when POPOV was assaulted and battered, the baseball was not loose and was securely within POPOV's baseball mitt." Declaration of Kathy Sorensen, October 20, 2001.

30. Preliminary Injunction, *Popov v. Hayashi*, No. 400545, 2001 WL 35828490 (Cal. Super. Ct. Nov. 27, 2001).

Notes — Chapter 1

31. Order Denying Defendant's Motion for Summary Judgment and Granting in Part and Denying in Part Defendant's Motion for Summary Adjudication, *Popov v. Hayashi*, No. 400545, 2002 WL 34127867 (Cal Super. Ct. Sept. 9, 2002).
32. *Popov*, 2002 WL 31833731, at 3.
33. Complaint for Injunctive Relief, Conversion, Battery, Assault, Punitive Damages and Constructive Trust, para. 7, No. CGC-01-400545, 2001 WL 35949995 (Cal. Super. Ct. Oct. 23, 2001).
34. Ibid., para. 9.
35. Ibid.
36. Ibid., para. 8.
37. Keppel's sworn declaration states, "As shown on the videotape, Alex Popov caught the baseball and then is attacked by a number of fans." Declaration of Josh Keppel in Support of Issuance of Temporary Restraining Order and OSC re Preliminary Injunction, No.: 400545 (Cal. Super. Ct. Oct. 23, 2001), para. 4.
38. Declaration of John Creech; Superior Court of the State of California in the City and County of San Francisco; Case No.: 400545, November 27, 2001.
39. Defendant Patrick Hayashi's Verified Answer to Complaint for Injunctive Relief, Conversion, Battery, Assault, Punitive Damages and Constructive Trust, No.: 400545, 2001 WL 35949996 (Cal. Super. Ct. Nov. 13, 2001).
40. Ibid. Dean and Professor of Law from the University of Illinois, John E. Cribbet, a noted scholar on property law, has stated: "Possession is nine points of law." This old saw happens to be true and in many a legal controversy involving property rights the principal issue can be phrased: "Who had the prior possession of this thing?" John E. Cribbet, *Principles of the Law of Property*, 2d ed. (New York: Foundation Press, 1962); 12.
41. Popov Complaint, para. 10.
42. Declaration of Kathy Sorensen, para. 5.
43. Declaration of Doug Yarris in Support of Issuance of Temporary Restraining Order and OSC Re Preliminary Injunction, para. 5, *Popov v. Hayashi*, 2002 WL 31833731 (Cal. Super. Ct. Dec. 18, 2002) (No. 400545), *available at* 2001 WL 34131856.
44. Popov, 2 n.5.
45. "If I were to recover Barry Bonds 73rd home run baseball in the above-entitled matter, I would have no intentions of selling Barry Bonds' Home Run Baseball." Declaration of Alex Popov Regarding Sale of Baseball, *Popov v. Hayashi*, 2002 WL 31833731 (Cal. Super. Ct. Dec. 18, 2002) (No. 400545); Superior Court of the State of California in the City and County of San Francisco; Case No.: 400545, November 27, 2001.
46. Matt Bean, *In the Battle for the Ball, A Mediator*, www.courttv.com (June 25, 2007).
47. *Up for Grabs* (2004).
48. The Anaheim Angels defeated the Giants 4–3 to win its first World Series. Bonds batted .471 in the series (8–17) with four home runs, six RBIs, two doubles, and eight runs scored. He walked 13 times for an on-base percentage of .700.
49. Declaration of Richard R. Garcia in Opposition to Motion for Preliminary Injunction, para 8, *Popov v. Hayashi*, 2002 WL 31833731 (Cal. Super. Ct. Dec. 18, 2002) (No. 400545), *available at* 2001 WL 35947036.
50. Ibid., para. 10.
51. Ibid., para. 11.
52. Ibid., para. 18.
53. Plaintiff Alex Popov's Reply Brief in Support of OSC Re Preliminary Injunction, para. 7, *Popov v. Hayashi*, 2002 WL 31833731 (Cal. Super. Ct. Dec. 18, 2002) (No. 400545). 54. "Ownership comes to the person who catches the ball by two different legal theories: the 'common law of baseball,' which is based on the traditions and evolution of baseball, and the 'traditional law of abandonment.'" Finkelman, "Fugitive Baseballs and Abandoned Property," 1610. "It has been the common practice in Professional Baseball since the 1940s that any baseball hit into the stands belongs to the fan who caught the baseball. Moreover, baseball teams encourage the fans to catch and keep baseballs. For example, fans are encouraged bring their baseball mitts to the game." Declaration of Paul Finkelman in Support of Issuance of Temporary Restraining Order and OSC Re Preliminary Injunction, para. 6, *Popov v. Hayashi*, 2002 WL 31833731 (Cal. Super. Ct. Dec. 18, 2002) (No. 400545), *available at* 2001 WL 34131848.
55. The Arizona Diamondbacks policy regarding balls hit into the stands states:

FOUL BALLS/HOME RUN BALLS

Guests are welcome to keep any foul ball hit into the stands. At no time should a foul ball be thrown back on the field. All guests are cautioned to stay alert for foul balls, bats and broken bats which could land in the seating area. If you would like to lessen the risk, the Arizona Diamondbacks will exchange your ticket for one in the upper deck, or will refund the ticket at any time before the first pitch.

Guests who catch D-backs' home run balls can arrange to have the ball autographed by the player who hit it. Simply contact the Guest Service Representative (usher) at the top of your seating section/area. The ball will be returned to the guest by mail, generally within three days. If they wish, guests are allowed to return a visitors' home run ball to the field; however, it must be done immediately and in such a way that it does not endanger any player. Interference with play in any way is not permissible.

Warning: Any guest interfering with a ball in play, or going onto the playing field, will be ejected from the ball park and subject to possible arrest.

Chase Field, A-to-Z Guide, http://arizona.diamondbacks.mlb.com/ari/ballpark/information/index.jsp?content=guide.

56. Once the ball is hit in the stands it is considered abandoned under property law. However, slugger Mike Piazza evidently did not understand this legal concept in depth when he demanded the ball he hit for his 300th home run from a Mets fan. Mets security guards forced the fan to give up the ball which was later given to Piazza. The Mets policy clearly stated fans can keep all balls hit into the stands. Rafael Vasquez had caught the ball and given it to his six-year-old daughter. Vasquez was promised he would get the bat used by Piazza when he hit the 300th home run. Vasquez did not get that bat but instead was given another bat. Piazza claimed to know nothing about the incident until a few weeks after the security guards seized the ball from Vasquez. He later stated the 300th home run ball was a "personal heirloom." Finkelman, "Fugitive Baseballs and Abandoned Property," 1624–1625.
57. *Popov*, 2002 WL 31833731, at 3 n.17.
58. Ibid.
59. Ibid.
60. Ibid., 3 n.21, quoting Roger Bernhardt & Ann M. Burkhart, *Real Property In A Nutshell* (St. Paul, MN: West Group, 2000), 3. Professor Bernhardt is one of the leading scholar's in the field of property law and has authorized several texts on the subject.
61. *Popov*, 4 n.22, quoting Ray Andrews Brown, *The Law of Personal Property*, 3rd ed. (Chicago: Callaghan, 1975), 21. Professor Brown is also a leading scholar in the property law field and has published widely in the field.
62. *Popov*, 2002 WL 31833731, at 4.
63. Ibid., 3.
64. Ibid.
65. Ibid., 4.
66. Ibid., 5.
67. Ibid.
68. Ibid.
69. Ibid., 3.
70. *See* Popov Complaint, 2001 WL 35949995.
71. Ibid., 6.
72. Ibid.
73. Ibid.
74. Ibid.
75. Ibid.
76. Ibid., 7.
77. Ibid.
78. 33 A. 1055 (N.J. Ch. 1896).
79. Ibid., 1056–1057.
80. *Popov*, 2002 WL 31833731, at 8.
81. Michael D. Barnes of the Barnes Group had indicated the ball would sell in the range of $1.2 million to $3 million in a public auction. Declaration of Michael D. Barnes in Opposition to Motion for Preliminary Injunction, para. 9, *Popov v. Hayashi*, 2002 WL 31833731 (Cal. Super. Ct. Dec. 18, 2002) (No. 400545), *available at* 2001 WL 35947037.
82. *Triano v. Popov*, 2005 WL 1230766 (Cal. Super. Ct. May 24, 2005) (No. A106857). Matt Bean, *Baseball Dispute in Court, Again* (9 July 2003), http://news.findlaw.com/court_tv/s/200 30709/09jul2003151330.html.
83. Bean, *Baseball Dispute in Court, Again.*
84. See *Bernhardt v. Popov*, No. c6c-03-421-765 (Cal. Super. Ct. 25, 2003).
85. *In Re Alexander Popov*, 2007 WL 1970102 (N.D. Cal. July 3, 2007) (No. C-06-2696 MMC).
86. Ibid., 1.
87. Ibid., 3.
88. Jonathan Saltzman, "Sox Play Tough on Memento: Lawyers File '04 Series Ball," *Boston Globe*, 1 December 2005. The lawsuit was filed by the Red Sox on November 30, 2005 in the Suffolk Superior Court.
89. Brian E. Tierney, "A Fielder's Choice: How Agency Law Decides the True Owner of the 2004 Red Sox Final-Out Baseball," *Willamette Sports Law Journal* 3 (2006): 1.
90. Chase Davis, "Sox Drop Suit Over Series Ball: Agree to Arbitration with Mientkiewicz," *Boston Globe*, 17 December 2005.
91. "Red Sox Resolve Dispute Over Ball," *BBC Sport*, 25 April 2006.

Chapter 2

1. 24 Abb. N. Cas. 393, 9 N.Y.S. 779 (N.Y. Sup. Ct. 1890)
2. The Ward case has the distinction of being the most significant early baseball case. This was partly due to the fame of Ward. Robert M. Jarvis and Phyllis Coleman, "Early Baseball Law," *American Journal of Legal History* 45 (April 2001): 125. A Westlaw search (May 5, 2010) revealed the case has been cited by 18 other cases as well as 24 law review articles and legal journals.
3. David Hinckley, "Clubhouse Lawyer John Montgomery Ward Chapter 165," *New York Daily News*, 12 October 2003. Ward was also extremely competitive, once punching an umpire.
4. Some of Ward's articles included: "Help Them with the Ball," *Chicago Daily Tribune*, 23 September 1888, 28; "Evolution of Baseball," *Chicago Daily Tribune*, 30 September 1888, 26; "Life of a Ball-Player," *Chicago Daily Tribune*, 9 September 1888, 28; "How Base-Ball is Run," *Chicago Daily*, 25 November 1888, 10; "Fans vs. Pitcher: John M. Ward on Baseball," *Baseball Magazine*, 7 (February 1912): 83–84; "Are Players Chattel, Abstracts from a Ball Player's Letter," *New York Times*, 17 July 1887; "A Batter's Prime," *Baseball Magazine* 20 (1918): 404–406; "Why Great Fielders Don't Hit," *Baseball Magazine* 11 (October 1913): 40–44; "Important Changes in the Baseball Rules," *Baseball Magazine* 25 (June 1920): 335–336, 357–358; "The Coming Southpaw," *Baseball Magazine* 17 (July 1916): 43–46; "The Science of the Game (Part I)," *Baseball Magazine* 11 (August 1913): 61–68; "The Famous Sisler Case," *Baseball Magazine* 21 (July 1918): 33–37; "The Proposed

Reform in Batting Records," *Baseball Magazine* 21 (July 1918): 283–284, 298–299; "Butch Schmidt, the Player-Worker," *Baseball Magazine* 16 (March 1916): 33–50.

5. John M. Ward, *Ward's Base Ball Book, How to Become a Player* (Montgomery, AL: Athletic Publishing, 1888).

6. Bryan Di Salvatore, *A Clever Base-Ballist: The Life and Times of John Montgomery Ward* (New York: Pantheon Books, 1999), quoting *Summer Snap: New York Clipper*, December 26, 1896. Di Salvatore's book provides a through and insightful look at Ward's life.

7. "It may or may not be a serious reflection upon the accuracy of his history that the circumstances of the invention of the first ball are developed in some doubt. Herodotus attributes it to the Lydians, but several other writers unite in conceding to a certain beautiful lady of Corcyra, Anagalla by name, the credit of first having made a ball for the purpose of pastime. Several passages in Homer rather sustain this latter view, and, therefore, with the weight of evidence, and to the glory of woman, we, too, shall adopt this theory. Anagalla did not apply for letters patent, but, whether from goodness of heart or inability to keep a secret, she lost no time in making known her invention and explaining its uses. Homer, then, relates how:

"O'er the green mead the sporting virgins play,
Their Shining veils unbound; along the skies,
Tost and retost, the ball incessant flies."

And this is the first ball game on record, though it is perhaps unnecessary to say that it was not yet base-ball." Ward, *Ward's Base Ball Book*, 9, citing to the Odyssey of Homer, Book VI.

8. Ward went to law school during the off-season. Even though he had never completed undergraduate studies, Ward would first receive a Bachelor of Law in the summer of 1885 and later a Bachelor of Philosophy degree. Ward graduated from law school on May 27, 1885, in the evening. That afternoon he played for the Giants against Buffalo in a 24–0 win. He scored three runs and had three hits in the game. Di Salvatore, *A Clever Base-Ballist*, 182–183.

9. Ward has been called the Marvin Miller of his day. Red Smith, "The Catfish Hunter of His Time," *New York Times*, 14 April 1975. For further study of John Ward and his extraordinary life, see Davin Stevens, *Baseball's Radical for All Seasons: A Biography of John Montgomery Ward* (Lanham, M.D.: Scarecrow Press, 1998).

10. Jerrey Malloy, *Sol White's History of Colored Base Ball: With Other Documents on the Early Black Game, 1886–1936* (Lincoln, N.E.: Bison Books, 1995). Di Salvatore says Ward wanted to sign Geroge Stovey and Moses Fleetwood Walker, Walker was a black player who had been educated at The University of Michigan. Ward was thrown out while attempting to steal by Walker and become so impressed with him he wanted to sign him to a contract as well. Cap. Anson was opposed, so Ward evidently dropped the matter. Di Salvatore, *A Clever Base-Ballist*, 235–237.

11. "Helen Dauvray's Choice," *New York Times*, 12 October 1887, 1.

12. Robert A. Gelzheiser, *Labor and Capital in 19th Century Baseball* (Jefferson, NC: McFarland, 1955), 121.

13. Ward, along with some other students, built the first baseball field on the Penn State campus.

14. Penn State faculty minutes, October 6, 1876, quoted in Di Salvatore, *A Clever Base-Ballist*, 55.

15. Penn State faculty minutes, January 26, 1877, quoted in Di Salvatore, *A Clever Base-Ballist*, 56. Attorney John Orvis wrote a letter to the president of Penn State on behalf of "Monte" Ward and his companion McCormick stating in part "I was chiefly instrumental in getting Mrs. Ward to send Monte up there. This I now regret, as I believe it has been a serious wrong to him; as I have no doubt he would have gone through any other college without any difficulty.... The Great trouble seems to be, that the Faculty do not have the confidence or respect of but a small proportion of the students. This causes large numbers to voluntarily leave, and others to conduct themselves as to be dismissed.... Instead of spending any more time and labor in canvassing for new students, we had better put forth our efforts to secure a Faculty that will possess both the disposition and skill to retain the students they do get." Di Salvatore, *A Clever Base-Ballist*, 57–58.

16. Ward's last record from Penn State indicates "left college."

17. Ward's hometown newspaper did not think much of his chances for success as a ball player. It wrote: "Monte Ward, youngest son of the late lamented James and Ruth Ward, of this place, a young man of talent and whom we had hoped to see a scholar and statesman, perhaps, has become a hired base-ball pitcher. There is no reason why a base-ball pitcher should not eventually become a great man, but the chances, for Monte's sake, we are sorry to say, are against it.... We trust he will pause and reconsider.... Monte, quit it, and go to your books again. Di Salvatore, *A Clever Base-Ballist*, quoting "Monte Ward, Youngest Son," *Democratic Watchman*, July 13, 1877.

18. "Monty Ward First to Use Curve Ball," *Altoona Mirror*, 4 June 1923, 17.

19. John Thorn and Pete Palmer, *Total Baseball: The Most Complete Baseball Encyclopedia Ever!* (New York: Warner Books, 1989), 1980.

20. Gary Gillete and Pete Palmer, *The ESPN Baseball Encyclopedia*, 4th ed. (New York: Sterling Publishing, 2007), 252.

21. Ibid.

22. "Fireman of the Year Award Began in 1960," *Sporting News*. In 2001 the name of the award was changed to The Sporting News Reliever of the Year.

23. Hy Turkin and S.C. Thompson, *The Official Encyclopedia of Baseball*, 3rd rev. ed. (New York: A.S. Barnes, 1963).
24. John Thorn and Pete Palmer, 1528.
25. Stolen bases records for Ward were not available before 1885. A base runner was also given credit for a stolen base if they took a base on either a hit or an out.
26. Norman MacLean, *All Time Greatest: Who's Who in Baseball 1872–1990* (New York: Who's Who in Baseball Magazine), 99–100.
27. Gillette and Palmer, *ESPN Baseball Encyclopedia*, 1682.
28. One interesting aspect of the divorce decree between the couple was that Ward could never remarry while Dauvray was still alive. This agreement would later be rescinded and Ward would remarry. Ward and Dauvray were at odds about whether she should go back to the stage. They separated and eventually divorced. The break up would reveal a very personal side to Ward. He was devastated about the breakup. He told the press he would keep his personal matters private, stating "I don't know what would become of me, I love my wife dearly, and would have done anything in the world to make her happy, but to consent to her return to the stage never." "Ward's Heart Broken," *Trenton Times* 8, 18 April 1890, 2292.
29. Ward also ran for Justice of the Peace in Long Island in 1907; "John Ward is Out for office," *Washington Post*, 16 March 1907, 8.
30. Gelzheiser, *Labor and Capital in 19th Century Baseball*, 84.
31. Ibid., 93.
32. "Mr. Ward Duly Received," *Chicago Daily*, 18 November 1887, 3.
33. Ibid.
34. Ibid.
35. "A Letter to the Brotherhood," *Washington Post*, 21 November 1887, 2.
36. Ibid. In his book on baseball, Ward addressed a player's training regimen and the use of alcohol: "If he finds it necessary to take some light stimulant, let it be done *with* the evening meal. Never take liquor at any other time. I do not favor the indiscriminate use of any drink, but, on the contrary, oppose it as a most harmful practice; I do believe, however, that a glass of ale, beer, or claret with one's meal is in some cases beneficial. A thin, nervous person, worn out with the excitement and fatigue of the day, will find it a genuine tonic; it will soothe and quit his nerves and send him earlier to bed and asleep. The 'beefy' individual, with plenty of reserve force, needs no stimulant, and should never touch liquor at any time. If taken at all, it should be solely as a tonic and never as a social beverage." Ward, *Ward's Base Ball Book*, 43.
37. Ibid.
38. Ibid.
39. Ibid.
40. Ibid.
41. Ibid.
42. For a good overview of the tour, see Mark Lamster, *Spalding's World Tour: The Epic Adventure that Took Baseball Around the Globe—and Made It America's Game* (New York: Public Affairs, 2006).
43. Geoffrey C. Ward and Ken Burns, *Baseball an Illustrated History* (New York: Alfred A. Knopf, 1994), 29.
44. Ibid., 31.
45. Dean A. Sullivan, *Early Innings: A Documentary History of Baseball, 1825–1908* (Lincoln, NE.: Bison Books, 1997), citing to *New York Clipper*, 1 December 1888.
46. Gelheiser, *Labor and Capital in 19th Century Baseball*, 95, citing to *The Sporting Life*, 8 January 1890.
47. The complete Manifesto can be found in Sullivan, *Early Innings*, 188–89.
48. Albert G. Spalding, *America's National Game 1839–1915* (Cleveland, OH: Halo Books, 1911), 173.
49. The league would have eight teams, Boston, New York, Brooklyn, Philadelphia, Pittsburgh, Cleveland, Buffalo, and Chicago. The clubs would be under the central administration of an eight-man board, four selected by the financial backers of the team and four by the players. The league itself was governed by a senate composed of 16 men, two representatives from each team.
50. "We're Not in the Swim," *Pittsburgh Post*, 10 October 1889.
51. Immediately after the establishment of the Players League it became clear Ward was its essential member: "John Montgomery Ward is the body, soul, and brains of the Players League. Without him it would be a ship without a rudder or a kite without a tail. Without the New York short stop the Players League would flounder around for a week or two and then go to pieces on the shoals of League opposition." "Exchange: Short Stops," *New York Times*, 22 December 1889, 16.
52. Gelzheiser, *Labor and Capital in 19th Century Baseball*, 121, citing to Harold Seymour and Dorothy Seymour Mills, *Baseball: The Early Years* (New York: Oxford University Press, 1960), 288.
53. Ward and Burns, *Baseball, an Illustrated History*, 39.
54. "The Ball Players' Revolt," *New York Times*, 23 September 1889, 2.
55. Ward and Burns, *Baseball, an Illustrated History*, 39.
56. Gelzheiser, *Labor and Capital in 19th Century Baseball*, 125, citing Bill James, *The Baseball Book* (New York: Villard Books, 1990).
57. Roger I. Abrams, *Legal Bases: Baseball and the Law* (Philadelphia: Temple University Press, 1998). Although not considered very reliable, the published attendance showed 980,887 for the Players League and 813, 678 for the National

Notes — Chapter 2

League; Seymour and Mills, *Baseball: The Early Years*, 237. *Reach's Official Base-Ball Guide 1889–1891* (1895) supports these figures.

58. "On the Baseball Field," *New York Times*, 1 May 1890, 3. Ward's Brooklyn squad prevailed 10–3. Ward went 1 for 1 but did commit an error in the field.

59. "Baseball Notes," *New York Times*, 24 January 1890.

60. Ibid.

61. Ibid.

62. *Black's Law Dictionary* defines an injunction as "A court order commanding or preventing an action. To get an injunction, the complainant must show that there is no plain, adequate, and complete remedy at law and that an irreparable injury will result unless the relief is granted." *Black's Law Dictionary*, 8th ed. (St. Paul, MN: West, 2004).

63. Seymour and Mills, *Baseball: The Early Years*, 108.

64. *Metropolitan Exhibition Co. v. Ward*, 24 Abb. N. Cas. 393, 401, 9 N.Y.S. 779 (N.Y. Sup. Ct. 1890).

65. Ibid.

66. Ibid., 402.

67. Ibid.

68. Ibid. Ward was arguing that the contract was unfair to him and "without equity." Ibid.

69. Ibid., 402–403, citing *Lumley v. Wagner*, 2 De Gex; *Hochester v. De la Tour*, 2 E. & B. 678; *Frost v. Knight*, L. R. 7 Ex. 111; *Howard v. Daly*, 61 N.Y. 362; *Daly v. Smith*, 33 Supr. Ct. 158; *Hayes v. Willis*, 11 Abb. Pr. N.S. 167; *McCaull v. Braham*, 16 Fed. Rep. 37.

70. Although the league argued that Ward's services were unique, others disagreed. When Ward went on the world tour in 1888 he indicated he might not be back in time for the season to start because he and his wife wanted to see the world. President Day of the New York Club objected. He said Ward would be treated like any other player and if he was not around when the season started someone would take his place. He stated, "I could get half a dozen men to fill his position better than he has this year. His work by long odds has been very unsatisfactory." "To Go Around The World," *New York Times*, 7 October 1888, 2. Napoleon Lajoie would face the same issue of "uniqueness" eleven years later in his lawsuit with the Philadelphia Phillies but unlike Ward, Lajoie would lose.

71. *Metropolitan*, 24 Abb. N. Cas. at 403. The Boston-New York baseball rivalry was alive and well in January 1890. As noted by one Boston writer: "The Ward suit is not interesting many down this way, as all the leading lawyers of this city say that it is impossible to keep him from playing ball where he sees fit next season. The directors of the Boston club would bring a lawsuit, but they know how the case would be treated in this State. Boston is out for the pennant next season, but I am afraid that your brotherhood team will walk off with that prize money." "T. H. Mur-

nane, "Base-Ball News from Boston," *Chicago Daily Tribune*, 19 January 1890, 7.

72. *Metropolitan*, 24 Abb. N. Cas. at 405.

73. Ward, *Ward's Base Ball Book*, 30–31

74. *Metropolitan*, 24 Abb. N. Cas. at 405.A contract can be declared unconscionable and therefore unenforceable. Unconscionable is defined by *Black Law's Dictionary* as: "An agreement that no promisor with any sense, and not under a delusion, would make, and that no honest and fair promise would accept."

75. *Metropolitan*, 24 Abb. N. Cas. at 405.

76. Ibid., 406.

77. 14 F. 257, 259 (C.C. Pa. 1882). The court held, "Specific performance will not be enforced, directly or indirectly, unless the agreement is mutual, its terms certain, its enforcement practicable, and the complainant is without adequate redress in an action at law ... and it will not be enforced when it is doubtful whether an agreement has been concluded, nor where the duties are continuous and require skill and judgment...." (citations omitted).

78. Gelzheiser, *Labor and Capital in 19th Century Baseball*, p. 132.

79. *Metropolitan*, 24 Abb. N. Cas. at 411.

80. Ibid., 418.

81. Ibid., 411.

82. Ibid., 407.

83. 49 How. Pr. 150 (N.Y. Super. Ct. 1874).

84. *Metropolitan*, 24 Abb. N. Cas. at 410.

85. Ibid., 412.

86. Ibid., 413.

87. Ibid.

88. Ibid., 414.

89. Ibid., 395 n.al. Ward's case was well publicized. It even became the subject of a *Harvard Law Review* article in 1890. The author wrote the article after the injunction had been denied but before the final resolution of the case in March 1890. The author stated that although Judge O'Brien refused to grant the preliminary injunction, "it seems to us that the plaintiff company has a very good chance of obtaining a permanent injunction on the hearing of the case, the plain construction of the word 'reserve' is this: it is the right to keep, to hold for future use." *Harvard Law Review* 3 (1890): 330. And: "The final judgment of the Supreme Court of New York on this bill will be watched for with interest." Ibid., 331.

90. *Metropolitan*, 24 Abb. N. Cas. at 395 n.al.

91. Ibid.

92. Ibid.

93. Ibid.

94. Ibid., 418–419.

95. Ibid., 418.

96. Ibid., 419 n.al.

97. 8 Pa. C.C. 57 (Ct. Com. Pl. 1890). This case was decided March 15, 1890. Other players were also successful in court including Tom Keefe, Hardie Richardson, and George Gore.

98. Seymour and Mills, *Baseball: The Early Years*, 239.

99. Why would Ward go back to National League after all the difficulties he had endured in overcoming the reserve clause and establishing a new league? Di Salvatore says, "The final answer is elusive." He contemplates that Ward, although "fiercely competitive," must have had his limits as well. Maybe he "could not contemplate another loss." Di Salvatore, *A Clever Base-Ballist*, 298–299.

100. "It will be taken for granted that the late John M. Ward was a smart ball player. His subsequent career, after he retired from baseball, proved that. He studied law and become a very successful lawyer in this city." John Kieran, "Sports of the Times," *New York Times*, 3 February 1931, 35.

101. "Ward Golf Champion of New Jersey Clubs," *New York Times*, 4 June 1905, 22.

102. A.B. Cratty, "Pirate Points," *Sporting Life*, 1 June 1912, 8.

103. "Pulliam, Self Shot, Dies on his Wound," *New York Times*, 30 July 1909, 14.

104. Ibid.

105. Di Salvatore, *A Clever Base-Ballist*, 374.

106. "Ward-Johnson: Result of Suit by Lawyer Against President," *Sporting Life*, 20 May 1911, 24.

107. Ibid.

108. His Cooperstown plaque states: "Pitching pioneer who won 158, lost 102 games in seven years. Pitched perfect game for Providence of N.L. in 1880. Turned to shortstop and made 2,151 hits. Managed New York and Brooklyn in N.L. president of Boston, N.L. 1911–1912. Played important part in establishing modern organized baseball." www.*baseballhalloffame.com*.

Chapter 3

1. 51 A. 973 (Pa. Sup. Ct. 1902); *see also Philadelphia Base-Ball Club v. Lajoie*, 10 Pa. D. 309, 1901 WL 4150 (Com. Pl. 1901); *Philadelphia Baseball Club v. Lajoie*, 13 Ohio Dec. 504, 1902 WL 1036 (Com. Pl. 1902).

2. Arthur Daley, "Sports of the Times," *New York Times*, 5 December 1954, S2.

3. After his playing days John Ward weighed in on who was the "super-player" of the day in an article he wrote. He found that Ty Cobb was "superior" to Lajoie and Honus Wagner but did state Lajoie was the greatest fielder on record. John J. Ward, "The Aristocracy of Baseball Stardom," *Baseball Magazine* 17 (May 1916): 37–41. Ward set forth "four acid tests" to determine the "super-players."

4. "Napoleon 'Nap' Lajoie combined graceful fielding with precision at the plate." *National Baseball Hall of Fame and Museum 2007 Yearbook* (Cooperstown, NY: Baseball Hall of Fame and Museum, 2007), 89. An early baseball article described Lajoie as follows: "An inch over six feet in height, he is a very heavy man, weighing nearly two hundred pounds, but he moves with the same light step and easy bearing which have made his fielding such a thing of absolute perfection." F. C. Lane, "The Inside Facts of the Great Lajoie Deal," *Baseball Magazine* 15 (June 1915): 50–62.

5. "Napoleon Lajoie, "One of Greats, Dies in Florida at 83," *New York Times*, 8 February 1959.

6. Ibid.

7. www.*baseball-reference.com*.

8. Ron Smith, "Baseball's Greatest Players: A Celebration of the 20th Century's Best," *Sporting News*, 1998.

9. Brad Sullivan, *Batting Four Thousand: Baseball in the Western Reserve* (Lincoln: University of Nebraska Press, 2008), 97–98.

10. www.*baseball-reference.com*.

11. The Lajoie case elicited several early scholarly articles dealing with specific performance of contracts. See "Specific Performance. Defenses. Clean Hands: Application of the Maxim to Baseball Contracts," *Harvard Law Review* 28 (1914): 213–214. "The Doctrine of Mutuality in Specific Performance Cases," *Yale Law Journal* 27 (1917): 261–262.

12. The Lajoie case proved to be the subject for law students as well. Before the Court of Common Pleas of Pennsylvania made its decision, the case was used as an example in a contracts class at the Penn Law School. The dean of the law school predicted the option clause would be upheld but the remainder of the contract would be unenforceable. He stated, "No court will uphold it." Norman L. Macht, *Connie Mack and the Early Years of Baseball* (Lincoln: University of Nebraska Press, 2007), 227.

13. www.*baseball-almanac.com*. Mike Shatzkin, *The Ballplayers: The One and Only Book That Tells the Stories Behind the Stats* (Westminster, MD: Arbor House, 1990), 595.

14. "Lajoie Signs with American League," *New York Times*, 21 March 1901, 7.

15. "Cross and Frazer Jump," *Washington Post*, 17 March 1901, 3.

16. "Trying to Get Players," *Chicago Daily Tribune*, 19 November 1889, 6.

17. "Baseball Gossip," *New York Times*, 5 December 1889, 5; Col. Rogers set forth the following proclamation in November 1889 which was unanimously adopted by the owners: "Resolved, that this League hereby declare that it will aid each of its club members in the enforcement of the contract rights of such clubs to the services of its reserve players for the season of 1890, and the League, with all power to act, and to formulate and carry out the best methods of enforcement of said contract rights of mid note clubs; and that said committee, be authorized to draw upon the guarantee fund of the League for such amount as may be necessary to carry out the intent and purpose of this resolution." "The Base Ball Bluffers, A Bluff at the Brotherhood," *Pittsburgh Post*, 16 November 1889, 6.

18. "Brush Will Keep his Men," *Chicago Daily Tribune*, 2 February 1890, 3.

Notes — Chapter 3

19. "Col. John I. Rogers," *New York Times*, 14 March 1910. See also "Its Labor Finished," *Tyrone Daily Herald*, 25 July 1889.
20. Col. Rogers originally purchased the Worchester Brown stockings and relocated them to Philadelphia. *www.mlb.com*. He would later sell the team after the death of twelve fans and hundreds more were hurt during a bleacher collapse on August 8, 1903. Multiple lawsuits were filed alleging the ballpark was faulty and that the club were responsible. Bob Warrington, "'Black Saturday': Philadelphia's Deadliest Sports Disaster," *Philadelphia Athletics Historical Society*, www.philadelphiaathletics.org; "Stands Falls at Philadelphia," *Chicago Daily Tribune*, 9 August 1903, 9. "We find that the accident was due to the rotten condition of the supporting timbers of the balcony, and we further find that the Philadelphia Base Ball Club (Limited) was responsible for not having a thorough examination made of these timbers throughout the time of their ownership and in stating at the time of the transfer for that the buildings were in first-class condition.... This verdict absolves from blame the *present* owners of the Philadelphia National League base ball club, who purchased the franchises early this year from the former company, of which John I. Rogers was the principal stockholder." "Timbers Were Rotten," *Tyrone Daily Harvard*, 20 August 1903.
21. "Trying to Hold Lajoie," *Washington Post*, 27 March 1901.
22. "Lajoie's Attorney Demur," *Washington Post*, 30 March 1901.
23. Ibid.
24. "Lajoie Case on Trial," *Washington Post*, 21 April 1901.
25. Ibid.
26. Ibid.
27. "Injunction Against Lajoie Dismissed," *New York Times*, 18 May 1901, 10.
28. "Captain Lajoie of the Philadelphias," *Chicago Daily Tribune*, 22 May 1901, 6.
29. The National League Philadelphia Club finished second without Lajoie, one place higher than the previous season.
30. "Baseball Appeal to Supreme Court," *New York Times*, 15 November 1901, 10.
31. "Baseball Case is Postponed: Lajoie is Not Dead," *Chicago Daily Tribune*, 21 December 1901, 6.
32. "Freedman is 'Spurned' Again," *Chicago Daily Tribune*, 5 April 1902, 8.
33. "Lajoie Refuses Big Offer," *Washington Post*, 5 April 1902, 8. "I have received nothing but the best treatment possible from President Shibe and Manager Mack. I am under contract to the Philadelphia American League club for two years longer. I have no intention of repudiating that contract, and all the offers of the National League will not induce me to desert the American League. I am satisfied with the treatment I have received from Manger Mack, and intend to show my appreciation of it by remaining loyal to him."
34. "The Lajoie Case Receives a Hearing in Pennsylvania's Supreme Court," *Sporting Life*, 25 January 1902, 7.
35. "This decision upholds the validity of the reserve clause in the National League contracts." "Upheld by Supreme Court," *Titusville Morning Herald*, 22 April 1902.
36. The court's opinion referred only to Lajoie even though Bernhard and Fraser were also defendants in the case. Injunctions were eventually issued against all three players.
37. "Hart Says Complete Victory," *Chicago Daily Tribune*, 22 April 1902. See also "In Meches of Law Again: The Lajoie Case," *Sporting Life*, 31 January 1914, 10.
38. "Rogers Wins in the Lajoie Case," *Chicago Daily Tribune*, 22 April 1902, 13.
39. "Calling Players to Time," *Washington Post*, 22 April 1902, 8.
40. Ibid.
41. "League Wins in Court," *Washington Post*, 22 April 1902, 8.
42. "Await Details of Decision," *Chicago Daily Tribune*, 22 April 1902, 13.
43. "Baseball Players Enjoined," *New York Times*, 24 April 1902, 6; "Lajoie Injunction," *Oil City Derrick*, 24 April 1902.
44. "Fierce Legal War: Temporary Injunction," *Sporting Life*, 3 May 1902, 6.
45. "Baseball War in Court," *Washington Post*, 24 April 1902, 8.
46. Ibid. He went 1–4 with 1 RBI and a stolen base in the game.
47. Ibid.
48. Ban Johnson stated the "American League would assume the aggressive and give the National League all the litigation it cared for." "Fight to a Finish," *Titusville Morning Herald*, 1 May 1902. The best defense is a good offense and, with that in mind, the Washington club of the American League filed a lawsuit against the National League on April 24, 1902, seeking an injunction to prevent them from tampering with any of its players. "Right to the Players," *Washington Post*, 24 April 1902, 8.
49. Ibid.
50. "Lajoie is Out of the Game," *Chicago Daily Tribune*, 29 April 1902, 13.
51. Ibid.
52. "Players Rejoin Athletics," *Chicago Daily Tribune*, 29 April 1902, 13.
53. "Hope to Elude Rogers," *Washington Post*, 2 May 1902, 9.
54. Lajoie actually traveled on a freight car when he had to pass though Pennsylvania during the years the injunction was in place. What a sight that must have been, the greatest second baseman in baseball history riding the rail to avoid jail and stay out of the grasp of Col. Rogers. "Lajoie, Hall of Fame Batsman, Dies at 83," *Chicago Tribune*, 8 February 1959, A1.

55. "Baseball Notes," *Washington Post*, 11 May 1902, 8.
56. "Lajoie and Fraser Jump," *Washington Post*, 16 May 1902, 9; Fraser would play for the Phillies in the 1902 season and compile a 12–13 record. In 1901, he went 22–16 with the Philadelphia Athletics.
57. Ibid.
58. "National League May get Lajoie," *New York Times*, 18 May 1902, 11.
59. "Baseball Notes," *Washington Post*, 21 May 1902, 9.
60. Macht, *Connie Mack and the Early Years of Baseball*, 272.
61. Ibid.; "Lajoie Holding Out," *Sporting Life*, 24 May 1902, 5.
62. Many thought that Lajoie would never sign with Philadelphia. "Reach and Rogers have about as much chance of signing Lajoie as they have of signing Grover Cleveland," said President Kilfoyle, of the Clevelands, when asked concerning the efforts of the Quakers to induce Larry to return." "American Affairs," *Sporting Life*, 19 July 1902, 11.
63. Ibid.
64. "Detroit to Get Lajoie," *Chicago Daily Tribune*, 11 May 1902, 10.
65. "The World of Base Ball," *The Sporting Life*, 7 June 1902, 2.
66. "Somers Succeeds," *Sporting Life*, 31 May 1902. Colonel Rogers took immediate action, sending a telegram to Robert Young which read "go to game to-day, and if Lajoie or Bernhard take part in same swear to affidavit of fact and send it to me immediately." Ibid.
67. "Cleveland Defeats Boston," *Chicago Daily Tribune*, 5 June 1902, 13.
68. "The Legal Warfare: Col. John I. Rogers Makes Another Move in Court," *Sporting Life*, 21 June 1902, 3.
69. "Lajoie Deal not yet Close," *Chicago Daily Tribune*, 29 May 1902, 13.
70. "Baseball Notes," *Washington Post*, 28 May 1902, 9. On June 17, 1902, approximately two weeks after Lajoie had made his debut with Cleveland, John Rogers was trying to get Judge Ralston in the court of common pleas to hold Lajoie and Bernhard in contempt of court for disobeying the injunction. Judge Ralston made no decision that day, with Rogers saying he would present the necessary authority to the judge in a few days to support his position. "On the Diamond: Lajoie and Bernhard," *Titusville Morning Herald*, 18 June 1902.
71. "Baseball Notes," *Washington Post*, 8 June 1902.
72. "American Wins in Lajoie Case," *Chicago Daily Tribune*, 10 July 1902, 6.
73. "Rain Stops White Sox," *Chicago Daily Tribune*, 25 July 1902, 4. Lajoie responded: "The $10,000 sounds good, but you know I am under contract to the Cleveland Club. Wait until I get back in Cleveland, and if I can get my release we will talk business. However, I cannot hold back any hope of the release." Ibid.
74. "Rogers in Court Again," *Washington Post*, 2 August 1902, 9.
75. "Turn Fire on Col. Rogers," *Chicago Daily Tribune*, 8 August 1902, 6. Colonel Rogers was less than complimentary of the judge. *See* "Cleveland Chatter," *Sporting Life*, 16 August 1902, 2.
76. "Fails to Enjoin Players," *Chicago Daily Tribune*, 17 August 1902, A11; "Roger's Rebuff," *Sporting Life*, 23 August 1902, 11.
77. "Players Selected as the Strongest Possible Team from the American League," *Chicago Daily Tribune*, 28 September 1902, 9.
78. Ibid.
79. Ibid.
80. "Cleveland 3, Philadelphia, 2," *New York Times*, 12 June 1903, 7.
81. "There is no right by the team to demand performance of a player for a player's non-performance as exhibited by his jumping to another team, however, they can obtain equitable performance by way of injunctive relief through a contractual clause." Walter T. Champion, Jr., *Sports Law In a Nutshell* (Eagan, MN: West, 2005), citing to *Philadelphia Ball Club v. Lajoie* (1902).
82. Ibid.
83. *Lumley v. Wagner*, (1852) 42 Eng. Rep. 687 (Ch.); 1 De G.M.&G. 604.
84. *Philadelphia Base-Ball Club, Limited, v. Lajoie*, 10 Pa.D. 309, 1901 WL 4150, 2 (Com. Pl. 1901).
85. Ibid., 1901 WL 4150, 6.
86. Ibid.
87. Ibid.
88. Sports Law Professor Walter T. Champion has presented it as follows: "The use of injunctions as a remedy in professional sports was established in *Philadelphia Ball Club v. Lajoie* (1902) which allowed a ball club to enjoin a professional baseball player, a future Hall of Fame member, one Napoleon Lajoie, when he attempted to play for another team. The injunction was authorized to restrain Lajoie from rendering services to another team since his services were of a unique character which would render them of peculiar value to the baseball club." Champion, *Sports Law In a Nutshell*, 10–11.
89. *Philadelphia Base-Ball Club, Limited*, 1901 WL 4150 at 7.
90. Ibid. (containing contract clause at issue).
91. Ibid., 9.
92. Macht, *Connie Mack and the Early Years of Baseball*, 229.
93. Ibid.
94. Ibid.
95. Ibid.
96. Ibid.
97. Ibid., 230.
98. At various times, Dryden wrote for both the *Chicago Daily Tribune* and the *Chicago Examiner*. He was the highest paid writer of his time. *www.baseballalmanac.com*.

99. Macht, *Connie Mack and the Early Years of Baseball*, 230.
100. Ibid.
101. Ibid.
102. Ibid.
103. Ibid., 231.
104. Ibid.
105. Ibid.
106. *Philadelphia Ball Club v. Lajoie*, 51 A. 973, 974 (Pa. Sup. Ct. 1902).
107. Ibid.
108. Ibid.
109. There have only been 14 Triple Crown winners in the 216 combined seasons of baseball's modern era, 1901–2008. Carl Yastrzemski was the last player to win it in 1967. Ted Williams and Rogers Hornsby both won it twice. John E. Daniels, "Where Have you Gone, Carl Yastrzemski? A Statistical Analysis of the Triple Crown," *Baseball Research Journal* 37 (2008).
110. *Philadelphia Ball Club*, 51 A. at 974.
111. Ibid., 975.
112. This was rather an odd statement since players had virtually no ability to negotiate terms of a contract. A player's contract was essentially a contract of adhesion. "In an adhesion contract, there is no adjustment of rights of the parties; the contract is on a take-it-or-leave-it basis." 1 Richard A. Lord, *Williston on Contracts* § 1:20, 4th ed., citing *Bilbrey v. Cingular Wireless, L.L.C.*, 2007 OK 54, 164 P.3d 131 (Okla. 2007).
113. *Philadelphia Baseball Club Co. v. Lajoie*, 13 Ohio Dec. 504, 1902 WL 1036, at *1 (Com. Pl.).
114. U.S. Constitution, art. IV, § 1: "Full Faith and Credit shall be given in each State to the public Acts, Records, and judicial Proceedings of every other State. And the Congress may by general Laws prescribe the Manner in which such Acts, Records and Proceedings shall be proved, and the Effect thereof."
115. *Philadelphia Baseball Club Co.*1902 WL 1036 at *4.
116. Professor Abrams deemed the Ohio decision as "a truly remarkable judgment." Roger I. Abrams, *Legal Bases: Baseball and the Law* (Philadelphia: Temple University Press, 1998), 40.
117. "A shrewd lawyer adept at the discovery and manipulation of legal technicalities." *The American Heritage Dictionary* (Orlando, FL: Houghton Mifflin, 1976), 931.
118. Rogers died of heart failure on March 17, 1910. It was noted he was "a prominent attorney of Philadelphia and for twenty years the biggest stockholder in the Philadelphia National League Baseball Club...." "Col. John L. Rogers Dies," *Wellsboro Gazette*, 17 March 1910.
119. Champion, *Sports Law In a Nutshell*.
120. *See generally* C. Paul III Rogers, "Napoleon Lajoie, Breach of Contract and the Great Baseball War," *SMU Law Review* 55 (2002): 325–345.
121. *Marchio v. Letterlough*, 237 F. Supp. 2d 580 (E.D. Pa. 2003).
122. Ibid., 586–87. The *Lajoie* decision has clearly had a significant impact on American contract Law. The *Lajoie* case continues to be read and analyzed by law students today. Two textbooks, which are widely used to teach sports law in U.S. law schools contain the court's opinion. Walter T. Champion, Jr., *Sports Law: Cases, Documents, and Materials* (New York: Aspen Publishers, 2005) and Paul C. Weiler, and Gary R. Roberts, *Sports and the Law: Cases, Materials, and Problems* (Eagan, MN:: West Publishing, 1993). It has also been cited in numerous sports-related cases. *See, e.g., Machen v. Johansson*, 174 F. Supp. 522 (S.D.N.Y. 1959) (boxing); *Connecticut Professional Sports Corp. v. Heyman*, 276 F. Supp. 618 (S.D.N.Y. 1967) (basketball); *Madison Square Garden Corp. v. Braddock*, 90 F.2d 924 (3d Cir. 1937) (case involving "The Cinderella Man," James J. Braddock); *Dallas Cowboys Football Club v. Harris*, 348 S.W.2d 37 (Tex. Civ. App.1961) (football); *American League Baseball Club of Chicago v. Chase*, 149 N.Y.S. 6 (N.Y. Sup. 1914) (baseball); *Winnipeg Rugby Football Club v. Freeman*, 140 F. Supp. 365 (N.D. Ohio 1955) (rugby); *Cincinnati Bengals, Inc. v. Bergey*, 453 F. Supp. 129 (S.D. Ohio 1974) (football); *Philadelphia Hockey Club v. Flett*, 58 Pa. D. & C.2d 367, 1972 WL 16067 (Pa.Com. Pl. 1972) (hockey).
123. Through August of the 1902 season the Athletics had attracted more than 290,000 fans, "averaging about 5,700 to the Phillies' 2,100." Macht, *Connie Mack and the Early Years of Baseball*, 291.
124. The standard player contract for Major League Baseball currently states in relation to the uniqueness of a player:

PLAYER REPRESENTATIONS
Ability
4.(a) The Player represents and agrees that he has exceptional and *unique* skill and ability as a baseball player; that his services to be rendered hereunder are of a special, unusual and extraordinary character which gives them peculiar value which cannot be reasonably or adequately compensated for in damage at law, and the Player's breach of this contract will cause the Club great and irreparable injury and damages. The Player agrees that, in addition to other remedies, the Club shall be entitled to injunctive and other equitable relief to prevent a breach of this contract by the Player, including, among others, the right to enjoin the Player from playing baseball for any other person or organization during the term of his contract. 2007–2011 Basic Agreement, Schedule A-Uniform Player's Contract, para. 4.(a), 210 (emphasis added).
125. "Lajoie, Hall of Fame Batsman, Dies at 83," *Chicago Tribune*, 8 February 1959, A1.

Chapter 4

1. 181 S.W. 1167 (Mo. Ct. App. 1916)
2. See Rob Neyer, *Rob Meyer's Big Book of Baseball Blunders* (New York: Fireside, 2006); G. Edward White, *Creating the National Pastime: Baseball Transforms Itself* (Princeton, NJ: Princeton University Press, 1996), 88.
3. For a good discussion of the batting race, see Al Stump, *Cobb: A Biography* (Chapel Hill, NC: Algonquin Books, 1996), 194–199; Daniel E. Ginsburg, *The Fix Is In: A History of Baseball Gambling and Game Fixing Scandals* (Jefferson, NC: McFarland, 1995).
4. "Chalmers Defends Lajoie," *New York Times*, 16 October 1910.
5. Gary Gillette and Pete Palmer, *The ESPN Baseball Encyclopedia*, 4th ed. (New York: Sterling Publishing, 2007), 396.
6. Ibid.
7. Ibid.
8. *All-Time Greatest Who's Who in Baseball 1872–1990* (New York: Who's Who In Baseball Magazine, 1990).
9. After the 1910 season was over the criteria for the Chalmers award were changed so that it no longer would be based on the highest batting average only. "After discussing the matter pro and con with the leading men in baseball and the leading baseball writers, Mr. Chalmers decided that he would offer a trophy on the broadest possible basis, namely, the basis of the greatest all around value of a player to his team in the pennant race." Ren Mulford, "The Chalmers Baseball Trophy: How this Famous Baseball Prize Originated — The Chalmers Commission — Object of the Award-System of Voting: A Typical Ballot," *Baseball Magazine* 12 (April 1914), 80.
10. Paul MacFarlane, "After 70 Years, Researchers Prove Lajoie Really Did Win," *Sporting News*, 18 April 1981, 1.
11. Cobb was inducted in the Baseball Hall of Fame's inaugural class in June of 1939. Ken Smith, *Baseball's Hall of Fame* (Mew York: Grosset & Dunlap, 1966), 3.
12. In the 1989 movie, *Field of Dreams*, Ray Liotta, playing Shoeless Joe Jackson, says "Ty Cobb wanted to come but none of us could stand the son of a bitch when we were alive so we told him to stick it." Twelve years after the disputed batting title, Cobb alleged he was being treated unfairly in New York when he was not credited with a hit. Ban Johnson, president of the American League, awarded Cobb a hit in December 1922 for a game played in May of that year. "Ty Cobb Calls for Scoring Clean-Up," *New York Times*, 9 December 1922.
13. Daniel Okrent and Harris Lewine, eds., *The Ultimate Baseball Book* (Boston: Houghton Mifflin, 2000), 82.
14. He was inducted into the Baseball Hall of Fame in 1939.
15. Gillette and Palmer, *The ESPN Baseball Encyclopedia*; http://cleveland.indians.mlb.com/cle/history/cle_history_overview.jsp.
16. Ibid.
17. "Odd Doings of Fans," *Washington Post*, 6 November 1910.
18. Ibid.
19. John Thorn and Pete Palmer, eds., *Total Baseball* (New York: Warner Books, 1989), 1353–1354.
20. Ibid.
21. Ibid.
22. Ibid.
23. Ginsburg, *The Fix Is In*, 78, citing 1892 *Spalding Guide*.
24. Alfred H. Spink, *The National Game*, 2nd ed. (St. Louis, Mo.: National Game Pub. Co., 1911; Carbondale: Southern Illinois University Press, 2000), 111.
25. Ibid.
26. Hy Turkin and S.C. Thompson, *The Official Encyclopedia of Baseball*, rev. ed. (New York: A. S. Barnes, 1956), 40.
27. "O'Connor On Way To See Johnson," *Washington Post*, 15 October 1910.
28. "Hedge Lets Out O'Connor," *Chicago Daily Tribune*, 16 October 1910.
29. *O'Connor v. St. Louis American League Baseball, Co.*, 181 S.W. 1167 (Mo. Ct. App. 1916).
30. "Player Corriden Explains," *New York Times*, 15 October 1910.
31. Turkin and Thompson, *The Official Encyclopedia of Baseball*, 113.
32. "Wanted Ninth Hit Badly," *Washington Post*, 14 October 1910, 8.
33. Stump, *Cobb: A Biography*, 194.
34. Ibid.
35. "Major League Records," *New York Times*, 7 August 1910.
36. "Major League Records," *New York Times*, 13 August 1910.
37. "Major League Records," *New York Times*, 4 September 1910.
38. Stump, *Cobb: A Biography*, 194.
39. "Tigers Score Runs in Bunches," *New York Times*, 7 September 1910.
40. "Naps Beat the Champions," *New York Times*, 8 September 1910.
41. Ibid.
42. Ibid.
43. "Detroit Takes One from Cleveland," *New York Times*, 10 September 1910.
44. Ibid.
45. "Tigers Blow Up in Sixth and Lose," *New York Times*, 14 September 1910.
46. Ibid.
47. "Tigers on Heels of Yanks and Red Sox," *New York Times*, 15 September 1910.
48. Ibid.
49. "Major League Records," *New York Times*, 18 September 1910.
50. "Texas Pitcher Beats Athletics," *New York Times*, 20 September 1910.

51. "Major League Records," *New York Times*, 25 September 1910.
52. "Boston and Naps in a Tie," *New York Times*, 27 September 1910.
53. "Boston Loses Two to Naps," *New York Times*, 28 September 1910.
54. Ibid.
55. "Red Sox Could Not Hit Kaler," *New York Times*, 29 September 1910.
56. "Yanks Make Clean Sweep In Detroit," *New York Times*, 29 September 1910.
57. "Lajoie Keeps Up His Batting," *New York Times*, 2 October 1910.
58. "Cobb and Lajoie Each Gets Three Hits," *New York Times*, 6 October 1910.
59. "Lajoie Gets Three More Hits," *New York Times*, 7 October 1910.
60. "League Baseball Records for the Week," *New York Times*, 9 October 1910. To qualify for the batting title, a player had to appear in 100 games. Richard Marazzi, *The Rules and Lore of Baseball* (New York: Stein and Day, 1980), 248–249. The rule was changed in 1953 to require players to have at least 502 plate appearances or 3.1 at-bats per game.
61. "Lajoie's Average Takes a Drop," *New York Times*, 9 October 1910.
62. "Cleveland Blanks Browns," *Washington Post*, 9 October 1910.
63. *Washington Post*, 9 October 1910.
64. MacFarlane, "After 70 Years, Researchers Prove Lajoie Really Did Win."
65. "Eight Hits in Eight Trials," *Chicago Daily Tribune*, 10 October 1910.
66. *New York Times*, 11 October 1910, 9.
67. Ibid.
68. Ibid.
69. "American League," *New York Times*, 10 October 1910.
70. "Lajoie Leads Cobb in Batting," *New York Times*, 10 October 1910.
71. "Lajoie's Bat Wins Prize Automobile," *Chicago Daily Tribune*, 10 October 1910.
72. Ibid.
73. "Corriden Helps Lajoie to Seven Out of Eight Hits," *Washington Post*, 10 October 1910.
74. Ibid.
75. Ibid.
76. Ibid.
77. Ibid.
78. Ibid.
79. Ibid.
80. Ibid.
81. Ibid.
82. Ibid. Although not known for his speed, Lajoie did have 380 stolen bases in his 21-year career.
83. Joseph L. Reichler, *The Baseball Encyclopedia*, 4th ed. (New York: Macmillan, 1979).
84. "Eight Hits In Eight Trials," *Chicago Daily Tribune*, 10 October 1910.
85. Ibid.
86. "Lajoie's Batting Causes Scandal," *New York Times*, 11 October 1910.
87. "Every Hit Genuine," *Washington Post*, 11 October 1910.
88. "Lajoie Fools Browns," *Washington Post*, 11 October 1910.
89. Cobb weighed in the controversy, showing a great deal of sportsmanship. "I have absolutely nothing to say detrimental to Lajoie.... The official scores gave Lajoie eight hits. They should know what they are doing. If the records show Lajoie got eight hits and through them jumped ahead of me in the batting percentages, that's the record and there is no going around.... I do not propose to get mixed up in any controversy. If there was a crooked deal pulled off in St. Louis sooner or later the persons implicated will suffer. That is a question for baseball authorities to take up. But I hardly think there will be an investigation if the commission waits for me to demand one." Bob Kuenster, "These Were the Majors' Closest Batting Races Ever!" *Baseball Digest* (July 1988), 60.
90. "Wanted Ninth Hit Badly," *Washington Post*, 14 October 1910.
91. Howell, a part-time Browns scout, was released along with manager Jack O'Connor. "O'-Connor Will Sue for $5,000 Salary," *New Castle News*, 24 August 1911.
92. Ibid.
93. "Cautious Corriden's Funny Fests Now Embalmed in Immortal Verse," *Washington Post*, 13 October 1910.
94. *New York Times*, 11 October 1910. It was widely reported that the Most Valuable Player Award was instituted in 1911 as a result of the disputed 1910 batting race. Ty Cobb won the first American League MVP award, batting .420.
95. Ibid.
96. "Lajoie Made Hits Fairly," *New York Times*, 13 October 1910.
97. Ibid.
98. Ibid.
99. "O'Connor May Lose Berth," *Washington Post*, 13 October 1910.
100. "Demands Explanation," *New York Times*, 14 October 1910.
101. "Player Corriden Explains," *New York Times*, 15 October 1910.
102. Ibid.
103. Ibid.
104. "O'Connor On Way to See Johnson," *Washington Post*, 15 October 1910; "Jack O'Connor May Be Kicked Out of League," *New Castle News*, 14 October 1910, 15; "O'Connor Must Report," *Lowell Sun*, 14 October 1910, 9.
105. "Hedges Lets Out O'Connor," *Chicago Daily Tribune*, 16 October 1910.
106. Ibid.
107. Ibid.
108. Ibid.
109. Ibid.

110. Ibid.
111. Ibid.
112. "Ty Cobb Is Champion," *Washington Post*, 16 October 1910.
113. Ibid.
114. Ibid.
115. Ibid. *See also* Geoffrey C. Ward and Ken Burns, *Baseball an Illustrated History* (New York: Alfred A. Knopf, 1994), 108.
116. "The Strangest Batting Race Ever," http://cleveland.indians.mlb.com/cle/history/story1.jsp.
117. "Magee Feels Slighted," *Washington Post*, 17 October 1910.
118. Ibid.
119. "Ty Cobb Is Champion," "*Washington Post,*" 16 October 1910.
120. Mr. Chalmers presented the cars on October 18, 1910, at the Philadelphia American League grounds just before the beginning of the first World Series game. For a history of baseball's Chalmers Award, see Mulford, "The Chalmers Baseball Trophy: How this Famous Baseball Prize Originated — The Chalmers Commission — Object of the Award System of Voting: A Typical Ballot," 79–82.
121. "Lajoie Fools Browns," *Washington Post*, 11 October 1910.
122. Ibid.
123. "Jack O'Connor After Hedges," *Chicago Daily Tribune*, 4 December 1910.
124. Ibid.
125. "O'Connor Plans Suit," *Washington Post*, 4 December 1910.
126. Ibid.
127. Ibid.
128. Ibid.
129. "Still Minus Manager," *Washington Post*, 7 December 1910.
130. Ibid.
131. "Approve of Transfer," *Washington Post*, 21 December 1910.
132. Ibid. President Hedges of the Browns indicated at one point that the parties had settled the case. "American League Notes," *Sporting Life*, 21 October 1911. O'Connor stated with regard to settlement: "I refused to compromise with Hedges.... My suit will be filed this week, as at present my lawyer is out of the city.... I have called on Hedges, but because he refused to pay me $5,000 we did not come to any understanding and I told him I would file suit. He didn't feel that he should pay me $5,000 and do any work for him. I was ready to again handle the club, if wanted, and so reported to him. But, as long as he didn't put me on the job, I'll expect him to pay me just the same, as the conditions are in black and white in the contract." "O'Connor's Case," *Sporting Life*, 19 August 1911.
133. "Approve of Transfer."
134. "'Social Standing' New Line In Which Manager Of Browns Must Show," *Washington Post*, 23 December 1910.
135. Ibid.
136. Ibid.
137. "H.P. Ziegler Killed by Rich Divorcee," *New York Times*, 2 May 1921, 1
138. "O'Connor has sued his wife for divorce and he names, or rather his petition says he will name two prominent men of St. Louis. The trouble between man and wife began last March, when O'Connor was informed he could find his wife at a road house with a certain party. He went to the place, found his wife, it is claimed, and there was a scene. The man in the case pulled a revolver, but the base ball player's right reached his jaw before the gun could be used. The O'Connor's separated, and a day or two ago the suit was filed. Mrs. O'Connor is a handsome young woman and has been married twelve years." "Jack O'Connor Troubles," *Sporting Life*, 9 September 1905, 19. It was also reported that Mrs. O'Connor and Ralph Orthwein were having an affair. O'Connor challenged Orthwein over his wife. "In 1902 O'Connor joined the St. Louis American League baseball club, of which Ralph Orthwein was then President. Mrs. O'Connor and Orthwein were often together at the all-night resorts and road houses that flourished around St. Louis at the time. In 1905, O'Connor came upon them in a wine room at the old Delmonico Restaurant at Kings Highway and Manchester. There was a violent scene, and, it was said, O'Connor tried to kill Orthwein, but was restrained by friends who had accompanied him. O'Connor soon afterward sued for divorce, naming Orthwein in his petition, and was granted a decree." "H.P. Ziegler Killed by Rich Divorcee."
139. "H.P. Ziegler Killed by Rich Divorcee."
140. "O'Connor Will Sue for $5,000 Salary," *New Castle News*, 24 August 1911, 11. The club filed an answer to the lawsuit, stating: "O'Connor brought baseball into disrepute by favoring Napoleon Lajoie in his contest with Ty Cobb for batting honors of the American League in 1910." "St. Louis Team Answers Suit," *Lowell Sun*, 8 May 1913.
141. "Browns Must Pay O'Connor's Salary," *New York Times*, 13 May 1913. After he was victorious in his lawsuit against the Browns, O'Connor even contemplated suing all eight clubs in the American League for "driving him out of that league." David L. Fultz, "The Baseball Player's Fraternity: A Monthly Department Devoted to the Activities of the Organized Ball Player," *Baseball Magazine* 11 (July 1913), 72.
142. "Browns Must Pay O'Connor's Salary."
143. Ibid.
144. Ibid.
145. Ibid.
146. Ibid.
147. Ibid.
148. Ibid.
149. Ibid.
150. Ibid.

151. Ibid.
152. Ibid.
153. *O'Connor v. St. Louis American Baseball*, 181 S.W. 1167 (Mo. Ct. App. 1916).
154. Ibid., 1168.
155. Ibid.
156. Ibid., 1170.
157. Ibid.
158. Ibid., 1173.
159. "Browns Must Pay O'Connor's Salary."
160. After leaving the Browns O'Connor would manage in the Federal League. He said he never backed down from a fight and he showed that when he managed in the newly created Federal League. On June 28, 1913, he engaged in a fist fight with an umpire, Jack McNulty, during a game. "Jack O'Connor Fights an Umpire," *New York Times*, 29 June 1913. McNulty's jaw was fractured and he retired after the game. "Punish Jack O'Connor," *Washington Post*, 1 July 1913. In July 1913, McNulty sued O'Connor for damages he sustained to the nerves of three of his teeth, his nose, and right eye. "Umpire McNulty Sues For $35,000," *Washington Post*, 25 July 1913. McNulty was eventually awarded $1,500 against O'Connor. "Must Pay Umpire McNulty," *Washington Post*, 18 July 1914.
161. *O'Connor v. St. Louis American Baseball*, 181 S.W. 1167, 1173 (Mo. Ct. App. 1916).
162. Alan Schwarz, "Numbers are Cast in Bronze, but are not Set in Stone," *New York Times*, 31 July 2005.
163. "Almost 90 years later, sports encyclopedias disagree on the final numbers" [referring to the 1910 American League batting race]. Dwight Chapin, "When History and Controversy go Hand-in-Hand Memorable Tales Arise from Races for Titles, Records," *San Francisco Examiner*, 4 September 1998. *See also* "Interview: Alan Schwarz Discusses the History of Baseball Statistics," *NPR Talk of the Nation*, 1 July 2004.
164. MacFarlane, "After 70 Years, Researchers Prove Lajoie Really Did Win."
165. Ibid.
166. Ibid., 3.
167. Ibid., 11.
168. Ibid.
169. "Committee Supports Cobb's 1910 Crown," *Sporting News*, 25 April 1981, 37.
170. "Cobb-Lajoie Appeal Rejected," *Sporting News*, 2 January 1982, 6.
171. Ibid.
172. Gillette and Palmer, *The ESPN Baseball Encyclopedia*, 3. There was a dispute at one time whether Babe Ruth had 714 or 715 home runs. Bill Fleischman, "Another Homer for the Babe? Debate Grows Hot, Heavy," *Sporting News*, 10 May 1969, 8. Barry Bonds passed Ruth's home run total when he hit 715. Tom Goldman, "Bonds Slides Past Ruth on All-Time Home Run List" (29 May 2006), www.npr.org/templates/story/story/php?storyid=5436936.
173. The 1910 batting race was not the only controversial batting race. George Brett won the 1976 American League title over teammate Hal McRae, .333 to .332. Brett got an inside-the-park home run on his last at-bat of the season in a controversial play. Twins outfielder Steve Brye allowed Brett's hit to drop in front of him and then bounce over his head. Hal McRae argued it was racially motivated.

Chapter 5

1. Criminal Court of Cook County, Illinois, February Term, 1921, Indictment No. 21868.
2. Frankie Bailey and Steven Chermak, *Crimes and Trials of the Century: From the Black Sox Scandal to the Attica Prison Riots, From Pine Ridge to Abu Ghraib* (Santa Barbara, CA: Greenwood Publishing, 2007).
3. Numerous books have been written about a variety of aspects of the Black Sox trial. The seminal work on the topic is considered to be Eliot Asinof, *Eight Men Out* (New York: Holt, Rinehart and Winston,1963). The film *Eight Men Out* was a major hit in theaters. In the *The Godfather II*, the character Hyman Roth (played by Lee Strasberg, for which he received an Academy Award nomination) said he fell in love with baseball when Arnold Rothstein fixed the 1919 World Series. For articles, see William B. Anderson, "Saving the National Pastime's Image: Crisis Management During the 1919 Black Sox Scandal," *Journalism History* 27 (Fall 2001): 105–111; Jay Bennett, "Did Shoeless Joe Jackson Throw the 1919 World Series?" *American Statistician* 47 (November 1998): 241–250; Gene Carney, "Uncovering the Fix of the 1919 World Series: The Role of High Fullerton, *Nine* 13 (Fall 2004): 33–49; Michael W. Klein, "Rose Is in Red, Black Sox Are Blue: A Comparison of *Rose v. Giamatti* and the 1921 Black Sox Trial," *Hastings Communication & Entertainment Law Journal* 13 (1990–1991): 551–588; Gene Carney, "Comiskey's Detectives," *Baseball Research Journal* 38 (Fall 2009), 108; Allen Boyer, "'The Great Gatsby,' the Black Sox, High Finance, and American Law," *Michigan Law Review* 88 (1989): 328–342.
4. Schalk was elected to the Baseball Hall of Fame in 1955. He hit .304 during the 1919 World Series, but he was elected largely on the basis of his defensive skills. His lifetime batting average of .253 is the lowest of any position player in the Hall of Fame. www.baseball-reference.com.
5. A convincing argument has been made that the Reds would have won the series anyway. *See* William A. Cook, *The 1919 World Series* (Jefferson, NC: McFarland, 2001).
6. J.G. Taylor Spink, *Judge Landis and Twenty-Five Years of Baseball* (New York: Crowell, 1947), 58.
7. Spink said Chick Gandil's failure to slide

into third base on a close play might have been just one of those boners one sees in some ball parks every day of the week. Ibid., 58.

8. "Tris Speaker Tells of Poor Playing of Sox in First Game," *Washington Post*, 1 October 1920.

9. Fred M. Loomis, "Is Anything Wrong With Sox?" *Chicago Daily Tribune*, 19 September 1920, A1. The letter signed by Loomis was actually written by *Tribune* sportswriter Jim Crusinberry who thought the truth about the 1919 World Series should finally come out. David L. Fleitz, *Shoeless: The Life and Times of Joe Jackson* (Jefferson, NC: McFarland, 2001), 220.

10. Spink, *Judge Landis and Twenty-Five Years of Baseball*, 63.

11. "Admit Guilt," *Chicago Daily Tribune*, 29 September 1920, 1.

12. "Eight White Sox Players are Indicted on Charge of Fixing 1919 World Series," *New York Times*, 29 September 1920, 1.

13. Ibid.
14. Ibid.
15. Ibid.
16. Ibid.

17. "Jackson's Story," *Chicago Daily Tribune*, 29 September 1920, 2.

18. This is clearly an objectionable question. The question assumes Jackson played "crooked" ball in the series. Jackson simply answered the question.

19. "Grand Jury Testimony of Joe Jackson," available at Shoeless Joe Jackson's Virtual Hall of Fame, http://www.blackbetsy.com/joejackson-1920-grand-jury-testimony-vhof.pdf.

20. "Admit Guilt." When Jackson died on December 6, 1951, he was still protesting his innocence. "Shoeless Jackson Dies Protesting Innocence in 1919 'Black Sox' Scandal," *Daily Register*, 6 December 1951.

21. "Eight White Sox Players are Indicted on Charge of Fixing 1919 World Series."

22. Ibid.

23. "More Players to Bare Plot," *Ironwood Daily Globe*, 29 September 1920. There was some evidence that Williams' family was threatened by gamblers the night before he was to pitch a game.

24. "Indict Two Gamblers in Baseball Plot: Men Named by Williams in Confession," *New York Times*, 30 September 1920, 1. *See also* "Excerpts of Statement of Claude 'Lefty' Williams," available at http://law2.umkc.edu/faculty/projects/ftrials/blacksox/williamsconfession.html.

25. "Indict Two Gamblers in Baseball Plot," 1.

26. "Eight Fired by Comiskey, Wreck Teams," *Chicago Daily Tribune*, 29 September 1920, 1.

27. "Two Sox Confess; Eight Indicted; Inquiry Goes On," *Chicago Daily Tribune*, 29 September 1920, 1.

28. Ibid.

29. "Again!" *Chicago Daily Tribune*, 27 March 1921, A1.

30. "More Players Face Trial," *New York Times*, 26 March 1921, 8; "7 'Black Sox' Indicted Again, 11 Others Named," *Chicago Daily Tribune*, 27 March 1921, A1.

31. "Seven Black Sox Go on Trial for Throwing Games," *Freeport Journal-Standard*, 29 June 1921, 1.

32. "White Sox Players are All Acquitted by Chicago Jury," *New York Times*, 3 August 1921, 1, 3.

33. "A formal, detailed statement of the claims or charges brought by a plaintiff or a prosecutor, usually filed in response to the defendant's request for a more specific complaint. The bill of particulars has been abolished in federal civil actions and replaced by the motion for a more definite statement. "Although it has been said that the bill of particulars is not a discovery device, it seems plain that it is a means of discovery, though of a limited nature. It is the one method open to a defendant in a criminal case to secure the details of the charge against him." 1 Charles Alan Wright, *Federal Practice and Procedure*, 3d ed., § 129, at 646–47 (St. Paul, MN: West, 1999).

34. Most states now refer to this as a motion for more definite statement.

35. Petition for Bill of Particulars, *People v. Cicotte*, No. 21868 (Crim. Ct., Cook County, Ill. Aug. 2, 1921), available from Clerk of the Circuit Court, Cook County, Records and Archives website , http://www.cookcountyclerkofcourt.org (copy on file with author).

36. For an in depth view of Chase's involvement in the Black Sox Scandal, see Martin Donell Kohout, *Hal Chase: The Defiant Life and Turbulent Times of Baseball's Biggest Crook* (Jefferson, NC: McFarland, 2001), 239–243, 244–246, 273–375.

37. Petition for Bill of Particulars, 4, 7, 8, 9–11.

38. Bill of Particulars, *People v. Cicotte*, No. 21868 (Crim Ct., Cook County, Ill. Aug. 2, 1921) (copy on file with author).

39. "Seven Black Sox Go on Trial for Throwing Games," *Freeport Journal-Standard*, 29 June 1921, 1.

40. "Baseball Scandal in Court Tomorrow," *New York Times*, 26 June 1921, 6.

41. "Voir Dire: *n.*[Law French "to speak the truth"] 1. A preliminary examination of a prospective juror by a judge or lawyer to decide whether the prospect is qualified and suitable to serve on a jury. Loosely, the term refers to the jury-selection phase of a trial." Bryan A. Garner, ed., *Black's Law Dictionary*, 8th ed. (St. Paul, MN: West, 2004). In Illinois in 1919, only men were allowed to serve as jurors. Women were finally allowed to vote by passage of the 19th amendment to the U.S. Constitution in August 1920.

42. "Black Sox Jury Chosen Trial Starts Monday," *Chicago Daily Tribune*, 16 July 1921, 5.

43. "'Master Mind' Hidden as Trial of Sox Starts," *Chicago Daily Tribune*, 27 June 1921, 2.

44. "Called 'Jumper,' Comiskey Rages at Trial of Sox," *Chicago Daily Tribune*, 19 July 1921, 2.
45. "Burns Tells Story of Plot to Throw 1919 World Series," *New York Times*, 26 July 1921, 1.
46. Ibid.
47. Ibid. Burns made no mention of Jackson in his testimony.
48. "Burns Tells Inside Story of Fixing World's Series," *The Decatur Review*, 20 July 1921, 10.
49. "Burns Tells Story of Plot to Throw 1919 World Series," 3.
50. "The Black Sox Trial: Trial Testimony (Excerpts)," available at http://www.law.umkc.edu/faculty/projects/ftrials/blacksox/trialtestimony.html
51. Ibid.
52. "Baseball Plot Confessions Gone," *New York Times*, 23 July 1921, 10.
53. "Admission of Confessions is Before Court," *Freeport Journal Standard*, 25 July 1921, 5.
54. The Miranda warnings arose from *U.S. v. Miranda*, 384 U.S. 436 (1968). Prior to the *Miranda* case no warning had to be given to criminal defendants by the police. The test of admissibility of a confession was whether the confessions were given voluntarily.
55. "Confessions of Three Players Go as Evidence," *Logansport Morning Press*, 26 July 1921, 7.
56. "Confessions Enter Trial of White Sox," *New York Times*, 26 July 1921, 13.
57. Ibid.
58. Ibid.
59. Ibid.
60. Ibid.
61. "Joe Jackson and Cicotte Testify for 'Black Sox,'" *Naugatuck Daily News*, 25 July 1921, 8.
62. "Judge Admits Confessions of 'Black Sox' Trio," *Chicago Daily Tribune*, 26 July 1921, 3.
63. Ibid. "Cicotte Tells World's Series "Fixing" Story," *Bismarck Tribune*, 25 July 1921.
64. Ibid.
65. "Confession to be Admitted in Baseball Trial," *Alton Evening Telegraph*, 25 July 1921, 2.
66. Ibid.
67. "Confessions of Three Black Sox Read in Court," *Freeport Journal-Standard*, 26 July 1921.
68. "State to Close Sox Case with Maharg Story," *Chicago Daily Tribune*, 27 July 1921. After the state completed its case, Judge Friend informed the prosecutors he was going direct the jury to return a verdict in favor of players Happy Flesch and Buck Weaver as well as defendant Carl Zack. (A judge may make this decision on his own if the evidence is lacking.) However, the judge temporarily overruled a defense motion to have the case dismissed against these three defendants when the state argued that the defendants might be incriminated by further testimony. The state rested its case after Judge Friend said he would not let the case go to the jury against defendants Louis and Ben Levi of Kokomo, Indiana. "Bully Maharg Confirms Burns," *Decatur Daily Review*, 27 July 1921.
69. "Prosecutors Today Rest Baseball Case," *New York Times*, 27 July 1921, 12. "Maharg Strong Witness Against Seven Black Sox," *Freeport Journal-Standard*, 27 July 1921. Most of the White Sox team had been called as witnesses.
70. "Defense Rests Case in Baseball Trial," *New York Times*, 29 July 1921, 15.
71. Ibid.
72. Ibid.
73. Ibid.
74. Ibid.
75. Ibid.
76. Ibid.
77. Ibid.
78. Ibid.
79. Ibid.
80. "Series Played Honestly, To Be Defense of Sox," *Chicago Daily Tribune*, 28 July 1921, 17.
81. Ibid.
82. "Defense Rests Case in Baseball Trial," 15.
83. Ibid.
84. Ibid.
85. Ibid.
86. Ibid.
87. J.G. Taylor Spink, *Baseball Guide and Record Book 1945* (St. Louis, MO: Charles C. Spink & Son, 1945), 170.
88. Ibid. *See also* "Fixing of Series Cost Innocent Players $1,952," *Washington Post*, 30 September 1920.
89. "Holds Confessions Convict White Sox," *New York Times*, 30 July 1921, 13. Each side was allotted ten hours for closing argument by the judge.
90. "White Sox Players are all Acquitted by Chicago Jury," *New York Times*, 3 August 1921, 2.
91. "Holds Confessions Convict White Sox," 13.
92. "Arguments in Ball Scandal," *Logansport Morning Press*, 30 July 1921, 11.
93. "Baseball's Ruin Seen if 'Black Sox' are Freed," *Chicago Daily Tribune*, 31 July 1921, 15.
94. "The Black Sox Trial: Trial Summations (Excerpts)," http://law2.umkc.edu/faculty/projects/ftrials/blacksox/trialsummations.html.
95. Jury Instructions, Criminal Court File (copy on file with author).
96. *Chicago Daily Tribune*, 3 August 1921.
97. "White Sox Players are all Acquitted by Chicago Jury," *New York Times*, 3 August 1921, 1.
98. Ibid., 3.
99. Ibid.
100. Jury Instructions, Criminal Court File. The criminal court file contains many proposed jury instructions. There were 45 refused jury instructions. It is difficult to determine from the criminal court file which jury instructions were actually read to the jury on the day of trial. One of the refused jury instructions stated: "The legislature of the State of Illinois recently enacted legislation defining it to be a crime to throw a ball game, and this fact you may consider as a circum-

stance in determining whether or not the State's evidence, even if you believe it to be true beyond a reasonable doubt is sufficient to establish a crime under the law as it heretofore existed at the time of the alleged conspiracy and before the passage of such act of the legislature."
101. Ibid.
102. Ibid.
103. Ibid.
104. Criminal Court File Cook County, Form of Verdicts 51-C.
105. Ibid.
106. "White Sox Players are all Acquitted by Chicago Jury," 1.
107. *Chicago Daily Tribune*, 3 August 1921.
108. "White Sox Players are All Acquited by Chicago Jury," 1.
109. "Nine Acquitted in World Series Scandal Trial," *Alton Evening Telegraph*, 5 August 1921, 8.
110. Ibid.
111. Ibid.
112. "White Sox Players are all Acquitted by Chicago Jury," 1.
113. Ibid.
114. Ibid.
115. Ibid.
116. Spink, *Judge Landis and Twenty-Five Years of Baseball*, 83. Gandil later told the press, "I guess that will learn Ban Johnson that he can't frame an honest bunch of players." Ibid.
117. Ibid., 83–84.
118. Benjamin G. Rader, *Baseball: A History of America's Game*, 2nd ed. (Champaign: University of Illinois Press, 2002).
119. "Weaver's Appeal Denied by Landis," *New York Times*, 12 December 1922, 21.
120. Spink, *Judge Landis and Twenty-Five Years of Baseball*, 85.
121. Ibid.
122. Ibid.
123. Weaver died in 1956.
124. "New Setback Halts Ball Players' Trial," *New York Times*, 28 June 1921, 7.
125. Joe Jackson and Furman Bisher, "This is the Truth!" *SPORT Magazine*, October 1949.
126. Ibid. Jackson concluded the article with this statement: "Well, that's my story. I repeat what I said when I started out — that I have no axe to grind, that I'm not asking anybody for anything. It's all water over the dam as far as I am concerned. I can say that my conscience is clear and that I'll stand on my record in that World Series. I'm not what you call a good Christian, but I believe in the Good Book, particularly where it says 'what you sow, so shall you reap.' I have asked the Lord for guidance before, and I am sure He gave it to me. I'm willing to let the Lord be my judge." Ibid.
127. "Barred White Sox Clean up in South," *New York Times*, 12 July 1923, 15.
128. "Two More Players Sue the White Sox," *New York Times*, 13 May 1922.
129. Ibid.
130. Ibid.
131. Ibid.
132. The jury awarded him damages for "two seasons and two weeks of ball playing." Ibid.
133. Ibid.
134. Fleitz, *Shoeless: The Life and Times of Joe Jackson*, 254–255. Jackson also sued for damages for slander, but later dropped that claim. Felsch was also arrested for making statements that differed from what he told the grand jury in 1920. Carney calls the 1924 civil trial, "The Trial Nobody Noticed." Gene Carney, *Burying the Black Sox: How Baseball's Cover-Up of the 1919 World Series Fix Almost Succeeded* (Dulles, VA: Potomac Books, 2006), 1.

Chapter 6

1. No. A8905178, 1989 WL 111447 (Ohio Com. Pl. June 26, 1989); *Rose v. Giamatti*, 721 F. Supp. 906 (S.D. Ohio 1989).
2. Murray Chass, "Spells Finish to a Sorry Episode," *Sporting News*, 4 September 1989, 12.
3. Pete Rose and Rick Hill, *My Prison Without Bars* (Emmaus, PA: Rodale Books, 2004), 143.
4. *See, e.g.*, 'Three Players Expelled for 'Selling' a Game," *New York Clipper*, 11 November 1865.
5. Daniel E. Ginsburg, *The Fix Is In: A History of Baseball Gambling and Game Fixing Scandals* (Jefferson, NC: McFarland, 1995).
6. Elliott Kalb and Chris Collinsworth, *The 25 Greatest Sports Conspiracy Theories of All-Time: Ranking Sports' Most Notorious Fixes, Cover-Ups, and Scandals* (New York: Skyhorse Publishing, 2007).
7. Ibid.
8. Thomas Rogers, "Leo Durocher, Fiery Ex-Manager, Dies at 86," *New York Times*, 8 October 1991.
9. Murray Chass, "Notebook; Steinbrenner vs. Ueberroth: You Make the Call," *New York Times*, 28 April 1991.
10. Ginsburg, *The Fix Is In*.
11. Tony Castro, *Mickey Mantle: America's Prodigal Son* (Dulles, VA: Potomac Books, Inc., 2009), 344.
12. *The Baseball Encyclopedia*, 10th ed. (New York: Macmillan, 1996). Rose has also made the most outs of any player in the history of the game.
13. Ibid.
14. Ira Berkow, "The Pete Rose Case: Man in the News, The Legend of Charlie Hustle: Peter Edward Rose," *New York Times*, 25 August 1989.
15. Ron Kroichick, "A Collision With Pete Rose in the 1970 All-Star Game Changed Ray Fosse's Career," *SF Gate*, 10 July 1999.
16. Pete Rose, *Pete Rose: Baseball's Charlie Hustle* (Nashville, TN: Cumberland House Publishing, 2003). Rose commented on the incident:

"Look, I'm the winning run in the all-star game in my hometown.... I just want to get to that place as quickly as I can. Besides, nobody told me they changed it to girls' softball between third and home." Ibid., citing Pete Rose and Roger Kahn, *Pete Rose: My Story* (New York: Macmillan, 1989).

17. See James Reston, Jr., *Collision at Home Plate: The Lives of Pete Rose and Bart Giamatti* (1991; repr., Lincoln: University of Nebraska, 1997).

18. For a few examples, see Matthew B. Pachman, "Limits on the Discretionary Powers of Professional Sports Commissioners: A Historical and Legal Analysis of Issues Raised by the Pete Rose Controversy," *Virginia Law Review* 76 (1990): 1409–1439; Michael W. Klein, "Rose is in Red, Black Sox are Blue: A Comparison of *Rose v. Giamatti* and the 1921 Black Sox Trial," *Hastings Communications and Entertainment Law Journal* 13 (1991): 551–588; Ronald J. Rychlak, "Pete Rose, Bart Giamatti, and the Dowd Report," *Mississippi Law Journal* 68 (1999): 889–902; Kimberly G. Winer, "Maintaining the Home Field Advantage: Rose vs. Federal Court," *Loyola of Los Angeles Entertainment Law Journal* 10 (1990): 695–713; Peter G. Neiman, "'Root, Root, Root for the Home Team': Pete Rose, Nominal Parties, and Diversity Jurisdiction," *New York University Law Review* 66 (1991): 148–188; Jason M. Pollack, "Take My Arbitrator, Please: Commissioner 'Best Interests' Disciplinary Authority in Professional Sports," *Fordham Law Review* 67 (1999): 1645–1712.

19. In a February 1989 meeting with Commissioner Ueberroth, Rose said he had lost $2,000 betting on the Super Bowl. Rose and Hill, *My Prison Without Bars*, 147.

20. John M. Dowd et al., "Report to the Commissioner, In The Matter of: Peter Edward Rose, Manager, Cincinnati Reds Baseball Club" (May 9, 1989), 1 [hereinafter Dowd Report].

21. Dowd was a former marine and prosecutor. He had the reputation of being a tough prosecutor and a very capable investigator. He received his law degree from Emory Law School.

22. It was the second day of spring training and the Reds announced that Rose was away on "personal business." Reston, *Collision at Home Plate*, 261.

23. Ibid., 262.

24. Murray Chass, "Rose is the Subject, Mum is the Word," *New York Times*, 22 February 1989, A24. Also present at the meeting was Edwin Durso, executive vice president of baseball as well as Giamatti's top assistant, Fay Vincent.

25. "Ueberroth Confirms Inquiry on Rose," *New York Times*, 21 March 1989. The only limitation on Attorney John Dowd was that he could not pay for information.

26. Ibid.

27. Richard Justice, "Rose Faces Charges He Bet on Baseball," *Washington Post*, 22 March 1989.

28. Craig Neff and Jill Lieber, "Rose's Grim Vigil," *Sports Illustrated*, 3 April 1989. *See also* Richard Justice, "Baseball's Probe of Rose Believed to be Widening," *Washington Post*, 24 March 1989, D9; "From the First Meeting to the Final Penalty," *New York Times*, 25 August 1989, A23. Peters was later sentenced on drug and tax evasion charges. Ibid.

29. "I.R.S. Is Said to Believe Rose Made Baseball Bets," *New York Times*, 5 April 1989, D26. The Dowd report discusses the activities of Paul Janszen and Ron Peters in detail. Dowd Report, 113–114.

30. Murray Chass, "Rose Said To Have Bet More than $1 Million," *New York Times*, 25 April 1989, D27.

31. "Rose Denies Report He Made Betting Signals," *Philadelphia Inquirer*, 26 March 1989.

32. Ira Berkow, "Some Quips, but Little More From Rose," *New York Times*, 23 March 1989, D23.

33. Ibid.

34. Ibid.; Hal McCoy, "Rose Mum on Baseball Bets," *Sporting News*, 3 April 1989.

35. "Rose Finally Breaks his Silence," *New York Times*, 26 March, 1989, S3.

36. Richard Justice, "No Preseason Action on Rose," *Washington Post*, 29 March 1989, F1.

37. Thomas Boswell, "Rose's Weight is Wait," *Washington Post*, 4 April 1989, D1.

38. Ibid. No ballplayer would attend the trial of Curt Flood when Flood sued baseball over the reserve clause and very few would even lend their support to Flood. However, 12 years later, the Players Association had made substantial headway in leveling the playing field against the owners. Some players came to the defense of Rose. Kirk Gibson, the 1988 National League Most Valuable Player, said: "If he were guilty of some wrongdoing, that wouldn't change my opinion of Pete Rose as a man. I make mistakes. I wouldn't crucify him. He's a Hall-of-Famer. I don't care what he's done." Ibid.

39. Ibid.

40. "I.R.S. Audits Rose," *Washington Post*, 9 April 1989, C10.

41. Ibid. Bench was elected to the Hall of Fame in January 1989, and the *Sporting News* named him the 16th greatest player of all time.

42. "Rose Reportedly Bet Reds to Win," *Washington Post*, 12 April 1989, D6.

43. "More Betting Links Surface on Rose," *New York Times*, 14 April 1989, A29.

44. "Rose Displays 3 Series Rings to Quell Rumors," *Washington Post*, 19 April 1989, C4A.

45. Ibid.

46. Ibid.

47. The full text of Giamatti's letter to Judge Rubin:

I am advised that Ron Peters will appear before you shortly in the above-entitled case to enter a plea of guilty to two felonies and to receive his sentence.

It is my purpose to bring to your attention the

significant and truthful cooperation Mr. Peters has provided to my special counsel who is conducting the investigation into allegations concerning the conduct and activities of Pete Rose, the manager of the Cincinnati Reds Baseball Club.

Mr. Peters has been readily available at all times to my special counsel and has provided critical sworn testimony about Mr. Rose and his associates. In addition, Mr. Peters has provided probative documentary evidence to support his testimony and the testimony of others. Based upon other information in our possession, I am satisfied Mr. Peters has been candid, forthright and truthful with my special counsel.

In view of the confidential nature of my inquiry, I would respectfully request this letter to remain under the Court's seal until the completion of my inquiry.

Thank you for your consideration of this letter on behalf of Mr. Peters.

"Text of Commissioner's Letter to Judge Rubin," *Chicago Tribune*, 26 June 1989.
48. Law school professor Roger Abrams has deemed Giamatti's letter "an error of Odyssean proportions." Roger I. Abrams, *Legal Bases: Baseball and the Law* (Philadelphia, PA: Temple University Press, 1998), 158.
49. Murray Chass, "Giamatti Notes Cooperation," *New York Times*, 24 April 1989, C4.
50. Ibid.
51. Chass, "Rose Said to Have Bet More than $1 Million," D27.
52. Ibid.
53. Ibid.
54. Ibid.
55. U.S. House Speaker Jim Wright of Texas was under investigation at the same time as Rose. A *Washington Post* poll showed more people were paying attention to the Rose investigation than that of the speaker, although half of those polled believed Rose bet on baseball. Support was growing for Rose. Richard Morin, "Poll Shoes Support for Rose," *Washington Post*, 25 April 1989, C6.
56. Murray Chass, "Criticism on Rose Inquiry from Judge," *New York Times*, 26 April 1989, D23. Five noted law professors stepped forward and criticized Judge Rubin's statements. Professor Freedman of Hofstra University said, "He should not be talking about it; it is a violation of the Code of Judicial Conduct." Noted Harvard law professor Alan Dershowitz said Rubin's comments were a violation of the American Bar Association's Code of Judicial Conduct and further noted about Judge Rubin: "It sounds like a bored old man who's vicariously rooting for the Cincinnati Reds and seeing one of his heroes' careers being ripped to shreds in front of him. He's totally out of line. He's butting his nose into affairs that are not his concern. He sounds like a kid." "Rose Awaiting 'Meet Me on Moon' Request," *Sporting News*, 8 May 1989, 12; "Lawyers Criticize Judge," *New York Times*, 27 April 1989, D30.
57. Murray Chass, "Judge Withdraws; Criticized Giamatti," *New York Times*, 28 April 1989, B14.
58. On the Sunday following the Rose deposition, Rueven Katz released Giamatti's letter to Judge Rubin.
59. Joe Sexton, "Rose Remains Defiant Over Report," *New York Times*, 2 July 1989, S1.
60. The report not only contained allegations that Rose had bet on baseball, but also contained testimony about Rose's "supposed affairs." "There's a Steamy Side, Too," *Sporting News*, 10 July 1989, 25.
61. During his deposition Rose was shown betting sheets that experts had determined to be in his handwriting. He was asked whether the handwriting was his and he said: "I couldn't tell you if that's my handwriting" and "I don't recognize it as my handwriting." Dowd Report, 18.
62. Ibid., 2.
63. Ibid., 221.
64. Steve Berkowitz, "Rose's 'Filibuster' May Be Near End," *Washington Post*, 3 August 1989, B3.
65. Murray Chass, "Giamatti Schedules a Hearing for Rose to Respond to Report," *New York Times*, 12 May 1989, B17.
66. Ibid.
67. "Former Union Chief Assails Giamatti Inquiry," *New York Times*, 25 May 1989, D26.
68. Steve Berkowitz, "Peters Amends Conditions for Talk with Rose's Lawyers," *Washington Post*, 10 June 1989, D4.
69. Murray Chass, "Rose, Citing Charges He Bet on Reds, Sues Commissioner," *New York Times*, 20 June 1989, A1.
70. The complaint was 36 pages long and requested that an independent arbiter hear the case. David Aldridge, "Rose Sues Giamatti, Targets Allegation He Bet on Reds," *Washington Post*, 20 June 1989, E1. On June 22, the FBI procured betting sheets with Rose's fingertips on them. Murray Chass, "F.B.I. is Said to Have Slips Linking Rose to Betting on Reds," *New York Times*, 22 June 1989, A1.
71. George Will wrote that "Rose's legal strategy was to find a judge willing to insinuate himself into baseball's disciplinary procedures. If Rose had succeeded, the Commissioner's office would have been irreparably damaged." George F. Will, "Foul Ball," *New York Review of Books*, 27 June 1991, 3.
72. For a timeline of all the activities of the Rose case, see "From the First Meeting to the Final Penalty," *New York Times*, 25 August 1989. Lajoie's legal dealings with Col. Rogers would cover almost two years while the Rose-Giamatti dispute would only cover a few months.
73. Motion for Temporary Restraining Order

and Preliminary Injunction at 1, *Rose v. Giamatti*, 1989 WL 111386 (Ohio Ct. Com. Pl. June 19, 1989) (No. A8905178).
74. Memorandum of Plaintiff Peter Edward Rose in Support of his Motion for Temporary Restraining Order and Preliminary Injunction, *Rose v. Giamatti*, 1989 WL 111386 (Ohio Ct. Com. Pl. June 19, 1989) (No. A8905178).
75. Ibid., 2–4.
76. Ibid., 6.
77. Ibid., 3.
78. Ibid., 5. Rose argued that the Commissioner acted more like an advocate not a judge. Ibid., 6. And further: "Pete Rose's career in baseball and his ability to exploit his accomplishments in the game, which is Pete Rose's only business, will be destroyed if he is suspended or banned from baseball for his alleged betting on baseball. Giamatti's obvious bias in favor of Pete Rose's accusers and his failure to follow Baseball's Rules of Procedure incalculably increase the likelihood that Pete Rose will be wrongfully branded and suffer irreparable tarnishment, including possible banishment from the game, unless Giamatti is restrained by the Court." Ibid., 10.
79. Ibid., 5.
80. Ibid.
81. Ibid., 7.
82. Ibid.
83. Ibid., quoting Major League Rules of Procedure, para. 2, 4, 6.
84. Ibid., 8.
85. Ibid.
86. Ibid., 4.
87. Ibid.
88. Ibid., 9.
89. Steve Berkowitz, "Baseball Investigator Says Rose Bet on Reds Games," *Washington Post*, 23 June 1989, A1.
90. Neither Rose nor Giamatti testified before Judge Nadel. Reston, *Collision at Home Plate*.
91. *Rose v. Giamatti*, No. A8905178, 1989 WL 111447 (Ohio Ct. Com. Pl. June 26, 1989). Noted sports law scholar Gary Roberts called Nadel's ruling "clearly wrong," noting that "the law is clear that the internal rules of a private association are not to be interfered with by the courts." He also said that although the Major League Rules stated that Rose was entitled to a "judicial" hearing, it was up to the commissioner of Baseball to determine how the hearing is conducted. Michael York, "Nadel's Words Crack Baseball's Shield," *Washington Post*, 26 June 1989.
92. *Rose v. Giamatti*, 1989 WL 111447, at 1.
93. Joe Gergen, "Nadel Proved Worth of Home-Court Advantage," *Sporting News*, 10 July 1989, 6.
94. The night of Nadel's decision, a banner appeared in Riverfront Stadium, "Pete 1, Bart 0." The fan was forced to remove the banner down by security. Reston, *Collision at Home Plate*, 9. In the next election, Judge Nadel resoundingly defeated his Democratic opponent to gain re-election to the bench.
95. *Rose v. Giamatti*, 1989 WL 111447, at 1.
96. The ruling was said to be "the most serious incursion into what has been the virtually dictatorial authority of the commissioner's office since it was created in 1920." Murray Chass, "Judge Blocks Giamatti's Hearing on Betting Charges Against Rose," *New York Times*, 26 June 1989, A1.
97. Ibid.
98. Stanford law professor William Gould said the judge's ruling was against legal precedent. Joe Sexton, "The Ruling Bucks Precedent," *New York Times*, 26 June 1989, C4.
99. Hal McCoy, "Judge Gives Pete Banner Day," *Sporting News*, 3 July 1989, 26; Gergen, "Nadel Proved Worth of Home-Court Advantage," 6.
100. Motion for Suspension of Temporary Restraining Order Pending Appeal and for Expedited Treatment, *Rose v. Giamatti*, No. A-8905178, 1989 WL 111453 (Ohio Ct. Com. Pl. June 26, 1089).
101. Ibid.
102. Ibid., 4.
103. The appeals court refused to rule on the motion for temporary injunction because it was not a final court order. *Rose v. Giamatti*, No. C-890390, 1989 WL 111451 (Ohio Ct. Com. Pl. June 28, 1989), at 1.
104. Rose had retained one of Cincinnati's best litigators, Robert Stachler, to handle his case.
105. He would give a deposition to Rose's attorneys on June 29, lasting most of the day.
106. *Rose v. Giamatti*, 721 F. Supp. 906, 915 (S.D. Ohio 1989).
107. Judge Rubin could not help himself one last time. In the order he signed transferring the case from the Western Division to the Eastern Division, he and Judge Weber stated: "Plaintiff is not just another litigant. He is instead a baseball figure of national reputation closely identified with the Cincinnati Reds and the City of Cincinnati. Under such circumstances, it would appear advisable that it be transferred to a city of the Southern District of Ohio other than Cincinnati." Ibid., 908.
108. The legal question presented to the court was an extremely complicated one. William Fox, a law professor at Catholic University, called it one of "the toughest in the book." Steve Berkowitz, "Don't Make a Federal Case of It, Rose Set to Ask Court," *Washington Post*, 5 July 1989.
109. Paul C. Weiler and Gary R. Roberts, *Sports and the Law: Cases, Materials and Problems* (Eagan MN: West Publishing, 1993), 3. Even Rose understood his iconic status: "Between the fans, media, and baseball purists, the commissioner was under enormous pressure to deal with the case fairly — no whitewash for a star player. On the other hand, I was Charlie Hustle, baseball legend. I would not go down without a fight." Rose and Hill, *My Prison Without Bars*, 157.

110. *Rose v. Giamatti*, 721 F. Supp 906.
111. Ibid., 924.
112. Ibid., 922.
113. Murray Chass, "Rose Accuser Reports Evidence of Tax Evasion by Manager," *New York Times*, 10 August 1989, D21.
114. "Rose Denied Home Court," *Sporting News*, 28 August 1989, 15.
115. Office of the Commissioner of Baseball, In the Matter of Peter Edward Rose, Manager, and Cincinnati Reds Baseball Club (August 23, 1989), reprinted in *Mississippi Law Journal* 68 (1999), 909.
116. Murray Chass, "Rose is Out, but He Says Wait Till Next Year," *New York Times*, 25 August 1989.
117. "Remarks Made by Giamatti Leave Rose 'Dumbfounded,'" *New York Times*, 29 August 1989, B11.
118. Giamatti was a well-respected commissioner of the national pastime. John Dowd called Giamatti "one of the finest and most decent men I've ever known." Murray Chass, "Giamatti: Popular and Respected," *Sporting News*, 11 September 1989, 12.
119. Ibid.
120. Giamatti received a doctorate from Yale in 1964. The majority of his scholarly work focused on English Renaissance literature and, more specifically, Edmund Spenser, the 16th-century English poet.
121. Judge S. Arthur Spiegel made the following introductory statement before sentencing Rose: "Foremost, we must recognize that there are two people here: Pete Rose, the living legend, the all-time hit leader, and the idol of millions; and Pete Rose, the individual, who appears today convicted of two counts of cheating on his taxes. Today, we are not dealing with the legend. History and the tincture of time will decide his place among the all-time greats of baseball. With regard to Pete Rose, the individual, he has broken the law, admitted his guilt, and stands ready to pay the penalty. Under our system of law and sense of fairness, when he has completed his sentence, he will have paid his debt to society and should be accepted by society as rehabilitated. Only time will tell whether he is to be restored to his position of honor for his accomplishment on the ball fields of America." At his sentencing on criminal charges, Rose said: "Your Honor, I would like to say that I am very sorry. I am very shameful to be here today in front of you. I think I'm perceived as a very aggressive, arrogant type of individual. But I want people to know that I do have emotion. I do have feelings, and I can be hurt like everybody else. And I hope no one has to go through what I went through the last year and a half. I lost my dignity. I lost my self-respect. I lost a lot of dear fans and almost lost some very dear friends. I have to take this opportunity to thank my wife for giving me so much moral support during this ordeal. It had to be very tough on her when your 5-year-old son would come home from school and tell her that his daddy is a jailbird. I really have no excuses because it's all my fault. And all I can say is, I hope somewhere, somehow in the future, I'm going to try to make it up to everybody that I disappointed and let down. Thank you very much." "The Pete Rose Case; Courtroom Statements By Rose and the Judge," *New York Times*, 20 July 1990.
122. Cesar Brioso and Peter Barzilai, "The Rose Scandal," *USA Today*, 5 January 2004.
123. "Pete Rose Chronology," *Sports Illustrated*, 4 January 2004; "Pete Rose Timeline," *The Cincinnati Inquirer*, 6 January 2004.
124. Murray Chass, "Selig is Said to be Opposed to Reinstatement of Pete Rose," *New York Times*, 12 September 1997.
125. John Dowd called this a travesty and said Rose should not have been allowed to appear.
126. Don Walker, "Rose Taking Another Swing at Reinstatement," *Milwaukee Sentinel*, 11 December 2002.
127. "$1 Million," *USA Today*, 20 August 2004; Jarrett Murphy, "IRS Woes for Pete Rose: Baseball Great Dunned for $1 Million in Back Taxes," CBS News, 20 August 2004.
128. "Pete Rose Admits to Betting on Baseball," 7 January 2004, www.pbs.org/newshour/extra/features/jan-june04/rose_1–07.html"; "Pete Rose Comes Clean: I Did Bet," CBS News, 5 January 2004. "I Bet on Baseball in 1987 and 1988," 5 January 2004, http://sports.espn.go.com/mlb/news/story?id=1700618. Early on in the investigation Rose had declared his innocence. "Look, I'm able to listen to all of this crap because I know one thing a lot of people don't seem to know. I'm not guilty." Dave Nightingale, "The Cloud Over Cincinnati," *Sporting News*, 24 April 1989.
129. Rose said, "I bet on my team every night. I didn't bet on my team four nights a week.... I bet on my team to win every night because I love my team, I believe in my team." "Rose Admits to Betting on Reds 'Every Night,'" March 16, 2007, http://sports.espn.go.com/mlb/news/story?id=2798498.
130. Rose and Hill, "*My Prison With Bars*, 147–148.
131. "Pete Rose Comes Clean: I Did Bet," CBS News, 5 January 2004.
132. Rose and Hill, *My Prison Without Bars*, 320.
133. Don Harrison, "Pete Rose Belongs in the Hall of Fame," *The Philadelphia Inquirer*, 10 August 2009.
134. Murray Chass, "'F' Spells Finish to a Sorry Episode," *Sporting News*, 4 September 1989.
135. Ken Gewertz, "Should Pete Rose be in the Hall of Fame?" *Harvard University Gazette*, 21 August 2003. "Pete Rose on Trial: Summary of Testimony," *ESPN.com*, 17 July 2003. There are some who think Rose will never make it in the Hall of

Fame. Jayson Stark, "Rose Induction Day will Never Happen," *ESPN.com*, 24 August, 2009. Cochran was, of course, famous for his closing argument in the O.J. Simpson murder trial stating, "If it doesn't fit, you must acquit." Associated Press, "'Dream Team' Lawyer Johnnie Cochran Dies," *MSNBC.com*, 30 March 2005.

136. Mike Schmidt, a former Rose teammate, said, "Pete has paid his dues," and fully supports Rose's reinstatement to baseball. Andrew R. Tripaldi, "Baseball; Schmidt Adds His Support to Have Rose Reinstated," *New York Times*, 18 April 2003. One of Rose's biggest supporters has been Bill James, who said Rose got a raw deal from baseball. Bill James, *The Politics of Glory: How Baseball's Hall of Fame Really Works* (New York: Macmillan, 1995), 355.

Chapter 7

1. Major League Baseball Players Ass'n v. Comm'r of Major League Baseball (John Rocker Arbitration Decision), *in Understanding Business and Legal Aspects of the Sports Industry 2001*, at 765 (PLI Intellectual Property Course Handbook Series No. G-638, 2001) [hereinafter Rocker Arbitration].
2. Rocker was asked during the interview if he felt a bond with NBA player, Latrell Sprewell. Sprewell had been suspended from the NBA two years before for choking his coach. Rocker said Sprewell should have been arrested and commented that if Sprewell had been white they would not have let him back in the NBA.
3. Jeff Pearlman, "At Full Blast," *Sports Illustrated*, 27 December 1999, 62.
4. Ibid., 62 & 64.
5. Rocker Arbitration, 774.
6. Jack Curry, "Baseball Orders Test for Rocker," *New York Times*, 7 January 2000. The resolution called on the Braves to release Rocker.
7. Murray Chass, "Remarks Could Hurt Rocker Most of All," *New York Times*, 24 December 1999, D1. Aaron was a senior vice president of baseball with the Braves at the time.
8. Ibid.
9. Rocker Arbitration, 776.
10. Rocker Arbitration, 777.
11. Ibid.
12. Curry, "Baseball Orders Test for Rocker."
13. For a general overview of the development of the Office of the Commissioner of Baseball and its powers, see Jeffrey A. Durney, "Fair or Foul? The Commissioner and Major League Baseball's Disciplinary Process," *Emory Law Journal* 41 (1992): 587–588.
14. *Finley v. Kuhn*, 569 F. 2d 527 (7th Cir. 1978). Art. I, sec. 2 provides in part:

> The functions of the Commissioner shall be as follows:

(a) TO INVESTIGATE, either upon complaint or upon his own initiative, any act, transaction or practice charged, alleged or suspected to be not in the best interests of the national game of Baseball, with authority to summon persons and to order the production of documents, and, in case of refusal to appeal or produce, to impose such penalties as are hereinafter provided.

15. See "Benny Kauff Acquitted," *New York Times*, 14 May 1921, 10; Andrew Zimbalist, *In The Best Interests of Baseball: The Revolutionary Reign of Bud Selig* (Indianapolis: Wiley, 2007), 44. Kauff won both batting titles of the Federal league. He captured the title in 1914 with a .370 average and again in 1915 with a .342 average. For further study, see Bennie Kauff, "The Inside Story of Bennie Kauff's Holdout," *Baseball Magazine* 17 (May 1916), 19.
16. "Benny Kauff will Sue Judge Landis," *Washington Post*, 8 September 1921, 10.
17. "Other Sports Gambling Scandals," *USA Today*, 9 February 2006.
18. Louis Effrat, "Chandler Bars Durocher for 1947 Baseball Season," *New York Times*, 10 April 1947, 1.
19. Lisa Swan, "Take My Wife ... Please," *New York Daily News*, 5 March 1973.
20. Ibid. Fritz Peterson and Suzanne Kekich later married each other and had four children together. Fritz Peterson later became an evangelist.
21. Ibid.
22. U.S. Const. amend. I.
23. *NCAA v. Tarkanian*, 488 U.S. 179 (1988).
24. *Ludtke v. Kuhn*, 461 F. Supp. 86 (S.D.N.Y. 1978).
25. Ibid., 93.
26. Ibid., 96.
27. Murray Chass, "Biased Words in '38 Led to a Suspension," *New York Times*, 3 February 2000, D7.
28. The arbitrator in the Rocker case did not seem to place much significance on the Powell case. He mentioned it in a footnote at the end of the case, but it never played a part in his decision to discipline Rocker. Rocker Arbitration, 807 n.2.
29. "Powell Suspended for Radio Remark," *New York Times*, 31 July 1938, 63.
30. Ibid.
31. "Landis Banishes Powell From Yankees for 10 Days When Negroes Claim Insult," *Syracuse Herald*, 31 July 1998.
32. *Washington Post*, 31 July 1938. Powell's manager defended the actions of his player: "The ball players do not want to engage in these broadcasts.... In fact, most of them are afraid of them and want no part of them. But they are pestered and pestered until finally one of them gives in. Then in an unguarded moment something is said, maybe only in a joke, but it's taken the wrong way and then there is trouble.... I don't know what

Powell said, but whatever it was, I'm pretty sure he meant no harm. Probably just meant to get off a wise crack. So the radio people ran out cold with apologies and I'm out a ball player for ten days in the thick of a pennant race." "Jake Powell Suspended for Radio Remark," *Chicago Tribune*, 31 July 1938, B1.

33. "Jake Powell Kills Himself as Police are Questioning Him," *Washington Post*, 5 November 1948.

34. Before the first pitch of the 1990 World Series, Schott took the microphone in front of a sold-out riverfront stadium and called for a moment of silence for U.S. troops "in the Far East" and also dedicated the game to the U.S. troops in "The Middle West." Jeff Merron, "The Strangest Series Moments," updated 25 October 2004, http://sports.espn.go.com/espn/page2/story?page=list/strangeWSmoments.

35. Claire Smith, "Baseball Bans Cincinnati Owner for a Year Over Racial Remarks," *New York Times*, 4 February 1993.

36. Ibid.

37. "Guillen Apologizes for Use of Homosexual Slur," updated 22 June 2006, http://sports.espn.go.com/mlb/news/story?id=2494491. NFL player Joey Porter was fined $10,000 for using term "fag" in describing another player. Mark Maske, "Steelers' Porter Fined for Slurring Winslow," *Washington Post*, 15 December 2006.

38. "Guillen Fined, Ordered to Take Sensitivity Training for Slur," updated 23 June 2006, http://sports.espn.go.com/mlb/news/story?id=2496753.

39. Harold Johnson, "*Who's Who in Major League Base Ball* (Chicago, IL: Buxton Pub., 1933); see also Jeffrey Powers-Beck, "'Chief': The American Indian Integration of Baseball, 1897–1945," *American Indian Quarterly* 25 (Autumn 2001): 528–29.

40. "Iverson Releases Album with Modified Lyrics," *SportsPickle.com*, 9 January 2002.

41. Ibid.

42. "NBA's Iverson to Change Offensive Rap Lyrics," ABC News/ESPN Sports, 13 October 2000, http://abcnews.go.com/Sports/story?id=100294&page=1; see also "Iverson Fined for Slur to Fans," *New York Times*, 3 February 2001.

43. Mike Wise, "N.B.A. Fines Rodman $50,000 for Remarks on Mormons," *New York Times*, 13 June 1997.

44. Ibid.; see also Karen Martin Dean, "Can the NBA Punish Dennis Rodman? An Analysis of First Amendment Rights in Professional Basketball," *Vermont Law Review* 23 (1998): 157–175.

45. Wise, "N.B.A. Fines Rodman $50,000 for Remarks on Mormons."

46. "N.H.L.: Notebook — Tampa Bay; N.H.L. Investigates Alleged Racial Slurs," *New York Times*, 7 October 1998.

47. "I just want to comment on how it's become like a common thing in the NHL for guys to fall in love with my sloppy seconds. I don't know what that's about." "Sean Avery Axed from Dallas Stars After 'Sloppy Seconds' Comment," Fox News, 15 December 2008, http://www.foxnews.com/story/0,2933,467085,00.html. The Stars owner backed the commissioner's decision and then cut Avery from the team. Avery checked into a 10-day treatment program after the incident.

48. Thomas Fielder, "Keep Your Mouth Shut and Listen: The NFL Player's Right of Free Expression," *University of Miami Business Law Review* 10 (2002): 549–550 n.20 (includes text of restricted speech addendum).

49. Mark Heisler, "Bengals Have Really Sharpened Their Clause," *Los Angeles Times*, 11 July 2000.

50. Braves Team President Stan Kasten said Rocker's remarks were "repugnant" and "unconscionable." He said if Rocker would have made the remarks during the season he would have definitely been suspended. Jack Curry, "Baseball Orders Test for Rocker," *New York Times*, 7 January 2000.

51. The parties agreed that article XII(A) of the Basic Agreement was applicable: "The Parties recognize that a Player may be subjected to disciplinary action for just cause by his Club, the Vice President, On-Field Operations or the Commissioner. Therefore, in Grievances regarding discipline, the issue to be resolved shall be whether there has been just cause for the penalty imposed. If discipline imposed upon a Player is determined to be improper by reason of a final decision under this Grievance Procedure, the Player shall promptly be made whole." 2007–2011 Basic Agreement, art. XII. sec. A, available at http://mlb.mlb.com/pa/pdf/cba_english.pdf.

52. Lewis Kurlantzick, "John Rocker and Employee Discipline for Speech," *Marquette Sports Law Review* 11 (2001): 186.

53. Rocker Arbitration, 778; see also Ethan Yale Bordman, "Freedom of Speech and Expression in Sports," *Michigan Bar Journal* 86 (September 2007), 36.

54. Rocker Arbitration, 779.

55. Ibid.

56. Ibid., 780.

57. Ibid., 781.

58. Ibid., 782.

59. Ibid., 784.

60. Ibid., 785.

61. Ibid.

62. Some states have statutes protecting an employee's First Amendment rights from private employers. See, e.g., Conn. Gen. Stat. Ann. § 31–51 (WL current through 2011 Jan. Reg. Sess.) (giving an employee an action for damages against their employer if the employer engages in conduct in violation of employee's first amendment rights); *Employment Coordinator* (St. Paul, MN: Thomson/West, 2011), 6: § 57:18 ("Off-duty activity may be used to support a lawful discharge. Such conduct may be in violation of the employer's

work rules, a conflict of interest with the employer's business, or simply evidence of unfitness for duty.") For cases dealing with this issue, see *Matthews v. A-I, Inc.*, 748 F.2d 975 (5th Cir. 1984); *Nix v. MLCY/Radio/Rahall Communications*, 738 F.2d 1181 (11th Cir. 1984).
63. Rocker Arbitration.
64. Ibid.
65. Ibid., 788. The term of the Uniform Player Contract begins in spring training and remains in force until the end of the World Series.
66. Ibid.
67. Ibid.
68. Ibid., 790.
69. Ibid., 789–90.
70. Ibid., 790.
71. " Knepper Apologizes," *New York Times*, 19 June 1988.
72. "Bell a No-Show for Turn at Bat," *Washington Post*, 18 May 1988.
73. Rocker Arbitration, 791.
74. Scott Williams, "Moguls Going Mano a Mano? Turner v. Murdoch: Here's How Titans Would Match Up," *New York Daily News*, 17 June 1997.
75. Rocker Arbitration, 792.
76. Rocker Arbitration, 794.
77. Das received a B.A. in history from Harvard, an M.A. in social sciences from the University of Chicago, and a law degree from Yale.
78. Professor Roger I. Abrams, a noted baseball and the law scholar, called this an "obvious error in the commissioner's sanctions" and he made that call even before the arbitration opinion was issued. Roger I. Abrams, "Off His Rocker: Sports Discipline and Labor Arbitration," *Marquette Sports Law Review* 11 (2001): 171.
79. Rocker Arbitration, 796.
80. Ibid.
81. Ibid., 799.
82. Ibid., 800.
83. Ibid.
84. Ibid., 799.
85. Ibid., 801.
86. Ibid., 803. The commissioner did receive correspondence supporting Rocker's First Amendment rights.
87. Ibid., 803.
88. Ibid., 802.
89. Ibid., 803.
90. Ibid.
91. Ibid., 804.
92. Ibid., citing to Howe, No. 95, 15.
93. Ibid., 804–805.
94. Ibid., 805.
95. Ibid. Harvard Professor Alan Dershowitz said the commissioner would been have been wise not to suspend Rocker but instead to issue a statement that said the league had a commitment to free speech but that it did not agree with Rocker's opinions. Alan M. Dershowitz, "Baseball's Speech Police," *New York Times*, 2 February 2000, A21.

96. "Rocker On: Braves Closer Gets Suspension and Fine Reduced," CNN/Sports Illustrated, 2 March 2000, http://sportsillustrated.cnn.com/baseball/mlb/news/2000/03/01/rocker_suspension_ap/.
97. In his career Rocker had an impressive 332 strikeouts in 255.3 innings pitched. He appeared in several league championship series and in the 1999 World Series.

Chapter 8

1. 320 N.Y.S.2d (App. Div. 1971)
2. 799 F. Supp. 1475 (S.D.N.Y. 1992)
3. *See generally* Sol White, *History of Colored Base Ball: With Other Documents on the Early Black Game, 1886–1936* (Lincoln, NE: Bison Books, 1995).
4. Much has been written about Jackie Robinson and his life. *See, e.g.*, Jules Tygiel, *Baseball's Great Experiment: Jackie Robinson and His Legacy* (New York: Oxford University Press, 1983; expanded ed., 1997); Margaret Davidson, *The Story of Jackie Robinson: Bravest Man in Baseball* (New York: Yearling, 1987); Arnold Rampersad, *Jackie Robinson: A Biography* (New York: Ballantine Books, 1998); Jonathan Eig, *Opening Day: The Story of Jackie Robinson's First Season* (New York: Simon & Schuster, 2008); Sharon Robinson, *Promises to Keep: How Jackie Robinson Changed America* (New York: Scholastic Press, 2004).
5. Robert Peterson, *Only the Ball was White: A History of Legendary Black Players and All-Black Professional Teams* (New York: Oxford University Press, 1970; repr., 1992).
6. "Emmett Ashford Becomes First Black Major League Umpire," *Boston Globe*, 18 September 1965.
7. For further study, see the film *The Life and Times of Hank Greenberg* (2000); Ira Berkow, *Hank Greenberg: Hall-of-Fame Slugger* (Philadelphia: Jewish Publication Society of America, 2001).
8. "The association of sports and masculinity, the gender-biased nurturing, and the media's perpetuation of sports-related gender stereotypes have all contributed to limiting women's athletic participation and accomplishments." Syda Kosofsky, "Toward Gender Equality in Professional Sports," *Hastings Women's Law Journal* 4 (1993): 226.
9. George Vecsey, "Worst Call Ever? Sure. Kill the Umpires? Never," *New York Times*, 3 June 2010. Galarraga showed great sportsmanship after the call. Commissioner Selig refused to overturn the call. In an ESPN poll in June 2010, Joyce was voted the best umpire in Major League Baseball by a poll of 100 players.
10. William. A. Phelon, "Baseball Customs Past and Present; How the Old Timers Roasted the Home Team and the Umpire — Former Cus-

toms Compared to Modern — The Real Pinch Hitter — Comments from the Side Lines," *Baseball Magazine* 15 (October 1915): 53–62.

11. In the 1950 Hollywood movie, *Kill The Umpire*, ex-baseball player Bill Johnson played by William Bendix, runs into some trouble as an umpire and attains the nickname of "two call" Johnson. William Bendix also played "The Babe" in *The Babe Ruth Story* (1948). Spalding also discussed the umpire in his early book on baseball: "I desire to speak a word for the umpire of the present and the future. As I have already said, he is essential to the game. There can be no Base Ball without his presence. His position at the best is not an enviable one. In every game there will need to be close decisions. He must give offense to somebody in each recurring contest. That every umpire will make mistakes is true." Albert G. Spalding, *America's National Game: Historic Facts Concerning the Beginning Evolution, Development and Popularity of Base Ball with Personal Reminiscences of Its Vicissitudes, Its Victories and Its Votaries* (New York: American Sports Pub., 1911), 413. It has also been stated: "Umpiring is a mixture of good physique, good eyes, plenty of courage, pride in your work, a knowledge of the rules, getting the right angle, a respect for the ability of others — managers, players and umpires — plus plenty of common sense. There is no greater asset than common property applied. Anticipation is an umpire's greatest trouble-maker. It is invariably the source of calling plays too quickly. Instead of anticipating the play, let it happen, follow it intently to its completion before reaching a decision." Hy Turkin and S.C. Thompson, *The Official Encyclopedia of Baseball* (New York: Copp Clark, 1956), 485 (condensed from William G. Evans, "Umpiring from the Inside," 1947).

12. Spalding, *America's National Game*, 405–406.

13. *Quoted in* Marty Payne, "The Undesirable Position: Umpiring in the American Association 1882–1891," *Base Ball: A Journal of the Early Game* 1 (Fall 2007): 104–114.

14. *Parks v. Steinbrenner*, 520 N.Y.S.2d 374, 376 (App. Div. 1987).

15. Ibid., 375.

16. Ibid.

17. Ibid.

18. Ibid., 378. The court gave a brief historical perspective of the umpire in arriving at its decision that Steinbrenner's statements constituted opinion and not fact and were therefore protected speech. "Since the late nineteenth century, the baseball umpire has had to tolerate extraordinary verbal abuse. Indeed, on occasion he has been the target of unlawful physical attacks by players and fans. For example, in 1940 one fan jumped out of the stands at Ebbets Field to 'flatten' Umpire George Magerkurth appeared in the newspaper the next day, it was learned that he had risked more than the exercise of his 'right to question the umpire'— the attacker was a paroled felon who was promptly returned to jail for violating his parole. Yet, Magerkurth, perhaps because his assailant had been imprisoned for the attack, never pressed charges for the assault. In the 1985 World Series, Pitcher Joaquin Andujar attacked umpire Don Denkinger on the field of play. Andujar was promptly fined and suspended. As in ordinary life, so in sports, the physical integrity of players, umpires, and fans are protected against unlawful intrusion." Ibid., 377 n.2. "For present day fans, a goodly part of the sport in a baseball game is goading and denouncing the umpire when they do not concur in his decisions, and most feel that, without one or more rhubarbs, they have not received their money's worth. Ordinarily, however, an umpire garners only vituperation — not fisticuffs. Fortified by the knowledge of his infallibility in all judgment decisions, he is able to shed billingsgate like water on the proverbial duck's back." Ibid., quoting *Toone v. Adams*, 137 S.E.2d 132, 136 (N.C. 1964).

19. Jeff Idelson, "Growing Experience in Cooperstown: Third Installment of a Four-Part Look at the History of the National Baseball Hall of Fame and Museum," 21 February 2007, available at *http://web.baseballhalloffame.org/news*.

20. Sharon L. Roan, "No One Yelled 'Kill The Ump' When Amanda Clement Was a Man in Blue," *Sports Illustrated*, 5 April 1982, W3.

21. *Quoted in* Gai Ingham Berlage, *Women in Baseball: The Forgotten History* (Santa Barbara, CA: Praeger, 1994).

22. Dorothy Seymour Mills and Harold Seymour, *Baseball: The People's Game* (New York: Oxford University Press, 1991), 85.

23. Ibid., 484.

24. Gai Ingham Berlage, "Women, Baseball, and the American Dream," in *Baseball and the American Dream, Race, Class, Gender, and the National Pastime*, ed. Robert Elias (Armonk: M.E. Sharpe, 2001), 242.

25. Ibid.

26. John D. Kelly, *The American Game: Capitalism, Decolonization, World Domination, and Baseball*, (Chicago: Prickly Press, 2006); John Henderson, "Women Go the Distance — Long Line of Sports Pioneers Led Way for Golfer Sorenstam," *Denver Post*, 22 May 2003; "Women in the Baseball Through the Years," *Kansas City Star*, 4 December, 2006; Leslia A. Heaphy, "More Than a Man's Game: Pennsylvania's Women Play Ball," Historical Society of Pennsylvania, http://www.hsp.org/node/2934; Society for American Baseball Research, *Women in Baseball Committee Newsletter* 21 (August 2000).

27. Kelly, *The American Game*, 16–17; Kaye Sharbono, *Jackie Mitchell, Baseball Player* (Upper Saddle River, NJ: Modern Curriculum Press, 1995); Joel Zoss and John Bowman, *Diamonds in the Rough: The Untold History of Baseball* (New York: Macmillan, 1989; repr., Lincoln: University

of Nebraska Press, 2004), 208–209; "Whiskers of New Nat Pitcher Stir in Nation's Capital," *Sporting News* 23 August 1934.

28. Dean A. Sullivan, *Late Innings: A Documentary History of Baseball, 1945–1972* (Lincoln: University of Nebraska Press, 2002), 60 ("Minor League Head Forbids Signing of Female Players").

29. "First Woman Among Largest Hall Class Ever," NBC Sports, 28 February 2006. For some books exploring the topic of women in baseball, see Jean Hastings Ardell, *Breaking into Baseball: Women and the National Pastime* (Carbondale: Southern Illinois University Press, 2005); Berlage, *Women in Baseball: The Forgotten History*; Barbara Gregorich, *Women at Play: The Story of Women in Baseball* (San Diego, CA: Harcourt Brace, 1993).

30. "Giants Dismiss Stadium Announcer," *New York Times*, 1 January 2000.

31. John Shea, "Giants' PA Announcer Living a Dream," *ESPN.com*, 4 May 2006.

32. Barry Janoff, "Parkes Named MLB CMO," *Brandweek.com*, 7 July 2008.

33. "Female Rice Alum Umpires MLB Game in Arizona," *Houston Chronicle*, 29 March 2007.

34. "Only Female Ump in Minors Released," SI.com, 31 October 2007, http://sportsillustrated.cnn.com/2007/baseball/more/10/31/woman.umpire.released.ap/index.html.

35. Richard Lapchick, *The 2008 Racial and Gender Report Card: Major League Baseball*, (15 April 2008), 5, available at http://tidesport.org/RGRC/2008/2008_MLB_RGRC_PR.pdf.

36. Tim Dahlberg, "Keith Hernandez Looking Like Sexist Moron," *NBC Sports*, 25 April 2006.

37. Marty Noble, "Hernandez Apologizes for Remarks," *mets.com*, 24 April 2006.

38. Cox also brought a lawsuit against MLB at the same time Postema did. Her case also was settled on a confidential basis.

39. *Postema v. Nat'l League of Prof'l Baseball Clubs*, 799 F. Supp. 1475, 1478 (S.D.N.Y. 1992).

40. John Garrity, "Waiting For the Call," *Sports Illustrated*, 14 March 1988, 26.

41. Sharlene A. McEvoy, "The Umpire Strikes Out: *Postema v. National League*: Major League Gender Discrimination," *University of Miami Entertainment and Sports Law Review* 11 (1993): 3–4.

42. *Postema*, 799 F. Supp. at 1478. Postema said in her book that if a player used this word when referring to her, they would be immediately ejected from the game.

43. Ibid., 1479.

44. There are no direct references to baseball umpires in either the Hebrew Bible or New Testament. However, Reverend Larry Coulter did cite to Job 9:33 from the Hebrew Bible:

> There is no umpire between us,
> Who may lay his hand upon us both.

Rev. Coulter received his M. Div. from Princeton Theological Seminary. "Interview with the Rev. Lawrence W. Coulter," 6 June 2010.

45. Pam Postema and Gene Wojciechowski, *You've Got to Have Balls to Make it in This League: My Life As An Umpire* (Lincoln: University of Nebraska Press, 1992, repr., 2003), 180.
46. Ibid., 181–182.
47. Ibid., 182.
48. Ibid., 183.
49. Ibid.
50. Ibid., 1479.
51. *Postema*, 799 F. Supp. at 1480.
52. Postema, 1477.
53. Ibid., 1479.
54. Ibid.
55. Ibid.
56. Ibid.
57. Ibid.
58. Ibid.
59. Ibid.
60. Ibid.
61. Postema and Wojciechowski, *You've Got to Have Balls to Make it in This League*, 185.
62. Ibid., 186.
63. Ibid.
64. *Postema*, 799 F. Supp. at 1480.
65. Ibid.
66. Ibid., 1475, citing 42 U.S.C. 32000 e-5(c).
67. Ibid.
68. Ibid. Timely filing with the EEOC is a mandatory prerequisite to the subsequent maintenance of a Title VII claim. *United Air Lines, Inc. v. Evans*, 431 U.S. 553, 555 (1977).
69. *Postema*, 799 F. Supp. at 1481. Postema admitted she did not file a claim with the EEOC until April 4, 1990. Since 1988 the American League had only one opening for an umpire and hired former minor league umpire Jim Joyce in April 1989.
70. Ibid., 1482.
71. Ibid.
72. Ibid., 1482–1483.
73. Ibid.
74. Ibid., 1489.
75. "The odds of a plaintiff's lawyer winning in civil court are two to one against. Think about that for a second. Your odds of surviving a game of Russian roulette are better than winning a case at trial. 12 times better. So why does anyone do it? They don't. They settle. Out of the 780,000, only 12,000 or 1 percent ever reach a verdict. The whole idea of lawsuits is to settle, to compel the other side to settle. And you do that by spending more money than you should, which forces them to spend more money than they should, and whoever comes to their senses first loses. Trials are a corruption of the entire process and only fools who have something to prove end up ensnared in them. Now when I say prove, I don't mean about the case, I mean about themselves." Quote from *A Civil Action*, directed by Steven Zaillian (Touchstone Pictures, 1999).
76. In 2009, the author discussed the case with attorney Daniel R. Shulman who represented Ms.

Postema in her lawsuit against baseball. Shulman was very professional in his approach and all matters relating to the case were discussed except the confidential settlement. 77. Postema and Wojciechowski, *You've Got to Have Balls to Make It in this League*, 254.

78. "Postema Loses," *New York Times*, 15 December 1989, A36.

79. "How to Become an Umpire," accessed 16 September 2011, http://mlb.mlb.com/mlb/official_info/umpires/how_to_become.jsp.

80. Ibid.

81. Gera was the first women to umpire a professional game. "Umpiring Timeline," accessed 16 September 2011, http://mlb.mlb.com/mlb/official_info/umpires/timeline.jsp.

82. *New York Times*, 15 August 1969.

83. Ibid.

84. Ibid. Most of the hitting exhibitions she gave raised money for charity.

85. Ibid.

86. "Court Orders Female Umpire Hired," *New York Times*, 13 January 1972.

87. *N.Y. State Div. of Human Rights, v. N.Y.-Pa. Prof'l Baseball League*, 320 N.Y.S.2d 788, 791 (App. Div. 1971) [hereinafter *Gera*].

88. Ibid., 791.

89. "Baseball is Sued for $25 Million by Woman Umpire," *New York Times*, 16 March 1971.

90. *Gera*, 320 N.Y.S.2d at 791.

91. Ibid.

92. Ibid., 791–792.

93. Ibid., 792.

94. Ibid., 790.

95. Ibid., 792.

96. "[I]t shall not be an unlawful employment practice for an employer to hire and employ employees ... on the basis of his religion, sex, or national origin in those certain instances where religion, sex, or national origin is a bona fide occupational qualification reasonably necessary to the normal operation of that particular business or enterprise." 42 U.S.C. § 2000e-2(e).

97. *Gera*, 320 N.Y.S.2d at 792.

98. Ibid.

99. Ibid., 792–793.

100. Ibid., 793, citing to C.F.R. § 1604.1(a)(ii).

101. Ibid.

102. Ibid., 793–794.

103. Ibid., 794.

104. Ibid.

105. Ibid.

106. Ibid., 796–797 (Gabrielli, J., dissenting). In a separate dissent, Justice Cardamme stated: "[W]e should acknowledge that in the regulation of baseball, a sport traditionally known as our national pastime the predominant concern is national, and recognize that, pragmatically, organized baseball is not amenable to effective state-by-state regulation. I vote to reverse and dismiss the complaint." Ibid., 799 (Cardamone, J., dissenting).

107. Zoss and Bowman, *Diamonds in the Rough*, 305.

108. "Bernice Gera, Umpire, 61" *New York Times*, 25 September 1992.

109. "Sound Off, Sports Fans!," *Chicago Tribune*, 21 April 1970, C3.

110. 461 F. Supp. 86 (S.D.N.Y. 1978).

111. Ibid., 98.

112. Ibid.

113. 867 F. Supp. 696 (N.D. Ill. 1994).

114. *Kesner v. Little Caesar's Enterprises, Inc.*, No. 01-719942002, WL 1480800 (E.D. Mich. June 13, 2002).

115. "Jury Awards Ex-Flight Attendant $200,000 in Tigers Harassment Suit," *Detroit Tigers*, 14 February 2003.

116. *Ortiz-Del Valle v. Nat'l Basketball Ass'n*, 42 F. Supp. 2d 334 (S.D.N.Y. 1999).

117. Ibid., 336.

118. "N.B.A.: Court News; Referee's Jury Award is Severely Reduced," *New York Times*, 2 April 1999.

119. Famed MLB Harry Wendelstadt, who trained Teresa Cox, has noted: "I have no doubt that someday there'll be a woman umpire in the major leagues; I just hope I'm the one who trains her." Anna Quindlen, "Public and Private: The Clement Floor," *New York Times*, 28 August 1991.

Chapter 9

1. 407 U.S. 258 (1972).

2. Walter T. Champion, Jr., *Sports Law In a Nutshell* (Eagan, MN: West, 2005), 58–59.

3. Ibid.

4. In *Radovich v. National Football League*, 352 U.S. 445 (1947), the U.S. Supreme Court held that professional football was subject to antitrust laws. *See also Smith v. Pro-Football*, 420 F. Supp. 738, 746 (D.D.C. 1976), judgment aff'd in part, rev'd in part, 593 F.2d 1173 (D.C. Cir. 1978) (player challenged NFL draft); *Mackey v. Nat'l Football League*, 543 F.2d 606, 621 (8th Cir. 1976) (former Colts great challenged NFL's version of baseball's reserve clause, the Rozelle Rule); *Kapp v. Nat'l Football League*, 586 F.2d 644 (9th Cir. 1978) (former Vikings quarterback challenged the NFL Standard Player Contract on antitrust grounds).

5. 259 U.S. 200 (1922).

6. 346 U.S. 356 (1953).

7. *See* Ed Edmonds, "The Impact of Curt Flood's Minor League Baseball Experience on His Lawsuit against Bowie Kuhn," *Nine* 9 (Spring 2008), 62.

8. Curt Flood with Richard Carter, *The Way It Is* (New York: Trident Press, 1971), 34. Flood thought that the sign meant club soda and coke. Ibid. "Like many of the black players of the period, Flood was visiting the South for the first time, and its ways came as a shock to the system. For their

part, major league organizations did almost nothing to prepare their young black players for the kind of discrimination they might encounter in the minor leagues. Players were assigned with little regard for the risks they would encounter in certain leagues and cities." Alex Belth, *Stepping Up: The Story of Curt Flood and his Fight for Baseball Players' Rights* (New York: Persea Books, 2006), 28.

9. George Vecsey, "$90,000-a-Year Rebel," *New York Times*, 17 January 1970, 36.

10. Flood, *The Way It Is*, 37.

11. Georgia law prohibited Flood and Cardenas from dressing with white players. A separate cubicle was put up for them. Ibid., 43.

12. Ibid., 34–47.

13. Geoffrey C. Ward and Ken Burns, *Baseball an Illustrated History* (New York: Borzoi Books, 1994), 339.

14. Belth, *Stepping Up*, 91.

15. Flood, *The Way It Is*, 77.

16. Ward and Burns, *Baseball an Illustrated History*, 411.

17. His full name was Franklin Delano Roosevelt Wieand.

18. He is tied with Luis Gonzalez, Danny Litwhier, and Tery Puhl. From 1958 to 1969, Flood ranked first in fielding average and double plays for center fielders. From September 3, 1965, to June 2, 1967, he did not commit an error, establishing a league record of 216 games. He handled 568 chances during that span. He led the National League in putouts four times and fielding percentage twice. When he retired he had played the third most games in center field behind Richie Ashburn and Willie Ways.

19. Dennis Purdy, *Team by Team Encyclopedia of Major League Baseball* (New York: Workman Publishing, 2006), 912–915.

20. Belth, *Stepping Up*, 143.

21. "Cards' Flood Quits After Allen Trade," *Chicago Tribune*, 9 October 1969

22. Ibid.

23. Ibid.

24. Bob Gibson, Carl Yastrzemski and Frank Robinson all made $125,000 in 1970.

25. Leonard Koppett, "Flood, Backed by Players, Plans Suit to Challenge Baseball Reserve Clause," *New York Times*, 30 December 1969, 42.

26. Miller told Flood: "Let me put it to you the simplest way possible: The way I see it, the moment you file that suit, you're probably through in baseball. And there could be more to it than that." Marvin Miller, *A Whole Different Ball Game: The Inside Story of the Baseball Revolution* (Chicago: Ivan R. Dee, 2004), 181.

27. Koppett, "Flood, Backed by Players, Plans Suit to Challenge Baseball Reserve Clause," 42.

28. Flood, 17.

29. "Flood to Sue for Reserve Clause Test," *Chicago Tribune*, 30 December 1969, B2.

30. Ibid.

31. According to Flood's autobiography, the players representatives at the meeting were "Jack Aker (Athletics), Max Alvis (Indians), Jim Bunning (Pension Committee), Roberto Clemente (Pirates), Don Drysdale (Dodgers), Jack Fisher (Mets), Bill Freehan (Tigers), Dave Giusti (Astros), Dick Hall (Phillies), Tom Haller (Giants), Steve Hamilton (Yankees), Bob Humphreys (Senators), Randy Hundley (Cubs), Dave Johnson (Orioles), Bob Locker (White Sox), Tim McCarver (Cardinals), Dave Morehead (Red Sox), Russ Nixon (Twins), Milt Pappas (Reds), Bob Rogers (Angels), and Joe Torre (Braves). All of them had been properly elected by their teammates. Faced with undeniable facts, all proved solid citizens who cared, really cared, about the well-being of their fellow professionals." Flood, *The Way It Is*, 165.

32. Brad Snyder, *A Well-Paid Slave: Curt Flood's Fight for Free Agency in Professional Sports* (New York: Penguin Group, 2006), 104, citing interview with Joe Torre, Tampa, Florida, February 24, 2005.

33. Leonard Koppett, "Kuhn Denied Flood's Request to 'Free' Him for Other Offers Besides Phils,'" *New York Times*, 31 December 1969, 32.

34. Ibid.

35. Snyder, *A Well-Paid Slave*, 104.

36. Ward was born in 1860, one year before the beginning of the Civil War.

37. *See* Elliot J. Gorn, *Muhammad Ali, The People's Champ* (Champaign: University of Illinois Press, 1998).

38. Robert Lipsyte, "Revolt of the Gladiators," *New York Times*, 5 January 1970, 52.

39. Robert Lipsyte, "The Lives They Lived: Curt Flood; Baseball's Last Martyr," *New York Times*, 4 January 1998.

40. Flood's lawsuit would create a massive amount of scholarly activity. For starters, see Andrew Zimbalist, "Baseball's Antitrust Exemption: Why It Still Matters," *Nine* 13 (Fall 2004), 1; Stephen F. Ross, "Reconsidering *Flood v. Kuhn*," *University of Miami Entertainment and Sports Law Review* 12 (1995): 169; William B. Tsimpris, "A Question of (Anti)Trust: *Flood v. Kuhn* and the Viability of Major League Baseball's Antitrust Exemption," *Richmond Journal of Law and the Public Interest* 8 (2004): 69; Lacie L. Kaiser, "Revisiting the Impact of the Curt Flood Act of 1998 on the Bargaining Relationship Between Players and Management in Major League Baseball," *DePaul Journal of Sports Law & Contemporary Problems* 2 (2004): 230.

41. "Curt Flood Files Suit; Asks to be Free Agent," *Chicago Tribune*, 17 January 1970, 62. For a general overview of the allegations of the Flood's complaint, see Leonard Koppett, "Baseball is Sued Under Trust Law," *New York Times*, 17 January 1970, 1.

42. The lawsuit also had separate antitrust claims against Anheuser-Busch and CBS which were later dismissed by the court. The most con-

troversial, but probably not the most legally significant, claim made by the Flood lawsuit was that the reserve clause was a violation of the Thirteenth Amendment to the U.S. Constitution, which states in part, "Neither slavery nor involuntary servitude, except as a punishment for crime whereof the party shall have been duly convicted, shall exist within the United States, or any place subject to their jurisdiction."

43. Yastrzemski was the last Triple Crown winner in either league in 1967 with 44 home runs, 121 RBI's, and a .326 batting average. Harmon Killebrew tied him for the home run lead.

44. Yastrzemski made $130,000 in 1969.

45. "Baseball Goes to Court Today," *New York Times*, 20 January 1970, 36. Yastrzemski sent an angry letter to Marvin Miller saying all the players should have been consulted first. Robert M. Goldman, *One Man Out: Curt Flood Versus Baseball* (Lawrence: University Press of Kansas, 2008), 5.

46. One episode involving Twins player Dave Boswell was insightful. Boswell was underperforming for the Twins and there were rumors that he might be traded. "When I heard these rumors I thought: Calvin Griffith (Twins president) owns me. I have no beef, if he wants to trade me. If he does, fine. If he does not, fine. I am not going to take him into court if I am traded." Mike Lamey, "Demotion to the Bullpen Bugs Boswell," *Sporting News*, 1970, 10.

47. Snyder, *A Well-Paid Slave*, 118.

48. Ibid.

49. Richard Dozer, "Players Want Change, Death of Reserve Clause," *Chicago Tribune*, 22 January 1970, D2.

50. "Williams Terms Flood 'Ill-Advised' in Lawsuit," *The Washington Post*, 23 January 1970, B2.

51. Snyder, *A Well-Paid Slave*22, citing *Los Angeles Times*, 11 April 1970. Koufax laid some of the groundwork for Flood's lawsuit with his 1966 hold-out and negotiation along with teammate Don Drysdale. *See* Jane Leavy, *Sandy Koufax A Lefty's Legacy* (New York: HarperCollins, 2002), 209.

52. "U.S. Delays Decision in Flood Suit," *Chicago Tribune*, 4 February 1970, C2.

53. Leonard Koppett, "Flood Asks for Injunction to Make Him a Free Agent Immediately," *New York Times*, 4 February 1970, 50.

54. *Flood v. Kuhn*, 309 F. Supp. 793 (S.D.N.Y. 1970); Flood, *The Way It Is*, 204. Judge Cooper also issued a 19-page opinion when he refused to rule on the owners' motion to dismiss but did dismiss CBS and Anheuser-Busch as defendants in the lawsuits. *See Flood v. Kuhn*, 312 F. Supp. 404 (S.D.N.Y. 1970).

55. Marvin Miller anticipated severe delays in the Flood's case but that never happened. "While we thought Flood's case was not complex, we certainly had no illusions that the trial was going to be easy or that it would move through the judicial system rapidly. The disposition of a case in federal court *always* involves a lot of time. The court dockets are always crowded, and lengthy postponements are easy to get. It's no surprise that some cases remain unresolved for many years, which is to say, we fully, expected serious delays in Flood's case." Miller, *A Whole Different Ball Game*, 192.

56. Marvin Miller said although he never communicated it to Goldberg he felt betrayed when Goldberg decided to run for governor. He said Goldberg performed well below expectations in arguing the case before the U.S. Supreme Court. Ibid., 198.

57. Snyder, *A Well-Paid Slave*.

58. Flood, *The Way It Is*, 204.

59. Space does not permit a detailed explanation of the 2000 pages of the Flood trial transcript. However, a willing party has already performed that task. *See* Neil F. Flynn, *Baseball's Reserve System: The Case and Trial of Curt Flood v. Major League Baseball*, (Springfield, IL: Walnut Park Group, 2006).

60. Ibid., 87.

61. Ibid., 71. In today's media frenzy, player's salaries are published in numerous places in newspapers and the Internet. *See, e.g.*, USA Today Salaries Data Bases, http://content.usatoday.com/ sportsdata/baseball/mlb/salaries/team. The database contains the salaries of all major league players on opening day rosters and disabled lists from 1998 to the present. Player salaries have always been the subject of much fanfare. *See* William H. Dunbar, "Baseball Salaries Thirty Years Ago," *Baseball Magazine* 21 (July 1918), 291–92. The article explores in depth the salaries of famous players. The highest paid players for 1881 to 1889 were as follows:

1881	J.H. O'Rourke	$2,000
1882	J.W. Ward	$2,400
1883	Wm. Ewing	$3,100
1884	Wm. Ewing	$3,100
1885	J.H. O'Rourke	$4,500
1886	Fred Dunlap	$4,500
1887	C. Radbourne	$4,500
1888	Fred Dunlap	$7,000
1889	Fred Dunlap	$5,000

See also "Senate Subcommittee on Antitrust and Monopoly," *Organized Professional Team Sports*, 85th Cong., 2nd sess., 1958, 793–810; Dean A. Sullivan, ed., *Late Innings: A Documentary History of Baseball, 1945–1972* (Lincoln: University of Nebraska Press, 2002).

62. Testifying in a federal court trial can be intimidating to anyone who has not spent a lot of time in the court system. For a full rendition of Flood's full testimony, see Flynn, *Baseball's Reserve System*, 59–88.

63. *Flood v. Kuhn*, 316 F. Supp 271, 282 n.17 (S.D.N.Y. 1970).

64. Leonard Koppett, "Flood is First at Bat as Baseball Antitrust Suit Starts," *New York Times*, 20 May 1970, 52.

65. Ibid.
66. "Hall of Famers Back Flood in Court," *Chicago Tribune*, 22 May 1970, C1. On May 26, 1970, in the middle of the trial, Marvin Miller announced that the Players Association and the owners had reached a new three-year labor agreement. Leonard Koppett, "Baseball's Pact Put at $4-Million," *New York Times*, 26 May 1970, 67.
67. Veeck had many great ideas for the game of baseball — some worked and some did not. *See generally* Bill Veeck with Ed Linn, *Veeck as in Wreck: The Autobiography of Bill Veeck* (New York: Putnam, 1962).
68. "Reserve Clause Modification Would Aid Baseball — Veeck," *Chicago Tribune*, 11 June 1970, E4.
69. Leonard Koppett, "Veeck is for Shift in Player Clause," *New York Times*, 11 June 1970, 59.
70. Snyder, *A Well-Paid Slave*, 176.
71. Flood, *The Way It Is*, 197.
72. Ibid.
73. *Flood v. Kuhn*, 316 F. Supp. 271 (S.D.N.Y. 1970).
74. Ibid., 284–285.
75. "Phils Hope Flood Decides to Play; Kuhn is Pleased," *Chicago Tribune*, 13 August 1970, B5.
76. Ibid.
77. The court only reviews the transcripts of the lower court's proceedings.
78. The 1971 season would be the Senators' last in Washington. They would move to Dallas and become the Texas Rangers. The 1971 Senators forfeited their last game 9–0 to the Yankees. They were winning 7–5 with two outs in the ninth inning when the fans began running on the field. The game was then forfeited in favor of the Yankees. All statistics of the game were official including a home run by the Senators' Frank Howard. Merrell Whittlesey, "It was a Whole New Ballgame!," *Washington Star*, 1 October 1971.
79. Flood wanted to make sure that Marvin Miller knew he was not giving up on the case. Flood, *The Way It Is*, 211.
80. The manager of the Senators was Ted Williams, who had been critical of Flood's filing the lawsuit.
81. "Flood Quits Again: Off to Europe," *Chicago Tribune*, 28 April 1971, C1.
82. "Flood's Good-by: 'I'll Go Crazy if I Don't Get Out,'" *New York Times*, 29 April 1971, 53.
83. Ibid.
84. Ibid.
85. The Supreme Court takes very few cases. *See* Saul Brenner, "Granting Certiorari by the United States Supreme Court: An Overview of the Social Science Studies," *Law Library Journal* 92 (2000), 193.
86. "Flood Case in Court," *Chicago Tribune*, 21 March 1972, C1.
87. Leonard Koppett, "High Court Hears Baseball Back Antitrust Exemption," *New York Times*, 21 March, 1972, 1.
88. Glen Elsasser, "Reserve Clause Upheld by Court," *Chicago Tribune*, 20 June 1972, C1.
89. *Flood v. Kuhn*, 407 U.S. 258, 259 (1972).
90. Professor Roger I. Abrams wrote a unique and insightful article on the list of ballplayers named by Justice Blackmun, in which he contended that the likely source for the list was Lawrence S. Ritter, *The Glory of Their Times* (New York: Macmillan, 1966). Roger I. Abrams, "Blackmun's List," *Virginia Sports and Entertainment Law Journal* 6 (2007), 191.
91. Abrams, "Blackmun's List," 189–190. For general discussion on the court's decision-making process, see Miller, *A Whole Different Ball Game*, 199–202.
92. Justice Blackmun never commented on the Flood opinion, but he did write a letter to the New Jersey Bar Association in 1980 refuting the idea that he only included the three names of the African-American players upon the insistence of Justice Marshall. Abrams, "Blackmun's List," 190–191, citing the Blackmun papers held by the Library of Congress.
93. 259 U.S. 200 (1922).
94. Ibid., 208–209.
95. *Flood v. Kuhn*, 407 U.S. at 272.
96. Ibid., 282–283.
97. Ibid., 283–284.
98. Ibid., 284.
99. Ibid., 285–286.
100. Ibid., 286.
101. Ibid.
102. Ibid.
103. Ibid., 288.
104. Ibid., 290.
105. Ibid., 291.
106. Ibid., 292.
107. Ibid., 296.
108. Murray Chass, "Curt Flood, Forgotten Man in Baseball Freedom Fight, Lives in Self-Imposed Exile," *New York Times*, 9 September 1976, 51.
109. Ibid.
110. Charles Finley may have hired Flood because of his ongoing feud with Bowie Kuhn.
111. Joe Hoppel, "Sacrifice Guy," *Sporting News*, 3 February 1997, 47.

Chapter 10

1. *Nat'l & Am. League Prof'l Baseball Clubs v. Major League Players Ass'n*, 66 Lab. Arb. Rep. (BNA) 101 (1975) (Seitz, Arb.) [hereinafter Messersmith & McNally Grievances].
2. Bowie Kuhn, *Hardball: The Education of a Baseball Commissioner* (New York: Times Books, 1987).
3. Marvin Miller, *A Whole Different Ball Game: The Inside Story of the Baseball Revolution* (Chicago: Ivan R. Dee, 2004), 238.
4. Ibid., 252.

5. Richard Dozer, "Catfish Hunter Opened Money-Grabbing Tourney," *Chicago Tribune*, 5 January 1975. Hunter's signing by the Yankees was a sign of things to come in baseball. Historically, the Yankees continued to try sign all the best free available agents every year.

6. *Am. & Nat'l Leagues of Prof'l Baseball Clubs v. Major League Baseball Players Ass'n*, 130 Cal. Rptr. 626, 627 (Ct. App. 1975).

7. Ibid., 628.

8. Arbitration Decision, In the Matter of the Arbitration between American and National Leagues of Professional Baseball Clubs (Oakland Athletics) and Major League Baseball Players Association (James A. "Catfish" Hunter), Decision No. 23, Grievance Nos. 74–18 and 74–20, Dec. 13, 1974 (claim of default under section 7(a) of Uniform Player's Contract) [hereinafter Hunter Arbitration Decision]. Notwithstanding the arbitration loss, Finley still hoped Hunter would play for Oakland. He later sent Hunter a letter telling him he valued his friendship and hoped to continue their close relationship. Jim Hunter "Catfish," *Catfish, My Life in Baseball* (New York: McGraw-Hill, 1988), 144.

9. Hunter Arbitration Decision, 40.

10. *Am. & Nat'l Leagues of Prof'l Baseball Clubs*, 130 Cal. Rptr. 626.

11. Although the Padres and Royals made higher offers than the Yankees, Hunter still signed with New York. The deal was negotiated between Hunter and Clyde Kluttz, Yankees scouting director, during breakfast at a restaurant. Kluttz made the following offer to Hunter on a napkin: $1 million bonus, $1 million life insurance, $750,000 salary over five years, $500,000 in deferred money, $200,000 for attorney's fees, and $50,000 each for college-education annuities. John Helyar, *Lords of the Realm: The Real History of Baseball* (New York: Ballantine Books, 1994), 157.

12. For further insight on this issue, *see generally* Tom Adelman, *The Long Ball: The Summer of '75 — Spaceman, Catfish, Charlie Hustle, and the Greatest World Series Ever Played* (Boston: Little, Brown, 2003).

13. Miller, *A Whole Different Ball Game*, 236.

14. Ibid. Miller said he had always respected and liked Hunter because of the way he fought the baseball establishment. However, Miller was flabbergasted by Hunter's remarks when Hunter was inducted into the Baseball Hall of Fame. Much to the dismay of Miller, Hunter's induction speech gave credit to the owners, specifically George Steinbrenner, for his economic security via baseball.

15. Mike Shatzkin, *The Ballplayers: Baseball's Ultimate Biographical Reference* (New York: Arbor House/William Morrow, 1990), 733.

16. Gary Gillette and Pete Palmer, *The ESPN Baseball Encyclopedia*, 4th ed. (New York: Sterling Publishing, 2007), 72.

17. Joseph G. Preston, *Major League Baseball in the 1970s: A Modern Game Emerges* (Jefferson, NC: McFarland, 2004), 123.

18. Ibid.

19. Helyar, *Lords of the Realm*, 164.

20. Ibid., 163.

21. Gillette and Palmer, *The ESPN Baseball Encyclopedia*, 70.

22. Miller, *A Whole Different Ball Game*, 242.

23. Ibid., 242–243.

24. Ibid.

25. Ibid., 242.

26. Ibid., 243.

27. Ibid.

28. Ibid.

29. Preston, *Major League Baseball in the 1970s*, 126.

30. Ibid.

31. Miller, *A Whole Different Ball Game*, 245.

32. *See* Chantel D. Carmouche, "Arbitration and Major League Baseball," *Journal of American Arbitration* 1 (2001): 1.

33. "Touching all Bases," *Chicago Tribune*, 16 October 1975, E2. The Dodgers said: "Andy ... we wouldn't dream of trading you but we can't make it official by putting it in your contract because that would set a bad precedent. All the fellows would want a no-trade contract." Red Smith, "The Men Who Run Baseball," *New York Times*, 1975 October 26, 221.

34. The Dodgers were the original respondent in the grievance filed by Messersmith and McNally. All 24 Major League Clubs and the National and American Leagues later intervened in the grievance because of their interests in the outcome of the decision.

35. At the arbitration hearing, Messersmith's case was presented by the counsel for the Major League Baseball Players Association, Dick Moss. "Dodger Begins Free-Agent Bid," *New York Times*, 27 November 1975, 21. Baseball commissioner Bowie Kuhn, American League President Lee MacPhail, and National League President Chub Feeney testified on behalf of the clubs and leagues. "MacPhail, Kuhn Testify," *Chicago Tribune*, 25 November 1975, D2.

36. "Baseball's Future was Not Issue — Seitz," *Chicago Tribune*, 14 December 1975, A3.

37. Kenneth Denlinger, "This Morning," *Washington Post*, 25 December 1975, E11.

38. Kuhn, *Hardball: The Education of a Baseball Commissioner*, 181.

39. Messersmith & McNally Grievances, 5.

40. Ibid., 110.

41. Ibid.

42. Ibid., 112.

43. Ibid., 113.

44. Ibid. Noted legal scholar and arbitrator Roger Abrams found this comparison "questionable and "very troubling." Abrams said Seitz was wrong to use New York real estate law as precedent in deciding the case. Abrams is an experienced baseball arbitrator himself and said an arbitrator

should only look to legal precedent outside the collective agreement if the parties knew or considered that law when they drafted the labor contract. Abrams went as far as to say baseball's most legal decision was "wrong," although just because it was wrong did not mean a court could vacate the decision. Roger I. Abrams, *Legal Bases: Baseball and the Law* (Philadelphia: Temple University Press, 1998), 130.
45. Messersmith & McNally Grievances, 113.
46. Ibid.
47. He cited and discussed the following cases: *Lemat Corporation v. Barry*, 80 Cal. Rptr. 240 (Ct. App. 1969); *Central N.Y. Basketball, Inc v. Barnett*, 181 N.E. 2d 506 (Ohio Com. Pl. 1961).
48. Messersmith & McNally Grievances, 114.
49. Ibid.
50. Ibid.
51. Ibid.
52. Ibid.114–115.
53. Ibid., 110–111.
54. Ibid., 111 (footnote omitted).
55. Ibid., 116. *See also* "Baseball Peace Assumed," *New York Times*, 23 January 1903.
56. Messersmith & McNally Grievances, 116.
57. Ibid., 117.
58. Ibid., 112.
59. Ibid.
60. Ibid.
61. Ibid.
62. Ibid.
63. Ibid., 117.
64. Ibid. Historically the clubs with the most money have been able to sign the best available free agents. For further study on the issue, see Ronald W. Cox, *Free Agency and Competitive Balance in Baseball* (Jefferson, NC: McFarland, 2006).
65. Messersmith & McNally Grievances, 117.
66. Ibid.
67. Ibid., 118.
68. Richard Dozer, "Court Tests Can't Shake Miller," *Chicago Tribune*, 6 January 1976, C3.
69. Ibid.
70. *Kansas City Royals Baseball Corp. v. Major League Baseball Players Ass'n*, 409 F. Supp. 233, 236 (W.D. Mo. 1976).
71. The cases were *United Steelworkers v. Am. Mfg. Co.*, 363 U.S. 564 (1960); *United Steelworkers v. Warrior & Gulf Navigation Co.*, 363 U.S. 574 (1960); and *United Steelworkers v. Enterprise Wheel & Car Corp.*, 363 U.S. 593 (1960).
72. *Kansas City Royals Baseball Corp.*, 409 F. Supp. at 248.
73. Ibid., 247–248.
74. Ibid., 249.
75. Ibid.
76. Ibid.
77. Ibid.
78. Ibid., 252.
79. Ibid., 253.
80. Ibid., 254.

81. Miller, *A Whole Different Ball Game*, 255; James B. Dworkin and Richard A. Poshuma, "Professional Sports: Collective Bargaining in the Spotlight," in ed. Paul F. Clark, John T. Dalaney and Ann C. Frost, *Collective Bargaining in the Private Sector* (Ithaca, NY: Industrial Relations Research Assn., 2002).
82. Miller, *A Whole Different Ball Game*, 256.
83. Ibid.
84. Cincinnati Reds Catcher Johnny Bench noted that only 4 percent of current players would have met the criteria.
85. Ibid., 256.
86. Ibid., 258.
87. Ibid., 264.
88. Ibid., 267.
89. Miller wanted five seasons but finally agreed to six after receiving more concessions from the owners in other areas.
90. Preston, *Major League Baseball in the 1970s*.
91. Ibid., 131.
92. Miller, *A Whole Different Ball Game*, 253.
93. Ibid. Marvin Miller called Andy Messersmith a "fine fellow but not a very astute business man."
94. Ibid.
95. Gillette and Palmer, *The ESPN Baseball Encyclopedia*, 70.
96. Shatzkin, *The Ballplayers*, 723. McNally hit the home run off Tony Cloninger, who was the only pitcher to hit two grand slams in one game.
97. When Alex Rodriguez signed a $252-million contract in 2000 with the Texas Rangers, McNally commented: "My first thought when I saw that was did Texas offer him $250 million and he wanted two more? How did they get to $252 million." "Dave McNally 60, Early Free Agent Dies," *New York Times*, 3 December 2002.
98. Benjamin G. Rader, *Baseball: A History of America's Game*, 2nd ed. (Champaign: University of Illinois Press, 2002), 206.
99. Ibid.
100. Ibid.
101. Daniel R. Marburger, *Stee-Rike Four!: What's Wrong with the Business of Baseball?* (Westport, CT: Praeger, 1997), 9–10.
102. Rader, *Baseball: A History of America's Game*, 206.
103. Ibid., 210.
104. George Vecsey, *Baseball, A History of America's Favorite Game* (New York: Modern Library, 2006), 146. In 2009, the New York Yankees had a team payroll in excess of $200 million. *ESPN.com*.
105. Miller, *A Whole Different Ball Game*, 241.

Chapter 11

1. Richard Justice, "Free Agents Batting .000, but Morris May Test System," *Washington Post*, 30 November 1986, D6.

2. Ibid.

3. In February 1986, Marvin Miller was retired from baseball but still had a voice in baseball's labor relations saying, "It was because we had so many individual players with guts, players who stood up. Curt Flood. Andy Messersmith. Ted Simmons on occasion. Catfish Hunter." Jerome Holtzman, "Miller Tries to Rally Union," *Chicago Tribune*, 4 February 1986.

4. Salary arbitration had been in place since the 1974 season.

5. Jeffrey S. Moorad, "Major League Baseball's Labor Turmoil: The Failure of the Counter-Revolution," *Villanova Sports and Entertainment Law Journal* 4 (1997): 66.

6. Ibid. Former baseball agent Jeff Moorad obtained these figures directly from the MLBPA.

7. Richard Justice, "Baseball's Salary System: It's a Whole New Game," *Washington Post*, 22 December 1988, B1. Another source has the average salary in July 1987 reported as $431,000. Bob Spitz, "Is Collusion the Name of the Game?" *New York Times*, 12 July 1987.

8. Moorad, "Major League Baseball's Labor Turmoil," 67.

9. Ibid.

10. The strike occurred in August.

11. The player compensation system was eliminated.

12. This concession by the players was the first since the Basic Agreement of 1976. For a good discussion of the reasons behind the concession, *see* Marvin Miller, *A Whole Different Ball Game: The Inside Story of the Baseball Revolution* (Chicago: Ivan R. Dee, 2004), 335–339.

13. *See* Brief for Players Association, *Major League Baseball Players Ass'n and the 26 Major League Clubs*, Grievance No. 87-3 (Aug. 31, 1988) (Nicolau, Chairman) [hereinafter Brief for Players Association, Collusion II].

14. Ibid.

15. John Helyar, *Lords of the Realm* (New York: Ballantine Books, 1995), 370.

16. "Free-Agency Test for Owners Must Wait Till New Year," *Washington Post*, 12 January 1986, S7. Rona later made application to the MLBPA to be a player agent. His application was rejected by the union and forcefully opposed. He appealed the ruling and an arbitrator overturned the union's decision denying Rona's application. Murray Chass, "Baseball; Union Sues to Bar Rona as Agent," *New York Times*, 21 December 1993; "Baseball: Notebook; Rona is Allowed to Return as Agent," *New York Times*, 10 February 1994. Marvin Miller called Barry Rona "the so-called technician" of collusion. "He told the powers that be — and I know this because he told us the same thing — that the language in the contract didn't prevent the owners from meeting and exchanging information about free agents. In effect, he said that as long as the owners didn't sit down and say, 'we're going to take concerted action against free agents,' they were safe from any repercussions. After all, he reasoned, the owners are allowed to be 'fiscally cautious' and 'financially prudent.' Apparently it was just a coincidence that they all became cautious and prudent in exactly the same way and at the same time." Miller, *A Whole Different Ball Game*, 391–392.

17. The hearing on the grievance took 32 days of hearing and produced 5,674 transcript pages and 788 exhibits.

18. Keeping all the dates straight for the collusion cases can be a nightmare! I have provided the reader with a collusion timeline at the end of this chapter.

19. *Major League Baseball Players Ass'n and Twenty-Six Major League Baseball Clubs*, Grievance No 86-2, Panel Decision no. 76 (Sept. 21, 1987) (Roberts, Chairman) [hereinafter Collusion I].

20. Ira Berkow, "Drysdale Could Laugh at Himself," *New York Times*, 5 July 1993. Each pitcher nearly doubled his salary with the holdout.

21. Arbitrator Thomas Roberts was a lawyer, a Navy pilot during World War II, and a season ticket holder for the Los Angeles Dodgers at the time of the arbitration. "Loyal Fan Changes the Rules," *New York Times*, 22 September 1987. Donald Fehr, the players' representative on the panel, and Barry Rona, the owner's representative, both dissented from the opinion. Attachment 13 of the current Basic Agreement is a side letter to Donald Fehr from the Labor Counsel for Major League Baseball, which states: "This is to confirm our understanding that during the term of this agreement the Clubs will not operate an Information Bank with respect to free agents." 2007–2011 Basic Agreement, 156, available at http://mlbplayers.mlb.com/pa/info/cba.jsp.

22. Collusion I.

23. Ibid., 3.

24. Ibid.

25. Ibid.

26. Ibid.

27. Ibid. Roberts noted that article XVIII (H) did not allow an exemption "based upon fiscal needs or constraints." Ibid., 7.

28. Ibid.

29. Justice, "Free Agents Batting .000, but Morris May Test System," D6.

30. Collusion I, 5.

31. Ibid.

32. Murray Chass, "Tough Union Stance in Free-Agent Case," *New York Times*, 14 July 1987. In 1988, Commissioner Peter Ueberroth said almost all teams were making money or were at least breaking even. He said baseball's 1987 fiscal season showed a net profit of $2.13 million, the sport's first profit since 1973. Richard Justice, "Baseball Owners Cash in on Ueberroth's Efforts," *Washington Post*, 16 December 1988.

33. Collusion I, 14.

34. Ibid., 15.

35. Ibid.
36. Ibid., 8.
37. Ibid., 11.
38. Ibid., 12.
39. Ibid., 13.
40. Ibid., 16.
41. *Major League Baseball Players Ass'n and Twenty-Six Major League Baseball Clubs*, Grievance No 86-2, First Interim Remedial Award (Jan. 22, 1988) (Roberts, Chairman).
42. Ibid.
43. Ibid.
44. Ibid. The new look free agents were given until March 1, 1988, to strike a new deal with a club. If the "new look" free agent had not signed a new contract by March 1, 1988, he was to advise his current club whether he would continue to seek other offers. If the player continued to seek other offers, his current contract would terminate. If the player chose not continue to stay in the free agent market, his contract with his current club would remain in place. The award specifically provided that if a "new look" free agent signed with another club, no compensation in the form of a draft pick or otherwise would be provided to the player's former team. Roberts also found: "For purposes of the repeater rights provisions of the Basic Agreement, any Player covered by this Award shall retain the status he had after his election of free agency following the 1985 championship season." Ibid.
45. *Major League Baseball Players Ass'n and Twenty-Six Major League Baseball Clubs*, Grievance No 86-2, Panel Decision No. 1, at 2 (Aug. 31, 1989) (Roberts, Chairman) [hereinafter Damages 86-2].
46. Ibid., 7. Roberts said the panel would not only consider the situation of players who were free agents at that time, but also five players with two or more years of major league service but less than six years.
47. Ibid., 5, citing to *Story Parchment Co. v. Paterson Parchment Paper Co.*, 282 U.S. 555 (1931).
48. Damages 86-2.
49. Ibid.
50. Ibid., 6.
51. Ibid., 7.
52. Ibid. Space does not allow for an in-depth discussion of the complicated economical models set forth by the players. A discussion of the models is found at Damages 86-2, 7-20.
53. Ibid., 23. The panel further stated: "A proper 'harmonizing' of the finding the $16,622,00 in total player claims submitted by the Players Association will be accomplished by the chairman of the arbitration panel should the parties be unable to do so themselves." Ibid.
54. Ibid.
55. Ibid.
56. Ibid.
57. Ibid. For players with 6 or more years of service, the percentage of new contracts containing option buyouts fell from 27.5 percent in 1985 to 14.6 percent in 1986. The arbitrator found that the average amount of the option buyout fell from $34,565 in 1985 to $7,396 in 1986. Option buyouts for players with five years of major league service fell from $45,909 to $4,000 during the same time period.
58. Ibid., 24.
59. Ibid. In 1985, 272 contracts that were signed had performance bonuses. In 1986, that number decreased to 173.
60. Ibid. For players in the two- to five-year range, the reduction was comparable.
61. Ibid.
62. Ibid., 25.
63. Those bonuses that averaged $365,278. In 1986, that average fell to $180,454. Two to five-year players had the same experience.
64. In the preceding eight years, the number of players receiving signing bonuses ranged from 47 to 88. Ibid.
65. The arbitrator noted that claims for lost free agency, lost employment, emotional distress, lost security, lost outside income, and "other consequential damages" were not part of the arbitration award. Gene Orza, the union's lawyer, said: "The clubs got together and decided no one would bid on other free agents. It's the only logical way to explain how someone with the talents of Kirk Gibson gets no offers. If you don't believe they got together and decided this, then you probably believe that the stork brings babies.'" "Union Will File Grievance Charging Owners' Collusion," *Washington Post*, 1 February 1986, D2.
66. Damages 86-2, 30.
67. It has been argued that game 6 of the 1986 NLCS Series was the greatest game ever played. The Mets won 7-6 in 16 innings. Jerry Izenberg, *The Greatest Game Ever Played* (New York: Henry Holt, 1988).
68. *See* "Buckner's Error Completes Stunning Sox Collapse," numgber 2 on "ESPN Counts Down the 100 Most Memorable Moments of the Past 25 Years," http://sports.espn.go.com/espn/espn25/moments/index.
69. *Major League Baseball Players Ass'n and Twenty-Six Major League Baseball Clubs*, Grievance No. 87-3, Panel Decision No. 79, 14 (August 31, 1988) (Nicolau, Chairman) [hereinafter Grievance 87-3]. Some of these included Jack Morris, Andre Dawson, Tim Raines, Reggie Jackson, Lance Parrish, and Harry Spilman. There were also nontender free agents who became free agents by either non-renewal or release by a club.
70. Dawson had been with the Expos for 11 seasons before signing with the Cubs. In 1986, with the Expos, he batted .284, with 20 home runs, 78 RBI's, and 18 stolen bases.
71. Ibid., 16.
72. Ibid.
73. Ibid., 16-17.
74. Ibid., 17.
75. Ibid., 19.

76. For example, Morris was born in St. Paul and wanted to pitch in his hometown.
77. Ibid., 20.
78. Ibid., 23.
79. Ibid., 23–24.
80. Ibid., 24. The arbitrator's opinion is 81 pages long. The length of the text does not allow a summary of the entire opinion so only the most significant portions of the opinion are addressed.
81. Morris was 21–8 in 1986. He was baseball's biggest winner as a pitcher in the 1980s. "Tiger Offer is Rejected by Morris," *Los Angeles Times*, 30 January 1991. The last contract Morris had with the Tigers was for 4 years (1983–1986) and averaged $862,500 a year. Morris had signed the contract against the advice of his agent.
82. Morris was considered one of baseball all time great competitors. He won 254 games, pitched for four World Series winners, and was a five-time all star. Craig Muder, "Big Game Pitcher: Jack Morris Earned Title as One of the Game's Toughest Competitors," *Nat'l Baseball Hall of Fame*, 27 December 2009, http://community.baseballhall.org/page.aspx?pid=489.
83. Morris refused a two-year, $1.2 million annual offer from the Tigers.
84. Arbitrator Nicolau noted, "It is doubtful, given subsequent events, that this uniform response was accidental or without design." Grievance 87-3, 31.
85. Morris now had until December 19 to accept. He had received no offers from other clubs.
86. Hearing Transcript, *Major League Baseball Players Ass'n and Twenty-Six Major League Clubs*, Grievance No. 87-3, 4032 (Aug. 31, 1988) (Nicolau, Chairman) (testimony of Minnesota Twins General Manager Andy MacPhail) [hereinafter Hearing Transcript, Grievance No. 87-3].
87. Ibid., 3959, 4175, 4218–19.
88. Ibid.
89. Ibid., 4035.
90. He mentioned that some had been "utter flops." Ibid., 4033–35.
91. Ibid., 4033–39.
92. Ibid. .
93. Dick Moss testified that he had talked to the Twins owner, Carl Pohlad, on the previous Friday and was advised a Tuesday meeting was more convenient for Pohlad, so Moss accepted. When Tuesday came, Pohlad was not at the meeting. MacPhail told Morris that Pohlad had "misread" his schedule and had a very important meeting at a bank he owned and could not attend the meeting.
94. Fernando Valenzuela had the same numbers.
95. Grievance No. 87-3, 35.
96. Ibid., 36.
97. One study compared Dodger pitcher Fernando Valenzuela's "drawing power" to that of Morris and another study estimated how much additional revenue would be needed to meet the demands of Morris and his agent.

98. MacPhail explained this approach was taken because of the actual contract value of Twins pitcher Bert Blyleven. He also said the offer was couched in this way because it would put the Twins in a better situation "public relations wise" with fans. They would not have to explain to the public or press how far the parties were apart in negotiations.
99. Mr. Pohlad did not testify during the arbitration proceedings.
100. Hearing Transcript, Grievance No. 87-3, 4057–58.
101. Ibid., 4058, 4062 (testimony of Andy MacPhail).
102. Ibid., 4060.
103. Ibid.
104. Ibid., 3413–3415 (testimony of Steven Fehr).
105. Ibid., 3414–17. Dick Moss testified similarly to Fehr. Ibid., 3047–54 (testimony of Richard Moss).
106. Grievance 87-3, 39.
107. Hearing Transcript, Grievance No. 87-3, 4063–66.
108. Ibid., 4223.
109. Grievance No. 87-3, 40.
110. Ibid., 25.
111. Ibid., 26.
112. Ibid., 29.
113. Ibid., 40.
114. Ibid.
115. Ibid.
116. Ibid., 40.
117. Ibid., 40–41.
118. Ibid., 41.
119. Ibid.
120. Steinbrenner said signing them (Randolph, Guidry) was his "first order of business." He had already offered salary arbitration to both. Hearing Transcript, Grievance No. 87-3, 133–34 (testimony of Richard Moss).
121. MacPhail was almost on the money; he said the Tigers' arbitration offer would be $1.4 million.
122. Morris went 18–11 in 1987 with an ERA of 3.38. He struck out 208 batters in 266 innings.
123. Grievance No. 87-3, 47.
124. Five other players returned to the former clubs. Raines and Gedman received other offers but returned to their former clubs. Guidry, Boone, and Alexander all returned to their former clubs. Horner went to Japan to play. Horner would later be the recipient of the largest individual collusion award. None of these players received other offers being dismissed as "too old, too cantankerous, or not versatile enough to warrant any interest." Ibid., 48–49. *See also* Richard Justice, "Free Agents May End Up Looking Like the Real Losers," *Washington Post*, 8 February 1987.
125. Grievance No. 87-3, 49.
126. Hearing Transcript, Grievance No. 87-3, 7113–94 (testimony of John Madigan).

127. Helyar, *Lords of the Realm*, 380.
128. Ibid., 380–381.
129. Ibid., 380.
130. Ibid.
131. Ibid.
132. Ibid., 381.
133. Dawson would be making less than every veteran on the team except for Thad Bosley, a spare outfielder.
134. Ibid.
135. Ibid.
136. Murray Chass, "Cubs Get Dawson for $650,000," *New York Times*, 7 May 1987, 47.
137. Ibid.
138. Grievance 87-33, 68–69.
139. Ibid., 73.
140. Ibid., 74.
141. Ibid., 74.
142. Ibid., 80.
143. Ibid., 81.
144. This arbitrator's opinion is a complicated 41-page opinion.
145. The arbitrator said that to invalidate those contracts would be prejudging the evidence of Grievance 88-1 (Collusion III) which had not yet been heard.
146. *Major League Baseball Players Ass'n and Twenty-Six Major League Clubs*, Grievance 88-1, Panel Decision No. 83 (July 18, 1990) (Nicolau, Chairman) [hereinafter Collusion III].
147. Ibid., 2.
148. Ibid., 14. Brief for Players Association Brief, Collusion II, 19–44.
149. Collusion III, 2. Evidently the information continued in the bank was not always complete, accurate or timely. Ibid.
150. Ibid.
151. Ibid.
152. Ibid., 17.
153. Ibid.
154. Ibid., 18.
155. Ibid., 30.
156. Ibid., 34.
157. Ibid.
158. "Negative Collusion Numbers," *New York Times*, 27 September 1991, B11.
159. Opinion of the Arbitration Panel Grievance 86-2, 87-3, and 88-1, Players' objections.
160. Ibid., 3.
161. The framework was mailed to players who had at least one day of major league service during the 1985–1990 seasons and to all players who were released during spring training pursuant to a major league contract (1985–1990), even if they had no major league service. Ibid., 3.
162. Ibid., 6. The players could also object under a category entitled "miscellaneous issues."
163. Ibid., 22.
164. "Around the Majors," *Washington Post*, 14 September 1991.
165. "Baseball," *Washington Post*, 22 December 1990.
166. Murray Chass, "End of the Owners' Error: The Collusion Checks Are In," *New York Times*, 25 May 2010.
167. Ibid. The list of players took up 67 single spaced pages. Ibid.
168. Ibid.
169. Ibid.
170. Murray Chass, "Collusion Case Grants Unusual Damages," *New York Times*, 18 January 1995.
171. Albert Theodore Powers, *The Business of Baseball* (Jefferson, NC: McFarland, 2003), 187–190. In 1979 Nolan Ryan became the first million-dollar player in baseball.
172. Ibid. Bonds later signed a five-year, 90-million deal. Barry M. Bloom, "Bonds, Giants Agree on One-Year Deal," *www.MLB.com*, 7 December, 2006.
173. Powers, *The Business of Baseball*, 190 n.662.
174. Paul D. Staudohar, "Baseball's Changing Salary Structure," *Compensation and Working Conditions* 2 (Fall 1997), 5.
175. "2010 Opening Day Average Salary Increases to $3,340,133," MLBPA Press Release, 6 April 2010, http://mlb.mlb.com/pa/pdf/20100406_opening_day_average_salary.pdf.
176. Miller, *A Whole Different Ball Game*, 399–400.
177. Ibid., 400.

Chapter 12

1. 173 Pa. Super. 179, 96 A.2d 181 (1953).
2. 635 N.W.2d 219 (Mich. Ct. App. 2001).
3. A "can of corn" is a common baseball term, defined as "[a]n easily caught fly ball; a high, lazy fly ball that allow a defensive player time to stand under the ball and catch it easily." Dickson, *The Dickson Baseball Dictionary*, 160.
4. Paul Dickson, *The Dickson Baseball Dictionary*, 3rd ed. (New York: W.W. Norton, 2009), 340, citing Jerry Howarth, *Baseball Lite* (San Francisco: Protocol Books, 1986).
5. "Steve Evans Stats," *Baseball Almanac*, www.baseball-almanac.com.
6. Ibid.
7. "A baseball Enthusiast, a fan." Dickson, *The Dickson Baseball Dictionary*, 142.
8. "Foul Ball Cured a 'Knocker,'" *Washington Post*, 7 June 1914.
9. Knocker has been defined as "a critical baseball fan; one who criticizes." Dickson, *The Dickson Baseball Dictionary*, 485.
10. "Foul Ball Cured a 'Knocker,'" *Washington Post*, 7 June 1914.
11. Ibid.
12. Ibid.
13. *See* Zachary Hample, *How to Snag a Major League Baseball* (Fullerton, CA: Aladdin, 1999).

14. Alou later said he would have never caught the ball anyway. Carrie Nuskat, "Bartman Exonerated by Alou Admission," *MLB.com*, 2 April 2008.

15. The ball, of course, finally landed in the hands of a lawyer who was sitting behind Bartman in the stands, once again cementing baseball's direct connection to the law. Darren Rovell, "Price Surpasses Even Buckner's Ball," *ESPN.com*, 19 December 2003.

16. It is an understatement to say Bartman was not the most popular person in Chicago. Bob Kimball, "Bartman Declines $25,000 Autograph, Remains in Hiding," *USA Today*, 24 July 2008.

17. Rovell, "Price Surpasses Even Buckner's Ball." Compare the "Bartman" foul ball to the infamous ball that went through the legs of Red Sox first baseman Bill Buckner. Actor Charlie Sheen bought the Buckner ball for $93,500 in 1992. Since the purchase of that ball, the Red Sox have won two World Series. Darren Rovell, "Auction House Confident of Ball's Authenticity," *ESPN.com*, 11 November 2003.

18. The authors of the *Baseball Field Guide* used the Bartman/Alou tussle to explore the rule dealing with spectator interference. It was the authors' opinion that Alou probably would have made the catch even though he has said otherwise. They also stated that no rules were broken by spectator Bartman because the ball had already crossed into the spectator area before he touched the ball. Dan Formosa and Paul Hamburger, *Baseball Field Guide: An In-Depth Illustrated Guide to the Complete Rules of Baseball* (Cambridge, MA: Da Capo Press, 2008), 184.

19. Monica Davey, "Long-Suffering Cubs Fans Hope Blasted Ball Puts End to 'Curse,'" *New York Times*, 27 February 2004. The Chicago Cubs last won the World Series in 1909. For further reading, see Steve Gatto, *Da Curse of the Billy Goat, The Chicago Cubs, Pennant Races, and Curses* (Lansing, MI: Protar House LLC, 2004).

20. "What He Saw of the Game," *Washington Post*, 6 September 1904, 6. A foul ball hit a fan in the nose. The fan said he could not see the ball coming because a girl with a big hat was sitting in front of him and he could not see anything but the hat.

21. "Foul Ball and Cupid," *Washington Post*, 1 November 1908, 8.

22. "Foul Ball Cupid's Arrow," *New York Times*, 4 July 1913.

23. Ibid. Miss Gibble was under the age of seventeen at the time so the couple had to receive the consent of bride's parents to marry, which they gladly gave.

24. "Man Dodges Foul Ball, Lets His Girlfriend Take It on Her Elbow at Astros Game," *ESPN.com*, 11 August 2010.

25. "Million-to-One Foul Ball by Gibbons Hits his Wife," *CBS Sports*, 24 September 2006.

26. Heather Fletcher, "This Wedding is Brought to You by...," *New York Times*, 11 June 2006; Christine Frey, "Eat, Drink and Be Married at the Ballpark," *Los Angeles Times*, 21 April 2002; Kim Lyons, "Singles Find They Have a Good Chance of Scoring at the Ballpark," *Pittsburgh Tribune Review*, 4 April 2005.

27. Colbert I. King, "When Life Knocks You in the Nose," *Washington Post*, 11 August 2007. Alice was the wife of Earl Ruth, sports editor of the *Philadelphia Bulletin*. See also Fran Zimmiuch, *Richie Ashburn Remembered* (Champaign, IL: Sports Publishing, 2005), 36.

28. Walt Schnert, "Hall of Famer, Nebraska's Richie Ashburn," *McCook Daily Gazette*, 12 May 2008.

29. "Hides Foul Ball in Hat," *Chicago Daily Tribune*, 22 June 1905.

30. "Baseball Pioneer Dead," *New York Times*, 19 July 1919.

31. "Hides Foul Ball in Hat." The newspaper did not report Mr. Stott's age at the time but it was clear he was an adult.

32. Ibid. Ironically, Hart initiated the foul strike rule in baseball. "Baseball Pioneer Dead."

33. A 13-year-old girl died after being hit by a puck at an NHL game in Columbus, Ohio. "13-year-old Fan Killed After Hit by Puck at NHL Game," *CBC News*, 20 March 2002; Edward Wong, "Girl, 13, Dies After Being Hit by Puck," *New York Times*, 20 March 2002; "Puck Snapped Girl's Head Back, Damaging Artery," *SI.com*, 20 March 2002.

34. The policy of the Detroit Tigers Baseball Club allows fans to keep all balls, whether a foul ball or home run, that are hit into the stands unless the fan interferes with a ball in play or trespasses on the field.

35. *See generally* Robert M. Gorman and David Weeks, *Death at the Ballpark: A Comprehensive Study of Game-Related Fatalities of Players, Other Personnel and Spectators in Amateur and Professional Baseball, 1862–2007* (Jefferson, NC: McFarland, 2008).

36. James E. Winslow and Adam O. Goldstein, "Spectator Risks at Sporting Events," *Internet Journal of Law, Healthcare and Ethics* 4 (2007, No. 2).

37. Ashby Jones, "In Foul Ball Injury Litigation, Clubs Have the Upper Hand," *Wall Street Journal*, 15 July 2008.

38. The following language is from the back of a Houston Astros ticket from the 2009 season.

> The holder assumes all risks and danger incidental to the game of baseball, whether occurring prior to (including but not limited to batting practice), during or subsequent to the actual playing of the game, including specifically (but not exclusively), the danger of being injured by thrown or broken bats or thrown or batted balls, and agrees that the Houston McLane Co, Inc., The Houston Astros Baseball Club, Major League Baseball, The Office of

the Commissioner of Major League Baseball, the National League, American League, Participating Clubs, their Agents, Players or other related entities or other individuals are not liable for damages or injuries resulting from such causes.

39. Cindy Hirschfeld, "Scene/Dog Days at the Ballpark," *New York Times*, 12 August 2005.
40. Promotion for Cincinnati Bearcats Baseball, May 2009: Allowing free admission to all women who wore bikinis. The game was a sell out.
41. The rule has even become the subject of state legislation. *See* New Jersey Baseball Spectator Safety Act of 2006, N.J. P.L 2005, c.362 (Jan. 12, 2006).
42. "Protecting Fans at Sporting Events, Just How Far Must you go to Keep Attendees Safe?" *Facility Manager* (December-January 2008), 8.
43. This chapter will not attempt to categorize and list all injuries and deaths that have occurred at baseball games but only give representative examples. That task has already been performed at a scholarly level. *See* Gorman and Weeks, *Death at the Ballpark*.
44. In 1910 there were at least ten fatal accidents in baseball, with the majority occurring at the minor league level. "Accidents on Diamond," *Washington Post*, 6 November 1910.
45. "Condition of Tim Hurst," *Washington Post*, 25 August 1897, 8.
46. "Catcher Conner Killed by a Foul Ball," *Washington Post*, 31 May 1899.
47. "Singular Accident at a Ball Game," *Chicago Daily Tribune*, 10 August 1889.
48. Ibid.
49. "Killed by a Foul Ball," *New York Times*, 4 September 1900, 9.
50. "Foul Ball Causes Death," *New York Times*, 28 October 1902, 1.
51. Ibid. He had been watching a game of baseball between "two nines" of boys in an open lot near Queens when the accident occurred.
52. "Boy Killed by Ball," *Sporting Life*, 17 September 1904, 11.
53. "A Fatality," *Sporting Life*, 2 July 1904, 4.
54. Ibid.
55. Ibid.
56. "Foul Ball Kills a Boy," *New York Times*, 13 September 1909, 1.
57. Ibid.
58. "Girl Killed by Foul Ball," *New York Times*, 31 May 1911, 20.
59. Ibid.
60. Ibid.
61. Ibid.
62. "Girl Struck by Baseball Dies," *Washington Post*, 6 September 1912, 9.
63. Kevin Baxter, "A Foul Part of the Game," *Los Angeles Times*, 20 June 2008.
64. Mota has contributed greatly to the game of baseball through his many years of involvement with the Dodgers organization and through his own foundation.
65. Tim State, "Boy Hit by Foul Ball to be Okay," *www.chicagoist.com*, 12 July 2009.
66. "Fan Hit by Bat at Marlins Game Hospitalized with Ruptured Spleen," *USA Today*, 11 August 2005.
67. Jeff Passan, "Fan's Injury Should Force Bat Policy Change," *Yahoo Sports*, 30 May 2008.
68. "Battered Fan Sues the Mets," *New York Post*, 6 July, 2008.
69. Ibid.
70. "MLB, MLBPA Adopt Recommendations of Safety and Health Advisory Committee," MLBPA News Release, 9 December 2008, http://mlb.mlb.com/pa/pdf/health_advisory_120908.pdf.
71. Ibid.
72. Ibid.
73. Ibid.
74. For a few examples, see James L. Rigelhaupt, Jr., "Liability to Spectator at Baseball Game Who is Hit by Ball or Injured as Result of Other Hazards of Game," *American Law Reports ALR 3d* 9 (1979): 24; Ted J. Tierney, "Heads Up!: The Baseball Facility Liability Act," *Northern Illinois University Law Review* 18 (1998): 601; Gil Fried and Robin Ammon, "Baseball Spectators' Assumption of Risk: Is It 'Fair' or 'Foul'?" *Marquette Sports Law Review* 13 (2002): 39; Gil Fried, "Plaintiffs in the Stands," *Entertainment and Sports Lawyer* 20 (Summer 2002): 8; J. Gordon Hylton, "A Foul Ball in the Courtroom: The Baseball Spectator Injury as a Case of First Impression," *Tulsa Law Review* 38 (2003): 485; Roger I. Abrams, "Two Sports Torts: The Historical Development of the Legal Rights of Baseball Spectators," *Tulsa Law Review* 38 (2003): 433; Kenneth R. Swift, "I Couldn't Watch the Ball Because I Was Watching the Ferris Wheel in Centerfield," *Entertainment and Sports Lawyer* 22 (Winter 2005): 1.
75. "Mr. Potts Broken Nose," *Washington Post*, 14 October 1890, 8.
76. "Ball Club Wins Case," *Washington Post*,14 November 1905, 9.
77. Ibid.
78. Ibid.
79. Ibid.
80. "New Items Gathered From All Quarters," *Sporting Life*, 8 February 1913, 7.
81. Ibid. This foul ball resulted in a tragedy of a different kind. Mrs. Dobkin's husband was a "well to do" blacksmith in Chicago and the couple had eight children. After Mrs. Dobkin became paralyzed, her husband eloped with the local grocer's wife and her six children to California. Her husband's disappearance was not kept quiet until the filing of the lawsuit. "'Foul' Ball Strikes Woman; Suit Reveals Love Tragedy," *Chicago Daily Tribune*, 7 February 1913.
82. "News Notes in Highlights," *Sporting Life*, 13 January 1917, 7.
83. Ibid.

84. "Condensed Dispatches," *Sporting Life*, 13 January 1912, 2
85. "American League Notes," *Sporting Life*, 28 January 1911, 5
86. Ibid.
87. Ibid.
88. "Court Awards Fan Claim," *Washington Post*, 30 May 1913, 8.
89. Ibid.
90. Ibid.
91. Edling v. Kansas City Baseball & Exhibition Co., 168 S.W. 908, 908 (Mo. Ct. App. 1914).
92. Ibid.
93. Ibid.
94. Ibid., 911.
95. Ibid., 910.
96. "Woman Hit by Foul; Sues Rochester Club," *New York Times*, 2 October 1925.
97. "Hit the Foul Fly, Gets $4,500," *New York Times*, 31 October 1941, 25.
98. Ibid.
99. 78 S.W.2d 2d 520 (Mo. Ct. App. 1935).
100. "Woman Hit By Foul Tip Gets Damages," *Jefferson City Post-Tribune*, 31 October 1933, 2.
101. *Grimes*, 78 S.W.2d at 522.
102. 840 N.Y.S.2d 527 (Sup. Ct. 2007).
103. Ibid., 529.
104. 96 A.2d 181 (Pa. Super. 1953). Noted sports scholar Walter T. Champion, the George Foreman Chair of Sports Law at Thurgood Marshall School of Law, suggested the use of *Schentzel* as a representative case in this chapter. It is worth noting, however, that Professor Champion is a lifetime Phillies fan and is a Philadelphia native.
105. See www.retrosheet.org.
106. *Schentzel*, 96 A.2d at 183.
107. Ibid.
108. Ibid. Mrs. Schentzel was standing by her husband in line but it is not known whether she heard the alleged conversation between Mr. Schentzel and the ticket seller.
109. Ibid.
110. Ibid.
111. Ibid. The Schentzels had been seated about ten minutes in total when the ball struck Mrs. Schentzel.
112. Ibid.
113. Ibid.
114. Ibid. Trespass to personal injury has been phased out over time as a cause of action. *See* Jenny Steele, *Tort Law: Text, Cases, & Materials* (New York: Oxford University Press, 2007), 38.
115. Loss of consortium has been defined as "a loss of the benefits that one spouse is entitled to receive from the other, including companionship, cooperation, aid, affection, and sexual relations. Loss of consortium can be recoverable as damages from a tortfeasor in a personal-injury or wrongful-death action." *Black's Law Dictionary*, 8th ed. (Eagan, MN: Thomson West, 2004).
116. *Schentzel*, 96 A.2d at 184.
117. Ibid.
118. Ibid.
119. "Woman Gets $500 Award for Baseball Accident," *Chester Times*, 11 January 1952. "The Schentzels Had Sued for $20,000. Phillies Fight Award to Woman Hit by Ball," *Tyrone Daily Herald*, 1 October 1952. The *Chester Times* reported the story from the International News Service but the newspaper account was obviously incorrect. The story refers to Mrs. Reba Schentzel receiving a verdict of $500 by a Philadelphia Common Pleas County Jury. That statement is correct, but the article states the verdict was against the "Philadelphia Athletic." The article further notes the game was between the A's and the Chicago Cubs. The article is clearly mistaken with regard to the identity of the defendant in the lawsuit. It was the National League Club, the Phillies, not the American League A's who was the defendant in the lawsuit. There was no inter-league play in 1953. (The A's moved to Kansas City in 1955.)
120. "Phillies File Appeal Over $500 Judgment," *Long Beach (Calif.) Press-Telegram*, 1 October 1952.
121. *Schentzel*, 96 A.2d 181.
122. Ibid., 184, citing *Haugh v. Harris Bros. Amusement Co.*, 315 Pa. 90, 172 A. 145 (1934); *Kallish v. American Base Ball Club of Philadelphia*, 138 Pa. Super. 602, 603, 10 A.2d 831, 832 (1940).
123. Ibid., 187.
124. Ibid., 184.
125. Ibid.
126. Ibid.
127. Ibid..
128. The upper deck and left-field stands were added to Shibe Park in 1925, with the mezzanine level later added in 1929. Shibe Park was the first concrete and steel baseball stadium in the Major Leagues. *www.ballparks.com*. The stadium was named after Ben Shibe, an A's stockholder and baseball manufacturer. Ibid. The stadium was renamed in 1953 for Connie Mack. The last game was played in the stadium on October 1, 1970, and it was torn down in June 1976. A church is now on the site where the stadium used to be. For a good discussion of Shibe Park and its history, see Edward G. White, *Creating the National Pastime: Baseball Transforms Itself*, (Princeton, N.J.: Princeton University Press, 1996), 21–29; Bruce Kuklick, *To Every Thing a Season: Shibe Park and Urban Philadelphia, 1909–1976* (Princeton, NJ: Princeton University Press, 1993). It is interesting to note that when Shibe Park was built, steel posts significantly obstructed the views of spectators
129. The court in *Schentzel* cited to the following cases, which detailed the number of seats behind the screening: *Curtis v. Portland Baseball Club*, 279 P. 277 (Ore. 1929); *Brown v. San Francisco Ball Club, Inc.*, 222 P.2d 19 (Cal Ct. App. 1950); *Grimes v. American League Baseball Co.*, 78 S.W.2d 520 (Mo. Ct. App. 1935).

Notes — Chapter 12

130. *Schentzel*, 96 A. 2d at 185.
131. Ibid.
132. Ibid., 186
133. Ibid.
134. Ibid.
135. Ibid., 187.
136. "Baseball Fans Attend Games at Own Risk," *Post-Standard* (Syracuse, N.Y.), 16 April 1953, 20.
137. A Westlaw search shows that the case has been cited 107 times as of May 5, 2010. Westlaw indicated that although the case has never been overruled, the assumption of the risk doctrine has been modified somewhat and now is called the no-duty rule. *See Romeo v. Pittsburgh Associates*, 787 A.2d 1027 (Pa. Super. 2001).
138. For examples, see Walter T. Champion, *Sports Law In a Nutshell*, 2nd ed. (Eagan, MN: West Group, 2000); Paul C. Weiler and Gary R. Roberts, *Sports and the Law: Cases, Materials and Problems* (Eagan, MN: West Group, 1993); Walter T. Champion, *Fundamentals of Sports Law* (Eagan, MN: West Group, 2004).
139. 635 N.W.2d 219 (Mich. Ct. App. 2001). This case was selected from the myriad of foul ball lawsuits that have been brought by spectators because of its unique fact situation and because the case has been cited extensively by multiple jurisdictions as binding legal precedent dealing with baseball's special limited duty rule. In *Baseball and the American Legal Mind*, the noted authors had the same difficulty this author did in selecting representative baseball tort cases. They wrote there were an "endless array of tort cases" to choose from which involved personal injury. They finally selected two cases dealing with projectiles entering the grandstands, *Maytnier v. Rush*, 225 N.E. 2d 83 (Ill. App. Ct. 1967) and *Marlowe v. Rush-Henrietta Cen. Sch. Dist.*, 561 N.Y.S.2d 934 (App. Div. 1990). *Maytnier* dealt with a fan who was hit by a ball thrown by a pitcher at Wrigley Field in Chicago. A jury found in favor of the spectator for $20,000 and the verdict was affirmed on appeal. The jury verdict found the spectator did not assume the risk of every thrown ball, in this case by a player from the field. Spencer W. Waller, Neil B. Cohen, Paul Finkelman, *Baseball and the American Legal Mind* (Princeton, NJ: Garland Publishing, 1995), 403. *Maytnier* was also referred to as a notable tort case in Frederick J. Day, *Clubhouse Lawyer: Law in the World of Sports* (Bloomington, IN: iUniverse Star Publishing, 2002).
140. *Benejam*, 635 N.W.2d at 220.
141. "Sports in Brief, Baseball," *Globe and Mail*, 22 October 1998.
142. "Team gets Tab for Fan Injury," *The Star-Ledger*, 22 October 1998.
143. *Benejam*, 635 N.W.2d at 220.
144. Ibid.
145. A motion for Summary Disposition can be made by either party asking the trial judge jury to dismiss the case. Michigan Civil Court Rules, 2.116.
146. Wayne County in Detroit has been known to be very favorable venue for a plaintiff's lawsuit.
147. *Benejam*, 635 N.W.2d at 220.
148. Ibid., 219.
149. Ibid., 220.
150. Ibid.
151. Ibid., 221.
152. For a few case examples that have adopted the limited duty rule, see *Lawson v. Salt Lake Trappers, Inc.*, 901 P.2d 1013 (Utah 1995); *Bellezzo v. Arizona*, 851 P.2d 847 (Ariz. Ct. App. 1992); *Arnold v. City of Cedar Rapids*, 443 N.W.2d 332 (Iowa 1989); *Friedman v. Houston Sports Ass'n*, 731 S.W.2d 572 (Tex. Ct. App. 1987); *Swagger v. City of Crystal*, 379 N.W.2d 183 (Minn. Ct. App. 1985); *Rudnick v. Golden West Broadcasters*, 202 Cal.Rptr. 900 (Ct. App. 1984).
153. *Benejam*, 635 N.W.2d at 222.
154. Ibid.
155. Ibid.
156. Ibid.
157. Ibid., 223.
158. Ibid.
159. Ibid.
160. Ibid., 224.
161. Ibid.
162. Ibid., 225.
163. Ibid.
164. Ibid.
165. Ibid.
166. Ibid., 225–226.
167. Ibid., 226.
168. "Tigers not Liable for Ballpark Injury," *Cincinnati Post*, 12 July 2001.
169. A Westlaw search shows the case has appeared in parties' briefs; court opinions; law review articles; and court documents, including trial motions, memoranda, affidavits and appellate briefs, 110 times. (Last search performed August 28, 2010.)
170. The *Benejam* case has been used in numerous legal textbooks, articles, and treaties. A few examples include Vincent R. Johnson and Gunn Alan, *Studies in American Tort Law*, 3rd ed. (Durham, NC: Carolina Academic Press, 2005); Adam Epstein, *Sports Law* (Florence, KY: Delmar Cengage Learning, 2002); Robert Jarvis and Phyllis Coleman, *Sports Law, Cases and Materials* (Eagan, MN: West Group, 1999); Frank A. Schubert, *Introduction to Law and the Legal System* (Florence, KY: Delmar Cengage Learning, 2007); Walter Champion, *Sports Law: Cases, Documents, and Materials* (New York: Aspen Publishing, 2004).
171. No. 0550000480, 2007 WL 2318331 (Conn. Super. Ct. July 27, 2006).
172. Ibid., 5.
173. Ibid.

Chapter 13

1. 443 F. Supp. 2d 1077 (E.D. Mo. 2006), *aff'd* 505 F.3d 818 (8th Cir. 2007).
2. *www.imdb.com*.
3. "Henry Chadwick," *2008 Yearbook* (Nat'l Baseball Hall of Fame & Museum, 2008), 55. Chadwick was the most famous sports journalist of his day. He also created statistics for batting average and the concept of earned and unearned runs. Ibid. Chadwick was involved in statistical analysis and scoring of games in the very early days of baseball. Chadwick performed a variety of functions as "the father of baseball." *See* "Jim Nolan's Gossip," *Galveston Daily News*, 19 January 1986, 4; Henry Chadwick, "Some League Rules," *Logansport Journal*, 25 August 1895 (Chadwick making suggestions for scoring); "Veteran Chadwick Writes," *Sunday Herald*, 4 December 1892, 5 (Chadwick discussing new rules in baseball). Chadwick said baseball was the sport of the future, dismissing boxing and football. "Sporting Gossip," *Manitoba Daily Free Press*, 24 March 1890, 6. "Notes About Sports," *New York Times*, 1 February 1886, 8 (Chadwick proposing Canadian Baseball League). "Father of Baseball," *Bismarck Daily Tribune*, 22 October 1920, 4 (Chadwick forming the New York State Cricketer Association). *See also* E. W. Whipple, "Daily Gazette," *Fort Wayne Daily Gazette*, 9 May 1871 (editor of *DeWitt's Baseball Guide* for 1871). Chadwick's grave has a huge baseball on top of the grave, as well as "crossed bats" and a mask. A photograph of the grave can be found at Alfred H. Spink, *The National Game*, 2nd ed. (Carbondale: Southern Illinois University Press, 2000), 375.
4. The box score of the first professional game between the Kekiongas of Fort Wayne and the Cleveland Forest Cities on May 4, 1871, can be found in the *Fort Wayne Daily Gazette*, Friday, 5 May 1871. *See generally* Chad Gramling, *Baseball in Fort Wayne* (Mount Pleasant, SC: Arcadia Publishing, 2007). For an early version of a box score, see *New York Times*, 2 July 1859. The game was called a "first rate match of base-ball." The Eckford Club prevailed over the Putnam Club, 23–17.
5. WHIP stands for Walks plus Hits per Inning Pitched. "A statistic used to measure the frequency with which pitchers allow baserunners. A figure of 1.20 is considered top level and one greater than 1.50 indicates poor performance." Paul Dickson, *The Dickson Baseball Dictionary*, 3rd ed. (New York: W.W. Norton, 2009), 920.
6. HOLD is defined as "[a]n unofficial Statistic credited to a relief pitcher who enters a game with a *save opportunity* and maintains the lead until replaced by another pitcher. The term and statistic were created to reward relief pitchers who are often overworked and underappreciated." Ibid., 420.
7. BABIP stands for Batting Average on Balls in Play. "A batting average for batted balls that could have been fielded, computed by subtracting home runs from hits and then dividing this number by the number of at-bats minus both home runs and strikeouts." Ibid., 89.
8. This is by no means an exhaustive list but a few excellent examples include Jim Albert and Jay Bennett, *Curve Ball: Baseball, Statistics, and the Role of Chance in the Game* (New York: Copernicus Books, 2003); Alan Schwarz, *The Numbers Game: Baseball's Lifelong Fascination with Statistics* (New York: Thomas Dunne Books, 2004); Joseph Adler, *Baseball Hacks* (Sebastopol, CA: O'Reilly Media, 2006).
9. Players' statistics also are used extensively during baseball salary arbitration proceedings with each side attempting to use them to persuade the arbitrator to rule in their favor. Renowned baseball agent Bob Woolf said, "When I negotiated Bob Stanley's contract with the Red Sox, we had statistics demonstrating he was the third-best pitcher in the league. They had a chart showing he was the sixtieth best pitcher on the Red Sox!" *www.baseball-almanac.com*.
10. Since 1982 at least four mistakes have been found in Cobb's batting record. When Pete Rose broke Cobb's all-time hit record on September 11, 1998, he had actually broken the record three days before. Gary Gillette and Pete Palmer, *The ESPN Baseball Encyclopedia*, 4th ed. (New York: Sterling Publishing, 2007).
11. Wilson lost the RBI in a second game of a doubleheader in 1930 when the league office awarded an RBI to his teammate Charlie Grimm that should have been credited to Wilson. Baseball fan and former *Sporting News* writer and editor Cliff Kachline discovered the error during a research project in 1977 and wrote to the *Sporting News* about the possible error. The proposal to change the record was debated for many years. Finally, in 1999, when Manny Ramirez was on a pace to break Wilson's RBI record, Commissioner Bud Selig weighed in on the matter. "There is no doubt Hack Wilson's RBI total should be 191 ... it is important to get it right." Tim Wiles, "75 Years After Hack Wilson's Record Season, One RBI is Credited to Cooperstown," www.baseballhalloffame.org, 15 February 2007. Kachline was the Baseball Hall of Fame historian from 1969 to 1982.
12. Sabermetrics is defined as: "The study and mathematical analysis of baseball statistics and records, with the goal of discovering objective knowledge about the basic principles that underlie the game.... The term was coined from the acronym 'SABR' by Bill James and used in the introduction of his self-published *Baseball Abstract* (1980) and first conventionally published *Baseball Abstract* (1982)...." Dickson, *The Dickson Baseball Dictionary*, 732.
13. A Century of Games from the Collection of Dr. Mark Cooper, National Baseball Hall of Fame and Museum Exhibit 2008. For a thorough

examination of sabermetrics, see Gabriel B. Costa, Michael R. Huber, and John T. Saccoman, *Understanding Sabermetrics: An Introduction to the Science of Baseball Statistics* (Jefferson, NC: McFarland, 2008).

14. Bill James has written numerous books on baseball. Some include Bill James, *Bill James Historical Baseball Abstract* (New York: Villard Publishing, 1985); Bill James, *This Time, Let's Not Eat the Bones: Bill James Without the Numbers* (Lady Lake, FL: Fireside, 1995); Bill James, *Whatever Happened to the Baseball Hall of Fame?* (Lady Lake, FL: Fireside, 1995); Bill James, *The Bill James Guide to Baseball Managers* (New York: Scribner's, 1997); Bill James, *The New Bill James Historical Baseball Abstract* (New York: Free Press, 2001); Bill James and Rob Neyer, *The Neyer/James Guide to Pitchers* (Lady Lake, FL: Fireside, 2004).

15. "'Home Baseball Game' (1886) Night Light," *The New York Times Store*. A later version of the game was marketed directly to women.

16. For further study, see Mark Cooper and Douglas Congdon-Martin, *Baseball Games: Home Versions of the National Pastime, 1860s 1960s* (Atglen, PA: Schiffer Publishing, 1995).

17. The game was sold at auction in 2007 by Robert Edwards Auctions for $6,960. Only three were known to exist at the time of the auction.

18. Clarkson was one of baseball's early stars. He led the National League in wins, starts, complete games, innings pitched, and strikeouts in 1885, 1887, and 1889. Mike Shatzkin, *The Ballplayers: Baseball's Ultimate Biographical Reference* (New York: Arbor House/William Morrow, 1990), 194.

19. Brouthers led the league in hitting five times. He had a lifetime average of .343, ninth best all time. Ibid., 121.

20. www.apbagames.com.

21. www.strat-o-matic.com/about.

22. *See* Mayer Schiller, "Goryl Killer," *Elysian Fields Quarterly* 17 (2000), available at http://www.efqreview.com/NewFiles/v17n4/numbersgame.html. The article argues that, although it was statistically based, Negamco's Major League Baseball was the least accurate of its type of baseball game.

23. Manufactured by Diamond Toy Co., Inc.

24. "Strike 3 by Carl Hubbell."

25. Manufactured by Nok-Out MFG Co. (1940s).

26. Manufactured by Gothan Pressed Steel Corp. (1970).

27. The previous year Maris had broken Babe Ruth's single-season home run record with 61 home runs. Babe Ruth had several baseball games, including the *Babe Ruth National Game of Baseball* (1921), manufactured by Keiter-Fry Marketing Company. Rick Tucker, *The Game Catalog*, 8th ed. (Dresher, PA: American Game Collectors Ass'n, 1998), 62.

28. Manufactured by Gotham (1969).

29. Manufactured by Transogram (1960).

30. Manufactured by Centennial Game Co. (1958).

31. Manufactured by Gothan Pressed Steel Corp. (1970).

32. Manufactured by the Perfect Game Co. (1971).

33. *See, e.g.*, Fantasy Dispute Resolution, http://fantasydispute.com. The "litigants" are charged $14.95 and they are guaranteed a same day response to their fantasy dispute.

34. This seems almost unworkable as a fantasy game considering the "set up" of wrestling and its penchant for entertainment.

35. *See* IBF Interactive Fantasy Game — Badminton Manager (19 April 2006), http://www.badmintonscotland.org.uk/content/view/357/116/.

36. Cindy Chang, "Fantasy Sports? Child's Play. Here, Politics is the Game," *New York Times*, 2006 October 23.

37. Dean A. Sullivan, *Late Innings: A Documentary History of Baseball, 1945–1972* (Lincoln, NE: Bison Books, 2002).

38. Ibid.

39. Ibid. Hall of Fame broadcaster Ernie Harwell was a participant in the game in Michigan.

40. Schwarz, *The Numbers Game*, 175.

41. Ibid. Okrent received a B.A. from The University of Michigan in 1969.

42. Daniel Okrent, "Biography: The Public Editor," *NYTimes.com*, 2004, http://www.nytimes.com/ref/weekinreview/okrent-bio.html; Arthur A. Raney and Jennings Bryant, *Handbook of Sports and Media* (New York: Routledge, 2006), 633.

43. Schwarz, *The Numbers Game*,175.

44. Expert Report & Affidavit of Daniel Okrent, para. 8, *C.B.C. Distribution and Marketing, Inc. v. Major League Baseball Advanced Media, L.P.*, 443 F. Supp.2d 1077 (E.D. Mo. 2006), 2006 WL 1587249.

45. "Believe Me," *Syracuse Herald-Journal*, 30 May 1988. President Nixon was also an attorney.

46. Jim Reisler, "Jack Kerouac: The Beat of Fantasy Baseball," *National Pastime* 28 (2008). Kerouac used a system of cards and boxes to record at-bats. For a photograph of the cards, see Ibid., 41. *See also* Charles McGrath, "Another Side of Kerouac: The Dharma Bum as Sports Nut," *New York Times*, 16 May 2009, C1.

47. "What Is the FTSA," http://www.fsta.org/what_is_the_fsta. The association states they represent over 100 member companies which all have an interest in the fantasy sports industry. Ibid.

48. Stephanie Dahle, "Fantasy Sports Become Big Business," *ABC News*, 2 April, 2008. There is an enormous amount of information available to the fantasy owner/manager to assist in the playing of the game. A sampling of some of the materials include David Dorey, *Fantasy Football The Next Level: How to Build a Championship Team Every Season* (Lebanon, IN: Grand Central Publishing,

2007); Sam Walker, *Fantasyland: A Season on Baseball's Lunatic Fringe* (New York: Viking Adult, 2006); Erik Barmack and Max Handelman, *Why Fantasy Matters (And Our Lives Do Not)* (New York: Simon Spotlight Entertainment, 2006); Dan Flockhart, *Fantasy Baseball and Mathematics: Student Workbook* (Hoboken, NJ: Jossey-Bass, 2007); Robert Zarzycki, *Fantasy Football's Big Six* (Bloomington, IN: Author House, 2008); Dan Flockhart, *Fantasy Basketball and Mathematics: A Resource Guide for Teachers, Parents, Grades 5 and Up* (Hoboken, NJ: Jossey-Bass, 2007); Robert Zarzycki, *Drafting to Win: The Ultimate Guide to Fantasy Football* (Bloomington, IN: Author House, 2005).

49. Linda Greenhouse, "No Ruling Means No Change for Fantasy Baseball Leagues," *New York Times*, 3 June 2008.

50. Greg Johnson, "Suing Over Statistics: Fantasy Leagues Challenge Major League Baseball's Right to Demand Licenses," *L.A. Times*, 2 January 2006, D1.

51. Fantasy managers can receive updates on their fantasy status via Twitter.

52. J. Thomas McCarthy, *McCarthy on Trademarks & Unfair Competition*, 4th ed. (Eagan, MN: West Group, 2006), vol. 4, § 28:1.

53. William L. Prosser, *Handbook in the Law of Torts*, 4th ed. (Eagan, M.N.: West Publishing, 1971); J. Thomas McCarthy, *Rights of Publicity and Privacy*, 2d ed (Eagan, MN: Thomson/West, 2008), vol. 1, §1:26.

54. Russell Christoff was a professional model and was paid $250 from Nestle to use his image on the label of Tasters Choice Instant Coffee. He sued on the ground that Nestle used his image without his consent, thereby violating his right of publicity. A jury awarded him over $15 million in lost profits. *Christoff v. Nestle USA, INC.*, No. BC 36163, 2005 WL 5490764 (Cal. Super. Ct. Feb. 27, 2005); Nancy Wolff, *The Professional Photographer's Legal Handbook* (New York: Allworth Press, 2007), 211.

55. 202 F.2d 866 (2d Cir. 1953).

56. The court stated: "[A] man has a right in the publicity value of his photograph, i.e., the right to grant the exclusive privilege of publishing his picture.... This right might be called a 'right of publicity.' For it is common knowledge that many prominent persons ... would feel sorely deprived if they no longer received money for authorizing advertisements...." Ibid., 868.

57. 433 U.S. 562 (1977).

58. Ibid., 573.

59. *Uhlaender v. Henricksen*, 316 F. Supp. 1277, 1279 (D. Minn. 1970).

60. 894 F.2d 579 (2d Cir. 1990).

61. N.Y. Civil Rights Law §§ 50–51. Babe Ruth passed away in 1939.

62. 157 F.3d 686 (9th Cir. 1998).

63. He also sued for defamation, negligence and intentional infliction of emotional distress.

64. Newcombe served as a spokesperson for the National Institute of Drug and Alcohol Abuse. He was appointed by Presidents Nixon, Ford and Reagan. At the time of the filing of the lawsuit, Newcombe was the Director of Community Relations with the Los Angeles Dodgers.

65. Newcombe's number during his career was 36.

66. *Newcombe*, 157 F.3d at 692, quoting Cal. Civ. Code § 3344 (b)(1).

67. 114 Cal. Rptr. 2d 307 (Ct. App. 2001). For other cases arising out of the same litigation as related to Gionfriddo, see *Block v. Major League Baseball*, 76 Cal. Rptr.2d 567 (Ct. App. 1998); *Coscarart v. Major League Baseball*, 1996 WL 400988 (N.D. Cal. 1996).

68. Gionfriddo played four seasons with Pittsburgh and Brooklyn from 1944 to 1947. He had a lifetime average of .266 with two career home runs. Gillette and Palmer, *The ESPN Baseball Encyclopedia*.

69. Camilli played from 1933 to 1945 with the Cubs, Phillies, Dodgers, and Red Sox. He led the league with 41 home runs and 120 RBIs in 1941 with Brooklyn. He had 239 career home runs and batted .277. Ibid.

70. Crosetti played 17 seasons with the Yankees, 1932 to 1948. He had a lifetime average of .245 and 98 career home runs. He led the league in hit by pitched balls seven times, 1934, 1936–40, 1942 and 1945. Ibid.

71. Coscarat played nine seasons with Brooklyn and Pittsburgh, 1938 to 1946. He had a lifetime batting average of .243, with 28 career home runs. Ibid.

72. *Gionfriddo*, 114 Cal. Rptr. at 313.

73. Ibid., 314.

74. Ibid.

75. Ibid., 315.

76. Ibid.

77. 335 F.3d 1161 (10th Cir. 2003).

78. The text of the card stated: Egotisticky Henderson, accepting the "Me-Me Award" from himself at the annual "Egotisticky Henderson Fan Club" banquet, sponsored by Egotistiquy Henderson: "I would just like to thank myself for all I have done. (Pause for cheers.) I am the greatest of all time. (Raise arms triumphantly.) I love myself. (Pause for more cheers) I am honored to know me. (Pause for louder cheers.) I wish there were two of me so I could spend more time with myself. (Wipe tears from eyes.) I couldn't have done it without me. (Remove cap and hold it aloft.) It's friends like me that keep me going. (Wave to crowd and acknowledge standing ovation.)"

79. The MLBPA was the exclusive group licensing agent for active MLB players.

80. No. 06 Civ. 2359 (DLC), 2007 WL 4547585 (S.D.N.Y.).

81. Ibid., 1.

82. The defamation claim was based upon the line on the back of the card that said that Bell

"earned his nickname after falling asleep right before a game." His daughter called this a "bogus painful lie." "Cool Papa's Daughter Sues Topps Over Daddy's Baseball Card," *Wall Street Journal*, 25 October 2006. Brooks later voluntarily dropped the defamation claim.

83. "Topps, Cool Papa Bell Lawsuit Settled," *St. Louis Business Journal*, 17 November 2008.

84. Greg Auman, Baseball Looking to Recapture Imaginations, *St. Petersburg Times*, 17 February 2005, C2.

85. *C.B.C. Distribution & Marketing, Inc. v. Major League Baseball Advanced Media, L.P.*, 443 F. Supp. 2d 1077, 1081 (E.D. Mo. 2006).

86. Ibid.

87. This case was closely watched by fantasy sports providers, professional sports leagues, and the many participants in fantasy sports. The NFL Players Association, NBA Properties, NHL Enterprises, the National Association for Stock Car Auto Racing (NASCAR), the PGA Tour, and WNBA Enterprises all filed amici curiae briefs in favor of the defendants.

88. The counterclaim alleged CBC violated the players' right of publicity by using their "names, nicknames, likenesses, signatures, jersey numbers, pictures, playing records and biographical data via all interactive media with respect to fantasy baseball games." Ibid., 1082. The Players Association intervened in the lawsuit and joined in the counterclaim filed by Advanced Media.

89. Ibid., 1082–1083.

90. Rudy Telscher, the attorney for CBC, agreed that trademarked material, such as the MLB logo, required permission for its use, but he argued that player performance statistics were in the public domain and therefore available to everyone. Legal scholars quickly jumped in on the topic of who owns professional sports statistics. Just a few sample articles include Patrick K. Thornton and Christopher James, "Down Two Strikes, is Major League Baseball Already Out?: How the 8th Circuit Balked to Protect the Right of Publicity in *C.B.C. v. MLB, Advanced Media*," *South Texas Law Review* 50 (2008): 173; "Intellectual Property — Eighth Circuit Holds that the First Amendment Protects Online Fantasy Baseball Providers' Use of Baseball Statistics in the Public Domain," *Harvard Law Review* 121 (2008): 1439; Jane Shane, "Who Owns a Home Run? The Battle of the Use of Player Performance Statistics by Fantasy Sports Websites," *Hastings Communications and Entertainment Law Journal* 29 (2007): 241; Zachary C. Bolitho, "When Fantasy Meets the Courtroom: An Examination of the Intellectual Property Issues Surrounding the Burgeoning Fantasy Sports Industry," *Ohio State Law Journal* 67 (2006): 911; Gustavo A. Otalvora, "Alfonso Soriano is Getting Robbed: Why the Eight Circuit Court of Appeals Made a Bad Call in *C.B.C. Distribution and Marketing v. Major League Baseball*," *University of Illinois Journal of Law, Technology and Policy*, Fall 2008, 383.

91. The reference to Advanced Media also includes the Players Association.

92. *CBC*, 443 F. Supp. 2d at 1084–85.

93. Ibid., 1089.

94. Ibid.

95. 110 S.W.3d 363 (Mo. 2003).

96. Ibid., 370.

97. "Appeals Court Upholds $15M Verdict for Twist," *St. Louis Business Journal*, 20 June 2006.

98. *CBC*, 443 F. Supp. at 1089.

99. Ibid.

100. Ibid., 1086.

101. 232 A.2d 458 (N.J. Super. Ct. 1967).

102. Ibid., 462. The court in *Palmer* did not address the legal issue of whether statistical information could be characterized as one's identity.

103. 316 F. Supp 1277 (D. Minn 1970).

104. Negamco's advertisement for the game stated:

> SCIENTIFICALLY COMPUTED Players are rated in every phase of baseball play. Each pitcher is different and each batter is different. You manage 520 big time players. Your strategy affects the outcome of every game. This game is Big, Colorful, and True. 220 pitchers and 300 fielders are included.
>
> Can be played solitaire, or leagues of 20 can be formed of neighborhood friends. As coach you call the infield positing, coach the base runners, select the line-ups, and make many, many other decisions. With BLM, good managing is needed. Ibid., 1277.

105. Ibid.

106. The income was distributed to the players equally and not based upon accomplishments. Ibid., 1279.

107. The case was decided in 1970. In 1969 both Kaat and Perry had very good years. From 1962 to 1969, Kaat won 152 games for the Twins. Perry won 59 games for the Twins from 1965 to1969, winning 20 in 1969 and 24 in 1970, leading the American League in 1970 along with Mike Cuellar and Dave McNally. Gillette and Palmer, *The ESPN Baseball Encyclopedia*, 81.

108. Uhlaender was the lead plaintiff who sued "on behalf of himself and all other professional league baseball players similarly situated."

109. *Uhlaender*, 316 F. Supp. at 1282–1283. *Uhlaender* did not discuss the First Amendment but found in favor of the players based on the premise that persons have the right to enjoy the fruits of their labor.

110. The court said that the use of the players' name and statistics did not "go to the heart of the players' ability to earn a living as baseball players; the baseball players earn a living by playing baseball and endorsing products, they do not earn a living by the publication of their playing records." *CBC*, 443 F. Supp.2d at 1091. Negamco's

net profit of the sale of its two baseball games were minimal, $3,727 in 1969 and $4,300 in 1970.

111. Ibid. Plaintiffs' expert, Kevin Saundry, also made this argument in his expert report. "Additionally, the owners of Major League Baseball teams benefit from fantasy baseball. Members of my fantasy baseball leagues, including myself, decide whether to attend professional games based on whether the opposing team contains players on their fantasy team that year. For example, if the Cardinals are playing in Pittsburgh, *I* would normally not care about attending the game. However, if I had Jeff Suppan, a pitcher for the Cardinals, on my team that year, it would be much more likely that I would attend the game to watch him.... Not only are the owners of Major League Baseball profiting from increased interest in baseball and increased attendance at games, spring training, and minor league games, the owners are profiting from increased revenue associated with cable and satellite packages as a direct result of fantasy baseball. For example, I subscribe to a Dish Network Package called Major League Baseball Extra Innings, which allows me to watch many Major League Baseball games that I could not watch on local or regular cable. I only purchase this service in order to keep up with my fantasy league players." Expert Report of Kevin Saundry, para. 15, 17, *C.B.C. Distribution & Marketing, Inc. v. Major League Baseball Advanced Media, L.P.*, 443 F. Supp.2d 1077 (E.D. Mo. 2006) (No.: 4:05-CV00252-MLM), 2006 WL 1587250.

112. "Believe Me," *Syracuse Herald-Journal*, 30 May 1988.

113. Approximately, two weeks after the district court's ruling, CBC sold CDM Fantasy Sports to a Canadian Company for up to $10 million cash and stock. Tim McLaughlin, "Canadian Company Buys CDM Fantasy Sports," *St. Louis Post-Dispatch*, 25 August 2006.

114. Courts will sometimes address all issues in a case even though it may not be required to do so. The district court may have addressed the First Amendment issue in anticipation of the court of appeals disagreeing with its analysis of plaintiffs' right of publicity claim.

115. *CBC*, 443 F. Supp.2d at 1091.

116. "Speech that entertains, like speech that informs, is protected under the first amendment...." *Winters v. New York*, 333 U.S. 507, 510 (1948).

117. The First Amendment also has been applied to "pictures, graphic design, concept art, sounds, music, stories, and narrative present in video games." *Interactive Digital Software Ass'n v. St. Louis County*, 329 F.3d 954, 957 (8th Cir. 2003).

118. *CBC*, 443 F. Supp.2d at 1095.

119. *Bonito Boats, Inc. v. Thunder Craft Boats, Inc.*, 489 U.S. 141, 152 (1989).

120. *Feist Publications, Inc. v. Rural Telephone Services Co.*, 499 U.S. 340 (1991).

121. Ibid.
122. Ibid.
123. Ibid.
124. Ibid.
125. Ibid.
126. Ibid., 350–351.

127. In *Baltimore Orioles v. Major League Baseball Players Ass'n*, 805 F.3d 663 (7th Cir. 1986), the question was who owned the copyright in the broadcast of Major League Baseball games. This opinion is of questionable precedential value.

128. 105 F.3d 841 (2d Cir 1997).
129. 937 F.2d 700 (2d Cir. 1991).

130. The court said Kregos could obtain a copyright if he was able to show the required creativity in his selection of material for his pitching forms. To compare the two forms, see *Kregos v. Associated Press*, 713 F.Supp 113, 122 App. 1 (S.D.N.Y. 1990).

131. Greg Ambrosius, "Appeals Heard in Case Between MLB, Fantasy Provider," *SI.com*, 15 June 2007.

132. Ibid.
133. Ibid.
134. Ibid.

135. *Major League Baseball Advanced Media v. C.B.C. Distribution and Marketing, Inc.*, 553 U.S. 1090 (2008).

136. *C.B.C. Distribution and Marketing, Inc. v. Major League Baseball Advanced Media, L.P.*, 505 F.3d 818, 822 (8th Cir. 2007). The reasoning seems to make sense. Fantasy games are only popular because the "owners" are using actual player names and corresponding statistics. Russell S. Jones, attorney for the Players Association made this argument: "When a team owner drafts Albert Pujols, and he spends his time telling himself and his friends that are playing in the game with him that he won Albert Pujols, it seems rather apparent to us that the name Albert Pujols that he's using in his fantasy league is a symbol of the real Albert Pujols — especially when his fantasy team accumulates points based upon how the real Albert Pujols plays next week." Donna Walter, "St. Louis-Based Fantasy Baseball Web Site Wins in Federal Court," *St. Louis Daily Record & St. Louis Countian* (10 August 2006).

137. *CBC*, 505 F.3d at 824.

138. Ibid., 823, quoting *Gionfriddo v. Major League Baseball*, 114 Cal. Rptr. 2d 307, 315 (Ct. App. 2001).

139. "Royalties on R.B.I.'s?" *New York Times*, 20 May 2006, A12.

Chapter 14

1. *Major League Baseball Players Ass'n v. Commissioner of Major League Baseball*, Grievance 92-7, Panel Decision 94 (November 12, 1992) (Steve Howe Arbitration Decision), in *Understanding Business & Legal Aspects of the Sports Industry*

Notes — Chapter 14

(PLI Patents, Copyrights, Trademarks, and Literary Property Course Handbook Series, No. G548) (New York: Practicing Law Institute, 1999), 539–594, available at WL 548 PLI/Pat 539.

2. The Dodgers won the Rookie of the Year award four years in a row beginning in 1979: Rick Sutcliffe, 1979; Steve Howe, 1980; Fernando Valenzuela, 1981; Steve Sax, 1982. Five Dodgers also won the award from 1992 to 1996.

3. Howe said he began drinking at the age of fifteen and experimented with marijuana and cocaine while in college. Howe Arbitration Decision, 557.

4. Ibid.

5. Ibid. 1981 was a strike-shortened season. Howe said he did not use cocaine during the season but did use it during the 51-day strike. Ibid.

6. Steve Howe and Jim Greenfield, *Between the Lines: One Athlete's Struggle to Escape the Nightmare of Addiction* (Grand Rapids, MI: Masters Press, 1989), 91.

7. Howe Arbitration Decision, 557.

8. Ibid.

9. "Kuhn Bans Howe, 3 Royals for Year," *Chicago Tribune*, 16 December 1983, C1.

10. *Washington Post*, 15 December 1983, A1.

11. "Howe, Dodgers Agree," *New York Times*, 8 February 1984, D23.

12. Ibid.

13. Howe Arbitration Decision, 558.

14. Ibid. All three of Howe's suspensions from the 1983 season (two from the Dodgers and one from the league) became the subject of grievances filed by the Players Association. All were eventually settled.

15. Ibid.

16. "Howe Won't Return Until '85," *New York Times*, 2 June 1984, 44.

17. Ibid.

18. "SPORTS PEOPLE: Bankruptcy Petition," *New York Times*, 24 December 1983. In his bankruptcy petition, Howe listed $340,000 in debts and $267,000 in assets.

19. Howe and Greenfield, *Between the Lines*, 4.

20. Howe Arbitration Decision, 558.

21. Ibid. Howe often drank in the company of coaches and other team personnel who thought alcohol was the best way to keep him away from drugs.

22. Ibid., 559.

23. Ibid.

24. Ibid.

25. Ibid.

26. Ibid., 560.

27. Associated Press, "Howe Called Up by Rangers," *New York Times*, 7 August, 1987.

28. McDowell compiled a 141–134 lifetime win-loss record, registering 2,453 strikeouts and a lifetime ERA of 3.17. He was a six-time all-star selection and the 1970 American League Sporting News Pitcher of the Year. After McDowell left baseball, he began drinking heavily. He finally checked himself into a rehabilitation center for alcoholism. He earned a degree from the University of Pittsburgh in Sports Psychology and Addictions and become a certified counselor. Jeff Pearlman, "Catching Up With ... Sam McDowell, Pitcher," *Sports Illustrated*, 17 February 2003, 14.

29. Howe Arbitration Decision.

30. Ibid. The association argued that the Commissioner's failure to respond to the letter meant he thought Howe was no longer eligible to play for "any major league team at any level." Howe Arbitration Decision, 556.

31. Ibid., 561.

32. Ibid.

33. Ibid., 562.

34. Howe Arbitration Decision, 562–563.

35. Howe started the season in AAA Columbus to get himself into shape. He had 5 saves in 12 games and a 0.00 ERA.

36. Ibid., 562.

37. Howe had not been tested in the previous off-season.

38. "Howe is Arrested on Cocaine Charge," *Washington Post*, 20 December 1991, B9. In a taped conversation with a government informant, Howe said that he wanted to party one last time before spring training and that he knew if he cleaned out his body three days before he was tested he could still pass a drug test. Murray Chass, "Yanks Profess Concern for Howe Far Too Late," *New York Times*, 2 July 1992, B11.

39. Howe Arbitration Decision, 569.

40. "Howe Pleads Not Guilty," *New York Times*, 8 February 1992, 31.

41. "Howe Gets Three Years on Probation," *New York Times*, 19 August 1992, B11. During his probation he was prohibited from going to bars.

42. Howe Arbitration Decision, 544–545. In his report to the commissioner, George Mitchell stated the Commissioner of Baseball always had the authority to discipline and suspend players for drug use notwithstanding the absence of a formalized drug policy between labor and management.

43. Ibid., 545.

44. Ibid., 546, quoting Commissioner's exhibit 15 from the arbitration hearing.

45. Ibid., 547.

46. "Angry Cubs Sue Vincent," *Washington Post*, 8 July 1992, B1.

47. John Snyder, *Cubs Journal: Year by Year and Day by Day with the Chicago Club Since 1876* (Cincinnati, OH: Clerisy Press, 2005).

48. Thomas Rogers, "BASEBALL: Aide Says Spira Got Steinbrenner's Ear," *New York Times*, 11 April 1991.

49. "Union Files Grievance," *New York Times*, 30 July 1992, B15.

50. Dave Anderson, "Sports of the Times; Howe, Vincent and the Yankees," *New York Times*, 5 July 1992.

51. "Union Files Grievance," B15.

52. Ibid.

53. "Vincent Gives Himself an Error and Drops Threat," *New York Times*, 4 July,1992, 27. See also "As Vincent Dispute Heats Up, Disagreement is Everywhere," *New York Times*, 30 August 1992, S3.
54. Claire Smith, "Haughty Owners are not a Measure of Vincent," *New York Times*, 13 September 1992, S5.
55. "Resigning 'In the Best Interests of Baseball,'" *New York Times*, 8 September 1992, B12.
56. "Owners, in an 18–9 Vote, Ask Vincent to Resign," *New York Times*, 4 September 1992, B7.
57. Ibid.
58. In support of their argument, the Players Association relied upon the arbitration decision of Vida Blue (Panel Decision 60, Bloch, 1984). Howe Arbitration Decision, 542.
59. Ibid.
60. Ibid., 571–572.
61. Ibid., 572.
62. Ibid., 555, citing Nixon (Panel Decision 84, Nicolau, 1992).
63. Ibid., citing Wilson/Martin (Panel Decision 54, Bloch, 1964).
64. Ibid.
65. Ibid., 555–556.
66. It made no difference whether Howe was trying to buy cocaine or use it. Baseball's drug policy at the time made no distinction between use, possession, or attempt to use illegal drugs.
67. Ibid., 583.
68. Ibid., 581.
69. Ibid.
70. Ibid., 583. The arbitrator spend a good deal of time in his opinion discussing prior drug cases in baseball, including cases involving Willie Wilson, Jerry Martin, Willie Aikens, numerous players involved in the Pittsburgh drug trials of 1985, Vida Blue, Lamar Hoyt, Otis Nixon, and Gilberto Reyes. Arbitrator Das presided over the arbitration case of Hoyt when the contract of the Padres pitcher was terminated by the team after he pled guilty to a federal crime and was incarcerated. Commissioner Peter Ueberroth suspended Hoyt for the entire 1987 season. Arbitrator Das overturned both decisions, reinstating the contract and reducing the suspension to 60 days. One of the bases for his decision was that, in his judgment, San Diego had failed to provide adequate "aftercare." Hoyt (Panel Decision 74, Das, 1987).
71. Howe Arbitration Decision, 572. Howe wrote in his book that his mother made him and his brother taken Ritalin because they were both hyperactive children. "Maybe it permanently altered my body in some way, because my reaction to cocaine was unusual. Coke wakes most people up, but it pacified me, at least after I became addicted to it." Howe and Greenfield, *Between the Lines*, 18; "Howe Cites Behavior as Hyperactive Child," *New York Times*, 24 June 1992, B10.
72. Howe Arbitration Decision, 572–573.
73. Ibid., 573.

74. Ibid., 574. The Chairman is granted the power to order medical evaluations under the rules of arbitration.
75. The arbitrator ordered the test pursuant to his authority under the rules of procedure and with agreement of the parties.
76. Ibid., 542.
77. Ibid., 543.
78. Ibid., 543–544.
79. Ibid., 544.
80. Ibid., 555.
81. Ibid., 584.
82. Kim Jasper, president of CDT, Inc., testified that Howe's testing did not begin with off-season testing until late 1981, 1 years after the commissioner's decision. She said that CDT began testing Howe on April 25, 1990. In 1990, Howe was tested 24 times, an average of 1.3 times a week. If Dr. Riordan's recommendations had been followed, Howe would have been tested 64 times. He was not tested at all from August 26, 1990, through March 3, 1991, in which there should have been 95 tests. Howe's testing resumed in 1991 when he was tested 42 times, an average of 1.36 times a week. Ibid., 563–564.
83. Ibid., 588.
84. The arbitrator said that it had long been his position that all evidence, including after-acquired medical evidence, be considered in reviewing the appropriateness of a particular penalty. Ibid., 584. He noted that there was a past practice of accepting after-acquired medical evidence. See *Alex Johnson v. The California Angels*, Panel Decision 6 (Gill, 1971).
85. Howe Arbitration Decision, 593–594.
86. Murray Chass, "Howe's Endless Game of Chance," *New York Times*, 13 November 1992, B11.
87. Claire Smith, "Howe and Yankees Hoping 7 Proves to Be the Charm," *New York Times*, 18 February 1993.
88. When he returned to spring training in 1993 for the Yankees, Howe was throwing the ball 92 miles an hour. Michael Martinez, "Howe Off to a Fast Start in Relief," *New York Times*, 23 March 1993, B13.
89. "Steve Howe, Eligible Season," http://www.whatifsports.com/mlb-1/profile_player.asp?pid=6619.
90. Jack Curry, "Howe Arrested at Airport on Gun Charge," *New York Times*, 25 June 1996, B11.
91. Jack Curry, "Howe's Pinstripes Have the Union Label," *New York Times*, 14 August 1994, S6.
92. Ibid.
93. Jack Curry, "New Job, Controversy Find Howe Once Again," *New York Times*, 26 February 1995, S1.
94. Ibid.
95. *Howe v. New York Post Co.*, No. 124519/93, 1995 WL 572884 (N.Y. Sup. Ct. Mar. 7, 1995).
96. Ibid., 1.
97. Ibid.

98. Ibid., 3. Howe was not the first baseball player to ever sue for defamation. Baseball is replete with defamation lawsuits dating back over one hundred years. They have involved owners, executives, writers, umpires, players, and fans. John Ward had the first known defamation lawsuit in baseball. A few others are listed for review. *See, e.g., Woy v. Turner*, 573 F. Supp. 35 (N.D. Ga. 1983) (sports agent sues Ted Turner); *King v. Burris*, 588 F. Supp 1152 (D. Colo. 1984); *Smith v. McMullen*, 589 F. Supp. 642 (S.D. Tex. 1984) (former GM Tal Smith sues Astros owner); *Montefusco v. ESPN Inc.*, 47 Fed. Appx. 124 (3d Cir. 2002) ("The Count" sues over ESPN's comparison of him to O.J. Simpson); *Fielder v. Greater Media, Inc.*, No. 267495, 2006 WL 2060404 (Mich. Ct. App. July 25, 2006); *Phillips v. Selig*, 2000 No. 1550, 2006 WL 2947667 (Pa. Ct. Com. Pl. Oct. 12, 2006) (former Major League Umpires' Association counsel sued commissioner and others); *Cepeda v. Cowles Magazines & Broadcasting*, 328 F.2d 869 (9th Cir. 1964) ("Baby Bill" sues for defamation). For further study, see Symposium, "Panel I: Defamation in Sports," *Fordham Intellectual Property Media and Entertainment Law Journal* 15 (2005): 335–390.

99. "Howe Tries Comeback," *New York Times*, 25 April 1997.

100. "Howe Charged with Drunken Driving," *New York Times*, 30 August 1997.

101. Murray Chass, "A Life Filled with Trouble Comes to a Sad End," *New York Times*, 29 April 2006.

102. "Autopsy: Howe had Meth in System at Time of Crash," *ESPN.com*, 28 June 2006.

Bibliography

Articles

Abrams, Roger I. "Blackmun's List." *Virginia Sports and Entertainment Law Journal* 6 (2007): 181–207.

_____. "Off His Rocker: Sports Discipline and Labor Arbitration." *Marquette Sports Law Review* 11 (2001): 167–74.

_____. "Two Sports Torts: The Historical Development of the Legal Rights of Baseball Spectators." *Tulsa Law Review* 38 (2003): 433–43.

Andomeit, Peter. "The Barry Bonds Baseball Case — An Empirical Approach — Is Fleeting Possession Five Tenths of the Ball?" *Saint Louis University Law Journal* 48 (2004): 475–502.

Anderson, William B. "Saving the National Pastime's Image: Crisis Management During the 1919 Black Sox Scandal." *Journalism History* 27 (Fall 2001): 105–11.

Bennett, Jay. "Did Shoeless Joe Jackson Throw the 1919 World Series?" *American Statistician* 47 (November 1998): 241–50.

Bolitho, Zachary C. "When Fantasy Meets the Courtroom: An Examination of the Intellectual Property Issues Surrounding the Burgeoning Fantasy Sports Industry." *Ohio State Law Journal* 67 (2006): 911–60.

Bordman, Ethan Yale. "Freedom of Speech and Expression in Sports." *Michigan Bar Journal* 86 (September 2007): 36–39.

Boyer, Allen. "'The Great Gatsby,' the Black Sox, High Finance, and American Law." *Michigan Law Review* 88 (1989): 328–42.

Brenner, Saul. "Granting Certiorari by United States Supreme Court: An Overview of the Social Science Studies." *Law Library Journal* 92 (2000): 193–201.

Carmouche, Chantel D. "Arbitration and Major League Baseball." *Journal of American Arbitration* 1 (2001): 91.

Carney, Gene. "Comiskey's Detectives." *Baseball Research Journal* 38 (Fall 2009): 108–16.

_____. "Uncovering the Fix of the 1919 World Series: The Role of Hugh Fullerton." *NINE: A Journal of Baseball History and Culture* 13 (Fall 2004): 33–49.

Cieslik, Jason. "There's a Drive ... Way Back ... It Might Be ... It Could Be ... Another Lawsuit: *Popov v. Hayashi*." *Thomas M. Cooley Law Review* 20 (2003): 605–38.

Daniels, John E. "Where Have You Gone, Carl Yastrzemski? A Statistical Analysis of the Triple Crown." *Baseball Research Journal* 37 (2008): 107–14.

Davies, Ross E., and Craig D. Rust. "Supreme Court Sluggers: Behind the Numbers." *Green Bag 2d* 13 (2010): 213–26.

Dean, Karen Martin. "Can the NBA Punish Dennis Rodman? An Analysis of First Amendment Rights in Professional Basketball Law Review." *Vermont Law Review* 23 (1998): 157–75.

"The Doctrine of Mutuality in Specific Performance Cases." *Yale Law Journal* 27 (1917): 261–62.

Durney, Jeffrey A. "Fair of Foul? The Commissioner and Major League Baseball's Disciplinary Process." *Emory Law Journal* 41 (1992): 582–631.

Edmonds, Ed. "The Impact of Curt Flood's Minor League Baseball Experience on His Lawsuit against Bowie Kuhn." *NINE: A Journal of Baseball History and Culture* 16 (Spring 2008): 67–72.

Fielder, Thomas. "Keep your Mouth Shut and Listen: The NFL Player's Right of Free Expression." *University of Miami Business Law Review* 10 (2002): 547–83.

Finkelman, Paul. "Fugitive Baseballs and Abandoned Property: Who Owns the Home Run Ball?" *Cardozo Law Review* 23 (2002): 1609–33.

Fred, Sheryl Y. "Fan's Death Spurs Legal Debate in the Front Office." *Corporate Legal Times*, June 2002, 18.

Fried, Gil. "Plaintiffs in the Stands." *Entertainment & Sports Lawyer* 20 (Spring-Summer 2002): 8–13, 18.

Fried, Gil, and Robin Ammon. "Baseball Spectators' Assumption of Risk: Is It 'Fair' or 'Foul?'" *Marquette Sports Law Review* 13 (2002): 39–62.

Gewertz, Ken. "Should Pete Rose be in the Hall of Fame?" *Harvard University Gazette*, August 21, 2003.

Gorman, Bob, and David Weeks. "Foul Play: Fan Fatalities in Twentieth-Century Organized Baseball." *NINE: A Journal of Baseball History and Culture* 12 (Fall 2003): 115–32.

Heaphy, Leslie A. "More Than a Man's Game: Pennsylvania's Women Play Ball." *Pennsylvania Legacies* 7, no. 1 (2000).

Hylton, J. Gordon. "A Foul Ball in the Courtroom: The Baseball Spectator Injury as a Case of First Impression." *Tulsa Law Review* 38 (2003): 485–502.

Jarvis, Robert M., and Phyllis Coleman. "Early Baseball Law." *American Journal of Legal History* 45 (2001): 117–31.

Jones, Ashby. "In Foul Ball Injury Litigation, Clubs Have the Upper Hand." *Wall Street Journal*, July 15, 2008.

Klein, Michael W. "Rose Is in Red, Black Sox Are Blue: A Comparison of *Rose v. Giamatti* and the 1921 Black Sox Trial." *Hastings Communications & Entertainment Law Journal* 13 (1991): 551–88.

Kosofsky, Syda. "Toward Gender Equality in Professional Sports." *Hastings Women's Law Journal* 4 (1993): 209–47.

Kurlantzick, Lewis. "John Rocker and Employee Discipline for Speech." *Marquette Sports Law Review* 11 (2001): 185–94.

McEvoy, Sharlene A. "The Umpire Strikes Out. *Postema v. National League*: Major League Gender Discrimination." *University Miami Entertainment & Sports Law Review* 11 (1993): 1–30.

Moorad, Jeffrey S. "Major League Baseball's Labor Turmoil: The Failure of the Counter-Revolution." *Villanova Sports & Entertainment Law Journal* 4 (1997): 53–86.

Neiman, Peter G. "Root, Root, Root for the Home Team: Pete Rose, Nominal Parties, and Diversity Jurisdiction. *New York University Law Review* 66 (1991): 148–88.

Otalvora, Gustavo A. "Alfonso Soriano is Getting Robbed: Why the Eight Circuit Court of Appeals Made a Bad Call in *C.B.C. Distribution and Marketing v. Major League Baseball*." *Journal of Law, Technology & Policy*, Fall 2008, 383–407.

Pachman, Matthew B. "Limits on the Discretionary Powers of Professional Sports Commissioners: A Historical and Legal Analysis of Issues Raised by the Pete Rose Controversy." *Virginia Law Review* 76 (1990): 1409–39.

Pastrick, Michael. "When a Day at the Ballpark Turns a 'Can of Corn' Into a Can of Worms: *Popov v. Hayashi*." *Buffalo Law Review* 51 (2003): 905–35.

Payne, Marty. "The Undesirable Position: Umpiring in the American Association 1882–1891." *Base Ball: A Journal of the Early Game* 1 (Fall 2007): 104–14.

Pollack, Jason M. "Take My Arbitration, Please: Commissioner 'Best Interest' Disciplinary Authority in Professional Sports." *Fordham Law Review* (1999): 1645–1712.

Powers-Beck, Jeffrey. "'Chief': The American Indian Integration of Baseball, 1897–1945." *American Indian Quarterly* 25 (Autumn 2001): 508–38.

Reisler, Jim. "Jack Kerouac: The Beat of Fantasy Baseball." *National Pastime* 28 (2008).

Rigelhaupt, James L. "Liability to Spectator at Baseball Game Who is Hit by Ball or Injured as Result of Other Hazards of Game." *American Law Reports 3d* 91 (2003): 24.

Rogers, C. Paul, III. "Napoleon Lajoie, Breach of Contract and the Great Baseball War." *Southern Methodist University Law Review* 55 (2002): 325–45.

Ross, Stephen F. "Reconsidering *Flood v. Kuhn*." *University of Miami Entertainment & Sports Law Review* 12 (1995): 169–206.

Rychlak, Ronald J. "Pete Rose, Bart Giamatti, and the Dowd Report." 68 *Mississippi Law Journal* 68 (1999): 889–902.

Schiller, Mayer. "Killer Goryl." *Elysian Fields Quarterly* 17 (No. 4, 2000).

Semeraro, Steven. "An Essay on Property Rights in Milestone Home Run Baseballs." *SMU Law Review* 56 (2003): 2281–2300.

Shane, Jane. "Who Owns a Home Run? The Battle of the Use of Player Performance Statistics by Fantasy Sports Websites." *Hastings Communications & Entertainment Law Journal* 29 (2007): 241–58.

Socolow, Brian R. "Protecting Fans at Sporting Events, Just How Far Must you go to Keep Attendees Safe?" *Facility Manager* (2008): 8–10.

"Specific Performance — Defenses — Clean Hands: Application or the Maxim to Baseball Contracts." *Harvard Law Review* 28 (1914): 213–14.

Staudohar, Paul D. "Baseball's Changing Salary Structure." *Compensation and Working Conditions* 2 (Fall 1997): 2–9.

Stoklas, Patrick. "*Popov v. Hayashi*, a Modern Day *Pierson v. Post*: A Comment on what the Court Should Have Done With the Seventy-third Home Run Baseball Hit by Barry Bonds." *Loyola University of Chicago Law Journal* 34 (2003): 901–43.

Swift, Kenneth R. "I Couldn't Watch the Ball Because I Was Watching the Ferris Wheel in Centerfield." *Entertainment and Sports Lawyer* 22 (2005): 1, 33–38.

Symposium, "Panel I: Defamation in Sports." *Fordham Intellectual Property Media and Entertainment Law Journal* 15 (2005): 335–90.

Thornton, Patrick K., and Christopher James. "Down Two Strikes, Is Major League Baseball Already Out? How the 8th Circuit Balked to Protect the Right of Publicity in *C.B.C. v. MLB, Advanced Media*." *South Texas Law Review* 50 (2008): 173–206.

Tierney, Brian E. "A Fielder's Choice: How Agency Law Decides the True Owner of the 2004 Red Sox Final-Out Baseball." *Willamette Sports Law Journal* 3 (2007): 1–26.

Tierney, Ted J. "Heads Up!: The Baseball Facility Liability Act." *Northern Illinois University Law Review* 18 (1998): 601–17.

Tsimpris, William B. "A Question of (Anti)trust: *Flood v. Kuhn* and the Liability of Major League Baseball's Antitrust Exemption." *Richmond Journal of Law and the Public Interest* 8 (2004): 69–86.

Wakamatsu, Aaron. "Spectator Injuries: Examining Owner Negligence and the Assumption of Risk Defense." *Willamette Sports Law Review* 6 (2009):1–15.

Ward, John M. "The Aristocracy of Baseball Stardom." *Baseball Magazine* 17 (May 1916): 37–41.

Warren, Earl. "A Majority Opinion on Baseball by the Chief Justice of the United States." *Sports Illustrated*, April 9, 1956, 23.

Will, George. "Foul Ball." *New York Review of Books*, June 27, 1991.

Winer, Kimberly G. "Maintaining the Home Field Advantage: *Rose vs. Federal Court*." *Loyola Entertainment Law Journal* 10 (1990): 695–713.

Woolley, Edward Mott. "The Business of Baseball." *McClure's Magazine*, July 1912.

Zelinsky, Aaron. "The Justice as Commissioner: Benching the Judge-Umpire Analogy." *Yale Law Journal Online* 119 (2010): 113–25.

Books

Abrams, Roger I. *Legal Bases: Baseball and the Law*. Philadelphia: Temple University Press, 1998.

Adelman, Tom. *The Long Ball: The Summer of '75 — Spaceman, Catfish, Charlie Hustle, and the Greatest World Series Ever Played*. New York: Little, Brown, 2003.

Adler, Joseph. *Baseball Hacks*. Sebastopol, CA: O'Reilly, 2006.

Albert, Jim, and Jay Bennett. *Curve Ball: Baseball, Statistics, and the Role of Chance in the Game*. New York: Copernicus Books, 2003.

Ardell, Jean H. *Breaking into Baseball: Women and the National Pastime*. Carbondale: Southern Illinois University Press, 2005.

Bailey, Frankie, and Steven Chermak. *Crimes and Trials of the Century*. Westport, CT: Greenwood, 2007.

Barmack, Erik, and Max Handelman. *Why Fantasy Football Matters (And Our Lives*

Do Not). New York: Simon Spotlight Entertainment, 2006.//
The Baseball Encyclopedia. 10th ed. New York: Macmillan, 1996.//
Belth, Alex. *Stepping Up: The Story of Curt Flood and His Fight for Baseball Players' Rights*. New York: Persea, 2006.//
Berkow, Ira. *Hank Greenberg: Hall-of-Fame Slugger*. Philadelphia: Jewish Publication Society, 2001.//
Berlage, Gia Ingham. *Women in Baseball: The Forgotten History*. New York: Praeger, 1994.//
Carney, Gene. *Burying the Black Sox: How Baseball's Cover-Up of the 1919 World Series Fix Almost Succeeded*. Dulles, VA: Potomac, 2006.//
Castro, Tony. *Mickey Mantle: America's Prodigal Son*. Dulles, VA: Potomac, 2009.//
Champion, Walter T., Jr. *Sports Law: Cases, Documents, and Materials*. New York: Aspen, 2005.//
_____. *Sports Law in a Nutshell*. 3rd ed. St. Paul, MN: Thomson/West, 2005.//
Clark, Paul F., John T. Dalaney, and Ann C. Frost. *Collective Bargaining in the Private Sector*. Champaign, IL: Industrial Relations Research Association, 2002.//
Cook, William A. *The 1919 World Series: What Really Happened?* Jefferson, NC: McFarland, 2001.//
Cooper, Mark, and Douglas Congdon-Martin. *Baseball Games: Home Versions of the National Pastime, 1860s–1960s: Price Guide*. Atglen, PA: Schiffer Books, 1995.//
Costa, Gabriel B., Michael R. Huber, and John T. Saccoman. *Understanding Sabermetrics: An Introduction to the Science of Baseball Statistics*. Jefferson, NC: McFarland, 2008.//
Cox, Ronald W. *Free Agency and Competitive Balance in Baseball*. Jefferson, NC: McFarland, 2006.//
Cozzillio, Michael J., and Mark S. Levinstein. *Sports Law: Cases and Materials*. Durham: Carolina Academic Press, 1997.//
Cribbet, John E. *Principles of the Law of Property*. New York: Foundation Press, 1962.//
Davidson, Margaret. *The Story of Jackie Robinson: Bravest Man in Baseball*. New York: Dell, 1987.//
Day, Frederick J. *Clubhouse Lawyer: Law in the World of Sports*. New York: iUniverse Star, 2002.//
Dickson, Paul. *The Dickson Baseball Dictionary*. 3rd ed. New York: W.W. Norton, 2009.//
Di Salvatore, Bryan. *A Clever Base-Ballist: The Life and Times of John Montgomery Ward*. Baltimore: Johns Hopkins University Press, 1999.//
Dorey, David. *Fantasy Football the Next Level: How to Build a Championship Team Every Season*. New York: Grand Central, 2007.//
Durant, John, and Alice K. Durant. *National Baseball Hall of Fame and Museum: Cooperstown, New York*. New York: National Baseball Hall of Fame, 1952.//
Eig, Jonathan. *Opening Day: The Story of Jackie Robinson's First Season*. New York: Simon & Schuster, 2008.//
Elias, Robert. *Baseball and the American Dream: Race, Gender, and the National Pastime*. New York: M.E. Sharpe, 2001.//
Fleitz, David L. *Shoeless: The Life and Times of Joe Jackson*. Jefferson, NC: McFarland, 2001.//
Flockhart, Dan. *Fantasy Basketball and Mathematics: A Resource Guide for Teachers, Parents*. San Francisco: Jossey-Bass, 2007.//
_____. *Fantasy Baseball and Mathematics: Student Workbook*. San Francisco: Jossey-Bass, 2007.//
Flood, Curt, with Richard Carter. *The Way It Is*. New York: Trident Press, 1971.//
Flynn, Neil F. *Baseball's Reserve System: The Case and Trial of Curt Flood v. Major League Baseball*. Springfield, IL: Walnut Park, 2006.//
Formosa, Dan, and Paul Hamburger. *Baseball Field Guide*. New York: Da Capo Press, 2008.//
Ganz, Howard L., and Jeffrey L. Kessler, editors. *Understanding Business & Legal Aspects of the Sports Industry*. New York: Practising Law Institute, 2001.//
Garner, Bryan, ed. *Black's Law Dictionary*. 8th ed. St. Paul, MN: West Publishing, 2004.//
Gatto, Steve. *Da Curse of the Billy Goat: The Chicago Cubs, Pennant Races, and Curses*. Lansing, MI: Protar, 2004.//
Gelzheiser, Robert A. *Labor and Capital in

Bibliography

Nineteenth Century Baseball. Jefferson, NC: McFarland, 2006.

Gillette, Gary, and Pete Palmer. *The ESPN Baseball Encyclopedia.* 4th ed. New York: Sterling, 2007.

Ginsburg, Daniel E. *The Fix Is In: A History of Baseball Gambling and Game Fixing Scandals.* Jefferson, NC: McFarland, 1995.

Goldman, Robert M. *One Man Out: Curt Flood Versus Baseball.* Lawrence: University Press of Kansas, 2008.

Gorman, Robert M., and David Weeks. *Death at the Ballpark: A Comprehensive Study of Game-Related Fatalities, 1862–2007.* Jefferson, NC: McFarland, 2008.

Gorn, Elliot J., ed. *Muhammad Ali, The People's Champ.* Urbana, IL: University of Illinois Press, 1998.

Gramling, Chad. *Baseball in Fort Wayne.* Charleston, SC: Arcadia, 2007.

Gregorich, Barbara. *Women at Play: The Story of Women in Baseball.* San Diego, CA: Harcourt, Brace, 1993.

Hample, Zachary. *How to Snag a Major League Baseball.* Fullerton, CA: Aladdin, 1999.

Helyar, John. *Lords of the Realm: The Real History of Baseball.* New York: Ballantine, 1994.

Howe, Steve, and Jim Greenfield. *Between the Lines: One Athlete's Struggle to Escape the Nightmare of Addiction.* Grand Rapids, MI: Masters Press, 1989.

Hunter, James A., Jim Catfish Hunter, and Armen Keteyian. *Catfish: My Life in Baseball.* New York: McGraw-Hill, 1988.

Izenberg, Jerry. *The Greatest Game Ever Played.* Baltimore: Henry Holt, 1987.

James, Bill. *The Baseball Book.* New York: Villard Books, 1990.

_____. *The Bill James Guide to Baseball Managers.* New York: Scribner's, 1997.

_____. *Bill James Historical Baseball Abstract.* New York: Villard Books, 1985.

_____. *The New Bill James Historical Baseball Abstract.* New York: Villard Books, 2001.

_____. *The Neyer/James Guide to Pitchers.* New York: Fireside, 2004.

_____. *This Time Let's Not Eat the Bones: Bill James without the Numbers,* New York: Villard Books, 1995.

_____. *Whatever Happened to the Baseball Hall of Fame?* New York: Fireside, 1995.

Jarvis, Robert, and Phyllis Coleman. *Sports Law, Cases, and Materials.* St. Paul, MN: West, 1999.

Jennings, Kenneth M. *Swings and Misses: Moribund Labor Relations in Professional Baseball.* Westport, CT: Praeger, 1997.

Johnson, Harold. *Who's Who in Major League Base Ball.* Chicago: B.C. Callahan, 1936.

Johnson, Vincent R., and Alan Gunn. *Studies in American Tort Law.* 3rd ed. Durham: Carolina Academic Press, 2005.

Kalb, Elliott. *The 25 Greatest Sports Conspiracy Theories of All-Time: Ranking Sports' Most Notorious Fixes, Cover-Ups, and Scandals.* New York: Skyhorse, 2007.

Kelly, John D. *The American Game: Capitalism, Decolonization, World Domination, and Baseball.* Chicago: Prickly Paradigm Press, 2006.

Kohout, Martin Donell. *Hal Chase: The Defiant Life and Turbulent Times of Baseball's Biggest Crook.* Jefferson, NC: McFarland, 2001.

Kuhn, Bowie. *Hardball: The Education of a Baseball Commissioner.* New York: Times Books, 1987.

Kuklick, Bruce. *To Every Thing a Season: Shibe Park and Urban Philadelphia, 1909–1976.* Princeton, NJ: Princeton University Press, 1993.

Lamster, Mark. *Spalding's World Tour: The Epic Adventure that Took Baseball around the Globe and Made It America's Game.* New York: PublicAffairs, 2006.

Leavy, Jane. *Sandy Koufax: A Lefty's Legacy.* New York: HarperCollins, 2002.

Lord, Richard A., and Samuel Williston. *A Treatise on the Law of Contracts.* 4th ed. New York: Thomson/West, 1990.

Macht, Norman L. *Connie Mack and the Early Years of Baseball.* Lincoln: University of Nebraska Press, 2007.

MacLean, Norman. *All Time Greatest: Who's Who in Baseball 1872–1990.* New York: Who's Who in Baseball Magazine, 1990.

Marburger, Daniel R., ed. *Stee-Rike Four!: What's Wrong with the Business of Baseball?* Westport, CT: Praeger, 1997.

Miller, Marvin. *A Whole Different Ball Game: The Inside Story of the Baseball Revolution.* Chicago: Ivan R. Dee, 2004.

Mills, Dorothy Seymour, and Harold Seymour. *Baseball: The People's Game.* New York: Oxford University Press, 1991.

Morris, William, ed. *The American Heritage Dictionary of the English Language.* Boston: Houghton Mifflin, 1976.

Neyer, Rob. *Rob Neyers' Big Book of Baseball Blunders.* New York: Fireside, 2006.

Okrent, Daniel, Harris Lewine, and David Nemec. *The Ultimate Baseball Book.* Boston: Houghton Mifflin, 2000.

Paisner, Daniel. *The Ball: Mark McGwire's Home Run Ball and the Marketing of the American Dream.* New York: Viking, 1999.

Peterson, Robert. *Only the Ball was White: A History of Legendary Black Players and All-Black Professional Teams.* New York: Oxford University Press, 1992.

Pietrusza, David. *Judge and Jury: The Life and Times of Judge Kenesaw Mountain Landis.* South Bend, IN: Diamond Communications, 1998.

Postema, Pam, and Gene Wojciechowski. *You've Got to Have Balls to Make It in This League: My Life as an Umpire.* Lincoln: University of Nebraska Press, 1992, repr. 2003.

Preston, Joseph G. *Major League Baseball in the 1970's: A Modern Game Emerges.* Jefferson, NC: McFarland, 2004.

Price, Joseph L. *Rounding the Bases: Baseball and Religion in America.* Macon, GA: Mercer University Press, 2006.

Prosser, William L. *Handbook on the Law of Torts.* 4th ed. St. Paul: West, 1981.

Purdy, Dennis; *Team by Team Encyclopedia of Major League Baseball.* New York: Workman, 2006.

Quirk, Charles E. *Sports and the Law: Major Legal Cases.* New York: Garland, 1996.

Rader, Benjamin G. *Baseball: A History of America's Game.* 2nd ed. Urbana, IL: University of Illinois Press, 2002.

Rampersad, Arnold. *Jackie Robinson: A Bibliography.* New York: Ballantine, 1998.

Raney, Arthur A., and Jennings Bryant. *Handbook of Sports and Media.* New York: Routledge, 2006

Reichler, Joseph L. *The Baseball Encyclopedia.* 4th ed. New York: Macmillan, 1979.

Reston, James, Jr. *The Lives of Pete Rose and Bart Giamatti: Collision at Home Plate.* Lincoln: University of Nebraska, 1997.

Ritter, Lawrence S. *The Glory of Their Times.* New York: Macmillan, 1966.

Robinson, Sharon. *Promises to Keep: How Jackie Robinson Changed America.* New York: Scholastic Press, 2004.

Rose, Pete. *Pete: Baseball's Charlie Hustle.* Nashville, TN: Cumberland House Publishing, 2003.

Rose, Pete, and Rick Hill. *My Prison Without Bars.* Emmaus, PA: Rodale Books, 2004.

Schubert, Frank A. *Introduction to Law and the Legal System.* Florence, KY: Cengage Learning, 2007.

Schwarz, Alan. *The Numbers Game: Baseball's Lifelong Fascination with Statistics.* New York: Thomas Dunne Books, 2004.

Seymour, Harold, and Dorothy Seymour Mills. *Baseball: The Early Years.* New York: Oxford University Press, 1960.

Sharbono, Kaye. *Jackie Mitchell. Baseball Player.* Morristown, NJ: Modern Curriculum Press, 1995.

Shatzkin, Mike. *The Ballplayers: Baseball's Ultimate Biographical Reference.* New York: Arbor House/William Morrow, 1990.

Smith, James C., Edward J. Larson, John C. Nagle, and John A. Kidwell. *Property: Cases & Materials.* New York: Aspen Publishers, 2008.

Smith, Ken. *Baseball's Hall of Fame.* New York: Grosset & Dunlap, 1966.

Smith, Ron. *The Sporting News Selects Baseball's 100 Greatest Players: A Celebration of the 20th Century's Best.* St. Louis, MO: Sporting News, 1998.

Snyder, Brad. *A Well-Paid Slave: Curt Flood's Fight for Free Agency in Professional Sports.* New York: Viking, 2006.

Snyder, John. *Cubs Journal: Year by Year and Day by Day with the Chicago Cubs Since 1876.* Cincinnati: Emmis Books, 2005.

Spalding, Albert G. *America's National Game.* New York: American Sports, 1911; repr. San Francisco: Halo Books, 1991.

Spink, Alfred H. *The National Game.* 2nd ed. St. Louis, MO: National Game Pub., 1911; repr. Carbondale: Southern Illinois University, 2000.

Spink, J.G. Taylor. *Judge Landis and Twenty-Five Years of Baseball.* New York: Crowell, 1947.

Steele, Jenny. *Tort Law: Text, Cases, and Ma-*

terials. New York: Oxford University Press, 2007.
Stevens, David. *Baseball's Radical for All Seasons: A Biography of John Montgomery Ward*. Lanham, MD: Scarecrow Press, 1998.
Stump, Al. *Cobb: A Biography*. Chapel Hill, NC: Algonquin Books, 1996.
Sullivan, Brad. *Batting Four Thousand: Baseball in the Western Reserve*. Cleveland, OH: Society for American Baseball Research, 2008.
Sullivan, Dean A. *Early Innings: A Documentary History of Baseball, 1825–1908*. Lincoln: University of Nebraska Press, 1997.
Thorn, John, and Pete Palmer, eds. *Total Baseball: The Most Complete Baseball Encyclopedia Ever!* New York: Warner Books, 1989.
Turkin, Hy, and S.C. Thompson. *The Official Encyclopedia of Baseball*. 3rd rev. ed. New York: A.S. Barnes, 1963.
Tygiel, Jules. *Baseball's Great Experiment: Jackie Robinson and His Legacy*. New York: Oxford University Press, 1983; expanded ed., 1997
Uberstine, Gary A. *Law of Professional and Amateur Sports*. New York: Thomson/West, 1988.
Ueberroth, Peter. *Made in America: His Own Story*. New York: William Morrow, 1988.
Vecsey, George. *Baseball: A History of America's Favorite Game*. New York: Modern Library, 2006.
Veeck, Bill, with Ed Linn. *Veeck as in Wreck: The Autobiography of Bill Veeck*. Chicago: Putnam, 1962.
Vincent, Fay. *The Last Commissioner: A Baseball Valentine*. New York: Simon & Schuster, 2002.
Walker, Sam. *Fantasyland: A Season on Baseball's Lunatic Fringe*. New York: Viking, 2006.
Waller, Spencer W., Neil B. Cohen, and Paul Finkelman. *Baseball and the American Legal Mind*. New York: Garland, 1995.
Ward, Geoffrey C., and Ken Burns. *Baseball: An Illustrated History*. Alfred A. Knopf, 1994.
Ward, John M. *Base-Ball: How to Become a Player*. Montgomery, AL: Athletic Publishing, 1888.
Weiler, Paul C., and Gary R. Roberts. *Sports and the Law: Cases, Materials, and Problems*. New York: West, 1993.
White, Edward G. *Creating the National Pastime: Baseball Transforms Itself*. Princeton, NJ: Princeton University Press, 1996.
White, Sol, and Jerry Malloy. *Sol White's History of Colored Base Ball: With Other Documents on the Early Black Game, 1886–1936*. Lincoln: University of Nebraska Press, 1995.
Wolf, Nancy. *The Professional Photographer's Legal Handbook*. New York: Allworth Press, 2007.
Yasser, Ray, James R. McCurdy, and Peter C. Goplerud. *Sports Law: Cases and Materials*. 2nd ed. Cincinnati: Anderson, 1990.
Zarzycki, Robert. *Drafting to Win: The Ultimate Guide to Fantasy Football*. Bloomington, IN: AuthorHouse, 2005.
_____. *Fantasy Football's Big Six*. Bloomington, IN: AuthorHouse, 2008.
Ziff, Bruce, et al. *A Property Law Reader: Cases, Questions, and Commentary*. Toronto, Ont.: Thomson/Carswell, 2005.
Zimbalist, Andrew. *In The Best Interest of Baseball: The Revolutionary Reign of Bud Selig*. Hoboken, NJ: Wiley, 2006.
Zoss, Joel and Josh Bowman. *Diamonds in the Rough: The Untold History of Baseball*. New York: Macmillan, 1989; repr., Chicago: Contemporary Books, 1996.

Cases and Arbitration Decisions

Alex Johnson v. The California Angels, Panel Decision 6, (Gill, 1971).
Am. and Nat'l Leagues of Prof'l Baseball Clubs (Oakland Athletics, Division of Charles O. Finley and Co., Inc. and Major League Baseball Players Ass'n) v. James A. ("Catfish") Hunter, Arb. 23 Griev. 74–18, 74–20 (1974).
Am. and Nat'l Leagues of Prof'l Baseball Clubs v. Major League Baseball Players Ass'n, 130 Cal. Rptr. 626 (Ct. App. 1976).
Am. League Baseball Club of Chicago v. Chase, 149 N.Y.S. 6 (N.Y. Sup. 1914).
Arnold v. City of Cedar Rapids, 443 N.W.2d 332 (Iowa Sup. Ct. 1989).
Baltimore Orioles v. Major League Baseball

Players Ass'n, 805 F.3d 663 (7th Cir. 1786).

Bellezzo v. Arizona, 851 P.2d 847 (Ariz. Ct. App. 1992).

Benejam v. Detroit Tigers Baseball Club, 635 N.W.2d 219 (Mich. Ct. App. 2001).

Bernhardt v. Popov, 2002 WL 31833731 (Cal. Super. Ct. 2002).

Bonito Boats, Inc. v. Thunder Craft Boats, Inc., 489 U.S. 141 (1989).

Brown v. San Francisco Ball Club, Inc., 484, 222 P. 2d 19 (Cal. Ct. App. 1950).

CBC Distribution and Marketing, Inc. v. Major League Baseball Advanced Media, L.P., 505 F.3d 818 (8th Cir. 2007).

Cent. New York Basketball, Inc. v. Barnett, 181 N.E.2d 506 (Ohio Ct. Com. Pl. 1961).

Cepeda v. Cowles Magazines and Broadcasting, 328 F.2d 869 (9th Cir. 1964).

Chicago Nat'l League Ball Club, Inc. v. Vincent, No. 92 C 4398, 1992 WL 179208 (N.D. Ill. July 23, 1992).

Christoff v. Nestle USA, Inc., 62 Cal. Rptr. 3d 122 (Ct. App. 2007).

Cincinnati Bengals, Inc. v. Bergey, 453 F. Supp. 129 (S.D. Ohio 1974).

Connecticut Prof'l Sports Corp. v. Heyman, 276 F. Supp. 618 (S.D.N.Y. 1967).

Curtis v. Portland Baseball Club, 279 P. 277 (Ore. Ct. App. 1929).

Dallas Cowboys Football Inc. v. Harris, 348 S.W.2d 37 (Tex. Civ. App. 1961).

Daly v. Smith, 33 Cal. Rptr. 920 (Ct. App. 1963).

Fielder v. Greater Media, Inc., No. 267495, 2006 WL 2060404 (Mich. Ct. App. July 25, 2006).

Fiest Publications v. Rural Telephone Services, 499 U.S. 340 (1991).

Finley v. Kuhn, 569 F. 2d 527 (7th Cir. 1978).

Flood v. Kuhn, 309 F. Supp. 793 (S.D.N.Y. 1970).

Flood v. Kuhn, 312 F. Supp. 404 (S.D.N.Y. 1970).

Friedman v. Houston Sports Ass'n, 731 S.W.2d 572 (Tex. Ct. App. 1987).

Frost v. Knight, 7 L.R. Exch. 111 (1872) (Eng.).

Gomes v. Avco Corp., 964 F.2d 1330 (2d Cir. 1992).

Grimes v. Am. League Baseball Co., 78 S.W.2d 520 (Mo. Ct. App. 1935).

Haugh v. Harris Bros. Amusement Co., 172 A. 145 (Pa. Ct. App. 1934).

Hayes v. Willis, 11 Abb. Pr. (n.s.) 167 (N.Y.C.P. 1871).

Hochester v. De La Tour, 2 E. & B. 678 (Q.B. 1853).

Howard v. Daly, 61 N.Y. 362 (1875).

Howe v. New York Post, Inc., No. 124519/93, 1995 WL 572884 (N.Y. Sup. Ct. Mar. 7, 1995).

Howe v. New York Post, Co., Inc., 1995 WL 372884 (N.Y. Sup. Ct. 1995).

Interactive Digital Software v. St. Louis County, Mo., 329 F.3d 954 (8th Cir. 2003).

Kallish v. Am. Base Ball Club of Philadelphia, 10 A.2d 831 (Pa. Super. 1940).

Kapp v. Nat'l Football League, 586 F.2d 644 (9th Cir. 1978).

Kesner v. Little Caesar's Enterprises, Inc., No. 01-719942002 ,WL 1480800 (E.D. Mich. June 13, 2002).

King v. Burris, 588 F. Supp. 1152 (D. Colo. 1984).

Lawson v. Salt Lake Trappers, Inc., 901 P.2d 1013 (Utah Sup. 1995).

Lemat Corp. v. Barry, 80 Cal. Rptr. 240 (Ct. App. 1969).

Ludtke v. Kuhn, 461 F. Supp. 86 (S.D.N.Y. 1978).

Lumley v. Wagner, 1 De GM & G. 604, (1852) 42 Eng. Rep. 687 (Ch.).

Machen v. Johansson, 174 F. Supp. 552 (S.D.N.Y. 1959).

Mackey v. Nat'l Football League, 543 F.2d 606 (8th Cir. 1976).

Madison Square Garden Corp. v. Braddock, 90 F. 2d 924 (3d Cir. 1937).

Major League Baseball Players Ass'n v. Comm'r of Major League Baseball, Grievance 92-7, Panel Decision 94 (Nov. 12, 1992) (Steve Howe Arbitration Decision).

Marchio v. Letterlough, 237 F. Supp.2d 580 (E.D. Pa. 2003).

Marlowe v. Rush-Henrietta Cen. Sch. Dist., 561 N.Y.S.2d 934 (App. Div. 1990).

Matthews v. A-1, Inc., 748 F.2d 975 (5th Cir. 1984).

Maytnier v. Rush, 225 N.E.2d 83 (III. App. Ct. 1967).

McCaull v. Braham, 16 F. 37 (S.D.N.Y. 1883).

Metropolitan Exhibition Co. v. Ward, 9 N.Y.S. 779 (Sup. Ct. 1890).

Miranda v. Arizona, 384 U.S. 436 (1968).
Montefusco v. ESPN Inc., 47 Fed. Appx. 124 (3d Cir. 2002).
NCAA v. Tarkanian, 488 U.S. 179 (1988).
New York State Div. of Human Rights v. New York Pennsylvania Prof'l Baseball League, 320 N.Y.S. 2d 788 (App. Div. 1971).
Nix v. WLCY Radio/Rahall Communications, 738 F.2d 1181 (11th Cir. 1984).
O'Connor v. St. Louis Am. League Baseball Co., 181 S.W. 1167 (Mo. Ct. App. 1916).
Ortiz-Del Valle v. Nat'l Basketball Ass'n, 42 F. Supp.2d 334 (S.D.N.Y. 1999).
Parks v. Steinbrenner, 520 N.Y.S.2d 374 (App. Div. 1987).
People v. Cicotte, No. 21868 (Crim. Ct., Cook County, Ill. Aug. 2, 1921).
Philadelphia Ball Club v. Lajoie, 51 A. 973 (Pa. Sup. Ct. 1902).
Philadelphia Hockey Club, Inc. v. Flett, 58 Pa. D. & C.2d 367, 1972 WL 16067 (Pa. Com. Pl. 1972).
Phillips v. Selig, 2000 No. 1550, 2006 WL 2947667 (Pa. Ct. Com. Pl. Oct. 12, 2006).
Popov v. Hayashi, No. 400545, 2002 WL 31833731 (Cal Super. Ct. Dec. 18, 2002).
Postema v. Nat'l League of Prof'l Baseball Clubs, 799 F. Supp. 1475 (S.D.N.Y. 1992).
Radovich v. Nat'l Football League, 352 U.S. 445 (1957).
Romeo v. Pittsburgh Associates, 787 A.2d 1027 (Pa. Sup. Ct. 2001).
Rose v. Giamatti, No. A8905178, 1989 WL 111386 (Ohio Com. Pl. June 19, 1989).
Rose v. Giamatti, No. A8905178, 1989 WL 111447 (Ohio Com. Pl. June 26, 1989).
Rose v. Giamatti, No. A8905178, 1989 WL 111453 (Ohio Com. Pl. June 26, 1989).
Rose v. Giamatti, 721 F. Supp 906 (S.D. Ohio 1989).
Rudnick v. Golden West Broadcasters, 202 Cal. Rptr. 900 (Ct. App. 1984).
Schentzel v. Philadelphia Nat'l League Club, 96 A.2d 181 (Pa. Super. Ct. 1953).
Smith v. McMullen, 589 F. Supp. 642 (S.D. Tex. 1984).
Smith v. Pro-Football, 420 F. Supp. 738 (D.D.C. 1976).
Swagger v. City of Crystal, 379 N.W.2d 183 (Minn. Ct. App. 1985).
Triano v. Popov, No. A106857, 2005 WL 1230766 (Cal. Super. Ct. App. May 24, 2005).

Twelve Clubs Comprising the Nat'l League of Prof'l Baseball Clubs and The Twelve Clubs Comprising the Am. League of Prof'l Baseball Clubs (Los Angeles Club and Montreal Club) v. Major League Baseball Players Ass'n (John A. Messersmith and David A. McNally), Arb. 29, Griev. 75-27, 75-28 (1975).
Uhlaender v. Henricksen, 316 F. Supp. 1277 (D. Minn. 1970).
United Air Lines, Inc. v. Evans, 431 U.S. 553 (1977).
United Steelworkers v. Am. Mfg. Co., 363 U.S. 564 (1960).
United Steelworkers v. Enterprise Wheel & Car Corp., 363 U.S. 593 (1960).
Winnipeg Rugby Football Club, Ltd. v. Freeman, 140 F. Supp. 365 (N.D. Ohio 1955).
Winters v. New York, 233 U.S. 507 (1948).
Woy v. Turner, 573 F. Supp. 35 (N.D. Ga. 1983).
Zacchini v. Scripps-Howard Broadcasting Co., 433 U.S. 562 (1977).

Reports

Dowd, John M., Esq. "Report to the Commissioner: In the Matter of Edward Rose, Manager, Cincinnati Reds Baseball Club" (May 9, 1989), available at http://www.thedowdreport.com.
Lapchick, Richard. "The 2008 Racial and Gender Report Card, Major League Baseball (April 15, 2008), available at http://tidesport.org/RGRC/2008/2008_MLB_RGRC_PR.pdf.
Mitchell, George. "Report to the Commissioner of Baseball of an Independent Investigation into the Illegal Use of Steroids and Other Performance Enhancing Substances by Players in Major League Baseball" (December 13, 2007), available at http://files.mlb.com/mitchrpt.pdf.

Court Documents

People v. Cicotte, *No. 21868 (Crim. Ct., Cook County, Ill. Aug. 2, 1921).*

Criminal File: CR-21867; Proposed Jury Instructions (1920–1921).

Criminal File: CR-21867; Proposed Verdict Forms (1920–1921).
Criminal File: CR-21867; True Bill, Grand Jury Indictment for Conspiracy 21868 (Oct. 29, 1920).
Criminal File: CR-21867; Notice of Hearing, Bill of Particulars (Feb. 14, 1921).
Criminal File: CR-21867; Petition for Bill of Particulars Criminal Court of Cook County (March Term, 1921).
Grand Jury Subpoenas (March 1921).
Criminal File: CR-21867; True Bill, Grand Jury Indictment for Conspiracy, 23909 (Mar. 26, 1921).
Criminal File: CR-21867; Affidavit of Harry C. Levinson (June 22, 1921).
Criminal File: CR-21867; Notice of Hearing, Motion for Continuation, Ben Franklin and Carl Zork (June 25, 1921).
Criminal File: CR-21867; Affidavit of Dr. George M. Gorin (June 28, 1921).
Criminal File: CR-21867; Order Regarding Objections at Trial (July 5, 1921).
Criminal File: CR-21867; Nine Verdicts (Aug. 2, 1921).

Demand for Trial:

Ben Levi (May 12, 1921).
George Weaver, Fred Risberg, Oscar Flesch, Claude Williams and Joe Jackson (May 28, 1921).

Writs of Arrest:

Abe Attel, $3,000 Bail (Sep. 17, 1921). (Nollied)
Ben Franklin, $3,000 Bail (Sep. 17, 1921).
Carl Zork, $3,000 Bail (Apr. 1, 1921).
Claude Williams, $3,000 Bail (Mar. 28, 1921).
Charles Risberg, $3,000 Bail (Mar. 28, 1921).
Edward Cicotte, $3,000 Bail (May 1, 1921).
Fred McMullen, $3,000 Bail (Sep. 17, 1921). (Nollied)
George Weaver, $3,000 Bail (Sep. 17, 1921).
Hal Chase, $3,000 Bail (Sep. 17, 1921). (Nollied)
Joe Jackson, $3,000 Bail (Mar. 28, 1921).
Joseph Sullivan, $3,000 Bail (Sep. 17, 1921). (Nollied)
Oscar Flesch, $3,000 Bail (Apr. 1, 1921).
Rachel Brown, $3,000 Bail (Sep. 17, 1921). (Nollied)
Williams Burns, $3,000 Bail (Sep. 17, 1921).

Popov v. Hayashi, No. 400545, 2002 WL 31833731 (Cal Super. Ct. Dec. 18, 2002).

Declaration of Kathy Sorensen in Support of Issuance of Temporary Restraining Order and OSC Regarding Preliminary Injunction (Oct. 4, 2001).
Declaration of Brian A. Zeiden in Support of Notice to Defendant Patrick Hayashi of Ex Parte Hearing for Issuance of Temporary Restraining Order (Oct. 23, 2001).
Declaration of Josh Keppel in Support of Issuance of Temporary Restraining Order and OSC Re Preliminary Injunction (Oct. 23, 2001).
Complaint for Injunctive Relief, Conversion, Battery, Assault, Punitive Damages and Constructive Trust (Oct. 24, 2001).
Declaration of Plaintiff Alex Popov in Support of Insurance of Temporary Restraining Order and OSC Re Preliminary Injunction (Oct. 24, 2001).
Declaration of Doug Yarris in Support of Issuance of Temporary Restraining Order and OSC Re Preliminary Injunction (Oct. 24, 2001).
Declaration of Paul Finkelman in Support of Issuance of Temporary Restraining Order and OSC Re Preliminary Injunction (Oct. 24, 2001).
Memorandum by Plaintiff of Points and Authorities of in Support of Issuance of Temporary Order and OSC Re Preliminary Injunction (Oct. 24, 2001).
Defendant Patrick Hayashi's Verified Answer to Complaint for Injunctive Relief, Conversion, Battery, Assault, Punitive Damages and Constructive Trust (Nov. 13, 2001).
Declaration of Robert A. Roth (Nov. 20, 2001).
Declaration of Robert Holmes (Nov. 20, 2001).
Declaration of Arlan Ettiner in Opposition to Motion for Preliminary Injunction (Nov. 21, 2001).
Declaration of Bill King (Nov. 27, 2001).
Declaration of Dan Puthoff (Nov. 27, 2001).
Declaration of Evan Knight (Nov. 27, 2001).
Declaration of Gail Creech (Nov. 27, 2001).
Declaration of Jeff Hacker (Nov. 27, 2001).

Declaration of Jeremy Puthoff (Nov. 27, 2001).
Declaration of John Creech (Nov. 27, 2001).
Declaration of Kelly Collins Regarding Production of Photographic Stills (Nov. 27, 2001).
Declaration of Kevin Griffin (Nov. 27, 2001).
Declaration of Martin F. Triano in support of ISC Re Preliminary Injunction (Nov. 27, 2001).
Declaration of Maurie Bennett (Nov. 27, 2001).
Declaration of Michael D. Barnes in Opposition to Motion for Preliminary Injunction (Nov. 27, 2001).
Declaration of Paul Castro (Nov. 27, 2001).
Declaration of Richard R. Garcia in Opposition to Motion for Preliminary Injunction (Nov. 27, 2001).
Declaration of Russ Reynolds (Nov. 27, 2001).
Declaration of Stephen Kowalski (Nov. 27, 2001).
Objections by Plaintiff Alex Popov to Declaration Submitted by Defendant Patrick Hayashi (Nov. 27, 2001).
Preliminary Documents (Nov. 27, 2001).
Reply Brief by Plaintiff Alex Popov in Support of OSC Regarding Preliminary Injunction (Nov. 27, 2001).
Order after Hearing on Plaintiff Alex Popov's Motion to Compel Production of Documents (July 3, 2002).
Order Denying Defendant's Motion for Summary Judgment and Granting in Part and Denying in Part Defendant's Motion for Summary Adjudication (Sept. 9, 2002).
Order Denying Plaintiff's Motion for Summary Judgment/Summary Adjudication (Sept. 9, 2002).
Brief of Defendant Patrick Hayashi (2003).

Rose v. Giamatti, *721 F. Supp. 906 (S.D. Ohio 1989).*

Reply Memorandum of Plaintiff-Appellee Peter E. Rose in Support of Motion for Temporary Restraining Order and Preliminary Injunction (June 23, 1989).
Memorandum of Plaintiff Pete Rose in Support of his Motion for Temporary Restraining Order and Preliminary Injunction (June 26, 1989).
Memorandum of Plaintiff Peter Edward Rose in Support of his Motion for Temporary Restraining Order and Preliminary Injunction (June 26, 1989).
Motion for Suspension of Temporary Restraining Order Pending Appeal and for Expedited Treatment (June 26, 1989).
Brief of Plaintiff-Appellee Peter E. Rose's in Opposition to Defendants- Appellants' Motion for Suspension of Temporary Restraining Order Pending Appeal and for Expedited Treatment (June 28, 1989).
Emergency Motion of Plaintiff-Appelle Peter E. Rose to Dismiss Appeal (June 28, 1989).

Interviews

Bernhardt, Professor. Golden Gate Law School, 2007. Telephone interview.

Media

The Babe Ruth Story (1948)
A Civil Action (1988)
Eight Men Out (1988)
Field of Dreams (1989)
Kill the Umpire (1950)
The Life and Times of Hank Greenberg (2000)
Up for Grabs: The Hysterical Battle for the Bonds Ball. Sports Junkie. TV Productions, 2003

Websites

www.apbagames.com
www.Arizona.diamondbacks.mlb.com
www.badmingtonscotland.org
www.ballparks.com
www.baseball-almanac.com
www.baseballhalloffame.com
www.baseball-reference.com
www.BBCSports.com
www.brandweek.com
www.bus.ecf.edu
www.CBCSports.com
www.CBSnews.com
www.chicagoist.com
www.cleveland.indians.mlb.com
www.cnnsi.com
www.Courttvnews.com
www.ESPN.com

www.exploratorium.edu
www.fantasydispute.com
www.Forbes.com
www.imdb.com
www.johnrocker.net
www.law.umkc.edu
www.mlb.com
www.mlbplayers.mlb.com
www.msnbc.com
www.NBCSports.com
www.npr.org

www.PBS.org
www.philadelphiaathletics.org
www.retrosheet.org
www.sabr.org
www.SI.com
www.sportspickle.com
www.strat-o-matic.com
www.time.com
www.totalinjury.com/sports-spectator-Injuries.asp.
www.wizofbaseball.com

Index

Allegheny Baseball Club v. Bennett 33
American Association 30, 33
antitrust 158–159, 173–174

Black Sox Scandal 77–108
Bonds, Barry 5–6, 11
Boston Red Sox Baseball Club v. Mientkiewicz 19–20
Burns, Bill "Sleepy" 79, 87 89–95

Chadwick, Henry 234
Cicotte, Eddie 77–82, 84, 90–91, 95–99
Clement, Amanda 144
Cobb, Ty 41–42, 59–60, 62–71, 74–76
collusion 196–216
Comiskey, Charles 78–79, 84–85, 90
conversion 14–17

Dawson, Andre 209–211
Dowd, John 111, 113–116

fantasy baseball 236–237, 242–250
Federal Civil Rights Act of 1964 140
Felsch, Oscar "Happy" 84
Flood, Curt 158–177

Garcia, Rich 12
Gera, Bernice 141, 151–156
Giamatti, A. Bartlett 1, 109, 111–112, 114–125
Gray, Brian 14–15
Gray's Rule 15
Guillen, Ozzie 131

Hayashi, Patrick 5–11, 13–14, 16–18
Howe, Steve 251–268
Hunter, James "Catfish" 179–180

Jackson, Joe 80–84, 87, 97–98
James, Bill 234–235

Johnson, Ban 44, 48–49, 62, 70–71, 73
just cause 138–139

Keppel, Josh 6–9; videotape 7–8, 12
Keron v. Cashman 17
Knepper, Bob 136–138
Kuhn, Commissioner Bowie 183

Lajoie, Napolean 41–58, 59–60, 62–71, 74–76
Landis, Commissioner Judge Mountain 129–131
limited duty rule 221, 227, 229–232
Ludtke, Mellisa 156
Ludtke v. Kuhn 156

Mack, Connie 44–45, 48
Maharg, Billy 99
Major League Baseball Rule 2.00, definition of a catch 12
McCarthy, Judge J. 11–17
McDonald, Chief Justice Charles A. 96–98, 101
McFarlane, Todd 6, 18
McNally, Dave 181–184, 186, 191
Messersmith, Andy 180–186, 190–192
Mientkiewicz, Doug 19–20
Miller, Marvin 114, 178, 181–182, 186–187, 189–191
Morris, Jack 205–209
mutuality 52–53, 55, 57

National Brotherhood of Professional Baseball Players 24–29
National League 21–31, 33, 38–39
new look free agency 199–200

O'Connor, Jack 60–62, 68, 70–74

Players League 22, 28–29, 31, 38

331

The Players Relation Committee (PRC) 197–198, 212–213
Popov, Alex 5–19
possession 13–16
Postema, Pam 141, 146–151

Reserve Clause 30–32, 34–35, 37
Rickey, Branch 60, 141
right of publicity 238–250
Roberts, Chief Justice John 1
Rocker, John 126–128, 130, 132–139
Rogers, Colonel John 44–51, 53, 56–57
Rose, Pete 109–125

sabermetrics 234
Schott, Marge 131, 135, 138

Seitz, Peter 179–180, 182–187
Selig, Bud 128, 131–136, 138–139
Spalding, Albert Goodwill 21, 25–29
Stern, David 132

trespass to chattel 14
Turner, Ted 128, 136–138

Ueberroth, Commissioner Peter 111–112, 198

Ward, John Montgomery 21–40, 45
Ward's Baseball Book, How to Become a Player 23, 32
Williams, Claude "Lefty" 80–84, 95–98

www.ingramcontent.com/pod-product-compliance
Lightning Source LLC
Chambersburg PA
CBHW051207300426
44116CB00006B/466